JOCK: a memoir of the counterculture

Robert Coe

ISBN-13: 978-1502398024
ISBN-10: 1502398028

Cover Design by David Braddock
Cover Photograph by Charles R. Dyer

FOR COACH MARSHALL CLARK

"…who gave us the bit, then handed us the reins…"

"rapid motion through space elates one"

James Joyce

"the rabbit's running in the ditch

must be the season of the witch"

Donovan

CONTENTS

Preface: A person who experiences a career as an athlete like the one I had – let's call it "checkered" – usually doesn't sit down and write a book about it. More typical sports memoirs feature a protagonist who may or may not have had an easy time of things, but in the end he (or she) will wring redemption from difficult events. My redemption, or perhaps better to call it my reward, has been the pleasure I have found writing about the rich and complicated adventure I had as a runner at Leland Stanford Junior University from 1968 to 1972.

This work began six years after I graduated, with an article I published in the *Village Voice,* entitled "Memoir of an Ex-Jogger." "For years," I wrote, "whenever I have felt uneasy, whenever my life seemed empty and I didn't know what was wrong with it, I have wondered if I should have kept running." (I read this today and think I sound like *Moby Dick's* Ishmael with a case of "the hypos," wondering if I should have gone to sea one more time.) The "jogging" boom was in full swing by 1978 – I never "jogged," I *ran* – but since I was living in the concrete jungle of Lower Manhattan, I wasn't part of it. I was about to begin dancing in the company of Bill T. Jones, a future Tony Award-winning choreographer, MacArthur Foundation "Genius" and Kennedy Center Honoree (and a pretty decent college sprinter, too: 9.8 Seconds for One-Hundred Yards at S.U.N.Y. Binghamton.) My *Voice* article went on to enumerate all the things I thought were wrong with the "jogging" craze – mostly how tough it was on bodies and how addictive it could become. The piece drew in dozens of Letters to the Editor full praise and denunciation, as well as a request from *The David Susskind Show* (the *Charlie Rose* of its day) for me to appear on camera denouncing the running "mania." Me, a runner's Benedict Arnold? That would not happen. Despite the many caveats in my *Voice* piece, I had far too much love and respect for a sport that had nourished me, mentally, physically and spiritually, since high school.

Training and racing over middle- and long-distances was my thing in college. The story of a high school also-ran who became a freshman track star and one of the top Varsity cross-country runners at Stanford has a certain interest, I suppose, but this alone does not qualify this book as a conventional sports memoir. At the simplest level, this book is a spiritual autobiography of one athlete's progress and derailment. I was one of those Jocks who never quite lived up to his "full potential." (How many of us ever do?) There are always athletes like me around, and usually we tend to keep our mouths shut. But *JOCK: a memoir of the counterculture* became about a great deal more than just my personal situation. When I first started writing, I thought I would be satisfied with simply recounting my runner's life, the worlds I ran through and the people I knew, what we did and how we did it. But as I delved more deeply into my subject matter – as I thought more about the history of the late Sixties and early Seventies, and as my scope expanded from college cross country and Track & Field to include Rose Bowl football, Olympic-caliber swimming, and college sports in general, and from there to campus life and the constantly-exploding politics of the outside world – I began to see how intercollegiate athletics could become a window on an era, offering a fresh perspective on that era's brightest hopes and dreams and, in some cases, its failures and defeats. I further came to understand how my own journey could be viewed as part of a generational passage through a countercultural revolution, during which millions of young people, athletes and non-athletes alike, stepped outside the bounds of normalcy and narrow definitions of good behavior and tradition, in order to challenge the rules, complacency, and flat-out madness of the age.

I wrote this book in a confessional spirit, crossed with some nerdy distance runners' fanzine I have yet to come across, interleaved with pages from *A People's History of the United States*. I added the second part of my title – *a memoir of the counterculture* – so that no one would mistake what I am going for here: an unexpurgated account of how the anti-war, anti-authoritarian, anti-racist counterculture found ways (with a little help from our friends) to be at the center of sports action, challenging the orthodoxies of what was supposed to be the counterculture's polar opposite: big-time college athletics. @ @ @

THE BIG ROCK CANDY MOUNTAIN

More than forty years have passed since I was a distance runner at Stanford University, but those years on campus are as alive to me now as if they were not quite yesterday, but not so long ago at all. Those of us who ran before the wind in our ships with painted sails imagined we would just do it forever, but life isn't like that, because life measures out an end-date for us all. Yet there have been hundreds if not thousands of occasions over the intervening years when I have returned to the Stanford Stadium Track, to the Golf Course where we sometimes trained, and to the roads encircling the campus, and in these dreams I am running *– from where and to where I almost never know. I only seldom know why I'm running, or when I started, or how long I have been at it, or how much further I have to go. But I am running: churning, pounding, swiftly, endlessly, with a ghostly lack of effort, almost always to nowhere. In other dreams I run across trackless wastes, along unidentifiable streets, in empty castles, endless concrete labyrinths, shattered rooms in abandoned buildings, or on primitive video game screens, and on one occasion, the interior of Disneyland's Matterhorn ride. Sometimes I run through a scrim of current events: I once completed the five-borough New York City Marathon in two hours and seventeen minutes, every step under cover of my duvet. On some of my nocturnal jaunts I see old friends, teammates and rivals, and we are all young again, eager to test ourselves against one another, as we used to do in daylight. There are seldom any finish lines in these oneiric competitions, but more than once I have*

1

found myself in the finishing chute after a hard-fought cross-country battle, exhausted by a race in which I have invariably performed like a Trojan, Spartan, Athenian, or Gaul. Or I am at the finish of a shorter, faster-paced race on a quarter-mile track, panting, wobbly, totally spent, knowing that the race is won and so feeling satisfied and complete, with the special sense that I have not been defeated and can still produce fast times on minimal training. Some of these night-time contests are so vivid that I wake up thinking that the race I had just run in my sleep may have actually occurred sometime in my past; that the dream had has revealed something to me that was otherwise forgotten or repressed. I always find this mildly unsettling, because my rational mind tells me that this event had no more substance than a dream. And then other dreams are so eerie, so profoundly weird or obstinately vague, that I don't waste any time thinking about them and rise to greet my day as if I had never been a runner at all.

But I was a runner. I ran for Leland Stanford Junior University. And in my dreams, I still am. @ @

On Wednesday, September 18th, 1968, my grandparents dropped me off at Los Angeles International Airport so I could board a Pacific Southwest Airlines flight to San Francisco International Airport. From there I boarded a bus down the peninsula to Palo Alto, where I hailed a taxi for my final mile to Branner Hall, my newly-designated freshman dorm. As the first of my two suitemates to arrive, I tossed my two suitcases to claim a lower bunk, unzipped a bag, and dug out my white Adidas for a run around campus. My first stop wouldn't be "The Quad," the heart of Frederick Law Olmstead's original campus design, or "MemChu," the Memorial Church where my grandparents married almost fifty years earlier; it wouldn't be the new student union, Tressider, the "handsome hacienda" *(Time)* named after Stanford's fourth President, or the two-year-old Undergraduate Library, a looming fortress in the heart of campus students had nicknamed UGLY, or even the old Tri-Delt sorority house on Mayfield Avenue, where my father and mother met for their first date more than a quarter-century before. I had never visited there before, and was curious to see it.

But no: my first stop was Stanford Stadium. Which was locked. Tight as a drum. I made sure by running around it twice. What did they do to trespassers around this place? Book them? Pepper spray 'em? *Shoot* them? Preparing my line for the cops – "I-I'm a freshman distance runner, Officer! I-I just got here, fresh off the boat... from... from Texas! I didn't *know* you're not supposed to climb this twelve-foot high fence looped and coiled with barbed wire!"

I tore my new white nylon running shorts and sliced the ball of my thumb (not badly) on the razor-sharp coil along the top, but I got over the fence and dropped on down to the other side.

Trotting stealthily down the asphalt incline toward the stadium floor, one eye peeled for watchmen, I entered the 85,000-seat bowl.

And there it was, the thing I had come to see, encircling the football field: the Stanford Stadium Track – site of the legendary 1962 U.S.-U.S.S.R. dual meet, which had drawn a two-day crowd of 155,000 at the height of the Cold War six years earlier. I had seen photographs in *Life*, so I instantly recognized that the historic cinders had been replaced by an all-weather, artificial surface, identical (I believed) to the track in Mexico City, where the XIXth Olympiad would open in a few weeks, and where the Head Coach of the powerhouse U.S. team was Payton Jordan, who would be my Head Coach at Stanford, too.

My heart was beating like a Tom-Tom. My skin tingled, and I needed to pee, but I knew that was only nerves. I took a deep breath, exhaled, and began jogging down to the stadium track at last – feeling as if I had arrived at the start of a Cosmic Marathon without beginning, middle or end – as if I was commencing down a long road laid out for me by my family and my past, but that I was freely choosing to follow. An irreducible drama – Life itself! – was stretching before me down a long path where ends were only means in motion and doing brought all things into being!

I had read about artificial tracks but had never set foot on one during my high school years in Texas. I felt the track come alive under my feet. The road rising up to greet me! I started trotting again and in seconds was running faster, then faster still, until I was sprinting down the long straightaway and around the broad curve of that terracotta oval, overwhelmed by the absolute certainty – as sure as I had ever been of anything in my life – that at that moment there was nowhere else on earth I wanted to be more. Stanford's motto – "Die Luft der Freiheit weht;" "The Winds of Freedom Blow" – was what I felt that day: the Winds of Freedom gusting around that empty bowl, under a ceiling of the bluest air! I was an eighteen-year-old Scholar-Athlete, and as far as I was concerned, I had made it to the Promised Land! @ @

How extraordinary, to be living away from home as a student on "The Farm," as the site of former California Governor Leland Stanford's thirteen-square-mile horse breeding operation was known! "The Quad," "MemChu," "MemAud" and other campus landmarks had been part of my dreams and my reality for as long as I could remember. I was ten months old on my first visit to campus, asleep in my mother's arms; at age five I posed in our family photo spot on the steps before the Quad, looking grumpy in a blue sailor suit; at eleven I stood alongside my two sisters in the Carillon of Hoover Tower – all these images captured by my grandfather, a retired Los Angeles County Superior Court Judge (Class of '19, J.D. '20) who began the family tradition I had always known I would follow. I didn't even sweat admission, since my sister had breezed through two years earlier.

That I also intended to train and race intercollegiately took my grandparents by surprise, since I had written them from my parents' house in Texas: "If I get an athletic scholarship, I'll run at Stanford; if not, I won't." I don't know why I lied about this. I had always meant to be a Stanford Jock. Maybe I lied because no one in our Stanford family had ever been a college athlete before. Or maybe I wanted them to know how committed I was to being a successful student, because I was, in full. I didn't have an athletic scholarship because I was only fast enough for "rides" at a few cow colleges in Texas and Louisiana – my parents, brothers and I had moved from California after the Shell Oil Company closed my father's lab in California and moved it to Deer Park, Texas. I was at a meet in Conroe when the Head Coach of Texas

A & M cornered me behind a grandstand with the meet still in progress, a flinty gleam in his eye, a crooked good ol' boy leer on his puss, to ask: "You wom be an *Aggie?*"

Aggie Jokes were everywhere at the moment. An "Aggie Shower" was a splash of cologne in your armpits and cR.O.T.C.h, in lieu of soap and water.

"No, sir," I replied. "I-I-I'm going to Stanford –"

"*Stan*-furd?" Texas A&M's Head Coach stared back at me in horror. "You mean where all them *hippies* come from?" Then he spun around on his boot heels and stomped away without another word, no doubt in search of some young buck not at all like me. *Damn Straight,* I thought, *where all them hippies come from...* Haight-Ashbury and the Summer of Love had come and gone the year before, thirty miles north of the campus in Palo Alto. I had read about San Francisco flower children in *Life* magazine, and listened to music that was already changing the world. *"Are you goin'/ to San Francisco..."* I wasn't fast enough to be recruited to Stanford, but I didn't need an athletic ride to go to the school of my choice because I had an academic scholarship that would cover two-thirds of my tuition: $640 a quarter. This was a huge relief to me because it meant my grandparents wouldn't be on the hook for all of it. They had always taken special care of my sister and me, ever since our mother was killed in a car crash at the age of twenty-seven, seven years after earning her Biology degree on The Farm, where she met my father, a Ph.D. candidate in Chemistry. At the time of her death she was a twenty-seven-year-old M.D. with three kids. Our eldest sister had died young, too, in a sledding accident in the mountains above L.A. before reaching seventeen. My two Aunts had met their future husbands, both engineers, where my sister was a junior now. I would have gone to Stanford if it didn't have a track, much less a track team, but since it had both, I intended to train for races ranging from One-Half Mile to Six. My grandparents voiced no objection to this plan, as long as I kept my grades up and put my studies first. They fully expected a lawyer to emerge from this process seven years or so down the road. And at that point in my young life, I more-or-less fully expected to oblige. @ @

Everyone I met during my first full day on campus – my suitemates, my dorm mates – was so outgoing, engaged and engaging, and so smart! Lost in a sea of fresh-faced hall mates and mess-hall faces, dormitory get-acquainted parties, a gathering of the Class of '72 in "MemAud" (Memorial Auditorium), and an outdoor convocation at a twenty-acre on-campus park known as Frost Amphitheater, I found time to take a placement test that landed me back in French One, after three years of crappy high school French in Texas. I shrugged it off. I knew I belonged here. At a freshman colloquy that evening at Memorial Church, I listened as Chapel Dean B. Davie Napier invited us all to join "the Brotherhood of Man," then rose along with my classmates, young men and women, for a thunderous standing ovation. Back at Branner that night I stayed up until one with a track teammate who lived just down the hall from me, chatting up two girls we just met. He was an Oregon State Mile Champion with a best time that would have made him the second-fastest Miler in Texas that spring, while my claims to fame were that I had been the eighth-ranked Miler in a state not known for distance running and second man on a state champion cross-country team. My best Mile time – 4:25.8 (four minutes twenty-five and eight-tenths seconds) – was almost ten seconds slower than the Oregonian's. I wondered if I was even in the same league with this guy. But the next morning when we went out for an easy five miles together I discovered that one of a handful of new freshmen on a partial Track scholarship was not only not in shape; he was unsure if he wanted to be running in college at all.

Hours later I was standing shoulder-to-shoulder with fellow students at a noontime rally in White Plaza, listening to Student Body President (and future "Earth Day" founder) Dennis Hayes as he urged us to rise up against a "genocidal" war and make sure the Stanford administration understood that we knew about its complicity in the ongoing disaster in Southeast Asia, and if changes weren't made, what had happened at Columbia University in New York the previous spring

– a campus-wide shut-down – could happen here, too. Dressed in skintight white jeans and a white cowboy hat, Hayes concluded his extemporaneous remarks with several observations about his adversary in the last student election, the topless coed Vicky Drake, who could be seen in all her mammary glory in the issue of *Playboy* on the newsstands that day, delivering several bad puns about how his opponent had not been "abreast" of the times, and how he had "udderly" defeated her. (A recent issue of *Time* magazine had reported, "Asked what her platform was last spring, the 21-year-old blonde answered: "38-22-36.")

Strolling back to Branner I pondered this most interesting event, wondering if I had really heard what I thought I heard: had our Student Body President really just said that unless the administration dropped its complicity in the war, we would shut down the school? Yes, that was what he said. My anti-war sentiments had been firmly in place for years, partially courtesy of my grandparents, who opposed the war as thoroughly as I did. Young Americans – men and boys, mostly – were being killed and were killing non-combatants and combatants in a war in Southeast Asia we should never have engaged. Like everyone arriving on a college campus in the fall of '68, I had a great deal more to think about than grades and the agony and ecstasy of sports. @ @

1968 was the most eventful international year since 1945, and it wasn't over yet. After years of bombings and broken promises, the North Vietnamese Lunar New Year ("Tet") Offensive in January had revealed LBJ's "Light at the End of the Tunnel" to be a terrible mirage. More than seven thousand American troops had been K.I.A. during the Tet Offensive. Young Americans our age, slaughtered and slaughtering daily by the hundreds! And in the name of what? With the obscenity of the facts, the moral groundlessness and the visual imagery of the Vietnam disaster fully revealed by Tet, hundreds of American campuses had exploded in protest. Stanford rocked to its foundations.

The Naval R.O.T.C. Clubhouse was burned to the ground in a February arson supposedly perpetrated by student radicals, although it was later believed that the fire was set by an agent provocateur in the

7

F.B.I. In April and May, student demonstrators seeking to halt C.I.A. recruitment on campus trashed the office of then-Stanford President J.E. Wallace Sterling, while a larger, peaceful group occupied the Old Student Union in a sit-in that resulted in hundreds of arrests. An extraordinary cavalcade of events had continued all that spring and summer: Soviet tanks had rolled into Czechoslovakia, and a revolution collapsed in France. In March, LBJ withdrew from his own re-election campaign; in April, Martin Luther King was assassinated, sparking racial riots across the nation; the June assassination of Robert F. Kennedy on the night of his Democratic primary victory in California would mean the sure defeat of the anti-war factions in the Democratic Party and the nomination of LBJ's Vice President Hubert Humphrey, a status quo candidate who insisted that the calamitous war policy was working, thereby guaranteeing an autumn of campus "unrest," along with a general election that the likely Republican nominee, the anti-Communist "law & order" man Richard M. Nixon, would doubtless characterize as a "referendum on youth." Everybody knew that more protests were coming and that things would likely get ugly, although just how ugly was anybody's guess. A campus-wide poll revealed that seventy percent of the Stanford student body objected to the more extreme forms of protest, especially violent ones: "Students are seeking access to the decision-making channels of the university," our Class of '68 Froshbook informed us, and the administration was supposedly willing to let this happen, but a not-insignificant number of students also believed that "the 'success' of coercive tactics were grounds for their continued use 'whenever there are student desires.'"

As I changed into my workout gear, I idly wondered how college sports, and distance running in particular, could possibly matter in this world I was entering. But as I lay down on my bed I found my thoughts drifting irresistibly to our first cross-country team meeting to be held that afternoon, and my real concern, which was this: was I ready to compete at the Division I level, or was I not? My training at Clear Creek High School in League City, Texas, had been retarded by stupid school rules that wouldn't allow anyone to train off-campus even after school was out. I had one 64-mile training week my senior year and two other weeks over 40, but basically averaged about thirty miles a week during my senior cross country and track. This with very rare exceptions is not enough to build a distance-running champion. So after graduation I had left Texas and moved back to California, where I had grown up in Long Beach until I was fifteen – to spend the summer at my grandparents' beach house in San Clemente, training under a program mailed to me by Stanford's new Assistant Coach for distance runners.

I had followed this program almost to the letter.

Two weeks before heading north, I had tested my fitness with a solo Two-Mile time trial on the San Clemente High School track. My time – ten minutes flat – was "no great shakes," to use one of my father's expressions. But it was a PR (Personal Record) by three seconds. I would now be the eighth-fastest entering freshman Two-Miler on The Farm, which made me wonder if I would crack the freshmen line-up, since cross-country teams compete with seven. I rationalized like crazy. I told myself that with competition I would certainly have run much faster. Plus I was the fifth-fastest incoming Miler. So I decided I had a very good chance of suiting up for Stanford's Frosh Cross Country team. There were other unknowns I might have pondered, but I pushed these thoughts aside, closed my eyes and tried to nap, but was too excited to sleep. So I did some light reading instead until just before three o'clock, when I slipped back into my shorts and Adidas and jogged over to our first team meeting at the Track & Field locker room in Encina Gym, a small brick building located between Branner Hall and the Stadium, near a cinder track called Angell Field. @ @

The Stanford Track and Cross-Country locker room came as something of a shock: a drab, battleship-gray concrete cube, maybe twenty feet by twenty-five feet, with a twelve-foot-high ceiling, it smelled of fresh paint, dire cleaning products, and decades of B.O. from sweaty t-shirts, rank socks and rancid jocks. Soft dull light streaming through yellowing windows laced with chicken wire cast an amber glow on dancing motes of dust and shiny gray walls covered with framed and fading black & white photographs of long-departed Stanford thinclads, alongside plaques bearing inspirational slogans such as "Sure Enough!" and *"For Stanford I Will"* The latter phrase was printed at the bottom of a Thirties-era framed color print, beneath an image of a short-haired Caucasian youth in an "S" jersey straining as he breaks a finish-line tape with his chest. The room looked as if it had been spruced up recently, but probably hadn't had a major renovation since the Great Depression. I couldn't imagine hanging out there much, snapping towels, telling jokes and so on, but I couldn't stop thinking: *I made it... I'm here... This is Stanford's Track & Field locker room... Adidas on the Ground...*

Freshman lined our side of the locker room, more plentiful than the upperclassmen: a dozen or so of us slender, faintly goofy-looking young men with our stringy muscles, pencil necks, and pulsing Adam's Apples, some leaning against a wall of battered gunmetal lockers, others half-squatting on extremely low grey benches, an unprepossessing gaggle, looking slightly overwhelmed by its new surroundings in the last year the N.C.A.A. wouldn't allow freshmen to compete with the Varsity.

On the other side of the room, the sophomores, juniors and seniors made quite a contrast: high-spirited, laughing, joking among themselves as all of us waited for the arrival of Stanford's first-year assistant coach for cross country, middle- and long-distance running, who was delayed for reasons unknown to us.

"Buncha geeks," someone whispered in my ear. I turned to face a freshman about my size and build, with a lumpy complexion, thick wiry hair and a Cheshire cat grin on his puss. "Skinny-ass motherfuckers," he added, letting a trace of irony cross his face for a moment, in recognition that he and I were as skinny as everybody else was.

"I'm Jack Lawson," he said. "Gimme five..."

I had read about Jack. He hailed from Modesto, where he had been an

All-Northern California cross country team member and a two-time Sacramento-Joaquin Valley Section Two-Mile Champ. He was a walk-on, same as I was. I slapped the palm he had extended for that purpose and told him my name. Jack snorted and pulled his upper lip away from his teeth, which I gathered was another rendition of his smile.

"Rapid Robert! You're the cocky motherfucker who challenged us all to a Marathon this summer!"

I had forgotten all about that. It was a little embarrassing now. In a letter to the Varsity Team Captain I had boasted about all the hard training I was doing, and made a tongue-in-cheek aside about challenging everybody to race twenty-six miles, 385 yards, never expecting Brook to copy it verbatim into the newsletter and distribute it in a mimeo to the team. I was nowhere near ready to run a Marathon. Marathons scared me. Plus I didn't like running on asphalt.

"You ever actually *run* a Marathon, Rapid Robert?"

"No, Jack. I can't say that I have." My high school teammates had run one, one Sunday in training, but I had begged off.

"I didn't think so," he chortled again, eyeing me closely. This exchange, which was entirely friendly, would have continued, except our coach came darting through the door, out of breath and thirty minutes late for his team's first meet-and-greet. @ @

Coach Marshall Clark and I had corresponded over the summer, so I thought I knew what to expect, but Coach Clark surprised me anyway. He was slightly over six feet tall and lanky, with a tanned, weather-creased face (like most West Coast Track Coaches) topped by a stubborn cowlick, he probably didn't look all that different at thirty-five than he had as a University of Southern California runner, Class of '57. The summer issue of the *Stanford Sports Quarterly* had this to say about him: "An extremely versatile athlete, Clark, at one time or another, ran every flat race from 100 yards through the mile, in addition to being a very fine cross country competitor." Three years after graduating from U.S.C. he anchored a Southern California

Striders sprint medley relay team to the third-fastest time in the world in 1960. And now he was a college freshman again, hired away from a successful Seaside High School program on the Monterrey Peninsula. Coach Jordan had allowed last year's team to interview his nominees to replace the old coach, and Marshall Clark was the unanimous selection.

"I apologize for my tardiness," he said, still winded from his run over. "Something came up that couldn't be avoided… Let's go around the room… and introduce ourselves, tell us your hometown."

It was like one of those TV player introduction routines on televised football: "Robert Coe, Clear Creek High School, El Lago, Texas." We came from all over the U.S., it turned out. No longer nomads, monads, or high school kids, we were college teammates now. It crossed my mind that I would know some of these guys, and quite possibly this coach, for years.

With these formalities out of the way, Coach cut to the chase: "Most of you have done good work this summer in preparation for the season, and I want us to continue that. I also want all of us to think about Arthur Lydiard's maxim, 'Train, don't strain.' This doesn't mean we won't train hard, because we will, but we're also going to stay relaxed and run within ourselves," he went on, in an unhurried manner that seemed native to him. "We'll put in enough miles, at quick enough tempos, for this approach to pay off in time. We'll have harder days and we'll have easier days, but the key to everything will be patience and consistency. If each one of you follows through and does the workouts, I think we could find ourselves – *you* could find yourself – running faster than you ever thought possible."

This "Train Don't Strain" line was one I knew from my library of running books. It originated with the New Zealand Coach Arthur Lydiard, one of the great innovators in long-distance training and the coach of multiple world-record holders and Olympic Champs Down Under. "Train Don't Strain" sounded strange coming from the mouth of a distance-running coach. Running long distances was supposed to hurt, wasn't it? Not all the time, but a lot, right?

"'Train, don't strain' means working together as a team," our Coach continued. "We have some good personnel coming back this season, and a strong Freshman Class —"

"Really," Jack murmured, in a tone pitched so perfectly between recognition and sarcasm that I wasn't sure where he meant it to land. *Did* we have a strong freshman class? And if we did, where did I fit into that picture? In the mix? Nowhere? To be determined? Again, on paper, seven guys faster than me —

"— so I'm anticipating that if we run as a group, we'll have a good chance of surprising a few people this season. There's no reason to think we can't achieve some quality times. Any of our past accomplishments aren't likely to impress our opposition in the A.A.W.U." — the formation of the Pacific Eight Conference was still a year away, so Stanford was still a member of the Athletic Association of Western Universities — "and it certainly won't win us any races. But consistent work just might..." @ @

Coach Clark continued in this vein for quite some time. He was soft-spoken, but not necessarily a man of few words. (There would be occasions in the future, listening to him talk, when I would see white foam gathering on the corners of his mouth.) What was interesting to me was that he didn't seem like a man driven by Ego. He wasn't the least bit self-promoting or paternalistic or rah-rah, like way too many coaches I knew. Coach Clark won the attention of every member of our team with a simple message: tough, consistent *moderation.* You might wonder what's so moderate about ninety-plus-mile training weeks, and I couldn't have explained it to you yet, but everything Coach Clark said, and the way he said it, made perfect sense to me. Dissuading me from attempting 120-mile training weeks, which I had written him about trying over the summer, after I had been running sub-40 mile weeks in high school, had been more-or-less a no-brainer.

"— running as much as we will, it's also important that we keep a balance," Coach went on. "Eat well, sleep right, shoot for two-a-day workouts if you're able —"

"And don't forget the books." This came from the senior who had introduced himself as the Varsity Team Captain. Brook Thomas had a narrow face, close-set eyes, dark wavy hair, a seemingly-muscle-less chest, but surprising sprinting speed: without any speed training at all that summer he had covered a quarter-mile in fifty seconds flat, which was fast for a distance runner. Brook was an English major; also the editor of our team's highly-entertaining and informative newsletters, which chronicled our various summer adventures and plans for the fall. "Freshmen," he had written in his first installment, mailed from his family home on "Far Hill S. Rolling Road" in Baltimore – about as auspicious an address for a Cross-Country Team Captain as one could invent: "Welcome to that diverse, devastating, and at times disgusting society of Stanford distance runners. Speaking for the team I'm sure you'll enjoy running and studying at Stanford. Speaking for myself – wait and see for yourself." Warning us that there was "no rigid structure on this team," he advised us to "read all about the existential quest in distance running from Alan Sillitoe's *The Loneliness of the Long Distance Runner.*"

Brook's reminder "don't forget the books" stopped Coach Clark for a second. Then he said, "Oh yeah, books," with a flicker of a half-smile to let us know he was joking, which gave us all permission to laugh.

Coach next opened the floor to questions. People asked about workout schedules, time trials, equipment issuance and the like. From the way he responded you could tell that he was a good listener. Very straight up and on-the-level. Very eye-to-eye. Even Jack stopped joking around and gave our new Coach his undivided attention.

"When do we get our shoes?" someone called out – a question that seemed to fluster Coach for a moment, I didn't know why. (Years later I would learn he was late to our first meeting because he had been arguing with some factotum in the Athletic Department about getting us more shoes than the Department was apparently willing to spare. It was not an argument he won, at least not entirely.)

"We'll be running in Onitsuka 'Tiger' training flats this year, and they will have to last us through fall cross country into spring track," Coach said. "In the past, only the top seven varsity runners have gotten shoes, but this year we'll have a little more leeway on that. Freshmen who run under 21:30 on our 4.2-mile course will also get a new pair of shoes. Unfortunately we won't be able to issue them until after the time trials…" I learned later that shoe companies had been giving our Head Coach free samples of their product lines for the past year, hoping to influence his decision on how to shoe the horses on the U.S. Olympic team. One of our top distance runners had product-tested several and recommended the Onitsuka Tigers, a shoe under development by a former Oregon Half-Miler and Stanford MBA, Class of '62, who was working with a Japanese company on early iterations of what became the Nike running shoe. (His name was Phil Knight.)

"The upperclassmen are going to lead us to the soccer fields for some easy 330s today," Coach said. "We'll keep it relaxed and meet here tomorrow at 3:30 sharp for a long run behind campus. Freshmen," he added, "you won't officially be able to work out until Registration on Monday, but you do have the option of joining us if you want, and you might want to learn the lay of the land." After this final implication that Freshmen had better come, too, he was done. "Let's head out."

As the team made final preparations to run into that Indian summer mid-peninsula afternoon – adjusting jocks, pulling up socks, double-knotting shoes – Jack leaned over and stage-whispered in my ear.

"We're gonna get one pair of flats to last the year? That's what we got at my junior high school!"

"And we have to pass a time trial to get a pair of shoes?" (I was actually worried about this.)

"My high school gave Adidas to guys who couldn't run a six-minute mile!"

"I wonder what you have to do to get a new pair of shorts!" I said, thrusting three fingers through the tear I had gotten climbing the Stadium fence.

"Fuck 'em, Rapid Robert!" Jack said as he rose to his feet. "What was it Coach said? 'No pain, no gain?' Let's go do our thing, brothuh…"

The 330-yard "intervals" we ran on the soccer field that day – repetitions of that distance interspersed with set periods of recovery – felt easy, which was no doubt Coach's intention. I had no trouble keeping up with the Varsity, although after a quick once-over Jack looked like the fittest of the freshmen hands down.

"Rapid Robert!" I looked and saw he was shooting me the Finger. I grinned and shot one back at him. That made me feel good. Jack wouldn't be messing with me if I didn't look strong, too. Strong enough to make the team? I had a strong feeling I was as good as on it already. @ @

I went alone to MemChu again that night, this time for an event that put a different spin on "the Brotherhood of Man." I sat on the aisle in the fifth pew to hear Joan Baez, the folk-singer-wife of former Stanford Student Body President David Harris, shortly to serve fifteen months in federal prison for felony Draft evasion, implore an overflow crowd to practice non-cooperation with a soulless war and its immoral conscription. In the echoing splendor of the Chapel she sang an *a cappella* version of Bob Dylan and Richard Manuel's "Tears of Rage" from The Band's three-month-old album, "Music from Big Pink,": *"But oh, what kind of love is this which goes from bad to worse? Tears of Rage… Tears of Grief… Why must I always… be the Thief?"* I nodded in recognition as she told us that we had all been brought up "schizophrenic" – an insight re-confirmed to my satisfaction later that week at a screening of Frederick Wiseman's *cinema verité* masterpiece "High School," a pitch-perfect exposé of a monochromatic secondary school in Philadelphia that could just as well have been shot at Clear Creek High in League City, Texas. The final speaker at MemChu that evening was the founder and chairman of the Black Panther Party, Bobby Seale, who climbed up to the pulpit of Stanford's chapel to warn incoming freshman: there would be no peace without justice in racist America.

Walking back to Branner under the barrel-tiled roofs along the thirty-five-million-year-old sandstone of the Quad, I pondered these efforts and appeals for justice and continued to do so until my head hit the pillow for ten hours of uninterrupted sleep, which ended at six-thirty, when I shut off my travel alarm clock, slipped out from under my sheet and blanket, laced up my old high school training flats and ran five miles, followed by a quick breakfast and my first class as a college freshman: eight a.m. Biology 101. @ @

The day before classes started my teammates had gathered at the locker room for an easy hour run in the hills, but I chose to go alone to the Stanford Golf Course, where Coach Clark had said we would have a "controlled" time-trial the day after. The prospect of training on one of the natural wonders of The Farm, a golf course regularly voted among the hundred most beautiful in the world, was an unexpected boon. The comfort of soft rye and Bermuda grass for my chronically-sore Achilles tendons and brittle knees! Afterwards I ran back to the locker room in time for a team meeting, where I learned that I was in the middle of a controversy, which I wrote about to my grandparents: "The Frosh cross country team has elected me to the Athletic Council, which is the policy committee of the Athletic dept... I have stepped into the middle of a fight, too, because one of the star Milers, Duncan Macdonald, refuses to shave his moustache. Brook Thomas, the Varsity cross-country captain, and me are behind him 100% and we are going to see what we can do to help him keep it. I don't see any reason why he should have to shave. It's totally his business."

There wasn't too much time to get too worked up over this, because the "controlled" Saturday morning time trial was the following day. This was not the trial that would determine the team, just a dry run that didn't turn out as I hoped. I tried to go with the Varsity over our newly-designed six-mile circuit, but once I knew I couldn't handle the pace I shut it down and cruised in, not wanting to hurt too much and happy to be the second freshman finisher, behind Jack. On our dog trot back to the locker room, Coach Clark ran up alongside me, his omnipresent clipboard tucked under his arm. As a runner he looked and ran more or less like we did.

"Good work today, Bob," he huffed. "Thirty-one minutes... fifteen seconds... for 5.6 miles... This course is about nine minutes longer... than our 4.2 mile course... So you can do the math..." Wrinkling his nose as he smiled at me, he went jogging off to tell some other kid to do the math, too. When I did it, I realized I had run about 22:15 over our 4.2-mile course. I would need to slice 45 seconds off during the time trial to earn myself that new pair of shoes. @ @

The price I paid for my room and board and one-third of my tuition (the rest was covered by my scholarship) was a weekly letter to my grandparents, a chore I didn't mind at all. I banged out my first letter (in red ink) on the blue Royal manual typewriter they had given me as a high school graduation gift.

"'Relevance' is the favorite word here," I pecked. "There's even a chance that after the ten-year study of Education at Stanford is completed (this year?) all requirements will be done away with. That'll be good, I think. I currently need 17 units of lab science towards my degree, and I'm not looking forward to it." (I was more of a Humanities & Social Science type – the most popular majors of the Class of '72 would be Psychology, English, and History – and the hard sciences at Stanford were tough.) Three days in, my second letter to the people footing my bills confirmed my classes: "Western Civ, First-Year French, Freshman English, and Biology – the latter at 8 a.m. Not many morning workouts the same days as those 8 o'clocks. I'm not about to get up at 6:30 for a five-mile run..." I would sometimes run on those mornings anyway. Western Civilization – "Western Civ" – had been a Stanford freshman requirement for generations: my mother, her sisters and my sister had taken it (although the course would be gone by the Eighties, expunged in the name of cultural diversity.) The *Stanford Daily*, our student newspaper, informed us that our entering class of 1,447 was 85% Caucasian, 6-7% "Oriental," 5% "Negro," and the rest Mexican-American, Filipino and "American Indian." The *Daily* failed to mention we were also about 2:1 male. The Kerner Commission Report in February had described an America "moving toward two societies, one black, one white – separate and unequal," less than five weeks before the King assassination ignited inner cities nationwide. Stanford responded by nearly doubling the number of incoming Black freshmen – from 37 to 72 – and asking the entering class to read Claude Brown's Harlem memoir *Manchild in the Promised Land* as a departure point for "affinity group" discussions. (I inhaled it in a day and a night.) A year-old Black Student Union was demanding the creation of a Black Studies program and expanded admission and financial aid for minorities, while my English instructor had us reading Eldridge Cleaver's *Soul on Ice*, which he described as a work of "genius."

"I think it's a fascinating book," I wrote home. "But genius? That's an awfully big word..." I could be opinionated, even disputatious in my letters home, but you wouldn't hear me disagreeing much in classrooms, where I was more interested in fitting in than in shaking things up during my early days in college. I had come to Stanford anti-war and pro-individual rights, but not a flaming radical by any stretch. I wore my hair short and neatly parted on the right. I could have passed for sixteen, since I barely shaved – just a bit of facial hair above my upper lip, short sideburns and some whiskers on my chin. In my laced-up wingtips, buttoned-down Oxford shirts and stay-pressed slacks, I seemed like most of the other preppy-looking Future-Leader-of-America types at Branner that fall, all of us outfitted for the Paper Chase and seriously impressed with ourselves for getting into a really good school. Stanford was not nearly as far-out as U.C. Berkeley, the public option across the Bay, but this was changing fast: *en loco parentis* had gone belly up on The Farm the year before. In my sister's freshman year she had to "sign out" of Branner before she could go to UGLY to study at night, but two years later, all of that prewar stuff – sign-outs, dress codes, and curfews – had gone the way of the dinosaur. Prohibitions against late-night opposite-sex visitors in dorm rooms: they were history, too. Men, women, freshmen, seniors: all of us were free to come and go as we pleased, enjoying unimpeded access to the many dazzling and myriad temptations of the night.

"We had our house meeting at 9," I wrote home towards the end of our first week. "We were told about rules – there are none, except the

Golden Rule: don't infringe on anyone's rights. Tonight they're having keg parties in all the Freshmen and women dorms – so there really are no rules, as you can see." "Free Your Mind" was the slogan of the day, but the Mantra of the Night, in the freshman dorms at least, was (to quote Jefferson Airplane) "Feed Your Head." Marijuana was moving mainstream at Stanford that fall in a big, big way. The Bay Area's hippie *zeitgeist* was in quantum formation, moving from underground to foreground with the speed of a neural synapse. Freaks, Mutant Longhairs, Deadheads, and Proto-Computer Geeks were sprouting like mushrooms all across the Stanford campus. Scoring a bag of weed at Branner was easier than getting your hands on a cold six-pack of beer. Resident Assistants lived on each floor, upperclassmen and grad students charged with keeping us out of trouble, but two of Branner's RAs doubled as small-time pot dealers, including the one down my hall. By Day. By Day Three people weren't even stuffing wet towels under their doors anymore. I had smoked marijuana a few times in Texas at the end of senior year, so my sympathies were there, just under-developed. I had always been a dutiful student, committed to my studies, toeing the line and playing by the rules, mostly, but also a "behavior problem" and already a veteran of battles over hair: on enrollment day for my senior year in high school our Principal – a former under-sized third-team All-American Guard at Rice – had grabbed the shaggy keratin at the back of my neck and told me, "You're going home to cut this off." I was also drawn to loner types – your pranksters, whip-smart nerds, bad kids, and iconoclasts – even as I continued to do a pretty fair impression of the Houston Optimist Club "Boy of the Month" for February I had been the previous spring.

But everything was changing now, and changing fast. Stanford University, Middle Earth of my family's dreams for me and my own sense of entitlement and belonging, was revealing itself to me in a shimmering atmosphere of personal freedom, trippy adventures, and radical analyses. We were unlike students of previous generations in that we did not think of ourselves as empty vessels to be filled at the pleasure and discretion of administration and faculty. We felt an obligation and responsibility to inform our own lives. Weed, along with other substances and events, was loosening our connections to old hierarchies and enhancing our abilities to see the beauty, complexity and novelty in everything, from the mundane to the sacred. Everywhere we looked, we saw revelations unfolding; everywhere we turned, revolutions were at hand. Very little I would encounter during my first weeks on campus failed to open my eyes and blow my mind, with a single conviction that would continue to light my way: *that I was entitled to as much experience as I could possibly devour.* @ @

The official team time trial to determine the composition of the Varsity and Freshman Cross-Country teams took place on the warm and clear Saturday morning of October 5th. I was not surprised that Jack finished 33 seconds ahead of me, hanging with the Varsity pack, which came through together in 20:40. Jack was Number Three All-Time on the Stanford freshmen list. And I wasn't even second, being out-kicked over the last hundred yards by a fellow freshman from Los Altos High School, Bernie Lahde, a 9:13.8 Two-Miler, three seconds faster than Jack and forty-six seconds faster than mine. Based on our recent workouts, I felt I should have beaten him, so as penance for being taken from behind so to speak, by someone who style-wise struck me as a relentless plodder, I gave myself an extra seven-mile run that afternoon. But my time over the course was the ninth fastest on the All-Time Stanford freshman list. And it also easily bettered the clocking I needed to get my new pair of shoes.

So on Monday afternoon at 3:00 p.m., I took my place in line at the Dutch doors between the locker room and the equipment room, waiting for my Onitsuka Tigers, Size Nine, Cortez model.

"Here you are, Bob," Coach Clark said. I hadn't been "Bob" since I was five years old, but I couldn't have cared less. I was looking at the coolest pair of shoes I had ever seen in my life: two glued-together slabs of foam and leather, white with blue and red stripes and a raised heel to ease the pounding was what I was being paid to run for Stanford University. These Conquistadorian flats were expected to last us the year, meaning all the way through track season. They were a little on the heavy side, but the extra cushioning would help prevent injury. Slipping them on and taking a few baby trots across the locker room, I couldn't have felt more privileged, or more jazzed. *"I got 'em... I earned 'em... I got the Magic Shoes..."* @ @

Saturday, October 12th, 1968, was the day of our season opener: the 12th Annual Sacramento State Invitational Cross-Country Championship. It was also opening day of the Olympic Games in Mexico City. A hard rain had fallen the night before and the course was a muddy mess, leaving standing pools of water everywhere except along a quarter-mile patch of rocky trail behind Hornet Stadium and the grassy infield where our 4.2-mile race would begin and end.

The field for our race, the day's first, was huge: over two hundred Frosh and Junior College runners from across the State and as far away as Nevada. This was three times larger than any race I had ever been part of. Stanford's principal rival was the University of California at Berkeley Golden Bears, which included the fastest Half-Miler in the nation last spring, the great Texas high school middle-distance star John Drew, as well as the California State Mile Champion and winner of the Mile at the Golden West Invitational, which annually assembled the greatest high school Track & Field athletes from around the country. His name was Clifton West.

A voice over a scratchy PA: "Five minutes to race time." I looked down at my half-worn-out blue Adidas racing spikes, which Coach had dug out of the supply closet and "loaned" me for the day.

"This is it, son," Jack muttered, jogging up alongside me – wearing the same glazed, half-haunted look I undoubtedly wore: a look of impenetrable focus that overcomes most serious distance runners preparing to give it their all. My warm-up had felt good. Jack and I both felt strong. Despite our heavy workouts our legs were full of life.

I noticed a hundred spectators in attendance, fewer people than racers. The bib safety-pinned to my chest read "321." Countdown? Ignition?

Lift-off? We would need luck on this muddy day.

"Runners take your mark," called an older gentleman in a brown tweed porkpie hat.

"Moment of truth, Rapid Robert," Jack muttered as we trotted briskly to the line. *Was this what I had trained for all that summer, through ascending weeks of 56, 62, 71, and 80.5 miles, while also working four days a week as a supermarket check-out clerk at the local Albertson's?... I had run along the shoulder of Pacific Coast Highway (PCH), the hard sand bordering Pacific surf, and the faded trim of the Shorecliffs Golf Course that wound through my grandparents' subdivision in San Clemente, eyes open for flying golf balls and cursing duffers... One broiling day in late July I had run for ninety minutes and thirteen miles, longer and farther than I had ever run in my life, along a high cliff overlooking the Pacific. A total of 33 miles that day and the next in four workouts left me with balky knees, so I had to cut back to the mid-fifties the week afterwards. My skinny, five-foot, nine-inch, 137-pound frame had sucked up this training, taken to it like gangbusters...*

The race starter had to yank twice to extract the starter's pistol from his corduroy jacket and hold it off to one side, elbow crooked, waiting while two hundred or more of us settled behind the ragged chalk line across the stadium devil grass... I was just another cold, skinny college freshman, fearful, untested, ready to race myself to exhaustion, half-crouched at the line in my quarter-inch spikes, fronting a throng assembled as if for Pickett's Charge – most of us wearing college singlets in earnest for the first time, each of us poised and ferocious (or trying to be), determined to stop at nothing except the finish line – each of us a mystic knot, knowing the suffering we were about to endure, but eager for the crack of the starter's pistol – which came out of nowhere (no "runners set"), jolting us pell-mell across the line in a thunderous herd, elbows jabbing, shoulders jostling...Anyone who started too slowly or tripped and fell risked being trampled by a stampede! Our path promptly narrowed around two tight turns, which meant that the runners in back were trotting in place until there was room to move forward, while those of us in front (I was with this group) made the tight left U-turn out of the stadium along a narrow trail of mud and stones for a few hundred yards, where course officials blocked our way, waving us left, left, left, left, down another muddy trail that led to a steep rock-strewn levee where still more officials stood in yellow slickers, gesturing at us like stressed-out traffic cops, guiding us into the no-man's-land of undergrowth along the banks of the American River, where the bulk of the race would be won or lost.

The first half-mile passed in a state of such wild hysteria and disarray that my mind had barely functioned at all. Nothing about this felt familiar. I had never raced farther than two miles in my life. As a matter of common sense I knew enough to tell myself: settle down. Get a grip! Assess! The pace felt too fast for the distance we were racing and I was hurting barely a mile in, moving over a trail along the river's floodplain lined with thick, thorny brush, through a passage so narrow in places that it would have been difficult to pass anyone even if you felt you could, unless you were prepared to be gored by twigs and branches. But I was where I wanted to be: still among the leaders – part of a group of a dozen or so racing through thigh-scraping brush "amidst confusion and mud," as the Sacramento *Bee* later reported. The realization that I was near the front of the field invigorated me. I had felt like I was pressing before, but now I felt back in control, or at least farther away from the edge of it. I felt so good in fact that when I saw an opening ahead of me – thirty yards of visible trail – I impulsively ran into it, and kept on running hard for another hundred yards. My move left the rest of the field behind. Nothing lay ahead of me now but empty trail. @ @

There was a dream I once had, but never thought would come true: to be all alone in first place on a tough cross country course... Behind me I heard splashing footsteps, heavy breathing, and shouted expletives, probably from people who had run too close to the brush. The racing hadn't stopped; I just couldn't see it, even though I knew I was being chased by more than two hundred runners. This thought produced another wild swing of emotion. I was running beyond my comfort level again, soon to enter a section of the course the upperclassmen had warned us about: a three-quarter-mile stretch of sandy river bottom. A week earlier the team had driven over the coastal range to train in the heavy sand of San Gregorio Beach, in preparation for this moment. No one likes to run in sand, but I hated it. But this was our course that day, so I bore down, pumping my arms more, which I knew was the best way to maintain my pace, more or less. I muscled through it. And no one passed me. No one even moved up alongside. I was still in first place when I left the sandy river bottom for another quarter-mile of trail hemmed in by brush.

I was the first runner to see the levee, I was sure of it – returning like some ancient memory from a parallel universe… and in fifteen seconds I was pounding up it on the way back to the Stadium for the final stretch of racing. At the crest I stole my first glance behind – it would have been futile to look back through brush that obscured everything more than twenty feet behind me – and good grief! A half-dozen runners were close behind me, still in rabid pursuit! And another pack of fifteen or so behind them! This race still belonged to anybody! A moment later I was flying over the top of the levee and descending down it towards several dozen spectators, no more, all running in our direction, waving their arms and cheering their favorites. I saw Coach Clark (in his first race as a college coach) running to where he knew we would pass, that clipboard tucked under his arm. I already knew Coach wasn't much of a shouter, but as I passed he cupped his hand around his mouth and cried out, "Come on, Bob! Hang tough, Jack!"

Lawson has materialized alongside me. Man was I ever glad to see Jack! He was hurting, too, I could tell, because he didn't acknowledge me even for a moment – just stared straight ahead and ran, preparing himself (as I should be, too) for some gut-check racing at the end of this thing. Any serious distance runner will tell you that the last thing you want at the close of a hard-fought distance battle is to have to go as hard as you possibly can all the way to the finish line. It is infinitely easier – better! – to close a race with a reasonable effort, rather than have to expend every molecule of effort and will. But that was what it would take to win this race today. And so a tremor of fear ran through me, which was not a good thing. Would I have the guts to close this race? I had a perfect excuse for backing off. My excuse was that nobody expected me to win this thing, so no one would accuse me of cowardice if I let these runners slip by, because no one would know I quit. But even if I didn't quit – what if I "died?" What if I was passed by a dozen runners? What if I experienced total humiliation and collapse? Letting these negative thoughts rattle around my brain for even a moment was very unwise. My body was in agony and more pain was coming, but I knew that it would all be over in a matter of minutes, and the prospect of losing my place in this drama felt worse than the pain of abandoning it. So I hung on.

A Varsity teammate, junior Chuck Menz, screamed at us like a banshee as we flew by him: "Come on, Lawson!!! Come on, Coe!!! Make it hurt!!!!! *Make it hurt!!!!!*"

That's what we were doing, Chuck! We were *making it hurt!!!*

With a half-mile to go or less, I was still a co-leader! Was this really *my* lungs searing, my legs screaming, *my* heart thundering like never before? Hornet Stadium loomed to my right. There were four runners now: two strangers had closed the gap on Jack and me and were just behind us, judging by the sounds of their footfalls, fierce gasps and pants. (Was it Drew and West stalking us, waiting to close?) We ran just behind the grandstand, preparing to make a sharp U-turn into the stadium bowl for the race's climax, where I realized for the first time since the race began exactly how much distance remained to the finish: two hundred and fifty yards, maybe more, not less. This knowledge provided me with a sudden surge of energy.

As we emerged on to the edge of the football grass, I turned to Jack and gasped, *"Let's go."* And to my astonishment I rose up on my toes and began to sprint like a god-damned lunatic down the long sidelines of that stadium grass, around the tight left-angle turn on the football field, and then a second left turn, still alone, still sprinting – to where? To *where? Where was the god-damned finish line?* A tape suddenly materialized in front of me, and after 21 minutes and 57 seconds of dial-to-eleven effort, I broke it.

I broke the tape. I had won the race. @ @

A race official must have caught me under my arms, because the next thing I knew I was being propped on my feet and flung away – "Good race! Keep going! Through the chute! Keep moving…" My vision was blurred, but as I stumbled down the roped-off corridor away from the finish line, I looked down to see my legs were splattered with mud and my blue Adidas spikes soaked through. I wheeled around, still half-blind with pain, in time to watch Jack cross the finish line eight seconds behind me, as I later learned – a huge amount of time to put between the two of us in a couple of hundred yards.

And then, in slow-motion, the rest of the field began to come crashing across the finish line – a few runners at first, then clumps of them, stampeding, smashing into stragglers and crying out, a few collapsing in the mud, every one of them as spent as I was.

It would take five minutes for the rest of the field to finish.

Still jelly-legged, too stunned to jump up and down or pump my fist, the way winners were supposed to do, and too trashed to do anything more than what I was told, I was still trying to get a handle on what had just happened when Jack came trotting up, the mud-splattered King of the Central Valley, totally cool with finishing second.

"Rapid Robert! Good job!" He laughed his familiar throttled chuckle. "I wish I could have gone with you at the end, but I was *toast,* man!"

We got ourselves together and ran an easy mile, recapping the race from start to finish.

"You'd think they'd put some flags out there, Jack! There were times I was practically guessing which way to go! It was unnerving!"

Teammates arrived with news: George Watson had finished 10th; the Oregon Mile Champion, a lucky 13th; Bernie Lahde, 22nd. When the points were totaled we had won the Freshman/J.C. race easily with 48 points, pounding U.C. Davis, second with 130, and Santa Ana J.C., third with 131 points. I had no idea what had happened to Cal; I suddenly wasn't sure if Golden West winners Drew and West had even raced, and was too timid to ask around. I had not yet commented to anyone on my first-place finish. I think I wanted to behave as if this sort of thing had happened to me many times before, when in truth I was still struggling to believe that it had happened at all.

The gun went off for the Varsity race and we cheered our guys out of the stadium. I noticed people studying me from afar – fellow racers, checking me out. Jack noticed, too, and noticed me noticing.

"You're the Stud, Rapid Robert!"

"I can't believe it, Jack!" I said at last. "I won that race!"

We stopped for burgers and fries at a fast food place on the road back to Palo Alto, where I found a pay phone to call home collect. I still recall the stillness of that ancient phone booth, the black cigarette burns on the dark brown wood, the heft of the old-fashioned black receiver, and the dull, thick whirling of the rotary dial.

"Mom! It's me! Guess what! You're not going to believe this, but I won the race in Sacramento! I took first place!" My stepmother, who had been my sisters' kindergarten teacher before my natural mother's death, had raised me since I was five. With a son from a previous marriage, she also had three younger brothers with my Dad: the five Coe Boys.

Hearing my news, my Mom gasped out loud, burst into tears, and without another word passed the phone to Dad.

"Dad? Dad! You're not going to believe this, Dad, but I won the race in Sacramento! I beat over two hundred runners!"

My father did not express pride in me easily or often – he believed in his kids doing what was expected of them. But I heard pride in his voice that day. "Robert," he told me, "that is *faaan*-tastic…"

"*Faaan*-tastic" was my father's highest praise. It capped the day for me. @ @

I sat alone on the back bench of the mini-van for the long ride home, feeling the caked mud on my legs drying under my sweatpants and reliving the race in my mind time and again. I had won a few dual meet Half-Miles and Miles in high school, and had been on many winning relay teams, but never as the "anchor" runner who broke the tape. I hadn't even qualified for a "Regional" Track championship, much less a Texas State Track Championship. Only a few weeks earlier I had been a ten-minute Two-Miler, worrying if I would make the team. But all the hard work I had done over the summer had paid off in my first college race – my first race at any distance longer than two miles, and my first race in the distance-running Mecca of California. And I had dominated the race from the beginning, running in front then destroying a huge field of freshman and J.C. harriers with my final kick. I felt as if I had arrived at the base camp of a Big Rock Candy Mountain so substantial and *real* that as our team van pulled into the parking lot of the Stanford locker rooms, I wanted to lean out the window and shout out what protestors had chanted at rioting police at the Democratic Convention in Chicago that summer: *"The Whole World is Watching! The Whole World is Watching! The Whole World is Watching..."*

I was well aware that the whole world wasn't watching *me*. I was as high as a kite, but I wasn't delusional. Nobody much cared about what had just happened to us except our competitors, our families, our close friends, and us. Winning a freshman cross country race wouldn't amount to a hill of beans on Stanford's campus, even after Brook Thomas fed six inches of news to the *Daily* for the Monday edition. The news would not be broadcast over the airwaves of KZSU, Stanford's underground radio station, wired in the basement of MemAud. Sunday would unfold pretty much same old same old: I would sleep in and take an easy hour run in the mid-afternoon with Jack, then study again until dinner. Afterwards I would meet up with some guys from our hallway to smoke some weed – a few hits on a joint never affected my training or anything else, except my Head – then stroll over to MemAud for "The Flicks," Stanford's Sunday night film series since 1937, which my father and Aunts remembered fondly from their years on The Farm. The film that night was "The Fox," about lesbian lovers living in an isolated farmhouse in Canada – red meat to us stoned knuckleheads in the balcony, who in another inglorious Flick tradition disrupted the film with many inappropriate heckles and cat calls. Afterwards we would stroll back to Branner and make a munchie run on the vending machines in the cafeteria hallway before tromping off to our late night beds.

And when Monday morning rolled around, I would roll out of bed, do my morning run, and show up for my eight a.m. Biology class, as if nothing much out of the ordinary had happened to me at all. @ @

My grandparents received the news about Sacramento in a letter I wrote and mailed on Monday afternoon. My grandmother responded in carbon copy, addressed to my sister and me: "We were very glad to get Robert's letter today and to hear of your running triumphs and devotion to studies." They would have to mention the studies part. But I was fine with it. If they couldn't appreciate running on their own terms, they would never understand it in mine.

That Wednesday I came home from my long road run to discover something waiting on my desk: a Western Union telegram, dated October 17th. It was from my Dad's best friend, a man with six kids (like my father), who lived a few houses away in our Texas subdivision. The telegram read in full: *"Congratulations on your track accomplishments I hope we will be able to do as well on the flight of Apollo 8. William A Anders NASA Astronaut"* Our neighbor Bill Anders was one of the three Apollo spacemen, later named *Time* magazine's "Men of the Year" for 1968, who were six weeks away from becoming the first humans to leave earth's gravity, enter deep space, and circle 'round the moon.

I told my family about this telegram and thanked Bill for it, but I never showed it to anyone at Stanford except Jack Lawson. It ended up in a box, which ended up inside another box. I would not look at it again for another twenty-five years. @ @ @

THE LAST OF THE PAPOOSES

That feeling I had in the van coming home from Sacramento – that the whole world was watching – penetrated every nook and cranny of our lives in the fall of '68. It was uncanny how the news of the day and sensations of the world seemed to flow through our daily thoughts and emotions. And yet the sport we pursued lay near the bottom of the campus food chain, somewhere close to gymnastics, or fencing. Intercollegiate cross country supposedly began at Stanford in 1917, maybe because Governor Stanford had poached his engineering faculty from Cornell, which may have had a cross-country tradition with roots in England, where the modern sport was invented. I was guessing, because by the time Payton Jordan arrived in 1956, he had to reinstate a program that had been discontinued at a date none of us could ascertain. We knew nothing about our history beyond the memories of participants over the past five years or so. Cross country was a sport that almost nobody else cared about. The "jogging" fad of the late Seventies was still a decade away. When the recent film *The Graduate* screened at the Flicks that fall, not even former Dartmouth cross country captain Benjamin Braddock (Dustin Hoffman) could lend so much as a glimmer of existential glamour to our sport.

Not many people "got" what we were up to at all. One person who didn't was my suitemate Zac, a former football benchwarmer at nearby Gunn High School. Zac went to some trouble one evening to explain

31

why he thought distance running was a third-rate sport. (Our other suitemate was a wrestler from West Covina and the only child of a single mom, who kept a giant portrait of his high school girlfriend on his desk and cried himself to sleep at night on the bunk above mine.)

"In football or baseball or basketball," Zac said, as I sat at my desk in our narrow study, untying my Tigers in growing annoyance, "you're using all your muscle groups, your upper-body strength, your hand-to-eye coordination, everything. You distance runners are basically just a cardiovascular system with legs. No," Zac concluded with great confidence in his opinion, "the best sports are ones that ask for a much more complete athleticism than what you guys do."

"Then go play club rugby, Zac," I said, and flung my Tigers under my desk. I resented this uninformed not to mention rude opinion, but in the end decided to cut Zac some slack. I was surely a familiar sight, leaving Branner in the early mornings and again in the afternoons, shirtless in running shorts and Onitsuka Tigers (always with no socks), and returning an hour or two or three later red-faced with sweat streaming from my body in rivulets. And yet I was never sure if anybody in my dorm ever realized I was an athlete at all. @ @

Being a Jock at Stanford was different than being one at other schools. This wasn't just my opinion; it was established fact – part of the ethos of the place. Athletes on The Farm weren't treated all that differently than any other students on campus. Being involved in sports didn't make you a demigod; it was simply part of your unique educational experience, which was something everyone was having. Athletes weren't sequestered in athletic dorms, because Stanford didn't have any – never had, never would – and no training tables, either, except for the football team, and only for them during football season. You could stroll the Quad on a normal school day and fail to see a single letterman's jacket. If a person wanted nothing much to do with college athletics in the fall of '68, The Farm was not a bad place to hang out.

This lack of profile didn't mean there weren't athletes around, because there were, lots of them. Some of the best were in Mexico City, representing the U.S. and other nations at the XIXth Olympiad. My victory in Sacramento made me feel enough like a Stanford Jock to think I was one, seated on a sofa in front of Branner's only TV set alongside a sixteen-year-old freshmen swimmer who had broken the world record in the 1,500-Meter Freestyle only a few months before, finishing second in the first of two heats at the U.S. Olympic Trials. Mark Shelley's time had ended up the third fastest of the day, but because he would finish fifth in the Final the next day (by a fraction of a second), he wasn't swimming South of the Border. Instead he was sitting next to me on a soft pink sofa in Branner Hall, watching the great Stanford Butterflyer and Individual Medley specialist John Ferris, his boyhood friend from Arden Hills Swim Club in Carmichael, California, mount the medal stand to accept a Bronze Medal in the 200 IM: a race involving Butterfly, Backstroke, Breaststroke, and Free.

The "Star Spangled Banner" was playing and Old Glory was rising up the flagpole for the Gold Medalist, Indiana University junior Charlie Hickcox, when John lifted his fingers to the bridge of his nose. His knees buckled, and he fainted dead away.

"No, John! *No!!!*" Mark cried out as his friend's slumping body, overcome by fatigue and the altitude in Mexico City – 7,469 feet – was caught mid-slump by Hickcox, World Swimmer of the Year in '68, and Silver Medalist Greg Buckingham, a three-time world-record holder who also happened to be Ferris's Stanford fraternity brother.

Mexico City was the first Olympics to be broadcast instantaneously via satellite to every corner of the globe. All that day and the next, images of Ferris fainting on the victory stand would be splashed on TV and on the front pages of newspapers on five continents around the planet.

In the case of Ferris' sporting feat and subsequent faint, the whole world really was watching. @ @

Being a Jock at Stanford, or feeling like I was one, entitled me (I thought) to form my own opinions about Stanford's athletic programs. Our Athletic Department billed itself as the "Home of Champions," and there was some truth to this, but my research suggested that Stanford was the "Home of Champions" about as often as it was the "Home of Free Radicals." The Indians' traditional strengths were in the country-club sports: swimming ('67 N.C.A.A. Champs), tennis (although not yet with the dominance of later years), and golf. The '67 baseball team was 36-6-1, the best record in school history, but Stanford had not sent a round ball quintet to an N.C.A.A. tournament since 1942, and the current one was only good for getting U.C.L.A's Lew Alcindor to town, or so I not-so-humbly thought. Stanford hadn't fielded a top-twenty pigskin eleven since 1955. Last year's team was the definition of average: 5-5 in '67. The Athletic Department blamed these lackluster showings on the hazards of getting athletes through a tough Admission process, and there was some truth to this. But the larger problem was that Stanford either didn't have the money, or wasn't spending it on Jocks. With a handful of exceptions, like the new Stadium track and a basketball pavilion set to open in January, Stanford's athletic facilities dated from the pre-war era. Locker rooms were shabby, tennis courts pebbled, and equipment, even towels, in short supply. The national championship swim team put in its watery miles in a twenty-five-yard pool. Other than the new track, the 85,000-seat Stadium hadn't changed much since 1930, the year it opened.

Figuring all this out on my own did nothing to dampen my enthusiasm for Stanford sports. With my always over-heated imagination for the glories of competition and my family's mythology of Stanford Win, Lose or Draw, I became a rabid football fan that autumn, sun-bathing in the student bleachers (not the shady side where alumni sat), screaming myself hoarse and holding up those little colored squares to help spell out support of a team whose starting Defensive Ends weighed two hundred pounds each and whose star middle linebacker busted the scales at 205. Few football players were lifting weights in those days. Stanford had yet to hire a full-time Conditioning Coach, and two trainers cared for all sports combined. I couldn't have cared less. I couldn't have cared less that I smoked pot, hated war, supported civil rights for all Americans, and was a distance-running geek. I felt no contradiction at all between my budding countercultural proclivities and my developing love of Leland Stanford Junior University Football. @ @

Care to hear "the Winds of Freedom blow?" All you had to do was check out "The Incomparable Leland Stanford Junior University Marching Band," an all-male ensemble scattering across football fields like so many boiling molecules, dressed in waiter's jackets, pink tutus, heart-covered boxer shorts, wet suits and snorkels while playing funky rock 'n' roll ("Up Tight," "Midnight Hour," Beatles and Stones hits), and poking fun at anything untoward or right-wing in the news that week. Arthur P. Barnes, the current band director, had replaced a popular figure back in '63, and several band members had gone on strike to protest; Barnes won them all back by basically promising that they could do whatever they wanted to do going forward. Explaining his role many years later, Barnes would tell a newspaper, "I wrote the music and kept them out of jail."

Care to hear the answers blowin' in the wind? Then harken to the voices being raised against the very symbol of Stanford football since 1930: a google-eyed, bulbous-nosed, Al Capp-like caricature of a Native American that made a Negro lawn jockey look like a statue of Martin Luther King. Brook Thomas' mimeographed newsletters arrived on shiny Athletic Department letterhead festooned with these cartoon representations of our racial mascot engaged in various athletic pursuits, including pole-vaulting; one had him diving into a swimming pool wearing nothing but moccasins. These "Indian" images had adorned the windshields of my family cars for as long as I could remember (years later I noticed the startling resemblance of Stanford's "Indian" to cross-dressing Corporal Klinger on TV's M*A*S*H*), but all the same, these images were so politically retrograde, it hurt. Of course losing this sideshow version of an oppressed minority would also mean waving bye-bye to "Prince Lightfoot," the Yurok Native American who had performed at every Stanford home game since the year after I was born. Prince Lightfoot in civilian life was Timm Williams, who worked for a variety of Native American causes, although his critics claimed that his stadium dances were desecrations of ancient religious practices. I should have disapproved of "Uncle Tom-Tom," a name I heard more than once that fall, but I still found it moving when the stadium hushed and Lightfoot appeared in his white moccasins, white chaps and turf-length feathered war bonnet, his bare chest lifted high as he stamped and soared with heart-rending beauty – almost as if our players were his totem animals, and he wasn't their show-business mascot. Years later, when Lightfoot's dances were authenticated as Native American, but from Plains Indians, not his Hurok people, I would wish we had heard this from Williams himself.

These antics of our Incomparable Band and the political battles over our mascot may have been timely, but of far more interest to cock-eyed optimists like yours truly was the promise evinced on the playing field, the primary source of which hailed from the gritty East San Jose neighborhood of Alum Park, where Jim Plunkett grew up. Both of Plunkett's parents were blind. His Dad ran a post office newsstand to support his wife and three kids. As a teenager Plunk had worked as a gas station attendant, grocery store clerk and day laborer at a time when Mexican-Americans were treated like second-class citizens throughout most of California. He was about to enter Stanford when a cancerous tumor was discovered on his thyroid, threatening to derail his football career before it began. A Stanford assistant coach whose mother had recently gone blind pledged to honor Plunkett's scholarship, whatever the outcome. The tumor proved benign, but when Plunkett was slow to heal, Stanford's fifth-year Head Coach John Ralston contemplated switching him to Defensive End, a position he had played with distinction in a Shriner high school all-star game. Ralston's main concern was that Plunkett did not appear to have your stereotypical QB personality: he was a quiet type, although extremely well-liked and valued as a great teammate and a solid guy. But Plunkett wanted to play QB, and to that end trained all summer, reportedly throwing 500 to 1,000 passes a day while holding down a tough job in construction.

And in his first start during my first fall on campus, this rocket-armed redshirt sophomore went 10 for 13 for 277 yards and four touchdowns in only a halftime of work against San Jose State, earning himself the starting job, along with the respect and regard of everyone involved in Stanford sports. His favorite target was senior flanker Gene Washington, who snared 71 passes for 1,117 yards, both school records, after sprinting 100-yards in 10.1 for the track team in the spring. The first Black member of Delta Tau Delta anywhere in the nation, Washington would go on to a become an All-Pro wide receiver with the San Francisco 49ers and the N.F.L.'s Director of Football Operations. And many decades later he would be seen squiring ex-Bush Security Advisor and Secretary of State and current Stanford Provost Condoleeza Rice around town, which made my blood run cold when I read about it, but there you are. @ @

In the final year that the Pac-8 fielded freshmen football teams, we had football heroes at Branner, too. Defensive Tackle Greg Sampson, a six-foot five-inch Baby Huey who sometimes shared my breakfast table, holding bowls of steaming oatmeal under his chin and spoon-feeding himself like a backhoe. With his bristly Jarhead haircut (no curls needed for this Sampson's divine strength) and pimply cheeks otherwise smooth as a baby's bottom, Sampson seemed like a great big innocent to me (as I was a skinny innocent), but also like your stereotypical football player, focused on the game and academically under-engaged – perhaps an unfair assessment, since I barely knew Greg at all. Not picking on Sampson, but Stanford football players did not entirely escape the clichés about meatheads and Neanderthals, not to mention right-wingers: during the Columbia University shut-down that past spring, football players had been among the leaders of counter-demonstrations opposing the occupation of university buildings.

The notion that a football player could be a "Scholar-Athlete" was still oxymoronic to most people, even though athletics had been a component of Rhodes Scholarships for generations, not to mention getting thumbs up in Plato's *Republic* and the *Tao Te Ching*. An important part of Stanford's appeal to smarter student-athletes was its high academic standards and a curriculum with few if any "gimme" classes – no "Rocks for Jocks" (Geology 101). Stanford generally attracted the kind of student-athletes who had ambitions in the classroom and for their lives beyond the Game. But if you needed anything to inflame your dislike of football, not to mention any anti-Greek prejudices you might be harboring, harken back just eighteen months to the night when several masked members of the Delta Tau Delta chapter at Stanford – the Jock Animal House on campus, despite the presence of good guys like Plunkett and Washington – accosted Student Body President David Harris on a shadowy corridor of the Quad and gave him a buzz haircut, to which Harris (a football letterman at Fresno High School and the future author of two books about the N.F.L.) submitted without "Resistance," or so I was told.

But any behavior that reinforced clichés about what idiots football players could be failed to conceal something far more interesting that was happening on The Farm: *the "Student-Athletes" I was meeting embodied as much cultural diversity as the student body-at-large.* Everything happening on campus touched Jocks, too: dorm life, recreational drug use, heroic quests for peak experiences and communal excellence, challenging academic work, radical political activism – athletes were part of the whole deal. Participating in sports didn't give anyone a free pass on anything, and if you thought it did, you probably weren't paying attention in class that day. In the season of "Broadway Joe" Namath's Superbowl guarantee and Muhammad Ali's Draft Resistance, football was up to its eyeballs in 1968, the same as everything else was.

"The whole campus is up to beat S.C.," I wrote home during my first month, exaggerating a little to keep the previous generations happy, and myself, too, for that matter. "Everybody seems to think we can do it. After the first game of the season against San Jose State" – a 68-20 shellacking of our peninsula rivals that generated the most points by a Stanford team since 1949 – "some people around here are 'smelling roses!'" S.C. had long been the insurmountable roadblock on any highway to New Year's Day in Pasadena. In '68 the Trojans were the number two team in the country, but our student body believed that an eighteenth-ranked Stanford team led by Jim Plunkett could take them down. I was in Sacramento on game day, so I couldn't join the 81,000 fans at Stanford Stadium, a crowd not seen on campus since the Nineteen-Thirties. What people saw that afternoon was a Trojan offense known as "Give it to the Juice and Set him Loose." The future Heisman Trophy winner Orenthal James "O.J." Simpson spent the entire afternoon knocking down Indian braves like so many bowling pins, rushing for 220 yards on get this: *47* carries. Even so, the game was tied late in the Fourth 24-24 behind three Plunkett TD arrows. With almost no time left on the clock, S.C.'s Quarterback threw a pass to O.J. in the flat, where he was immediately hit by two defenders. But Simpson shook them off and improvised a miracle pass that set up the Trojan's last-second 34-yard game-winning field goal, ending Stanford's Rose Bowl hopes for another year. This crushing defeat did not seem to crush us. Our team would finish the season 6-3-1, with a nucleus of returning players that left many observers believing that gridiron greatness lay just around the corner. I certainly thought so, even during the dismal home loss to Oregon State, 29-7, on November 2nd, during which I preferred to focus on the Stanford Dollies (cheerleaders) in their Indian-Maiden-Meets-Mondrian pleated short skirts and blood-red panties, rather than observe the drubbing being administered by the Beavers on our Stadium grass. @ @

I followed everything on The Farm that fall, and everything followed me. What of my desideratum: Stanford Track & Field? I had barely investigated it in high school, since I was going to Stanford, end of story. But now I thumbed through the record books and learned about Stanford track immortal Ben Eastman, who set world records in the Half- and Quarter-Miles as an undergrad in the Thirties, and Decathlete Bob Mathias, who showed up on campus as a freshman in 1949 with an Olympic Gold Medal from the '48 London Games. (His world record of 7,887 points, set during the Helsinki Games four years later, remains Stanford's school record in the twenty-first century.) More recent seasons had produced more spring stars, among them Larry Questad, a binge-drinking frat boy from Livingston, Montana, shortly to finish sixth in the 200-Meter Olympic final in Mexico City. A Questad-led sprint quartet and a national discus champion had carried the 1963 team to a second place finish at the N.C.A.A. Championships; two years later, a Questad-anchored 4 x 110 yard sprint relay team set a world record of 39.7 seconds, but managed only fifth at the N.C.A.A. Championship that year.

The Athletic Department saw fit to boast about last year's tenth-place finish at the N.C.A.A. meet, led by Australian Olympian Peter Boyce's third-place in the high jump; junior Tom Colby, a recent Tulane transfer, third in the javelin; and sophomore Greg Brock, fifth over 10,000-Meters. Not so bad. But a closer reading of the sixteen-page media brochure delivered the harder truth: Stanford Track & Field was a perennial doormat, last at the conference championship this past spring after a 2-8 dual meet season that included ritual slaughters at the hands of U.S.C. and U.C.L.A., our two downstate rivals and consistent national championship title contenders, by scores so lopsided they looked like misprints: like, say, 120-40. Stanford hadn't beaten the University of Oregon in decades. Washington State had pounded us last spring, 109-36. And arch-rival Cal had grabbed the latest "Big Meet," 100-45. This record of futility made it difficult to comprehend how the current Head Coach of the U.S. Olympic Track & Field team, getting ready to lace 'em up in Mexico City, and the mastermind behind the historic Cold War U.S.-Russia dual meet in 1962, was our own Head Coach Payton Jordan. This was another mystery I would need to figure out, with a little help from my friends. @ @

Coach Clark had told us at the start of the year that we wouldn't have a lot of team meetings, but after the Varsity upset of U.S.C at Sac State, despite Trojan runners finishing 1-2 overall, he called us together for a pow-wow. The AP had picked up a story that the San Jose *Mercury* had right: "Stanford's cross country runners produced the biggest shakeup of the year in national collegiate cross country ratings by nipping U.S.C. in the Sacramento State Invitational meet on Saturday. Stanford, behind Brook Thomas's 4th place finish and 7th, 8th, 14th, and 16th place efforts by Allen Sanford, Don Kardong, Greg Brock, and Chuck Menz respectively, trimmed the top rated Trojans 49-50."

"We were major underdogs on Saturday," Coach told our assembly. "The race director had predicted we would finish no better than fourth in the team competition. Instead we really took it to S.C. Great job, fellows." A golf clap for the lads: Here, Here, Hip Hip, Tally-Ho, and all that. The day before the meet, Coach Clark told the *Daily* that he thought this year's squad might be "the strongest in school history."

"I also think it's important to acknowledge," Coach went on, "that while Duncan didn't score among our top five, he did finish ahead of S.C.'s fifth man, which enabled us to win the meet by a single point."

Duncan was sitting on the concrete floor lacing up his shoes when Coach ladled out this dollop of praise. He seemed momentarily startled to see the team applauding him vigorously. Finally getting what this was about, he held up one palm to stop us, saying – "Really, guys, it was nothing – *nothing...*" while wiggling his fingers on the hand below, inaudibly declaring "come on guys, more, *more...*"

"Keep believing in each other and this team has a chance to go far," Coach said after the clapping died down. Let's head out to the golf course. One-mile reps today."

Without hesitation we rose in one body, shoe-horned ourselves through the locker room door, and left the building at a quick dog-trot, hanging a hard left to set off across the heart of campus towards the lush green rolling fairways where we trained and raced.

On the way Coach Clark located me among the ragged harriers and trotted up alongside, clipboard tucked under his arm.

"You're doing well, Bob. I told Coach Jordan about you." Then he jogged ahead to share a few words with the Varsity.

I had already picked up a little about what our upperclassmen thought about Coach Jordan, and it wasn't good. Coach Clark was never anything less than respectful, even reverential towards our Head Coach, who had given him his first college job, although with an assist from our team, which voted him in. Whenever any of us started cracking wise or sounding judgmental about Coach Jordan, Coach

Clark became visibly uncomfortable, which of course made us drop our riffs instantly. For my part, I felt jazzed to be on Jordan's radar, even if he was a right-wing fanatic who had denounced "liberal loudmouths" in the pages of *Track & Field News*. He was the U.S. Olympic Coach and the Head Coach at Stanford, and I was a captive of the mythologies of the Olympics and Stanford U. @ @

Coach Clark was out of earshot, running with some of the J.V. freshman well behind us, while a group of Varsity runners passed the fountain and statue in White Plaza known as "The Claw," heading towards the golf course for our workout and gabbing, as usual. I already had the impression that getting to know my new teammates would be interesting. The fact that all of us were committed to the same challenging endeavor gave us an opportunity to get to know one another in ways we probably would never have done otherwise. Some of the most memorable conversations I would have in college would be with these guys. We were out of breath a lot, because we were running, but that didn't stop us from talking, or trying to talk. A leading topic that fall was the rampant absurdities of our Head Coach.

"So what's the skinny on Coach Jordan?" I shouted to no one in particular and everyone in general. "What's he all about?"

"He's a screaming Bircher!" someone shrieked in reply.

"Somewhere to the right…"

"…of Attila the Hun!"

"That is so weird!" I huffed. "My old high school Coach… taught 'Senior Government'… using literature from the John Birch Society… The day I challenged him… on a few 'facts…' about the 'International Communist Conspiracy…' I ran extra laps at practice…"

"Smart!"

"Punish someone – "

"– by making him train more…"

"Good messaging!"

"Eisenhower *was* a Commie! You know that, don't you?"

"Damn straight he was!"

"As Red as a… as a fire truck!"

"Don't let those 'Liberal Loudmouths' fool you!"

"Full-blown agent… of *Moscow,* that Eisenhower fellow."

"Better Red… than Dead …"

"Better Dead than *Red!*"

"Anti-Communist dyslexia!" General laughter.

"Birchers… what a buncha –"

"How do you know –"

"Might as well be…"

"So you don't really know –"

"Somewhere to the Right –"

"– of Attila the *Hun!*"

"Don't sweat it," said Brook Thomas, sliding up alongside me in one fluid move. "If it's something Payt said… we basically just tune it out… Have you heard the story of Pat Morrison?" @ @

I had heard pieces of the Pat Morrison saga: how this much-heralded English freshman had arrived on campus in the spring of '66 as the British national 200-Meter sprint champion although only a teenager – a surprise, given that The Farm attracted fast sprinters about as often as the football team had a strong defense, meaning almost never. Morrison was in a Stanford uniform the day he defeated the world-record holder and future Olympic Gold Medalist, San Jose State's Tommie Smith, over 220 yards. After the race he introduced himself to his competitor and was enjoying their conversation when a Stanford assistant coach pulled Morrison aside and informed him that Stanford athletes don't fraternize with the opposition. My views on this I shared with Morrison: you respect your rivals if they are worthy of it and you don't necessarily snub them or treat them with disdain. But this was only the first in a string of "subversive" actions on the part of Pat Morrison. His blonde Beatle mop-top and refusal to trim it was the stated reason Jordan kicked him off the team, although the real reason was that Jordan had personally caught him smoking weed in his hotel room on a road trip to L.A., and concocted this cover story to spare Morrison any legal repercussion, or so I would hear it claimed.

Hair being the cutting edge of the Culture Wars in '67, Patrick Morrison's coif, like David Harris's pate, had been big news on campus last spring, with his expulsion written up in the *Daily*. This might have been the end of it if Coach Jordan hadn't exercised a serious lapse in judgment: he actually mailed letters to the parents of all of Morrison's teammates, warning them not to let their sons be duped by Leftwing elements on campus and to keep their son away from a man whom Jordan claimed on paper was literally a member of the Communist Party – an accusation so preposterous that Morrison reportedly had a lawsuit filed for defamation. Jordan was lucky he wasn't fired. His refusal to re-instate Morrison for the "Big Meet" against Cal prompted several teammates to quit the team in solidarity. Stanford's other great long sprinter, Larry Questad, was so incensed by this long-haired Limey Pinko Freak who ran the same event he did exceptionally well (and had broken his freshman school record) that Questad allegedly assembled a posse of like-minded teammates to literally Tar & Feather the man. (I would learn this from Morrison himself fifteen years later, when I saw a man waiting outside a theater office in Downtown L.A. and asked, "Are you Pat Morrison?" A painter with a celebrity clientele in the entertainment world, Morrison would tell me that he believed Jordan and Assistant Coach Jerry Barland knew all about the Tar & Feather Plot, but had not lifted a finger to stop it.)

So that was the deal! My future college Head Coach of Record was the most reviled conservative on campus, if just this side of William Shockley, the Nobel-prize-winning inventor of the transistor, who was out there peddling his cockamamie theories of eugenics and calling for the mass sterilization of ghetto blacks who were "down-breeding" humanity. Jordan wasn't racist, but he was not in support of the Black Power movement, informing *Track & Field News* before the Games that the proposed boycott by black American Olympians wasn't a response to "real grievances." What about second-class citizenship? Wasn't that a grievance worth making some fuss about? How could anyone, especially a West Coast Track Coach, be that blind? @ @

"I knew none of this, Brook!" I huffed. "I had no idea... Coach Jordan... was like some kind of right-wing... *nut* job!"

We were running now past Lake Lagunita, along a wide dirt road under towering Eucalypti, soon to pass the Stanford Stables on the way to our favorite spot to stretch before our golf course workout. We had to be careful on this patch of road not to step on a Eucalyptus button, some of which were large enough to tweak your ankle.

"Don't worry about it," Brook said. "We're on our own a lot... But Coach Jer...'" His face brightened at the mere mention of last year's Assistant Coach for distance running. "Now Ol' Jer... Now there was a piece of work..."

I had heard about the old distance coach Jerry Barland already: how he coached the team with unrelenting intervals and various "Missions Impossible" before departing only months ago to become Chairman of the P.E. Department at Butte College in Chico, and later a distance Coach at Iowa State University in Ames. "Train don't strain" was not anywhere on Jer's menu, but around-the-oval monotony was. (During one of our sophomore's campus visit as a high school senior, Don Kardong had been waiting in the locker room for Barland to show up, and the upperclassman who was showing him around campus leaned in and said, "Why would you want to come *here?*")

"You don't wanna know about Coach Jer," Brook huffed, before launching into his story anyway. "For starters, Jer was the Coach... who told Pat Morrison... not to fraternize... with Tommie Smith..."

"As if there's something's wrong... with being friendly... with your competition – got it –"

"Coach Jer' told us once" – here Brook assumed a pompous, know-it-all tone – "'Boys, I want you to go out five miles… at ninety percent effort… then I want you to come back… five minutes faster!' We were all like, 'Uh – Coach…'"

"What's wrong with that? Sounds like a decent workout to me…"

Brook glanced over at me. "Figure it out, Coe! Five miles… at ninety percent effort… then come back… a minute faster per mile? That isn't hard… that's physically impossible! Large!" Brook swiveled around. "D'jew hear what Coe just said?"

Senior Allen Sanford – aka "Big Al," aka "Large" – was a very good cross country runner, seventh overall in Sacramento, and even better on the track, where he would be gunning for an unprecedented third consecutive victory in the Big Meet Mile that spring – a string no one had put together in the history of a rivalry going back seventy-five years. A happy-go-lucky soul with a croaking laugh and a constant expression of merriment on his face, Large jetted up to his best friend Brook and me and shouted, "Coe! You *weenie!*" He was ten feet away before I could manage a reply. (Whenever anyone said anything remotely stupid or even better, painfully naïve, Large would laugh in the person's face and say, "You *weenie!*" I would hear it a lot that fall.)

"Sounds like I dodged a bullet," I said. While Brook and Allen laughed at me I spent a moment contemplating the relief our upperclassmen must feel, after the absurdities of Coach Jer, to be working with Coach Clark, who actually listened to what we thought and expected to learn from *us* – a coach who gave us the bit, then handed us the reins.

"Hang in there, rookie…" said Greg Brock, pounding up alongside me with that jarring stride of his, on his heels – funky, but strong. "Let's see if we can't win some cross-country meets this fall…" @ @

Greg Brock was an interesting person to get to know, and even more interesting to train with. Nothing much seemed to get past Brock, which was what everybody called him. Last year's cross country M.V.P. and a track All-American over 10,000 meters, Greg had taken Jack and me out on a fourteen-mile run during our first week on campus, and while I never let on that I had never run that far in my life, Brock figured it out and teased me about it. A junior psychology major from Sacramento, he wore Pre-Retro, NASA desk jockey black horn rim glasses and had been blind in his right eye since the age of two, which left him 4F in the Draft, lucky stiff. He was also the fastest distance runner in Stanford history: the school record holder in the Two- and Three-Miles since the previous spring, when he rounded off a great sophomore campaign with a fifth-place in the 10,000-Meters at the N.C.A.A. championship, just nine seconds out of second place, thus guaranteeing himself (at age nineteen) a spot in the U.S. Olympic trials, for which he over-trained, resulting in a big DNF (Did Not Finish.) Brock ran with his elbows cocked at a funny angle and never seemed to get up on his toes to sprint, but he more than made up for it by being the team's hardest worker: prior to his senior year in high school Greg had averaged 97-miles a week for the entire summer, and he had done 100-mile weeks for most of this past one. Brock worked hard, but he was also extremely shrewd about what it would take to maximize his talent and lift his running to the next level. Having Brock on your team was almost like having a second Coach around – not because he gave us workouts, just a lot of good ideas.

Our fifth scorer at Sac State that day on the golf course was junior Chuck Menz, an Electrical Engineering major from nearby Cupertino High School and a thoroughly lovely guy – with his shy sincerity and smiling over-bite almost a cartoon cross country nerd, which made him the vessel of a certain holiness for us all. Chuck you could always count on for a little insane positive reinforcement: he had practically torn his own tonsils out in Sacramento, screaming at Jack and me to *'Make it hurt!'* Having a teammate like Chuck around, willing to go all psychotic for you while you raced, screaming like a man who had lost his mind, was energizing, I swear it was. When Chuck used his name for himself – "Tiger" – you believed him, and you wouldn't have been wrong. His kind, mild-mannered father wouldn't miss a single meet that fall. I liked having him around because he seemed like a kind of stand-in for all of our absent, World War Two-generation Dads.

To complete the Varsity snapshot, two sophomores: Don Kardong, our third man in Sacramento, a psychology major from Bellevue, Washington: six-foot-three inches of reed slimness, with a loopy, lopsided grin and an antic disposition, loping along in the middle of the pack in those days with eyes wide open for the nearest irony to feast upon. Don hadn't started running until his sophomore year at Seattle Prep, but as a senior had been runner-up for a Washington State cross country title. Arriving on The Farm as a walk-on in the fall of '67, he was unsure if he wanted to run at all. He had just managed a 4:22 Mile at an All-Comers meet over the summer; his lifetime PR was 4:16. Our other sophomore trained when he felt like it or when he could, which wasn't often, and even less often at the same time: Duncan Macdonald had been out of touch all summer, living in his home state of Hawaii and "his own time zone," as Brock quipped. His time at Sac State was only four seconds faster than mine, but Duncan was the high school state record-holder in Hawaii (his Dad was a Volcanologist) in both the Half-Mile and the Mile, despite his irregular training habits and a well-known love of brew that earned him the soubriquet "Drunken Duncan." A Biology major and a Phi Delt, Dunc was very funny, very mischievous, and very private, as far as I could tell. He was also, in the opinion of many more people than me, the most naturally-gifted runner on campus: the owner of one of those classic middle-distance gears that allowed him to run ungodly fast for stirring lengths of time. If Duncan ever got his act together and trained as hard and as consistently as we did, there would be little he couldn't do in our sport. But in the fall of '68 – after giving up the fight and shaving his 'stache – Duncan was Stanford's sixth cross-country man.

Ten or twelve other upperclassmen trained with us, too, but our Varsity was basically the Magnificent Seven: Brook, Large, Brock, Tiger, Don, Drunken Duncan and a third senior, Bob Anchondo from El Paso, Texas. Seven was also the number of runners a school could enter in a cross-country competition, with only five scoring, according to place, which means low score wins – just like golf. A 1-2-3-4-5 finish equaled 15, which was cross-country's version of perfection. Sixth and seventh runners scored no points themselves, but they could factor in if they finished ahead of a rival team's scorer, thus increasing the other team's total, as Duncan had done in Sacramento. The way scoring worked means that cross-country teams try to run as a pack, in order to pull slower runners along with swifter ones, because a team's fifth scorer could be as important as its first – arguably more important, because it was usually easier to improve a runner from a fortieth-place finish to a thirtieth, say, and drop ten points from your score, than it was to improve someone from a third-place finish to first, and drop only two. With Macdonald and Anchondo too far out of the mix to matter at this point early in the season, our top five runners would need to keep it together until late November – because only an undefeated season would inspire the Athletic Department to send a full squad to the Nationals, to be held that year at a legendary cross-county citadel: Van Cortlandt Park in the Bronx, New York. Not even our outstanding team in '62 had been deemed worthy to travel and compete against the nation's best. Brook had been beating the drums for an N.C.A.A. trip in his summer newsletters, frequently mentioning that we should think of ways to raise the money ourselves. @ @

"Listen, Brook," I called out to our Team Captain, still on our way to the golf course that day, after our loose discussion of Jordan's Far Right politics. "Large can call me a weenie… all he wants to… but I've been wanting to say… I haven't read… *Loneliness….. of the Long Distance Runner* … but my parents let me stay up late… to watch the movie… on TV… on a school night…"

Brook found this amusing for some reason. "What did you think of it, Bob?"

"I loved it! Beautiful black & white… cinematography! It really captured what it's like… to be caught… in a brutal race… But I have to say… I was disappointed… that Colin didn't win …"

Brook glanced sharply at me. "What do you mean, he didn't win? He *did* win, Bob… He just stopped short of the finish line… He was thirty seconds ahead of everybody… He just didn't cross the finish line… because he didn't want to share the glory… with a corrupt boy's reformatory! That was the whole point of the film!"

"Yes, I know that," I went on. "But I still think… he should have won… then he could have gone and told the Man… to shove it!"

"He won the race! He was three feet short of the –"

"Exactly! He didn't cross the finish line! He just stood there… staring at the Headmaster…"

"He *won* the damn *race*, Robert! What better way… to tell the Man… to go screw himself … than not to score points for the school?"

"Maybe," I said. "But I still wish he'd won…"

Brook exhaled loudly and glanced over his shoulder. "Large!" he cried. "The idea of an existential victory… seems to have passed Coe by!"

Large didn't need to be advised; he was eavesdropping. He zoomed up alongside, still with that huge smile on his face, as if he practically loved me because I was the most ridiculous thing on the planet.

"Coe!" he declared. "You are a weenie!" Then he jetted by again, ten feet ahead in four strides, where Brook caught up with him to continue their private laugh at my expense. Brook liked to jest, or at least I thought he was joking but was never sure, that there was something genuinely "off" about Sanford – as in, Big Al was "mental." But Al couldn't care less what Brook or you or I or anybody thought of him. The idiocies of Coach Jer, on the other hand, had caused him to quit the Track team more than once last season, before his teammates, mainly his best friend Brook, talked him back on again.

"Stop it, you guys," I called out to the two seniors. "I *do* get it! I'm not some… victory-at-all-costs guy… I just think… you should finish… what you start! You don't stop and go, 'See? I could win if I wanted to…'"

I could see that Al and Brook weren't going to stop snickering at me, so I threw up my arms mid-stride and said, "Okay! I'm an idiot!" This

50

further convulsed Brook and Large, such that they surged even farther ahead of me, presumably to discuss what a weenie I *ipso facto* was. At this point Senior Bob Anchondo, my "senior sponsor" who had written me over the summer to ask how my workouts were going, sidled up alongside me: the Varsity's seventh man and a 4:11 Miler was a sloe-eyed, doe-eyed Latino minority of one and our team's only other Texan. (Bob's a lawyer in El Paso to this day.)

"Don't worry, Bob," he said, grinning like Peter Lorre and the Cheshire Cat. "Get ready for a fun fall…" @ @

Every long-distance crew has its own distinct personality, and ours was – what was the best term to use? How about "Loose?" I was not a member of the Varsity yet, but I fed off its signature blend of competition and cooperation, although not so much its "Sal Bando Fan Club," a running gag I never found half as hilarious as Brook and Large seemed to think it was. Were they mocking the gung-ho enthusiasm of the Oakland A's third baseman, or ironically celebrating it? I was never a hundred percent sure, but I played along in a manner that seemed appropriate. Training as hard as we did and as consistently as we did over many months worked best in a positive motivational atmosphere of collegial friendship, because in the end you would either do the workout or you wouldn't do the workout, and your choice and effort would be reflected in how you performed on Saturday. The Varsity upperclassmen seemed immune from the cultural forces sweeping over the Class of '72, at Branner and elsewhere. What the Varsity was, was a standup bunch of guys: bright (distance runners often are), funny, good-natured, even-tempered, respectful of what mattered and disdainful of what didn't. I wanted to be part of this team more than I had ever wanted to be part of any group in my life because this was a team that let you be an individual and a teammate, running through your own pain, after your own promise, for a shared reward.

I had come across a quote in my Western Civ class from the imperial apologist Rudyard Kipling, who got this much right: "For the strength of the Pack is the Wolf, and the strength of the Wolf is the Pack." I liked this better than "One for All, and All for One," but it was a similar idea. Stanford's Cross Country team was a Pack of Wolves and a Gang of Warriors, running for ourselves and one another, the respect of our rivals and the amazement of anyone who cared to watch and understand. Being on this crew made us part of a conspiracy, something clandestine and full of adventure. Free shoes aside, we were amateurs in the purest sense: there was no pay-off for what we did, beyond doing it, and that was okay, because what we did was enough.

We finally arrived at our patch of golf course grass – the spot we considered ours – and stretched for a few minutes. Stretching was neither here nor there with us, compared to the miles we ran, and even then I knew we probably should be paying more attention to it than we did. We were running easy striders when Coach called us to the starting line of our new cross country course. He had recently measured it out himself, expanding the distance from 4.2 miles to six.

"One-mile reps, five of them, at race pace, with a three-minute jog between each," Coach said. "The Varsity should shoot for about 4:50 miles. We'll jog for three minutes between each rep."

With these instructions in mind, we trotted to the line and hovered there, our vision drifting into the middle distance and the wide expanse of green lawn with its sand traps and towering oaks.

"Keep it relaxed… Ready… *go…*"

And off we went, we skinny thinclads, passing some of the course's three hundred oaks across a rolling circuit for golfers in play. I have no idea how often we ran past a certain former star football cornerback for his high school in Kansas City, the future links immortal Tom Watson, who was a year ahead of me in school and lived in Alpha Sigma Phi, a golf geek fraternity, so I never met him. But what sounded like Athletic Department hyperbole – "the brilliant sophomore shot maker, [who] has people around the Stanford Golf Course murmuring comparisons to Jack and Arnie!"– would come to pass, not so far into a future that few to none of us could have predicted with any reliability at all. @ @

I sometimes wondered if there was a dark side to what we did. If there was, the argument would run like this: enormous feats of endurance – training and racing over distances ranging from 4 to 6 miles – involve considerable suffering. Even "training not straining" can hurt like hell sometimes, and racing is supposed to hurt, or you're not really trying. But why inflict such pain on yourself when it is not humanly necessary? What deep-seated masochism or rage was seeking expression or relief in all these miles? Did we run because we had nothing better to do, and it was better to hurt than to feel nothing at all? There were days when running felt fantastic, but "making it hurt" was also part of the game. There was self-expression and creativity involved, too, in racing and training, along with a healthy urge to compete and enjoy the camaraderie of friends. Were we striving to forge spirit into matter? Was running our means for transforming into our truer, purer, more ethereal selves? Or were we escaping the more complicated nether regions of our lives for the chaste clarity of running long distances? You could sound like a pretentious twit, trying to figure all this out. Better to *just do it*, and leave your motives at least partially unexamined, lest you upset the delicate balance of your running nature.

But I couldn't stop wondering: were we fleeing something? The opposite sex, for instance? (Or had girls fled us?) "No rigid structure on this team" was putting it mildly: to the best of my knowledge nobody on the team had a girlfriend. I am not saying we were a bunch of limp dicks; we were just kids – teenagers, mostly. All the same, Chuck Menz's joke in a summer newsletter about a broken love affair, "which shows how one-half of the minds on this squad originally started running," probably wasn't far off the mark for many of us, including me. I had always had close female friends in high school, but never a "girlfriend." But now I had a secret lover at Branner. We were "secret" because we spent most of our time together on a mattress on the floor of her room at Branner when her roommates were out. I had lost my virginity during my senior year to a classmate I barely knew, but a dorm mattress on the floor at Branner Hall was better. The gossamer-haired daughter of a San Francisco Beat novelist and the most gifted fiction writer in our class, she had a Vargas Girl figure, nicotine-stained fingers and a lopsided smile. She was articulate and fiercely smart. She seemed glued together in some ways, but as my first unabashed lover, my long-sought introduction to the universe of sex.

"This 'secret' thing isn't working for me anymore," she announced not long into the quarter. We had never presented ourselves as a couple to anyone. I said something about my romantic side not responding to hers, or some such total drivel, and we parted ways soon afterwards on faintly-sour terms. I had a great deal to learn about relationships outside of my academic studies and athletic pursuits. But I do remember mornings waking up in her room before dawn and feeling more will to go then care to stay, quietly sneaking back to my Branner suite, being careful not to rouse my roommates, slipping on my Tigers, jock and shorts and heading out the door for my first run in what was still the most passionate activity of my day. @ @

I asked Brook and Large if I could join them for one of their 6:30 a.m. runs into the hills along the winding cattle trails behind campus.

A light fog hugged the ground outside Dinkelspiel, the music and speaker's auditorium, and the air was chilly that morning, but Brook and Large were dressed the same as I was, in next to nothing: no t-shirts, only jocks, shorts and Onitsuka Tigers, no socks. I was a few minutes late, and Sanford and Thomas were mildly annoyed.

"We're running to the Dish and back," Brook announced, barely looking at me. (The radio dish behind campus had been in operation since 1961, probing the atmosphere and communicating with distant spacecraft.) "Five miles, some hills," he added, and without any more fuss wheeled around with Large, leaving me to follow. They had done me a favor by waiting for me, and now it was my business to keep up.

Within minutes we were leaping over cow styles and pumping over dirt roads not far from the Dish, where on a clear day you could see all the way to San Francisco. Churning up some nasty inclines, I discovered

Large was what everybody said he was: a monster hill runner. Large was a veritable Beast on Grades. He could also "fartlek" better than anyone I had ever run with. "Fartlek" – a Swedish word meaning "speed play" – was a training fad from the Forties and Fifties that we practiced sometimes, combining various speeds over various times and distances. In a phenomenon linked only by a linguistic coincidence, Large was also the team's best passer of gas on consecutive footfalls: when his feet struck pavement, Al could squeeze off a half-dozen or more percussive toots before the rest of us lost our ability to count.

Keeping up with Large and Brook had me in the hurtbox ten minutes in. "'Some… hills…' is right!" I said, sucking wind between each word. "These… are… forty percent… grades!" They had told me this would be an "easy" run, but when they saw me struggling, they glanced at one another and without a word of farewell left me in the dust. Torched me. Spat me out. Left me high and dry. By the time I got back to Branner they were probably already showered and dressed.

I felt no resentment at all. None. Zero. Getting my clock cleaned in an early morning workout I had volunteered to join was a serious wake-up call. The discovery that two of my teammates were pushing themselves that hard before breakfast – *Moderation, Schmoderation* – inspired me to pick up my morning tempos, too. Being a member of the Stanford distance crew involved some serious dues, but I was determined to pay them. I wasn't there yet, but I also wasn't that far behind the Varsity in our interval sessions, and I believed I would catch up sooner rather than later, if desire and talent had anything to do with it, which they do. As in almost everything having to do with running, it was only a matter of time. @ @

"Most of these 'Papoose' motherfuckers are so out of shape, you and me got the edge right now, Rapid Robert," Jack said.

Our team "mascot" was the Indian, so we freshmen were "Papooses" to some people. (We didn't know we would be the last Class to spend all four years as "Indians.") Our class was a breed apart: a pack of runts, stoners, and one Born-Again Christian. Jack and I were staking out territory as the team's Subterraneans: cocky and smart-mouthed (among ourselves), but also hard-working and hyper-competitive. Jack and I talked the talk; but we wanted to walk the walk, too. We did most of our optional runs together, and on Friday nights hung out and smoked weed (if there was no race the next day) in Jack's filthy dorm room at Cedro, across the street from Branner Hall, in a Kafka-esque warren of eight dorms, home to seven hundred students, known as Wilbur Hall.

Jack sat on the floor that night, slouched against his bed frame in a ratty t-shirt, cut-off jeans and sockless Tigers. He picked up the fat joint he had burning in an ashtray while turning the pages of a tattered notebook with his free hand.

"We were 1.7 seconds faster on those 330s this week than we were last week. Gettin' *quicka*. And *slicka*..."

"We should pick up the second set next time," I said. "Wanna go for an easy five next Tuesday, after the workout?"

Our conversations, which were almost always about training, were like nerdy baseball freaks' or CPAs'. We spoke mostly in stats. To train properly for long distance running meant paying strict attention to every step you took, every interval you nailed. Being in serious training meant holding hundreds of races, workouts, times and distances in your head, the way a baseball fan knows detail about batting averages and E.R.A.'s and more esoteric matters. Our brains teemed with "splits" – interim times – mileage, target goals and records of past races from *Track & Field News*, "the Bible of the Sport." Relying on capacious memories was not enough. We kept training logs, too, chronicling every split, every rep, every mile, every warm-up and cool-down of every workout of every day – results we studied like tea leaves or some occult calculus, always on the lookout for signs of improvement and ways to improve that might surface on Race Day.

Jack's roommate, at his desk with his head bent over his (real) calculus textbook, chose this moment to butt in. "Would you guys mind taking it outside? I'm trying to study here."

"Take a pill, Siegfried, it's Friday night," said Jack, who returned his joint to the edge of his ashtray, scooped up a tennis ball and started bouncing it against the wall: his imitation of Steve McQueen in *The Great Escape*. His roommate must have Jack figured out by now, because he simply shook his head in disgust and returned to his studies while we continued to wait for the other Cross-Country Papooses – weekend tokers like Jack and me, looking for a party, same as we were.

George Watson slumped through the door first. With his thick wavy hair, sunken chest and cheerful smile, George sometimes looked as if he was a hundred years old, but George was fast: a 9:23.4 Two-Miler from South Torrance High School, a distance powerhouse in Southern California. We did have some talent on our Frosh cross-country team.

"Watson my man!" Jack called out. "Want a fat one?" George barely had time to re-light Jack's joint before Bernie Lahde slouched in behind him, a laconic, pimply-faced freshman from Los Altos who rarely spoke and would say not a word that entire night, but was soon Bogarting Jack's joint like there was no tomorrow, which felt possible, along with a great many things at that early moment in the night.

"Hello you sorry-ass motherfuckers stoned outta yer fuckin' *wazoos...*"

The Hulk had strolled in without knocking, of course, grinning like a fool and holding his own joint, which he had fired up in the hall: One of Brook's summer newsletters had mentioned that The Hulk sounded "confused and mentally and physically unprepared for college life, but he continues to run." The Hulk – his last name was what everybody actually called him, but here I'll just call him The Hulk – was a brilliant, six-foot four-inch shuffling brute from suburban Arizona who had run a 51.5 Quarter-Mile in high school, faster long-sprinting speed than any of us, and had a best High School Mile (4:24) that was faster than mine, too. He also had a cleft hand since birth – basically a thumb and two fingers, which he had employed earlier that week to hypnotize the Oregon Miler, who had smoked some super-strong Oaxacan that had left him far too open to suggestion.

"Listen... to *me*," The Hulk had intoned, waving his cleft paw in front of his teammate's face in a public hallway at Branner. "You... are... *a chicken!*" Our teammate instantly transformed himself into a clucking, scratching barnyard fowl in front of a dozen Brannerites who practically wet their pants laughing. I grant you this was excessively cruel, but I did nothing to intervene. Our teammate had violated the Stoner's Prime Directive – "Keep Your Shit Together" – and he had shown up on campus out of shape so he didn't deserve much mercy anyway. We were his teammates, but we were on our own. All of us were. Lawson was on his own. The Hulk sure was. And so was I.

Baking in the Hulk's insulting patter, I needed a few seconds to realize that one final freshman teammate had slipped into our smoke-filled room: Arvid Kretz, a four-eyed, Born-Again-Christian Bassoonist from Millbrae, just up the peninsula. Seeing that he had just walked into a pot party in progress, Arvid thrust his hands into his pockets and stood there, blinking. Watching him smiling through a haze of marijuana smoke (had he ever even *smelled* marijuana before?), and knowing he hadn't run at Sac State for reasons I was not privy to, made it easy to under-estimate Arvid Kretz, who had let Jesus Christ "take over his body" (his words) during his senior year in high school. You need to understand: Arvid was skinny. We were all skinny, but at five-nine, maybe 115, Arvid was *really* skinny. He was also the fastest of us all: at last fall's "Postals," the event in which cross-country teams across the country mail-in results so *Track & Field News* can crown an imaginary distance running champion and championship team, Arv had posted a Two-Mile time that made him third in the country in a competition as close as anything else to what the Footlocker Championships would become a few decades later. Arvid had been top man on a Mills High School team that had crushed the three-year-old national Postals record, which meant that Arv was the fastest runner on the best high school cross-country team America had ever produced. He had finished sixth at the Cal State Two-Mile Track championship that spring. I knew none of this at the time, however, because this son of a

Marine Corps lifer didn't have a boastful bone in his body. All I knew about Arv was that he was on an athletic scholarship (this turned out to be faulty information), that his best Two-Mile was 9:11.0, which was almost fifty seconds faster than mine; and that Jack and I were stronger than he was, at least for now.

"Arv! What's shakin', son?" Jack cried. "Not to worry, nothing's gonna happen to you. We're just smokin' some reefer... You're not gonna turn into a dope fiend or nothin'. You wanna toke?"

Jack let out a world-class, ghoulish, cartoonish, throttled chuckle, since he knew full well that Arv didn't wanna toke, and Arvid knew Jack knew he was messing with him.

Without losing his smile, Arvid replied, "Thanks, I'll pass."

Hoping to avoid another one of Jack's rag-on-Arv sessions, I employed my best Boy Scout voice: "Hey guys! We're all here now! Let's go check out the dance at Serra!"

"Good idea," said Siegfried, or whatever his name was.

"I hear there's a band," said Watson, I presumed.

"Cool!" Jack's throttled, phlegm-y laugh was contagious. He never played anything straight, which was one of the things I liked about him.

And so four of the Papoose Cross Country Scoring Five gathered their things in preparation for heading out into the night, while one took a moment to walk over to the graffiti Jack had scrawled in permanent marker on the cinderblock wall near the head of his bed: "You will _run_ against U.S.C.!" This was the spring meet against the Trojans that would mark the only occasion where freshman would be allowed to compete against the Varsity in Track. I pressed my palm against this inscription, envisioning myself on the starting line some months away, poised beneath a garish canopy of blue, preparing to push body and soul over ineffable distances at indelible speeds. @ @

Psychotropic substances of one kind or another were omnipresent in Stanford's freshman dorms and athletic teams that fall, foreshocks of counter cultural earthquakes to come. I had it on good authority that a heavily-recruited Black Quarterback-Wide Receiver duo from the same Dallas high school – the wide-out had also been one of the fastest high school Quarter-Milers in the nation that spring –actually dropped mescaline for the Stanford-U.S.C. Freshman Football game, an action by two skill players in a violent sport that struck The Hulk and me as –

The Hulk used his best stoner's drawl as he humped it alongside me down the sidewalk one mid-peninsular night.

"Can you feature a QB in the huddle tripping his brains out? 'Uh.... like... *you* go *long,* man... really, reaaaally, *loooonnnnngggggg.....* Whoa! Dig our *uniforms, man!* They're so *RED!* And *WHITE!* White is the *absence* of color... Did you know that? That's so *heavy!* Can I touch your chin strap?"

"Get your 'Claw' off me," I said as I slapped it away. The Hulk called his hand his "Claw," why couldn't I?

"Did they win the game, Roberto?"

"I didn't hear, so I can't tell you, you Freak. But I'm predicting these guys won't last 'til Christmas."

And guess what? They didn't make it past Thanksgiving.

I had no plans to self-administer a powerful psychedelic on a football field, in the comfort of my dorm room, or Yosemite, or anywhere. What we observed happening to the common sense of students who smoked too much weed and gobbled too many psychotropic substances wasn't going to happen to us. We didn't do stupid shit like that. We were in it for the long haul and the next workout, which I for one craved like oxygen. We smoked some weed on the weekends, big deal – that didn't change who we were, or what we were doing. We were Going for the Guts and the Glory! Taking One Day at a Time! Preparing For a Long Season With a Lot of Hard Work!

We were Distance Runners, Nailing Intervals and Polishing Off Road Miles for Stanford U! @ @ @

UNDEFEATED (ALMOST)

That was what I became that fall: a Division I college distance runner. Whatever pain & suffering I experienced training and racing, and whatever joys reached me apart from it, were nothing compared to the exhilaration and commitment I felt as a member of Stanford's cross country crew. All through my afternoon Western Civ class I would day-dream about the up-coming workout, only half attending to lectures about fleet Achilles on the fields of Troy and Virgil leading Dante into the underworld, as I was thinking instead about the Intervals we would run that afternoon. I could feel my skin grow hotter, my bladder quiver and butterflies cross my belly, which meant my adrenals were in good shape and I was ready to have a great workout that afternoon. Chronically stiff and sore, I would rise from my classroom seats like Frankenstein's Monster, stifling groans and waddling flat-footed for my first few steps to avoid tweaking my Achilles tendons, which I did anyway from time to time. I had to avoid sudden starts and stops, especially when I worked out, or else I would limp for days. But without fail, if healthy, I would do what distance runners do: I showed up and did the workout. Whether before breakfast, lunch or dinner, in scouring rain or scorching heat; whether or not I was so stiff and sore and tired and even bored that I felt like I was going to scream, I did the run. Even when I had a flawless excuse for not showing up and doing what I had to do, I did the workout.

When I woke up in the morning, if I could, I ran. I averaged four and one-half morning runs out of seven possible each week that fall, covering six and even eight miles, logged in the three-by-five inch green spiral notebook I used through the '68-'69 season. That mileage included a mile-plus warm-up before intervals, plus the mile cool-down I never failed to perform. Adding these miles to the morning run – occasionally before that despised 8 a.m. biology class on Mondays, Wednesdays and Fridays – my weekly mileage stayed consistently in the sixty- to eighty-mile range, with almost none of it slower than 6:30 minute per mile pace. During workouts every inch of my body would glisten with sweat, and I became quite red-faced. I must have been a scary sight sometimes. But as time went on I think even my rugby-playing roommate Zac, who had told me I was nothing but a cardio-vascular system with legs, started showing some respect, once he understood that I was training alongside a Varsity team that had its sights set on competing for a national title in late November. @ @

Our afternoon training routine involved a week-long cycle of workouts from 3:00 p.m. to 5:30 p.m., door to door, Mondays through Fridays. Mondays were mile reps on the golf course, at race pace or faster, as I have described. Tuesdays were speed days and our first anaerobic workout of the week: fifteen 550s in the 78 to 82-second range, or eighteen to twenty-four 330s in the 48- to 52-second range, with an 80-yard jog back to the starting line – three or four sets of these in six reps, each set separated by a mile jog. The purpose of Tuesdays was to stress our bodies so they would adapt to the mechanical and physiological demands of running faster, and to improve our ability to surge during the middle and at the end of races as well. Later in the season we would do forty 110s – one hundred and ten yards, at quicker tempos. All of these intervals were closely monitored by Coach Clark, pumping his stopwatch, noting our times on his ever-present brown clipboard, and providing us with the rhythm of each rep: *"Ready… Go."* Rightly or wrongly, I decided that except for Large and Dunc, I had as much natural speed as anyone on the team.

I experimented with a new arm carriage that fall, copped from a twenty-one-year-old University of Kansas senior who had set world records in the Half-Mile and Mile as college freshman, not much older than I was then. Jim Ryun was to our sport what Muhammad Ali, Joe Namath, Lew Alcindor and Arnold Palmer were to theirs: a distant hero who did the same things you did, only at levels that made you feel like they had come from a different planet far, far away. I had always thought that imposing a running style on yourself was the height of mannerism, but Ryun's arm motion felt comfortable on my body, so I started holding my elbows close to my ribs and rocking my forearms in front of me as I ran, like I was playing maracas or pretending to be a running metronome. I copied Jim Ryun not to pretend I was Ryun, but because I wanted to see what it felt like to run in the way he did. Eventually I would get bored with imitating him and stop. @ @

Wednesdays we hit the roads: from the foothills to the sea! We trained on and off our 8,180-acre campus, in soft air, crackling lightning and rain, brilliant sunlight and swollen clouds that darkened the day like an eclipse until lightening flashed, thunder clattered and the air reeked of ozone. We met at the locker room and broke into groups for runs of anywhere from ten to thirteen miles, and sometimes fifteen, on local routes that I soon could run in my sleep. My favorite run was Arastradero Road, or "Arastradero" – my default workout, winding eleven miles through Eucalyptus groves and a few moderate hills to test you if you felt like pushing. I liked Arastradero best because its broad dirt shoulders were easier on my legs. The thirteen-mile Woodside circuit would get the better of me more than once that fall, so I approached it infrequently, with trepidation and dislike. Any distance runner will tell you that there are few things as unpleasant as having a long road run go south on you when you're still miles from the barn, stiff, sore, and dead-legged. There were also matters of the bowels, something that should be familiar to anyone who has ever run hard over long distances a lot: there are few sensations as uncomfortable as being miles into a long road-run with your teammates and suddenly discovering you badly need a toilet. (At least twice that year I would evacuate in the bushes, and wipe with leaves.)

The fifteen-mile Portola Valley and Page Mill loops were epic treks that I attempted only rarely my freshman year, when I happened to feel immodestly ambitious – routes that swung through low rolling hills, along asphalt bike paths under more towering Eucalypti. And there was the original monster run I tried only once that fall, a seventeen-mile jaunt along Sand Hill Road, now the Champs Elysée of Silicon Valley, back then a dusty haul through a forest until you reached I-280 in the last stages of construction: a vast slash of powdery red dirt too soft for running but also too monumental not to think about at least trying.

"You'll get to know 'em all, Coe," Brock said, pretending to be a wizened Old-Timer out on a lark – and he was a trail-hardened veteran compared to my webfeet, although only a junior. One Wednesday that fall Brock led a group of us into the steep horse trails of Los Altos Hills, a ten-mile loop with too many hills and too much asphalt for my liking, where "Train don't strain" became platitudinous: Big Al and Brook got into a little friendly competition, Brock, Don and Chuck followed suit, and suddenly we were in some ninety-percent effort footrace back to the locker room. This wasn't supposed to happen, but competitive urges took hold sometimes. I would have gone with the leaders if I could have, but had to settle instead for one hard hilly ten-miler. God those hills hurt! – but in a good way. I was so stiff and sore afterwards that it was all I could do to walk from the locker room back to Branner for dinner. Hard road-runs like these, even when they're of the "train don't strain" variety, were never about feeling good all of the time, or even most of the time. On some of these longer runs, with your bodies totally stiff and sore and your bowels acting up with five more miles still to run just to get back to the stable, you couldn't say you were enjoying yourself at all. And yet these runs were among the most memorable. "To get the full value of a joy," Mark Twain wrote, "you must have somebody to divide it with." Agreed. And to get the full value of suffering? Same deal. @ @

Of all our weekday workouts my favorite was Thursday, because it was the most focused and the most competitive. Fifteen or twenty of us would trot out to the soccer fields, psyched for our toughest interval sessions of the week: six to eight one-thousand-yard reps. Those Thousands opened you up, seared your lungs, burned your quads, tore up your guts – made you hurt real bad! On the first few reps I would hang just behind the Varsity pack until the half-mile mark, when I would try to move up if I could, hoping not to twist an ankle on the Eucalyptus berries scattered on those final hundred yards of rocks and dirt. Thursday was the one day of the week when guys threw up on a regular basis. Between the later reps, there would almost always be at least one poor guy leaning against a Eucalyptus tree dry-heaving his guts out, having emptied his stomach after the rep before. And yet he would invariably – truly without fail – re-join us at the starting line, looking slightly green around the gills but otherwise more-or-less ready for another rep. (Thursdays: a good day for an early lunch.) Nerves had caused Jim Plunkett to toss his cookies before his first game in the Stadium, but I never threw up during a workout or from running in my life – not once. The stories of Jim Ryun hurling at every other session made me wonder why he bothered. The goal of our Thursday Thousands wasn't to make you blow lunch, or to run on fumes, either. Coach Clark's constant refrain to everyone, and to me in particular, was: "Take it easy... Don't force it... Stay within yourself... Run smart... This isn't race day..." Coach allowed for our enthusiasm, but mostly he seemed there to ground us, which is part of what any good distance-running coach should do. Coach Clark built us into a team by nurturing what was inside each one of us: a passion for training and competition and a hunger to improve. Sometimes he nurtured by pushing us forward; sometimes by holding us back. Harder and faster did not always result in improvement, because it also raised the possibilities of injury and burn-out. To train for long-distance racing meant listening to your body and being smart, patient, and relentless.

And yet those final few Thousands on Thursday usually contained an element of savagery, as the efficiencies that had kept us at or near our usual pace were thrown out the window and it was all I could do to stay near enough to eat the Varsity's dust. Some Thursday workouts were so intense that they left me without enough energy to jog back to

Branner, and I had to walk back to my dorm, eat a huge cafeteria dinner, take a long hot shower, read a little of the *Odyssey*, and drift off to dreamland, knowing I would be up in ten hours to run five miles, if I wanted. @ @

Fridays we tapered, maybe an easy six in the afternoon. Some guys would run on Friday mornings, too, which meant their legs wouldn't be as fresh for Saturday's race, but also that they got some extra work in. Brock was a two-a-day Friday runner. He always seemed to have a bigger picture in his head, looking at goals beyond this Saturday, which was when we raced. Sundays we participated in a tradition practiced by distance runners on every continent in every race, religion and creed: we took a long run, on one of the same trails we circumnavigated on Wednesdays. These ten-, twelve-, or fourteen-mile workout were viewed as recovery days before we started our weekly cycle over again.

And through all this I slept. My gawd how I slept! Ten hours almost every night – nine weren't enough. And I ate. Gawd how I ate! – until my jaw felt unhinged! I stuffed myself like a Christmas goose three times a day, plus seconds, plus thirds, plus snacks. Dinner would take me forty minutes to consume. My Mom used to say I didn't eat, I refueled. My 140-pound body continued to inhale these calories and training weeks as it had all summer, week after week after week. I probably could have logged more miles, because there were almost always more miles you could try to run. But I was staying healthy and improving within our program. Miracles seldom happen in long-distance running. All the talent in the world won't get you to the finish ahead of a lesser runner who worked harder than you did.

That's one of the wonders of long-distance training: some things matter enough that you're willing to suffer for them. @ @

Being a freshman long-distance runner in the fall of '68 felt special because the Mexico City Olympics were in progress. Jack, me, and all of us followed every step of the Track & Field competitions, where world records were set in all the sprints – the 100, 200 and 400-Meters – and equaled in the 800. The 7,469-foot altitude made endurance events extremely challenging, and yet miracles were occurring: Jim Ryun's 3:37.8 in the 1,500-Meters was two seconds faster than he had believed possible at altitude, but it only good enough for Silver, as Kip Keino's Olympic record 3:34.9 beggared belief, given that the Ryun's sea level world mark was less than two seconds faster and Keino had run the Final with gallstones so severe that doctors had warned that the race might kill him. In the glare of Bob Beamon's other-worldly 29-feet, 2-inch Long Jump – no one had ever leapt beyond 28 feet before – it went almost noticed that the Triple Jump world record was surpassed five times by three different athletes. Oregon State's Dick Fosbury went over the High Jump bar head first and on to his back, winning him Gold and re-inventing his event; Al Oerter won an unprecedented fourth consecutive discus title; and the U.S. 4x100 and 4x400 relay teams dominated in world-record times. In terms of Track & Field performances, the extreme altitude in Mexico City was a major factor in what was quite arguably the greatest Olympic Track & Field competition in history.

We had only inklings of other events surrounding the most politicized Olympiad since the Berlin Games of '36. We did know that the Black American boycott had been called off only after South Africa's apartheid regime was booted out of the Games entirely. But horrific events had unfolded in Mexico City that barely made the evening news. Ten days before the Opening Ceremonies, six thousand students had gathered in a plaza to march on the National Polytechnic Institute in protest of the army's continuing occupation of campus, chanting *¡No queremos olimpiadas, queremos revolución!* ("We don't want Olympic games, we want revolution!") Then the Mexican army arrived. The Tlatelolco Massacre, or "Night of Sorrows," began at sunset when police and military forces equipped with armored cars and tanks surrounded the square and began firing live rounds into the crowd. Demonstrators and passersby, including children, were caught in a slaughter that lasted nearly all night. What we knew about Tlatelolco didn't come from major media, but from flyers passed out in White Plaza with horrifying photographs of heaps of bodies left unattended in the streets and mutilated protesters airlifted out in fishnets by helicopters or removed in garbage trucks while soldiers conducted mop-up operations door-to-door in buildings adjoining the square. Reliable reports later stated that as many as two hundred demonstrators were murdered by the State, with another two to five hundred wounded, and fifteen hundred jailed, in one fell swoop achieving its purpose of ridding the city of protestors so that the world could pretend that a civilized global event was proceeding without misadventure. The *San Francisco Examiner*," quoting the Mexican government, reported "4 dead, 20 wounded; "25 dead," said the BBC.

Black protest wasn't over: on Wednesday, October 16th, four days after my win at Sac State, Tommie Smith and John Carlos accepted their Gold and Bronze medals in the 200-Meter dash, each wearing black socks on shoeless feet and a single black glove. Together they lowered their heads and raised a gloved fist while the "Star Spangled Banner" played in honor of Smith's world-record-setting victory. When those black-gloved fists went up, "you coulda heard a frog pissin' on cotton," Carlos later recalled. Given what they knew had happened in the streets of Mexico City, both men weren't being paranoid in imagining that they might actually be shot as they stood on the victory stand.

"Right on, bruthuhs," I thought as I watched them live on TV at Branner Hall. "Black *Pow*-uh..."

Then the booing started. Chicago newspaper columnist Brent Mussburger heinously referred to them on the air as "black-skinned Storm Troopers." I shouldn't have been shocked, but I was when word came down the next day that Smith and Carlos had been booted off the team by the U.S. Olympic Committee at the insistence of arch-right-wing Olympic President (and former Nazi sympathizer) Avery Brundage, who also stripped them of their medals, expelled them from the Olympic Village, and deported them back to a country where Smith anticipated being treated like "just another nigger." What followed was a national disgrace: the new 200-Meter Gold Medalist and World Record Holder (19.83) was unable to find a decent job and ended up washing cars at a Pontiac dealership in San Jose. His wife left him, and he had to move in with his San Jose State teammate, 400-Meter Gold Medalist Lee Evans. Carlos' wife left him, too, and committed suicide nine years later. At one point Carlos would burn his furniture to keep his children warm. Smith would claim many years later that their brave action in Mexico City ruined his life.

And where did Olympic Head Coach Payton Jordan stand in this controversy? Remember that he was on record saying that he thought an American Olympic boycott was uncalled-for, because Blacks had no real grievances in this country. But when Olympic authorities approached him to join in the denunciation of Smith and Carlos, Jordan declined to do so. He later claimed that he knew about their plan ahead of time and would "defend them 'til hell froze over. They were part of the team. They did their job and competed like champions. We never had a harsh word or a recriminating word." (In 2011 I would meet John Carlos at a book signing in New York; he told me, "I had complete respect and love for Payton Jordan.") In light of what I had heard about Jordan's delusional views on race relations (which were that he didn't really "see" a person's race, which created a whole other set of problems), his response to Smith and Carlos was mystifying and more than a little astonishing. Was there more, or was there less, to Payton Jordan than I was anticipating? @ @

Jack and I loitered in his dorm room discussing all of these events, including the death threats that Smith and Carlos were receiving back in the States. I told Jack about hitchhiking home from track practice on the day of the Martin Luther King assassination.

"I climbed into this battered pickup with this drunken thirty-year-old redneck behind the wheel, reeking of stale beer. 'Dja hear what happened? Martin Luther King got hisself shot and killed.' Then he says, 'Nother dead nigger.' Then he eyeballs me, like he wants to know what I'll have to say about that. I didn't want to be trapped in a truck with this racist asshole, but my Mom was keeping my dinner warm in the oven, so I blurted out where I was going and climbed in the cab, where I turned my face to the window and wept the whole rest of the ride. By the time he let me out at my corner, neither of us had said another word."

"This is the fuckin' Amerika we're livin' in, Rapid Robert. And now we have racism in our own fuckin' sport..." We had to do something in solidarity with Smith and Carlos. So the week after the Sac State race, Jack and I decided to wear black socks ourselves. @ @

The occasion was a late morning meet on Saturday, October 19th, two weeks after Sac State: our second meet of the year, contested on our 4.2-mile home course, and not much more than a walkover for us freshman against significantly-weaker opponents Cal Poly San Luis Obispo and Foothill and Butte J.C.s. An injured teammate snapped some photos of Jack and me mugging in our politically-symbolic black socks, patting each other on the butt as we crossed the finish line in a four-way tie with Watson and Kretz. A Cal Poly runner slipped in ahead of our fifth freshman, Half-Miler Dave Whiteing, denying us the perfect score. But sixteen points was not too shabby.

Watson was the first to notice our footwear. "Cool!" Arv glanced down at our socks and looked up at us in bewilderment.

"This could be national, maybe even world news!" Jack chortled. "We could end up on network television!" As usual with Jack, you didn't know whether he was joking or not, but I decided that what he said wasn't impossible.

A few minutes later I was talking with Coach Clark when I saw him glance down at my ankles. He instantly looked up at me with an expression of pinched incredulity and unhappiness. That was when it occurred to me that if our shenanigans actually were picked up by local media, we would be putting Coach Clark in a terrible bind. It would appear that he couldn't control his team. He never said a word to Jack or me about the socks – not then or later – but by the end of my second workout of the day – an easy eight-mile afternoon run – I was feeling a little ashamed about how irresponsibly Jack and I had acted.

70

What we had done was more anarchist goof than a serious protest, but we had been running in an intercollegiate competition for the school where the American Olympic Coach was the Big Boss – publicly expressing solidarity with Smith and Carlos during a sanctioned school event. We should have thought this through more carefully than we did, because if we had, we might not have gone through with it. I made a mental note to find other ways to express my political views, and other places to do it, than on fields of athletic glory. @ @

I thought this would be the end of the incident of the black socks (I later learned that a pair of black Yale cheerleaders did the black-glove thing at a football game Back East), but on Monday morning I paid my first visit to the Stanford training room to deal with a nasty blister I had developed under the joint of a big toe. I had instinctively known to steer clear of Stanford's Head Trainer Dave Blanchard, a short, blockish, crew-cutted knot of Napoleonic fury known far and wide as "Dave." But I had no choice. I introduced myself as a freshman cross country runner, described my ailment, and pointed down at my (white) socks and shoes. Dave looked at my feet, then up into my face again. Something clicked in his head, because suddenly he turned beet red, reached out his hand, and slapped me upside the head with the flat of his palm, hard enough to ring my bell. Then he got up in my grill and cursed me out like a like a Marine Boot Camp Drill Sergeant.

"What the *fuck* were you doing wearing black socks? Huh? You wanna get *an infection?* You fucking *idiot!* How did you get into this school? Huh? *Huh?*" He actually wanted me to answer these questions.

How did Dave know about my black socks? Was he at the meet and I just hadn't seen him? I was speechless. I had never been hit growing up. I had hardly ever been spanked – thank you, Doctor Spock, the pediatrician of the Baby Boom who advised against such corporal punishment (and who I would vote for President in 1972) – and Stanford was the last place on earth I would have imagined such treatment starting. Dave looked like he wanted to hit me again, but just as suddenly regained composure, wheeled around and stalked over to

71

the other side of the room, where he wheeled around again and looked back at me with an expression of apoplectic fury.

"Am I talking to a fucking wall? Get the fuck over here, Coe! Sit down and take off your fucking shoe! *Now!*"

I did as I was told.

Dave stared at the fat bubble of skin behind my big toe, pure hatred streaming from his eyes.

"God-*dammit!* Jesus *fuck*-ing Christ..."

Then he turned away to root through a cabinet for a tool.

As my initial astonishment faded, I felt an anger welling up that would have stood me in good stead in a rice paddy in Vietnam, if I had been bent that way. But my anger quickly subsided as I watched Dave work. Dave had a brilliant method for dealing with blisters, the bane of my running life since high school. First he lanced it with a scalpel large enough to castrate a goat. Then he pressed the blister with his thumb, which sent a tiny jet of clear liquid shooting halfway across the training room floor. Then he took out a small, old-fashioned lady's atomizer – the kind Grandma used to put on cologne – and shoved the tiny nozzle inside the flap of skin. Then he squeezed the bulb, and – Poof! – packed the empty blister tight with sulfa powder. Then he taped over the thing and bingo! Pain and blister gone, replaced by a moleskin-soft pad of antiseptic powder that would peel off like a callous.

Dave was a first-rate trainer, but he was also a world-class asshole. I mumbled thanks, he grunted sideways at me as if I was beneath any renewed contempt, and we went our separate ways.

I never told this story to anyone – especially not Coach Clark – other than Jack. I never considered doing so. I suppose I could have filed a grievance with the Athletic Department, demanding that abuse like this not be tolerated. I could have gone out on a limb and filed an assault charge. But what good would that have done me, making a powerful enemy like Dave? This final event surrounding the black socks helped me re-confirm my earlier resolve never again to leap on an athletic barricade or rock the boat with a stunt like that. At least not in my Jock persona. I would stay out of Dave's way and not do anything to jeopardize my involvement with Stanford's distance crew. @ @

The S.C.-Stanford Varsity Cross-Country race, contested just after the frosh race, was serenaded by members of the Stanford Band, who hadn't showed up in time for our freshman race. Last year's score in the Varsity competition had been 20-32, Trojans; this year we prevailed, 23-34, with only thirty-four seconds separating our top five over 4.2 miles. The team's cumulative time of 1:41:19.4 shaved 28 seconds off the school and course record, set by the 1962 team that our Athletic Department should have sent to Nationals.

"That tight grouping was excellent, and what we're looking for," Coach Clark told us in a locker room meeting on Monday. "I'm predicting great things if we can just hold it together!"

The next weekend the Varsity traveled to Westwood to battle a strong U.C.L.A. team over their hilly 5.5-mile course. The Bruins were called the winner until it was determined that officials had failed to count Don Kardong among the scorers. One L.A. paper called him a "Mystery Man." With Mystery Man tallied, our guys had just edged the Bruins, 26-30. We were the best college Varsity cross country team in the State of California – and while the Varsity battled the Bruins, the freshmen were to travel to South Lake Tahoe, California, for the Tahoe Invitational. But after the Olympics ended on October 27th, Coach Clark received a phone call saying that nobody wanted to race at altitude but the Stanford Papooses, so they were calling the whole thing off. We Papooses had a time trial instead, which I trained through with a tough 13-mile road run the day before. On an unseasonably warm day with temperatures reaching 86 degrees, Jack finished 38 seconds ahead of me in 30:57.2 over our new six-mile course – a course record because it was the first time anyone had ever raced on it. I didn't sweat it, and stayed in training groove by running four miles the following morning, then competed as an unofficial afternoon entry in Stanford's intramural Two-Mile championship, winning in a far-from-all-out 9:28.0 – not an impressive time, but a PR by more than half a minute.

My ten-minute Two-Mile in San Clemente two months earlier was ancient history. In two months I had quantum-leaped. @ @

The Varsity squeaker over U.C.L.A. was followed by a much-needed bye week, which we celebrated with an off-campus Sunday run in nearby Foothill Park, a gorgeous setting with incredible views and some truly monstrous hills. One three-quarter-mile climb at a thirty-degree angle left your legs and lungs burning in agony.

That week and the next we continued to push ourselves harder in training, introducing more speed work than we had all season. Everything looked good – so good that Coach Clark informed the Varsity that a strong performance against San Jose State, the local powerhouse in recent years and the national champion in 1962 and 1963, might be enough to inspire the Athletic Department to send a full squad Back East. Stanford Cross Country had sent only one runner to Nationals in its history: Harry McCalla, a Black distance star who had run a 4:01.5 Mile in 1963, finished twelfth in 1964. San Jose had beaten us easily last year, 22-37, behind two Senior All-Americans, but on a perfect Friday morning, November 8th, 1968, our Varsity destroyed the Spartans on the Stanford links with a 1-2-3-4-5 finish. Four Stanford runners broke 30 minutes on the new course, and a fifth ran 30:01. Only fifteen seconds separated our top five, whose cumulative time over the old, shorter 4.2-mile course was sixteen seconds faster than the school record the same group had set three weeks earlier – and they had kept right on running for another 1.8 miles. This was the Varsity's most impressive performance to date.

I was in that race. Freshmen were allowed to compete simultaneously in the Varsity competition, scoring against San Jose State's JV. Jack thought he might have to go home to Modesto that day, but in the end showed up. I won anyway, in 30:48.0, breaking Jack's freshman course record by nine seconds. Three months earlier I could barely run two miles at that pace, and now I could have run for a half-hour or so with the men you see on TV in the second pack of some lesser Marathon. I was now also faster than Bob Anchondo and Duncan, who DNF'ed that day. This meant I was fast enough to be sixth man on the Varsity. Too bad 1968-69 was the last year of freshmen ineligibility. Because if not for N.C.A.A. rules intended to protect freshmen from Varsity competition so they could get off on a good foot in their college studies, I would have been part of the team that hoped to compete for an N.C.A.A. Championship, if – *if* – our guys could get past Cal. @ @

Our Papoose cross-country season ended on November 16th against the University of California Bearcubs, the team that starred Texas State High School 4-A Mile winner John Drew and Cliff West, the California State and Golden West Mile Champion. The Heap Big Little Cross-Country Meet, Papoose on Bearcub, was the freshman race of the year, no doubt about it. A heavy rainstorm the night before had left the Berkeley golf course a sodden mess, so the race would be contested at an alternative venue: an asphalt road surrounding a reservoir in the hills above the Berkeley campus. A late start and snarling traffic got us to the venue so late that freshmen had only ten minutes to warm-up. With my chronic Achilles miseries I dreaded going all-out on blacktop. I also had a fetish about racing in light shoes, so I did not feel good about racing in my heavy Tigers. So without consulting anyone I unscrewed the spikes on my second-hand blue Adidas Tokyos and wrapped white adhesive tape around the holes. I figured that these super-light, un-spiked shoes would be faster than my thick-heeled training flats. After jogging a half-mile on the abrasive asphalt, the tape around the spike holes was already torn to shreds.

I have no idea what I was thinking, but I trotted to the starting line in shoes with plastic-soles.

I immediately discovered the huge mistake I had made. I felt as if I was running in an ice-skating rink. I slipped badly for the first six hundred yards until we reached a modest hill, where I discovered that climbing asphalt in these de-spiked shoes was impossible. So I stopped running, ripped the shoes from my feet, and set out barefoot after the field. I caught them soon enough and somehow ran another lead mile on harsh asphalt, sand-papering my soles. Then we hit a long patch of gravel and I had no choice: I quit a race for the first time in my life.

A minute later Coach Clark came walking towards me while the racers vanished around a bend in the course. Hot tears were coursing down my cheeks. "It's these damned shoes!" I said, holding up my blue Adidas spikes for Coach to see. (I would cry again six weeks later, over Christmas vacation, when I had to tell my Dad about my fender-bender in his big blue Chrysler Saratoga.) Coach Clark glanced at the footwear I held out to him, then at my bare feet, then over his own shoulder in the direction of the vanishing racers, his apprehension perhaps mixed with guilt over losing his top runner to the wrong pair of shoes: a coaching mistake. Should he have noticed what I was wearing?

Fortunately our Papooses sucked it up and we squeezed past Cal by three points, ending our season undefeated. Back home that afternoon for penance, I slathered the raw undersoles of my feet with Vaseline, put on my Tiger training flats and ran Arastradero –11 miles – in 63 minutes. My cross country season had ended on a sour note, even if our team was unbeaten; but after the Varsity mauling of the Bears, 20-38 and by virtue of a magnificent undefeated season, the Athletic Department agreed to send a full squad to the N.C.A.A. Cross Country Championship for the first time in history. "It's going to take nothing short of a plane crash at Kennedy to keep us from finishing high," Coach Clark told the *Daily*. "My main concern from here on is keeping the guys relaxed and letting me do the worrying for them..." @ @

Sightseeing in New York the day before the race, Don and Large decided to run to the top of the Statue of Liberty in their street clothes. This would be one of the rare occasions when anyone ever saw Coach Clark blow his stack – and I was told that seeing Coach lose it was not something you felt good about afterwards.

Van Cortlandt Park, the nation's most hallowed cross country turf, had been a muddy mess for the IC4A Championship the week before, and was in only slightly better shape in time for Nationals. A field of 233 runners made the start a madhouse, but our guys found each other early and raced together, the way they knew how, as a pack, for two loops of the freshman Three-Mile course, which omitted the murderous, slippery incline known as Cemetery Hill. Don later told me that the last half-mile of that race was the most brutal of his life – he couldn't get enough oxygen to breathe – but Stanford's top four runners came home bunched between 17th and 39th places, 22 seconds apart. The problem was that one of us finished more than a half-minute behind our fourth runner, buried in 71st place. (It wasn't Allen or Don, if you must know.) I didn't doubt the heart of a single one of my teammates, who had all proven themselves many times before, and I don't think any of us blamed just one guy (except maybe Brook.) But one bad day for one Indian runner meant that Stanford lost a national title by 24 points to the Wildcats of Villanova, who took home their third consecutive N.C.A.A. championship with a five-man team, just like we had. (Their sixth man finished 127th.) Coach Clark would tell the *Paly Times* that "there wasn't a word about us in the New York newspapers, nor of any of the other West Coast schools. Yet we finished second, U.S.C. was third, San Diego State sixth and Cal Poly of Pomona eighth." Oregon State and San Jose State had outstanding teams in the early Sixties, but a very serious argument could be made that this day marked the birth of West Coast cross country on the national stage.

After their initial disappointment wore off, our guys felt proud of their runner-up finish, and I thought they should be. Coach Clark had done a phenomenal job assembling a team left in ruins by the previous Coach. Years later, he would recall that magical '68 season in a *Runners World* interview with Kardong: "That team didn't have a history of success, but it was evident from the start of that season that the runners believed in one another and would succeed." My own thoughts were this: if I had been eligible, I would have found a way to finish in the top fifty, which would have given Stanford a National Cross-Country Title. This may or may not have been true; I had finished over 45 seconds behind our fifth man in the San Jose meet. But this wasn't the reason I never mentioned this aloud to anyone. It would have been obnoxious, first of all – our fifth man felt bad enough already – plus there was no point in scapegoating, because no one runner wins or loses a cross country meet. From the point of view of scoring, there is no "I" in "Team" or in "Cross Country," either.

And at Stanford there were no free rides, either, as Brook Thomas pointed out after an East Coast newspaper remarked on how extraordinary it was that Villanova had won a national championship with one runner on the team who wasn't even on an athletic scholarship. How many Stanford runners were on athletic scholarships? With Duncan home, not a single competitor on Stanford's N.C.A.A. runner-up cross country team was at The Farm on a running scholarship. Every one of our guys was running for the love of the sport and the greater glory of an Athletic Department that did buy air tickets and hotel beds and subway tokens, but otherwise couldn't see clear to give guys a new pair of shoes. @ @

The night before the N.C.A.A. Cross Country Championship I was at Lake Lagunita guarding the Big Game Bonfire from Cal's Zippos. At a rally on the boat deck that night, an undergraduate dressed up as Cal's mascot, "Oski the Bear," and pranced along the dock of the empty lake and hundreds of Indian boosters as an object of comic abuse. "The Big Game" (as it had been known for decades) was an event rich in symbolism and ritual befitting the oldest college football rivalry in the Western United States. The first game had been played on San Francisco's Haight Street Grounds on March 19, 1892, with the future U.S. President Herbert Hoover serving as Stanford's team manager in a 14-10 victory. None of the pomp and circumstance surrounding the event was more important than the disposition of a fifteen-inch-long lumberman's implement, which made its first public appearance at a Stanford bonfire in 1899, when it had proved useful in decapitating an effigy of a Bear. Soon after that first game the Stanford Axe was stolen by a gang of ingenious Cal students and, after a wild chase through the streets of San Francisco, the handle was broken off and the Axe vanished, only to turn up at a Berkeley fraternity house. It remained there until 1930, when twenty-one Stanford students – a gang known as "The Immortal 21" – stole it back. Three years later both sides agreed to make to make the Axe the symbol of victory in the Big Game, with ties leaving it in the hands of the previous year's winner.

Since 1930 the Axe had been stolen four times by Stanford students and thrice by Cal folks, most recently only two years before, when one or more Cal boosters pulled off a heist worthy of Topkapi by somehow managing to kipe the thing from its display case in the Stanford Student Union, where it had been for the previous six seasons, all Stanford wins. Cal officials (graciously?) returned the Axe it to Farm officials hours before last season's game, a 26-3 rout by the Golden Bears (highlighted by three fourth-quarter TDs), after which Berkeley fans poured on to our field to destroy our Stadium goal posts and mass in front of our rooting section to arrogantly retrieve their prize. For this year's Big Game, played not long after my friends raced in the Bronx, I was in the stands at Berkeley's Edwards Stadium, eager to see our football squad pull off an upset and bring the Axe home on the same day we would or would not also bring home a national championship.

We were seven-point underdogs that day, but dominated every phase of the game. Our much-maligned defense allowed just 126 total yards and intercepted four passes. The final score – Indians 20, Golden Bears Zip – was Stanford's first shut-out of Cal since 1955.

With two minutes left in the game, I watched the Cal Rally Committee carrying the Axe to the fifty-yard sideline, where the chairman of Cal's committee and the Stanford Axe Committee waited until game's end to determine who would take possession of the prize. This time-honored ceremony was known to some as "The Stare Down."

Like I said, for the Big Game, the oldest college game of the West, Stanford and Cal had as much ritual as Alabama-Auburn.

With the final whistle I remained in the stands, watching as hundreds of fellow students traversed the field to retrieve the Axe for its trip home to Palo Alto, where we knew it belonged. The Axe was called the Stanford Axe for a reason: it was our Axe. Cal only got to borrow it from time to time. @ @ @

"THE BABY-FACED ASSASSIN"

I didn't run a step for three days over Thanksgiving, spent at my grandparents' apartment in L.A. When I returned to Palo Alto I had finals to think about, so running remained on the backburner for a while. I had been a willing Spartan all fall, but a happy Athenian, too, stuffing my head full of Biology, English, French and Western Civ: "We're studying the ecology of Lake Lag as it fills up with water," I wrote home in early December, before my first finals. "Civ is the usual – Charlemagne, Gregory VII, all that. We've finally arrived at the past tense in French. Days fly by..." A B-plus/A-minus kind of under-achiever in those days of serious grade inflation, I was not nearly as bold in my studies as I was in my sport, which I pursued with the uncomplicated ardor of the teenager I was. My days flew by with the rhythm of miles, past campus sandstone and Eucalypti, on open roads and verdant fairways; my nights, with dreams of the future. I couldn't have been happier than I was then, running for myself, my teammates and my school, even if my family didn't fully understand or care to. Running was my choice, and mine alone: "For Stanford I Will."

But I also decided I had to become someone more than just a spectator in the theater of Resistance. I didn't want to stage another protest inside the athletic department, but my outrage over the war mingled with a vein of self-dramatization until the Greater Houston Optimist Club's "Boy of the Month" for February decided to participate in National "Turn in Your Draft Card Day" on November 14th, an event held concurrently on campuses coast to coast. Stanford Chaplain Robert McAfee Brown, after speaking eloquently on the moral numbness of Christians in the face of the rise of Nazism, had surrendered his Draft card; why shouldn't I do it? I also wanted to "Resist the Draft" publicly, so I drove to Kepler's Books in Menlo Park one morning – our grandparents had given my sister and me their old '62 Chevy Impala station wagon to share – and nervously fell in line with two dozen other newbie Resisters in the book store parking lot. I scanned the crowd for F.B.I. cameramen. I was about to commit a federal crime. I wasn't doing this because I thought it was cool; a felony conviction would destroy my future as a lawyer, not to mention my status in college, where my II-S student deferment was currently golden. My dilemma was that I couldn't stand carrying that card in my wallet anymore, and I wanted my giving it up to mean something.

At the last moment I got cold feet. I was turning away when I realized I was at the head of the line and Joan Baez was gazing placidly at me, holding out an ancient Zippo with a guttering flame. My hand shook as I extended my wallet-sized document and watched as the fire blackened the edges of it for a second before it burst into flame. Then the preppie-looking Jock dropped his Draft Card's curling ashes into a stranger's bowler hat. Or maybe I am remembering this wrong. Maybe Joanie just confiscated my card and that was all that happened. I have imagined for the longest time that she burned it, but I don't trust this memory anymore. All I know for sure, then and now, was that I would never join the armed forces during the Vietnam War. I would move to Canada first. (Suppose they gave a War and nobody came?) And if the Athletic Department ever found out about it, what would they do? I had no way to know for sure, but I suspected they wouldn't have given a tinker's dam one way or the other. @ @

The outdoor track season wouldn't begin until early March, which left us several months to prepare. I loved cross country. In cross country you didn't look at the clock, check your splits and worry about the weather, you just go out with your team and compete. But track I loved even more. Track was the heat of summer, the murmur of crowds. Track was the Olympic Games – the only foot racing that ordinary Americans cared about and the only glamour our sport provided. Some claimed that if cross country was Woodstock and indoor track was Las Vegas, then outdoor track and field was Carnegie Hall, and Carnegie Hall was where I wanted to play. But indoor Track came first, so for now Vegas would have to do. And how did you get to Vegas? Practice, Practice, Practice: "December 2nd: Three mile warm-up, 10 x 220s, 220 jog, average: 26.7 seconds; five mile run. December 3rd: 2 x 1000s, 5 x 550s, 8 x 330s, 10 x 110s. December 4th: 8 x 880s on the golf course..." Doing this kind of interval training on my own and mixing it up with only a couple of long runs a week, I saw my weekly mileage total drop to around 45, which may have been unwise at that time of year, but I didn't see it that way then. I wanted to reclaim the elation I had felt rounding the curves of the stadium track on my first day on campus. Before heading out for workouts, I would play the Beatles' "White Album" loud on the tinny Hi-Fi I had squeezed on top of my desk.

"Five thousand people showed up to watch the Soviets work out at Angell Field back in '62," Jack joked. "You think we might get one or two someday for our team? Maybe we should threaten the world with nuclear destruction! You think that might draw a crowd?"

"Fat chance, Jack! And what do you care, anyway? I like that nobody cares about us! My theory is that nobody messes with you when they don't know who you are."

Our Pack was good enough for me. @ @

With my first report card in hand – I had made the Dean's List and an A-minus in Western Civ – my sister and I found a drive-away on a Stanford bulletin board and headed home for Christmas, stopping at Carlsbad Caverns along the way. My first Sunday in Texas I ran five miles in the morning and in the afternoon got lost on the Farm-to-

Market roads between El Lago and La Porte. Using a map, I later calculated that I had covered 20 miles, the longest run of my life. Combined with my morning workout, it was also the farthest I had ever run in a day. ("I'm a little stiff," I wrote my grandparents after my near-Marathon.) I drove to my old high school track to throw down some intervals, too: my journal entry for Christmas Day 1968 noted, "2 x 660, 1:32, 1:34, 660 jog between each; 440 in 59 seconds, 440 jog; 10 x 110, fast-slow; 4 ½ mile jog. 8 ½ miles total. Felt good."

I skipped a few workouts over the holiday to follow our neighbor Bill Anders on his flight to the Moon and (hopefully) back. My father flew to Florida to witness the December 21st launching of his best friend faster than anyone had ever traveled in history: 25,000 miles per hour on top of an under-tested thirty-story-tall rocket ship burning 20 tons of fuel a second. Home from the launch, my Dad followed the mission on TV from the moment he woke up in the morning until he went to bed at night, without ever seeming to enjoy a single minute of it, which I didn't understand. I wouldn't learn until years later that Bill had dropped by our house one afternoon prior to launch to divulge a national secret: six months before Apollo 8's scheduled lift-off, American spies had discovered (incorrectly) that the Soviet Union was poised to launch a manned flight to orbit the moon. On orders from LBJ, Apollo 8's launch date was pushed up and its mission revamped: NASA engineers had been given three months to throw together the mechanics of the first moon shot. Anders, Borman and Lovell were also the first human beings strapped atop America's massive new Saturn V rocket, even though NASA placed no better than even money on the capsule surviving re-entry, given that this little trick had never been performed before. (Decades later, Bill would publicly declare that he thought the mission had a thirty percent chance, based on the number of times he and the crew had died in simulation. No wonder Bill hoped to do as well on Apollo 8 as I had done in Sacramento!) The purpose of Bill's visit to our house was to ask my Dad a favor: would he be his executor and look after his widow and six kids? My father didn't hesitate to say yes, but no wonder he sweated bullets the whole flight. Anders, Lovell and Borman did make it back to earth, becoming the first men to return from deep space, the first to voyage to a celestial body, and the first to see the dark side of the moon with naked eyes. Bill's photograph of the first earthrise ever seen by mankind with their naked eyes would become one of the most widely-published images in history and a major inspiration for the environmental movement just beginning to build muscle and spirit.

Prior to his historic voyage, Bill had cut a deal with all five Coe Boys.

"Haircuts," he said. "Get one, and I'll give you an Apollo 8 Moon patch I'll be carrying onboard." I was wearing my hair longer since cross country had ended and I didn't have Coach Jordan breathing down my neck, but I wanted a moon patch. So I self-trimmed some of the hair off in front and tucked the rest behind my ears. I was sure I didn't fool Bill, but he acknowledged my effort and gave me my Apollo 8 moon patch, which I would frame decades later, along with his telegram for my victory at Sacramento State, and hang above the desk where I type these words, and remember heroes, and wonder if that was what I hoped to become myself.

The voyage of Apollo 8 was unquestionably heroic, nothing could change that, but I was not aware of the physical hardship in the capsule, which was kept from the public and only revealed years later. Borman had caught a nasty intestinal flu prior to lift-off and didn't reveal it to Mission Control for days. Jim Lovell caught it in flight; only Bill did not. The vomiting wasn't the worst of it; the diarrhea was. They cleaned it up as best they could, but never got all of it. Weightless shit and puke floated all around the cockpit for the entire flight. Bill said that after a day or two they got used to the stench, but the Navy frogman who opened the hatch after touchdown nearly vomited. The Apollo 8 capsule had been a flying American Port-a-Can that went around the moon. @ @

"I am so keyed up for some fast times this year," I wrote my grandparents early in the new quarter. "I want to run a 4:10 in the first outdoor meet, and then maybe get down to around 4:07 before the season ends, which qualifies me to run at the N.C.A.A. championships in Tennessee, about a week after school gets out." But first we had that indoor season, although not much of one: Coach Clark tried to enter Jack and me in the Two-Mile at the Golden State Invitational at the Cow Palace in San Francisco that month – one of the biggest indoor meets in the country – but not a chance: some of America's greatest distance stars, like Gerry Lindgren and two-time Olympian George Young, would be racing. Our indoor season would consist of one meet: the "Athens" track meet at the two-year-old Oakland Coliseum Arena (where in a few more years I would go back to hear Bob Dylan perform with The Band as his back-up group.)

Six thousand, three hundred and seventy-seven fans filled half the Coliseum seats for our Friday night, January 24th, 1969, and the noise they produced was deafening. My warm-up was the first time I had ever set foot on a 160-yard wooden track, and none of my teammates in the Frosh Two-Mile Relay had ever run on one, either. The Coliseum boards felt super-fast, but the curves were so steeply banked that I felt like I was running them on my side, and the sharp crackling sound my short spikes made on the wood was disconcerting, doo.

The opening-leg runners settled at the starting line and off they went with the crack of the starter's pistol. Our first runner was the Oregon Mile champion, who ran with an expression of unbridled terror on his face.

"How many more?" he shrieked at me as he flew by.

"Three laps!" I screamed, holding up four fingers, which probably only confused him further. Did three fingers mean three laps down, or three to go?

With one lap left, he raced by me shrieking, *"Where am I?"*

"One more lap!" I screamed again, wind-milling my arms, but I wasn't sure he heard me, much less understood what I was trying to say. Thirty seconds after handing off to George Watson, he was still breathless and wild-eyed.

"You can't hear a thing out there!" he told me and Dave Whiteing, who would run the third leg. "The noise... is deafening! You can't understand... a word... the announcer... is saying! You can't even *think*, man! You have no idea... how much race is *left!*" Watson returned with the same report: "It's pandemonium! You don't know... where you are... five and a half... laps, how many, *what?*"

Trotting to my position near the baton exchange zone, ready to play my part in this debacle, I snatched the baton from Dave Whiteing's outstretched hand – my teammates had given me a six-foot lead – and launched myself around the steep banks of the track, trying with every ounce of concentration I had to count each lap as I passed the starting point. I got to "two." After that I had no idea where I was, other than first. How unspeakable – to be racing in a foreign environment with five competitors hot on your tail, not knowing where the finish line was or how many laps you had to run! This was as close to a runner's nightmare as you could get, without running off a cliff or into a wall.

I still have a photograph of myself breaking the tape that night, my eyes scrunched and mouth agape, arms stretched overhead in what I hoped was an image of triumph. All this picture reminds me of today is how that race hurt. My split (1:57.9) was nothing special, but it was a PR, and I had done it in my first-ever turn on the boards. Our team time, 8:03.6, wasn't much faster than what my high school quartet had managed outdoors, but it was a solid four seconds ahead of Laney College and five seconds ahead of the pre-race favorite, Fresno City College. The Oregonian, George, Dave and I were glad to collect our modest trophies, but we all wished the race hadn't been so hard. @ @

One of the beautiful things about being a Stanford Jock was the opportunities afforded you to see the very best there was, do what they did. The big event of an otherwise surprisingly-dull meet in Oakland wasn't the original "Fosbury Flopper," Dick, failing to clear opening height, or the Olympic 400-Meter Gold Medalist Lee Evans, who was supposed to be there but never showed up. The star of the night was the Australian distance running legend Ron Clarke, who had let the world know that he would be attempting to break the world indoor record for Three Miles... *"the whole world is watching"*... Three months earlier Clarke had crossed the finish line in sixth place at the Olympic 10,000-Meter Final in Mexico City and collapsed on the track. Doctors initially thought that the lack of air at altitude had killed him, but he revived a few minutes later with an oxygen mask strapped over his mouth, his tongue so badly swollen he couldn't talk. He had damaged the mitral valve in his heart (and would have it surgically corrected fifteen years later), but somehow he made it to the starting line of a 5,000-Meter heat and the final a few days later, where he finished fifth. Still the outdoor world-record holder at 5K and 10K, Clark would be lining up in Oakland against an elite four-man field. A month shy of his thirty-second birthday and a year away from retirement, he looked lean and wizened to me, but he was taking a shot at his seventeenth WR.

I found it incredible to be competing in a meet with the world's most prolific distance record-setter since "The Flying Finn," Paavo Nurmi, when less than a year ago I was running dual meets against Alvin and Dickinson High Schools. Knowing what it was like to race in that raucous fishbowl – and knowing that Clarke wouldn't be able to hear a word of what the announcer was letting everyone else in the Coliseum was hearing with perfect clarity – I snuck on to the infield and positioned myself inside the boards, thinking I could help by calling out splits. Another Australian, University of Texas at El Paso's Kerry Pearce, the world indoor record holder in the Two-Mile, led the field through the Mile in 4:26.7, at which point Clarke assumed the lead.

"8:48 at two miles!" I called out to Clarke as he raced by. "Sixty-five-second quarter! Eleven laps to go!"

Coming around to the start of lap twenty-three, I noticed Clarke studying me from fifteen yards out, knitting his eyebrows expectantly. The world's greatest distance runner was asking me – *me!* – for information! So I cupped my hands and shouted as loudly as I could as he flew by: "World record pace, Ron! Hang tough!" With nine laps to go, I told him where the competition was: "You're thirty yards ahead!"

With five laps left, the announcer let the crowd know that Clarke was still close to world record pace – "but he'll need to go hard that last half-mile!"

As Clarke approached I yelled loudly, "You gotta go hard, Ron! World record!" I saw him, his body, visibly react. He pushed those last few laps, sprinting for all he was worth. The Coliseum crowd rose to its collective feet, screaming *Go-Go-Go-Go!* The Coliseum was on fire! When Clarke leaned at the tape, his time – 13:12.6 – obliterated by over four seconds the old world indoor standard set in the Oakland Coliseum two years earlier by the former Oregon State runner and '68 Olympian Tracy Smith, a distant fourth in tonight's race. This was the seventeenth world-record-shattering performance by the Australian distance immortal, in only his second indoor attempt at the distance.

The first world record I had ever seen in person was Ron Clarke's last.

Mission accomplished, the man trotted off the boards, bent over and rested his hands on his knees for a few seconds. Then he straightened up, turned around and came trotting straight up to me, flung his arms around my neck and half-collapsed there, as a half-dozen cameramen converged on the two of us, flashbulbs popping.

I staggered for a moment, half-supporting his weight, feeling his thick sweat on my shoulders.

After a few seconds he righted himself, patted my arm, and said, "Thanks, mate!" Then off he jogged waving at the crowd, to corral Tracey Smith and Kerry Pearce so they could share his victory lap around the wooden oval. "I never heard a crowd yell like that anywhere," Clarke would tell the press later. "They must have knocked three or four seconds off my time themselves."

I remained on the infield, too stunned to move. When I turned I saw Coach Clark studying me from ten feet away, a half-smile creasing his face. I knew he knew what I was feeling. I had been greased by greatness! In a *frisson* of Sixties' *verité*, I had just played a tiny role in the fastest indoor Three-Mile race in human history. And the whole world of Track & Field was watching! @ @

Dennis Hayes' prediction the previous fall about a student-led shutdown of Stanford almost came to pass. "Unrest" at various state university campuses became the excuse California Governor Ronald Reagan needed to declare a state of emergency on February 2nd that nearly resulted in public school shutdowns across the state. Later that month, the Stanford chapter of Students for a Democratic Society (S.D.S.) demanded that the university and its wholly-owned Stanford Research Institute (S.R.I.) cease all military-related research immediately. Half of S.R.I.'s budget came from the Department of Defense, mostly for classified research, including research into biological and chemical warfare. Many of us believed this secrecy ran counter to the university's most fundamental principles of open inquiry, and that some of the work being performed at S.R.I. was immoral and possibly even illegal. The school administration had nothing whatsoever to do with the planning or administration of S.R.I. at that point in its history, but this didn't matter to those of us who believed (correctly) that the university's pursuit of truth carried a system of values that ought to make it unthinkable to cooperate with the war effort in any way shape or form. And yet Stanford's enormous expansion in the postwar era had been largely funded by increased D.O.D. spending on technological and military-related research.

For these interlocking reasons, the Radical Left was entering a new phase of campus protest: "Bringing the War Home." Dignified civil disobedience and protest would merge with the antics of hippiedom and the middle finger of polarizing, Berkeley-style politics.

I knew "the Radical Left" at Stanford. The Radical Left was everywhere, in every dorm, frat house and off-campus crash pad I knew about. We were the majority of the Student Body that had come to college to learn about injustices, among other things, and when we learned about injustices, it was only natural that we would want to see them ended. I never met a single "outside agitator" on the Stanford campus. The "outside agitator" was a straw man of Right Wing opponents who wanted to suppress student activism. I never even met an S.D.S. member, since most of them were upperclassmen and altogether too serious for my taste – although they did have a sense of humor on occasions, like when fifty of them broke into a closed meeting of Stanford trustees to reiterate their demands, filmed the trustees filing out the door, and stayed around long enough to polish off the trustees' chocolate éclairs. These people were not the Radical Leftists I knew. Growing numbers of ordinary students felt that something had to be done to stop the Southeast Asian war.

I protested but remained more-or-less a gung-ho fellow traveler – less interested in the nuts & bolts of political action than in the "counterculture,' a term coined only the year before to describe a vast international conspiracy to disrupt and replace bourgeois culture, lifestyles and values. The posters above my desk said it all: the Beatles, Ernest Hemingway, and Jim Ryun. On Friday nights dormitory groups would pile into cars to Winterland, one of the big rock palaces in "The City" – San Francisco – to speaker-dance and lip-sync along with Iron Butterfly – *"Innagaddadvida, baby"* – and maybe watch the naked Haight-Ashbury hippies fling themselves on stage like salmon up a fish ladder. I listened to the music, and music was everywhere. I read the books, which were everywhere, too. And I ran 1,789 miles in '68, the distance from L.A. to Chicago, averaging less than thirty-five miles a week but the bulk of it in the second half, with my road-run times noted on the Mickey Mouse Watch I wore for that expressed purpose. @ @

I planned to run more miles in to prepare for a 4:10 Mile (the freshman school record was 4:10.5) in our first outdoor meet in early spring. Except it rained in the Bay Area for forty-three straight days, from early January until late February – 22 inches in all. I averaged only 50 miles a week that first month and through most of February, when the latter month dried out I upped it to 60. My goal was to log six miles every Tuesday and Thursday morning and three miles and lift weights every Monday, Wednesday and Friday morning, in addition to the team workouts. I didn't always manage it because of various knee, calf and Achilles miseries, but I did do my morning run more often than not.

The rainout of February's "Red-White" intrasquad meet was a disappointment, because it meant missing my only chance to race a Mile against Duncan, Brook, and Large; the latter would finish third in the Mile at Conference that year, running 4:08.5. But on a bone-chilling February 28th afternoon, we had a 1½-mile time trial on the pebbled artificial track at Menlo College in Menlo Park. We plodded the first mile in 4:36. The pace felt snail-like to me. So with one lap to go I decided to hell with it and stepped on it, leaving the upperclassmen behind with a 62.4-second final lap. Running a mile and a half in 6:46.0 wasn't other-worldly – a bit over nine-minute Two-Mile pace – but the great thing about it for me was how easy it felt.

We were running an easy cool-down mile prior to finishing the workout with 8 x 220s in 28 to 30 seconds with a 220 jog between each, when Brook Thomas jogged up alongside me in a disgruntled mood and said, "That wasn't supposed to be a race."

I couldn't believe what he just said. Our cross-country Captain, bitching out a freshman for showing him up? I had no doubt that Large, Duncan and others could have gone with me, and beaten me, too, if they wanted to make the effort. Coach Clark had let my fast last lap slide. Why couldn't Brook?

"If you don't wanna race, then don't let me win" was what I wanted to say in reply, but as a freshman I kept my mouth shut and jogged ahead without a word. If I had needed a confidence boost, this time-trial in the middle of an eighty-mile training week would have been it. Was it possible that a freshman had caught up with the upperclassmen already? I couldn't answer have answered that question yet, but I would know if we could ever get ourselves into the same race. @ @

Outdoor track opened a week later at our Stadium, the Varsity opposing Occidental and Fresno State and the Frosh battling Laney and Santa Ana Junior Colleges. Coach Clark had me penciled in to double in the Mile and Half-Mile in the same half-worn-out blue Adidas I had worn in cross country. I decided to break the bank and buy myself a pair of top-of-the-line, Olympic-quality "Azteca." I couldn't afford the $16 price tag on the $25 a month allowance my grandparents sent north, but I couldn't resist these shoes. My golden Aztecs were my pride, my honor – my wings of Hermes! Slipping them on, I felt almost invincible, or at least ready to give my all.

I trotted to the starting line on a perfect spring day for a track meet, the azure sky overhead vast and the air soft, sweet and windless, for a race that would pit me against Keith Strodle, an outstanding Santa Ana Miler, whose lifetime best – 4:10.0 – was a full thirteen seconds faster than mine – seventy yards ahead. What makes the Mile a great race went beyond the drama of the four-minute barrier, which was once thought an impossible boundary of body and will. To run a fast Mile requires strength and speed: you can't run well off cardiovascular fitness alone, or leg speed alone; you need both in equal and optimum measure. The starter's pistol went off and I felt someone step on my foot, but regained my balance and settled in behind Strodle's shoulder.

The pace was preposterously slow. My opponent clearly intended to have an easy day of it by waiting until the last lap and out-kicking this no-name freshman. We plodded along through 67-second quarter-miles for three laps, but then I anticipated his move ten feet before the bell lap and blew by him before he had a chance to react. Seeing that the race had started my teammates rushed to the edge of the track, screaming and waving as we tore around the penultimate curve and down the backstretch in a full sprint, with Strodle inching up on me. I could only watch as he slipped smoothly by. I tucked in behind him on the backstretch and held on, drafting around the final curve – the actual drafting was probably minimal on that windless day, but I knew that he was working harder than I was. On the final straightaway I swung wide and within seconds we were shoulder-to-shoulder. Our 1,760-yard race became an eighty-yard, balls-out dash to the finish line.

I still have the yellowing Polaroid someone took of me lunging through the tape with Strodle eight inches behind. My last lap took 57.3 seconds, faster than I had ever closed a race over half that distance. My time, 4:19.0, was a PR and over a second faster than the winners of the

Varsity race that day, a three-way tie for Sanford, Macdonald and Anchondo in their tactical encounter with Milers from Oxy and Fresno State.

The applause of our few hundred spectators was dying down when I looked down at my left foot. I'd been spiked. My brand-new Azteca was shredded! Whoever stepped on my foot at the start of the race had torn my shoe open from toe to heel! My wings of Hermes had been totaled! I had been lucky the damn thing stayed on.

I sat down on the grass and pulled off the remains of my golden shoe to reveal a long red scratch that ran the length of my instep. It looked as if I had been clawed by a very large and angry cat.

Coaches Clark and Jordan – the latter long back from the Olympic Games in Mexico City, although I had yet to formally meet the man – converged around me, along with Dave the Trainer. "How does it feel?" Dead serious inquiry from Dave. No attitude whatsoever.

"It's nothing. It's superficial." It was, actually. It barely bled at all. "Tape it up. I have to run the Half in half an hour."

Dave glanced at the Coaches and the Coaches glanced at one another, perhaps to reassure themselves that they were making the right decision, and then nodded their assent. With stubby fingers as swift and practiced as a cashier in a Chinese restaurant, Dave taped up my wound, and a half-hour later I was at the starting line for the Half-Mile in a pair of borrowed spikes.

Knowing I had no competition I dawdled through a slow 58.9 first lap, comfortable but well back in fourth place. I saw Jordan and Clark standing side by side at the one-lap mark, looking at me with expressions that seemed to say, "What the heck are you doing?"

Right in front of them I shifted gears and blew past the field and around the second-to-last curve, almost like I was showing off – rocketing down the backstretch and sweeping around the final curve into the home straight in full-throttle, running with that fantastic feeling you have sometimes of running effortlessly, but fast. I broke the tape to wild cheers and applause – well, there were a few hundred people in the Stadium stands, and some of them were cheering. @ @

What happened next was like someone else's memory in Hollywood Technicolor – like an image from a more innocent time, perhaps when my parents were on The Farm. I wheeled around and looked up at the huge Stadium scoreboard and saw my results against a dazzling mid-peninsula sky: *"1:54.9."* Not an earth-shattering time, but one that bested my Oakland Coliseum PR by three seconds. My final lap took 56-seconds flat; my final 220, 27.1 seconds. And then the U.S. Olympic Head Coach was standing beside me, one hand on my shoulder and his mouth to my ear, as if he was my closest intimate:

"Bobby," he whispered – a name only my father used for me – "you are a *Champion!*" I nodded without making eye contact and went trotting away. My legs still felt full of life. I had more race in me. Ten minutes later I went looking for Coach Clark on the infield.

"Coach, let me give the Two Mile a shot. I tripled in an All-Comers meet in San Mateo a month ago." (That was true, although I did it for a workout.) "I'd like to give it a try. Yeah? I'm good to go!"

One of the team's volunteer assistants grabbed my wrist. It took me a moment to realize he was checking my pulse.

"Forty-four beats a minute," he told Coach Clark. "I'd say he's recovered already." After a few seconds of pondering, Coach said, "We'll get you in." I thought he was curious to see what I could do.

I quickly found I had nothing to contest with Arvid Kretz, who was rounding into shape after his slow cross country start His 9:11.2 that day was nearly his lifetime best, but second to the solid 9:08.4 effort turned in by Santa Ana's Rick Muth, who was heading to U.S.C. in the fall. My third-place finish (ahead of Jack) was the fastest Two-Mile of my life – 9:25.5. Three PRs in one day. Not quite up to Jesse Owens's three world records and a fourth tied in a spag257n of 45 minutes on the afternoon of May 25, 1935 at the Big Ten Conference meet in Ann Arbor, Michigan. But by my paltry standards, it was that kind of a day.

95

Brock spoke to me afterwards with his arms folded across his chest, in a manner declaring that as far as he was concerned, I could do what I wanted. But all the same: "You did good, Coe. But if you ask me, it's not very smart running three races in the season's first meet."

Thinking about it later, I had to agree. Greg was right. But I couldn't regret what I had done at my first outdoor college meet. It was everything I could have wished for and more. @ @

The following morning I was waiting in the Branner breakfast line, still in sweaty workout clothes after my Sunday run, holding a starter bowl of Cheerios in one hand and the "Sporting Green" of the *San Francisco Examiner* in the other, when I came across an article about a meet which started our Varsity season off on the good foot: Stanford 90, Occidental 62, Fresno 29. Under a rhythmic Tom-Tom headline – "Young Injun Spikers Breeze" – I read something that made me put down my cereal bowl. "Considering the rain and all that had limited preparation, Jordan couldn't help but wind up pleased at the day's happenings… He mentioned 'toughness,' too, and here he had to place an unheralded Indian Freshman from faraway Seabrook, Texas, one Robert Coe, high on the list… Not ranked among the best of the prospects, the driving Frosh rattled off a 4:19.0 mile win, then raced half that distance in a strong 1:54.9, not too far from the school yearling mark of 1:52.2."

I was a "driving Frosh!" In the San Francisco Sporting Green!

Monday morning I heard a knock on my dorm room door. A classmate stuck his head in and said, "Robert, your Coach is calling you. He's on the payphone in the hall."

Coach Clark had never called before.

"Hey Coach! What's up?"

"Can you come into the office this afternoon before the workout?" I heard pleasure in his voice. "Coach Jordan wants to meet you." @ @

I had been at school over six months without meeting our Head

Coach. I had barely seen him around at all since his return from Mexico City, where the American Track & Field team had won an unprecedented twenty-four medals, including twelve Golds. Distance guys didn't see Jordan generally, although he hovered over our program. I had only seen him in action at two team meetings, on January 14th and 15th – "quite heated meetings as a matter of fact," I reported home by mail. "Jordan commands absolutely zero respect among the team members, and I can't blame them." (This was not entirely true, as I later discovered; Jordan had a small but loyal coterie of team members, mostly conservative Republicans, in his corner.) "He talks about the honor of the school, etc., but when we're filling out eligibility forms, Tom Colby (one of the major thorns in his side) said that he once competed under an assumed name. Jordan says in front of everybody, 'Don't mention it on the form,' even though the form (for the N.C.A.A.) says that if you're caught lying, you're off the squad. You see, Colby was third in the nation in the javelin last year... Also, we had a vote about appearance" – addressing the heart of the Culture Wars that had torn the team apart two years before – "and nearly everyone said let it be a matter of personal discretion how long you allow your hair to get, mustaches, etc. Jordan went along with it, but far from cheerfully. I'm glad to see him give in. Stanford track has been lousy ever since he kicked Pat Morrison off the team a few years ago, and this year's squad should be great." (After the Pat Morrison debacle in 1967, Stanford had lost its first Big Meet against Cal in five years by a narrow score of 76-69, and then had our Indian scalps handed to us this past spring with a 100-45 drubbing.)

Was I being groomed and scripted to play a role in a Stanford turnaround? The morning edition of the *Palo Alto Times*, taking its lead from Jordan and the *Examiner*, singled me out as "looking like a great future prospect." @ @

I showed up at Coach Clark's office, the anteroom to Jordan's, at the appointed hour.

"Go right in, Bob." Coach wore a mild smile. "He's waiting for you."

Coach Jordan's "office" was not much more than a glorified broom closet. There with was enough room for Jordan's imposing desk and a single guest chair. Behind that desk sat our Head Coach, who upon seeing me sprang to his feet, squeezed from behind his desk and came around to grab my hand and pump it vigorously, his other hand resting on my shoulder. His laugh was an explosion of complicit merriment; his smile a mass of crow's feet and gleaming teeth.

"Well hallow, Bobby! How's that foot doing? Fine? My goodness, you were one tough son-of-a-gun on Saturday! You blew those other boys off the track!"

While he fussed over me, I looked around, slack-jawed. Nearly every inch of wall space was covered with framed photographs of Jordan himself, standing alongside various Stanford luminaries and Olympic Track & Field legends past and present. This was the world headquarters of a man who wanted you to know of his success an Agoraphobe's Olympus. Jordan hadn't stopped gushing: "We were worried that spike wound might bother you in the Half, but I guess we didn't have to, did we! My goodness – please, have a seat," he said, gesturing at the guest chair while he squeezed back behind his desk to sit across from me, a beaming Zeus enthroned before the honored supplicant in a chair ten inches lower than his own. @ @

Payton Jordan came at people like a force of nature. Pigeon-toed and pigeon-chested, with a helmet of perfectly-coiffed hair and a permanent tan, like most California track coaches, he reminded me a little of George Putnam, the stentorian right-wing newscaster I had grown up watching on Metro TV in L.A., who also never let a word pass his lips that he didn't believe with all the fervor that made America great. Jordan's success in Mexico City had led to gossip about him becoming Governor Ronald Reagan's Secretary of State, a largely honorary position he would have been well suited for. A track and football legend at U.S.C., where he had run on a world-record Quarter-Mile Relay team and starred at Running Back in the '39 Rose Bowl, he had unofficially tied Jesse Owen's world record in the 100-Meter Dash

(10.2), set a world record for the 100-Yard Dash on grass (9.3), and long-jumped "only" 24 feet, 11-inches, as he would tell me on another occasion. He had graced the cover of *Life* magazine bare chested in shorts and shoes for an article about Olympic hopefuls in 1939 – the contemporary equivalent of being feted on *The Today Show* and *60 Minutes* on the same day. World War Two, which caused the cancellation of the 1940 Olympics in Tokyo, Jordan spent working stateside for the Navy, while his best friend at S.C., Louie Zamperini, the N.C.A.A. Mile Champion, became a Pacific P.O.W. and much later the subject of Lauren Hillenbrand's best-selling book *Unbroken*. Prior to Jordan's arrival on The Farm in 1956, he had turned Occidental College in Glendale, California into a Division II Track & Field powerhouse, fielding teams that set world records in several relay events and sent a number of athletes on to the Olympic Games that Jordan never reached himself. At Stanford he had been named N.C.A.A. Division I Coach of the Year in 1965, after his team's second-place finish at Nationals and his Quarter-Mile Relay team's world record, employing a novel method of exchanging the baton that Jordan had devised. Frequently described as one of the most popular Americans the sport of Track & Field had ever produced, Jordan remained to us distance runners "Payt," or "Paytriot"– a man pathologically inured to reason who we had no choice but to live with. And now he was leaning across his desk, gazing deeply into my eyes. *En loco parentis* was over in freshman dorms, but not in Track & Field:

"What do you hope to get from this program, Bobby? What are your hopes and dreams? Because you have the potential to do great things for us!"

I don't remember how I answered him that day, but I do remember thinking that I had never invited Coach to infantilize me as "Bobby." (Thanks to Jordan, this nickname would percolate through the program as time went on.) Mostly I remember being in a mild state of shock. It was truly surreal to find myself the fair-haired boy of one of the biggest right-wingers on campus. After all, I was a pot-smoking, Draft-card-burning, black-sock-wearing Pinko who had marched behind Joan Baez and others in a "wake" down Campus Drive after Nixon's election to the Presidency last November, an event co-sponsored by S.D.S. and the "Resistance," the anti-Draft crusade, which provided marchers with 4,000 candles to dramatize our state of mourning over the death of the democratic process and the prospect of four years with Tricky ("Peace with Honor") Dick, whose "Secret Peace Plan" (as we would learn many years later, without being terribly surprised) began with his secret bombing of Cambodia two weeks after he moved into the White House. That election night march down Campus Drive ended at Lytton Plaza with a Country Joe and the Fish concert, where nine more people turned in their Draft cards and one burned it. I had left the concert early – I had to get up for my morning run – so I missed seeing the cops arrive at eleven p.m. to arrest twenty people for failure to disperse. "They were blocking traffic and throwing stuff from the roofs and a brick went through a police car window," I would write my grandparents. "So I can't blame the police in most cases. There were a few unfair instances, however…"

Of course I was not the first promising athlete to get "the Jordan Treatment." Years later I would read the account of Jack Kemp, a Republican Congressman and Vice Presidential nominee who had a similar encounter in the Fifties with his freshman football Coach at Occidental. Payton Jordan had launched a charm offensive that day, too, telling young Jack that if he worked hard and made all the right moves, he had the talent to become a starting quarterback in the N.F.L. one day, which was what happened. Kemp walked out of that meeting with Jordan "on cloud nine," he later said. "I would run through a brick wall for that man." I would have run through a brick wall for Coach Jordan, too, if it made me run faster. But my meeting with Coach left me feeling less like a future Olympian and more like the English Group Captain Lionel Mandrake in Stanley Kubrick's 1964 black comedy masterpiece *Doctor Strangelove* – the brilliant scene in which Mandrake (Peter Sellers) finds himself trapped on a sofa alongside a drunk, cigar-chomping General Jack D. Ripper (Sterling Hayden), who slings an arm over Mandrake's shoulder and explains how the "Commies" are destroying America's "precious bodily fluids" through fluoridation, which is why he has just ordered nuclear-armed bombers into the air to obliterate the Soviet Union.

The smile frozen on Mandrake's face is unforgettable and hilarious. You can literally read his thoughts: "This man is a complete lunatic and he's going to kill us all!" That was what I felt like that day in Jordan's office: I was Group Captain Mandrake. But I would not be completely truthful if I didn't admit that a part of me enjoyed the attention. The leader of the most successful Olympic Track team in history was asking me, *me*, "What can we do for you, Bobby? What do you want that we can offer? We want nothing from you but the very best you can give us!" I was young enough to be flattered, even a little starry-eyed in Coach's presence. But his intensity was weird, too. The man gazing back at me from across his desk wore a look of such paternal fondness and good will that I knew it had to be partly bullshit.

He sent me away that day with a nickname, meant to commemorate the murderous kicks I had unleashed in that weekend's Mile and Half.

"Ah, Bobby," he said as he showed me the door, one hand on my shoulder, an index finger in my face: "You're the Baby-Faced Assassin!!!" This is mildly funny now, but at the time I was glad it never caught on. @ @

My first meeting with Payton Jordan may have been more inspirational than I was willing to admit, because my training log records that I had my first 90-mile training week soon thereafter – although the fact that it was "Dead Week," a period of no classes in preparation for Finals, was probably more liberating than anything Jordan told me.

Just before our Monday workout, Coach Clark jogged up, with his clipboard under his arm, on our way from the locker room to the golf course to knock down some more Mile Reps.

"I've got news for you, Bob," he said. "Coach Jordan wants you in the Open Mile at the Easter Relays in Santa Barbara."

The Easter Relays! That meant world-class athletes in attendance! U.S.

Olympians! This was just the break I had been looking for! A chance to race against some of the best collegiate and open Milers in the State of California! I had planned to travel up to the University of Oregon that weekend to train alongside my old high school teammate Mike McClendon from Clear Creek High. The former Texas 3-A Mile Champion had been recruited to run at the great incubator of Milers in Eugene. Mike invited me, as he wrote in a letter, to "run me into the ground." (I figured he had probably read about me the San Francisco paper and was burning with jealousy.) Instead, without consulting anyone, I gave myself a small mid-season "Peak," skipping the Thursday Thousands and resting on Friday prior to the Easter Relays, doing some warm-ups and nothing more.

Our bus left Palo Alto on Friday at 3:00 p.m. and rolled into Santa Barbara five hours later for a team meal and bed. The next morning I got up early for a light jog on a nearby beach, only to find it ruined by the infamous offshore oil well blowout of January 28th, 1969, which led to laws restricting many forms of offshore drilling. Tons of tar balls had washed ashore all along the coast. I gave up trying to find a clear stretch of sand and jogged back to the motel to await the team bus to La Playa Stadium on the campus of Santa Barbara City College. @ @

That afternoon in Santa Barbara – Saturday, March 22nd, 1969 – was not a time or place anyone would have chosen to run a fast Mile. Steady twenty-five mile-an-hour winds brought gusts to thirty-five. In my warm-up I huffed and puffed and chugged, head down, bulling my way against the wind; in the other direction, I flew down the track like a clipper ship rounding the Cape of Good Hope. The cinders were busy with non-stop races, including some local high school events; we also to wait for a ceremony that crowned the Easter Relay "Queen," a Santa Barbara City College coed and her two Princesses. At 2:35 p.m. I trotted to the starting line of the Easter Mile.

The first thing I did there was locate U.C. Berkeley's freshman phenom and last spring's California State High School Mile champion, three runners to my right. Cliff West had won the Golden West title with a powerful kick in a relatively slow 4:14.0. The Golden West Mile winner the year before had been the future Olympian and teenage 1,500-Meter finalist Marty Liquori; the winner this year would be a Coos Bay, Oregon high school star named Steve Prefontaine. On the day of my 4:19.0–1:54.9 double in the Stadium, Cliff had doubled in times only slightly faster than mine, but his PR Mile was ten seconds quicker than I had ever managed, and only a second off the best high school time in the nation last year. Cliff had also run a 4:10.0 in the Open Mile at the Athens Indoor Meet, where I had anchored our winning Two-Mile Relay in an ordinary 1:57.9. Cliff had a reputation as a Warrior, which was something that ran in his family: his younger brother Cornel would become one of the leading Black intellectuals in America; Cliff taught Cornel to read. If I was a "phenom," as Cliff already was, we would be waging some epic battles over the next four years. Despite the glowing remarks about me in the Sunday *Examiner & Chronicle*, my hope was that Cliff would under-estimate me, or even better, overlook me entirely, so I could catch him unaware. @ @

The gun went off and I tucked in behind West. By the half-mile mark we were part of a three-man pack moving away from the field. I decided to pass Cliff in an unexpected place, on the backstretch of lap three – against the wind, chasing after Westmont College's Dennis Savage, a future Division II national Mile champion, who was leaving us both behind. Cliff did a double-take, literally, as I whizzed smoothly by. I was still in second place with less than three hundred yards remaining when Cliff made an even better move on me: I was running too wide on the backstretch and Cliff exploited my mistake with lightning quickness, darting by me on the rail and pulling four feet ahead in a half-dozen strides. I drafted behind him around the curve until we hit the last straightaway, where I swung wide... He was coming back to me... *Where was the god-damn finish line?* I leaned at what I thought was the end of the race and thought I had him beat, but race officials saw it differently, and they were probably right; my time was two-tenths of a second behind Cliff's. With his victory Dennis Savage was named Athlete of the Meet, his time of 4:06.5 just missing the meet record of 4:06.1, shared since 1960 in a tie race between Jim Beatty, the world's first sub-four-minute indoor Miler (1962, in Los Angeles), and Hungary's Laszlo Tabori, the third man to break four-minutes outdoors with his 3.59.0 on May 28th, 1955.

Recovered immediately, I pranced over to where Coach Clark stood at the thirty-yard-line. He read me the news from his stopwatch. "Four-oh-nine-five, Robert." I had just run a 4:09.5 Mile: a ten second PR! And I had run it in a gale, two weeks shy of my 19th birthday! On that day in Santa Barbara Cliff and I were surely two of the fastest eighteen-year-old Milers in America, as well as our new school record-holders: the first Papoose and Bearcub Milers under 4:10. When I heard my splits I understood the damage the wind had done: I had run 2:09 on the half-laps against the wind, and 2-flat with the wind to my back.

I went looking for my rival and found him on the infield.

"Hey Cliff!" I called out, jogging up with my hand extended and turning it into a soul shake, which surprised the hell out of him. "I thought I had you there at the end, but I guess not, huh?"

Cliff, a guarded black kid with a big Afro and even less facial hair than I had, kept his game face on. But near the end of our brief conversation he conceded something that surprised and pleased me.

"I talked to Brock before the race" – they knew one another from Sacramento high school days – "and he told me you'd be tough."

Hearing that my school's Two- and Three-Mile record-holder had told last year's California State and Golden West Mile Champion that I would be tough meant more to me than Coach Jordan's praise in the *San Francisco Examiner*. "Tough" wasn't a title anybody involved in distance running just handed to people. It wasn't a reputation you could win overnight. Tough wasn't just about how you competed on Saturday. Tough was the whole package. In another sport it might be called professionalism. In distance running, being tough meant you trained hard week in and week out, then showed up on race day.

That Greg had also blown my cover would not occur to me until many years later as I sit here at my desk, writing this story down. @ @ @

"...FIGURES TO BE ONE OF THE GREATEST..."

My new stature as a freshman track star came in the middle of having to figure out where the hell to live during my sophomore year. One option was a fraternity house, which I was not initially inclined to pursue, since I had mocked frat houses, frat boys and the whole fraternal mentality since I was old enough to ponder. My father, who was Sigma Chi at Wesleyan, used to sing a verse or two of "Let's go piss on the Beta House," but that had nothing to do with anything; my mother had been a Tri-Delt, shortly before Stanford outlawed sororities after a young woman hung herself on the lawn of the house that turned her down. My anti-Greek prejudice was simple: I thought fraternities were culturally backward, congenitally moronic, and probably Republican. The David Harris head-shearing incident in the spring of '67, conducted by a gang of "Brothers" from Delta Tau Delta, was a factor in the empty beds and shrinking budgets of fraternities across campus. But there were still three Jock fraternities – the Delts, Zeta Psi and Beta Theta Pi, omitting one other on the wildly-unfair bias that golf is not a sport – that had long taken the place of the athletic dormitories Stanford historically disallowed.

I considered pledging the Phi Delt house because Duncan lived there, but Duncan seemed under-enthused so I dropped the idea; it was difficult to tell if Duncan and I had a problem because we always got along fine, but we never had much of a personal friendship at all. So I looked elsewhere and in the end acted on the recommendation of my roommate Zac by checking out the Beta House and its world-class swimmers, hip football players, and future leaders of what many of us hoped would be a new and radically-improved America. @ @

The Beta who lured me to the bosom of fraternal hipness was Skip, a senior who under-weighed the second-lightest Beta bro by at least thirty pounds, meaning he was about my size. Brother Skip wasn't bummed by this a jot, because Skip was too cool for school, and certainly too hip to be concerned with anything as trivial as someone's perceptions of who or what he was. Wearing his dirty blonde hair down to his shoulders, a knowing smirk 24/7, and a serious gift of gab, Skip functioned as a kind of House Whip, or so he seemed to me. It was interesting and a little wild to meet someone so removed from any cliché of a frat rat, but who still wanted to be part of the place.

"Be part of 'the undercurrent of hipness,' Robert," Skip told me at one of the early Rush parties. The two of us were standing around two beer kegs on a sticky dining room floor, sharing a joint while the Rolling Stones' "Beggars Banquet" blared over the fraternity's fiendishly-good stereo system, which means it was really good.

"What does 'the undercurrent of hipness' mean in a frat house, Skip!"

"Dig it, man! The Beta House is the preferred house for stoner jocks! You do know that, right? Ken Kesey – you know who he is, right? The novelist who wrote *One Flew Over the Cuckoo's Nest* and dropped Acid at the Stanford Medical Center? Yeah, of course you know Kesey... Before Ken Kesey got into Stanford's Creative Writing Program, he was an intercollegiate wrestler at Oregon who almost made the U.S. Olympic team in 1960. And dig it: Kesey was an Oregon Beta, bro!" Skip said, patting my chest for friendly emphasis. "For what that's worth..." We both shared a chuckle over this. We both knew he was playing me, of course, but we were both enjoying it.

"I know, I know," he continued, "this notion of a buncha pot-smokers living in a Jock house is ludicrous to most people! Or counterintuitive! Conventional wisdom says that hippies replace competition with co-operation, and aggression with gentleness, right? While playing sports means you seek *dominance* over your opponents, even when you don't *feel* like it, right? Like 'We're fuckin' Jocks! Let's go invade Poland!'"

I laughed so hard trying to give Skip a low five that I spilled half my beer.

"Sports are the perpetuation of War by other means, right? Being an athlete means being *macho!* It means filling your *soul* with the *poisons* of desire – and-and-and-and *pride!* You embrace pain, you live through *pain* – not a hippie attribute, right? Can I get a witness here tonight?"

"Wrong?"

"That is exactly *right,* sir! *Dead* wrong! Competition is *not* conquest! We're not *buying* that crap at the Beta House, son! We're marrying the exuberance of fraternal hi-jinks to countercultural extremities, can you dig what I'm saying? You wanna be part of that? Well, do you? Of course you do. Right on, brothuh… Low Five…"

I had not decided to join this undercurrent of hipness, but that's what some Betas were spinning, or thought they were doing already: re-inventing frat houses for hippies. That was the fantasy Skip was laying down. (I thought "hippies" were mostly a media stereotype, but never mind that.) The Delts were the Animal House on campus; the Zetes were Jocks with a house on Lake Lag, but also morbidly square; the Betas – the Betas were God-Spun Heroes of the Freakazoid who understood that being an intercollegiate athlete meant opening yourself to some wild out-of-body experiences and a whole lot of high-wire fun.

My roommate Zac was surprised when I got a bid, given that he thought I participated in a second-rate sport, but I was even more surprised that I accepted and made plans to become a full-time resident of Beta Theta Pi in the fall of '69. @ @

Rush Week did not impede the progress of track on a campus on medium-boil. Kenneth Pitzer, a Stanford-trained chemist (like my father!), had been appointed the school's Sixth President on December 1st. The founder of NASA's Department of Aerospace Engineering, Pitzer had also run a chemical warfare project during World War Two, and as a past director of research for the Atomic Energy Commission had been influential in the decision to build the H-Bomb, later testifying against continuing security clearances for Robert Oppenheimer, the pacifist former head of the Manhattan Project. Campus radicals celebrated "Greet Pitzer" week by swarming his office, which as a committed hardliner against student activism he apparently didn't appreciate. In early April, Pitzer declined a meeting with the Black Student Union and its membership responded by stealing food from the cafeteria at Tressider and trashing the bookstore. Things would get far scarier: two days before his formal inauguration in June, somebody decided to blow up a phone booth not far from Frost Amphitheater, the scheduled site of the ceremony.

"Not a great start for the Pitz, Jack, don't you think?"

Lounging on his bed in Cedro, Jack nodded languorously in agreement. His season hadn't gone well so far. Like a lot of us freshmen – almost everyone except me – Jack had yet to equal his best high school marks.

We remained sympathetic political agnostics over those two weeks after the Easter Relays, watching the anti-war movement take its biggest action since the previous spring: student organizers invited the entire campus to attend a meeting to galvanize action against on-campus war-related research. From this meeting several hundred student demonstrators re-emerged as the "April 3rd Movement," which six days later led a group of at least four hundred students and some outside activists against the Applied Electronics Laboratory, an on-campus center (built with money from alumni William Hewlett and David Packard) where a number of classified, military-related research projects were being actively conducted. A3M demonstrators occupied the building and shut it down, as one protester declared, because "You have no academic freedom to help blow up Vietnamese children."

On Thursday after practice at the Stadium, I jogged over to the AEL

Labs to visit the newly-opened child daycare center, a "Red Guard" Book Store, an "Eldridge Cleaver Room," a "Che Guevara Room," and a United Student Movement office in the basement for the April 3rd movement's high school auxiliary. All righteous stuff, as far as I was concerned. Some of the more hard-core radicals, on the other hand, failed to impress me, as I wrote my grandparents: "They should realize they're trying to work with a bunch of thick-headed bureaucrats who consider students to be what they very well may be – a slew of irresponsible rebels… For some people, temper tantrums feel like the only way to get any attention around this place." The peaceful occupation of buildings made more sense to me, but instead of linking arms with A3M, I focused on schoolwork and our upcoming meet at San Jose State College – aka "Speed City," home to Olympic legends Tommie Smith, John Carlos, Lee Evans, and a team that would win the N.C.A.A. Track & Field Championship in Knoxville that year. My plan was to take a shot at the freshman school record in the Half-Mile, but unfortunately I wouldn't be able to compete in the Varsity Half-Mile, against a field that would include the world-record holder and Mexico City Gold Medalist over 400 meters, Lee Evans, experimenting with a move up. Based on his past attempts, he would most likely run a time not much faster than I thought I could manage. Wouldn't that have been cool, to race and defeat Lee Evans? Didn't happen. I had no competition in my freshman race on San Jose's green Tartan oval, and a stiff wind to contend with, but I still tore up the last half-lap and finished in a PR 1:54.2, two full seconds short of the freshman school mark. Without the wind I was sure I would have broken it.

The highlight of the meet that year was Chuck Menz's epic Two-Mile duel against Spartan distance star Ralph Gamez, a quasi-juvenile delinquent who was also a two-time California State High School Champion over Two-Miles, back when Chuck was a decent Also-Ran at Cupertino High. Gamez had the lead coming off the final curve, but "Tiger" was closing. Our entire team lined the rail, cheering like sailors as Chuck caught Gamez, both men gutting out shoulder to shoulder, each tying up badly, faces locked in masks of mortal agony. On a good day Chuck ran as ugly as Emil Zátopek, the grimacing Czech distance star of the Fifties, but on that day he held off Gamez for a thrilling victory, breaking nine minutes for the first time (8:57.4) with a 4:22 last mile that had every one of his teammates sharing his elation.

"A great competition and the Underdog wins," Brook Thomas said as we ran our cool-down together. "What's not to like about that?"

While all this went down, the AEL Occupation ended after nine days, when scary rumors circulated that Federal Marshals were coming to protect the government's secrets and vital interests there. @ @

A college Track & Field season is a long campaign that unfolds with lightning quickness. I knew that much from high school. People who have never competed for their school could never fully understand the pleasures and tolls that accompany a long season from beginning to end. Our next meet was rained-out, which gave us a welcome rest but was discouraging to me because I had planned to hammer the first two laps of a Mile in 2:02 and see if I could hang on. I had to settle for an 81-mile training week, at quicker tempos than I had managed before.

Ten days later the Coaches Jordan and Clark called me in to discuss my chances of competing in the June N.C.A.A. championship meet in Knoxville, where freshmen would be eligible. Back in January I had hoped to get my Mile under the 4:07 qualifying time, but now I learned that this wouldn't be good enough from Coach Jordan's perspective:

"Jordan only wants to bring people who have a chance to score," I told my parents in a letter I typed at my desk in Branner. "He says he wants me in the 4:03 – 3:59 range… Unfortunately, since they want such a fast mile, Coach Clark thinks I may stand a better chance running the three instead of the one. If only they had the Two-Mile at the nationals; that would be my bowl of meat…" I was already anticipating the upcoming Two-Mile against the Trojans that had inspired Jack to scribble *"You will run against U.S.C.!"* on the wall above his bed in Cedro during cross country season. This was our only opportunity to compete (as a Varsity non-scorer) in a dual meet race against upperclassmen.

Only opportunity now came with a hitch.

"It's been a long season, and I'll have already run the Mile," Brook told me at practice that week. "We don't want a fast pace, so don't even think about taking it out." Without a fast pace, my chances of breaking the freshman record of 9:04.0 would be seriously hampered.

I was sure I could break nine minutes, which would give me an equivalent N.C.A.A. qualifying time in the Three – and if I got under 8:55, the Coaches said they would enter me in the Two-Mile at the 42nd annual running of the West Coast Relays in Fresno, racing against some of the finest American middle-distance runners of the day – people like Tom von Ruden, ninth in the 1,500-Meters in Mexico City, and Bob Day, the former U.C.L.A. Bruin who had won the 5,000-Meters at the U.S. Olympic trials the year before. A fast time in the U.S.C. Two-Mile was imperative, but from a team perspective a tactical race was called for. And as a freshman, I had to go along with the upperclassmates' plan, especially after Brock signed off on it, too.

Brock had been lifting a lot of weights that spring, but had cut back when he noticed added bulk on his pecs.

"If we could bring a bench press down to the starting line," Brock joked, "S.C. wouldn't have a prayer!" @ @

The U.S.C.-Stanford Dual Meet on Saturday afternoon, April 19th, 1969 ran par for the course for this long-standing rivalry. Stanford was getting its butt kicked. O.J. Simpson ran the third leg on the Trojan's world-record 4x110 relay team, in a race that wasn't remotely competitive. The worst humiliation wasn't the one-lap relay or the final score, which was the more-or-less as expected – S.C. 111, Stanford 43. The worst part was watching Bob Seagren, U.S.C.'s Olympic Gold Medal Pole Vaulter and the United States Track & Field Federation's Athlete of the Year that year, defeat Stanford's talented school record holder Randy White in the 440-hurdles. Seagren had set his first world record in the vault at the age of nineteen and would go on to win the Silver in the Munich Games in '72 and also the inaugural "American

Superstars" competition on ABC-TV. "There's so little competition for me in the pole vault that I get bored," Seagren told the press that day at Stanford Stadium. "I'm U.S.C.'s No. 2 [hurdler], so why shouldn't I run them?"

My warm-up went beautifully. My legs felt alive. The weather was perfect: sixty degrees, no wind. All Systems were Go! I was so nervous I peed twice during my warm-up in the dilapidated lavatory under the stands, and was literally standing over the urinal a third time when I heard the announcement over the P.A.: "Final Call for the Two-Mile!" I made it to starting line with ten seconds to spare.

The gun went off and away we went, three little Indians and two Trojans in a dog trot: in a clump, plodding out seventy-second laps within a second or two of one another. We should have been averaging three or four seconds faster, but the S.C. runners didn't want to take out the pace, either. A mile and a half in my frustration overwhelmed me and I moved into lane three, preparing to move into the lead and push the last half-mile hard. Brook saw me on his shoulder and didn't even turn his head – only spoke in a voice loud enough for me alone to hear: *"Wait."* I had no choice: I settled into Lane Two, just outside the clump, knowing I would be running an extra six feet per lap but not wanting to miss the start of the real racing. When the bell lap sounded all five of us took off like we were fired from cannons. I shot past Brock and Brook, but couldn't get around the Trojans. The three of us stayed bunched around the second-to-last curve, the back straightaway, and the final curve, too. I made up ground in the final 80 yards and almost caught them, but ran out of race: I finished third, two-tenths of a second behind the winner, S.C. sophomore Jeff Marsee, an 8:47 Two-Miler the previous year, and almost shoulder-to-shoulder with S.C. sophomore Andy Herrity

The result was no different than if my teammates had let me try for the record. I later realized that our guys' real goal was to have an easy race that wouldn't embarrass them or tire them out too badly. Herrity and I had run 9:07 flat to Marsee's 9:06.8. Brock, our school record holder

(8:49.0), was fourth, more than two seconds behind me after a 61.7 final lap. Brook Thomas, who had eaten me for breakfast during a morning run six months earlier, was fifth, after running the Mile earlier in the meet. I ran my last lap in 58-flat, but missed the freshman school record by three seconds. (Arvid had missed it by four against San Jose, running a PR 9:08.0 but dying over a 69-second last lap.) I had improved my Two-Mile PR by 56 seconds in nine months. I was sure I could have run at least ten seconds faster and given myself a chance to race in Knoxville, but I hadn't been allowed to try.

All the same, a skinny freshman had beaten Stanford's two cross country All-Americans with an impressive closing kick. Running my cool-down in one of the outside lanes, I could hear the buzz among my Varsity teammates. Sprinters and weight men were checking me out, offering palms to slap: "Great race, Coe!" "You're the man!" "Good goin', Bobby!" "Alright!"

The Varsity Mile Relay, the last race in most track meets, was already in progress – with Stanford thirty yards behind after two carries – when out of nowhere Dave the Trainer came striding up to me on those stumpy legs of his.

"Bobby! You're overheated!"

"Dave, I'm fine! I always get red-faced like this!"

"No you're *not* fine! You're coming to the training room – *now!*" What was *this* about? Stanford's Head Trainer, abandoning a meet-in-progress to escort a freshman to the training room for some undisclosed treatment? I thought I knew what this was about.

I followed him down the gravelly quarter-mile and watched him unlock the training room from a thick ring of keys dangling from his belt. After testing a tub of water with his hand, he said, "Strip and hop in."

As I took off my clothes and slid as ordered into the cool water, Dave pulled up a slat-back chair and quietly and very respectfully talked to me for twenty minutes while I soaked. Following Jordan's lead, he was calling me "Bobby" now. I had no doubt he was going to all this trouble to make up for smacking me six months before. The point of my soak was to keep me from getting him into any hot water. And by being there, I was acknowledging that the two of us were square. @ @

I got the star treatment again in the *San Francisco Examiner* on Monday morning: "[Assistant Sprint Coach Bill] Moultrie, Head Coach Payton Jordan and everybody else connected with Stanford track are excited by Freshman Bill [sic] Coe, who outran the Indian varsity men while setting a school frosh Two-Mile mark [sic] of 9:07... Coe is equally brilliant in the half, mile and two mile and Jordan said after Saturday's meet, 'He's the best long-distance prospect to enter Stanford since I've been here.'" That Jordan was wrong – everybody knew that Duncan was his best prospect – did nothing to dampen my pride. From Walk-On to Chosen One, in ten short months! I was better in Jordan's eyes than Mike Ryan, who had transferred to the Air Force Academy after his freshman year and won the 1968 N.C.A.A. Cross-Country Championship for; better than Ernie Cunliffe, Stanford's school record holder in the Mile, a 1960 Olympian at 800 Meters and a former Indoor World Record Holder in the 1,000-Meter Run!

Stats rattled around my head as I tried to fall asleep the night after the S.C. meet. That Easter Relay Mile had proven that I could run much faster, right now, on a day without gale-force winds. That race was worth maybe a 4:07, an N.C.A.A. qualifying time! I would run a 4:05 later that spring, then go 4:04, 4:03... Duncan had run 4:11.8 as a freshman; Large, 4:12.8; the old freshmen record holder, who ran a 4:10.5, got down to a 4:02.3 before he graduated. Why couldn't I run a 3:59 at 19, or 20, or 21? And 3:54 at 25? What's the Varsity Record? Harry McCalla's 4:01.5 in the famous Peter Snell-Jim Beatty "Modesto Mile" in '63. No, the school record holder was Ernie Cunliffe, 4:00.4, 1960, the Rome Olympic year... Sub-four... *Roger Bannister*... The impossible barrier... The numbers... *I'm going... going... under* ... @ @

In the morning I put the *Examiner* clipping in an envelope and wrote my parents about the Coaches' plans for me: "With my solid background, we're going to try hard-soft days, instead of hard-medium, or medium-medium days like we've been doing. They're going to run me into the ground, really tough one day, and the next have me just relax and do a little striding..." The Coaches never went through with this; not surprising, since few people got individualized workouts at Stanford, because it wasn't usually Jordan's way. Just as well: my golden season as our Head Coach's fair-haired boy might have continued – I logged a solid 70-mile training week after the S.C. meet – but a nasty head cold that moved into my chest and "got my strength," as my Mom used to say. "For three days I was barely able to breathe," I wrote home on April 29th. "I could only do long runs, 8-10 miles, so as not to open my chest. It was killing me. I coughed my way through workouts. My Achilles were aching, too. I woke up this morning feeling great – spitting a little blood – I think that whatever I had in my chest broke up or something. Don't be alarmed..." I told the Coaches about my bloody cough when I showed up at practice that afternoon, but I also said I felt fine, so Coach Jordan threw me into a special workout meant to give me the feeling of a sub-four Mile: he had me run a Half-Mile (in 1:58.1), and follow it with a brisk 3-minute jog, then close with a second 880 (in 2:00.1.)

I had done those Halves back-to-back, but I didn't feel like I was anywhere near putting them together without stopping in a 3:58.2 Mile. My cold had kicked the stuffing out of me. I needed to do everything I could to get myself better, and I needed to do it fast. @ @

The following evening, Wednesday April 30th, I joined seven hundred anti-war activists and marched on Encina Hall, then three hundred who occupied it to protest the on-going war-related research abetting the rivers of blood in Southeast Asia. My thinking had changed since April 3rd. I felt I could no longer sit by while Stanford participated and even profited from the pursuit of an unjust war. I had to leave Encina early to get my ten hours' sleep, which meant I missed the pre-dawn hours of May Day, when the university called in the cops, who told the hundred or so remaining students to leave the premises or be arrested. People complied. I was with them in spirit. I, too, wanted to put my body "upon the gears and upon the wheels, upon the levers, upon all the apparatus," as Mario Savio had urged Berkeley students to do five years earlier. Only I planned to put my body upon the apparatus by resting up to run against Berkeley students in the seventy-fifth Big Meet, the traditional highlight of Stanford's track calendar and Cal's, too, which would be contested at our Stadium in two days' time. @ @

The long campaign that was our Track & Field season had followed its opening victory against Oxy and Fresno State with losses on successive weekends in all its dual meets leading up to Cal: beaten soundly by the future N.C.A.A. titlist San Jose State, Washington State, U.S.C., U.C.L.A. and Oregon. The Athletic Department contended that we had "the toughest dual-meet schedule in the country" and had been "close" against Cougars, Bruins and Ducks, which was true only if you thought "close" meant coming within 50 points. Our last dual meet was usually the most competitive: if you Beat Cal in any Stanford sport in those days, you could consider your season a success. Big Meets attracted Track & Field mavens from across the Bay Area to a much-anticipated gathering, famous for inspired competitions and personal bests, as athletes from both schools ran, threw, leapt and jumped faster, higher and farther than they ever had before.

The Bay Area papers had declared "the race of the meet" the face-off of each school's freshman Mile Record Holders: Cliff West and Robert Coe were due to "lock horns again" after their "epic battle" in Santa Barbara, said the Paly *Times*. Unfortunately it didn't work out that way. From Lap One Cliff toyed with me. Whenever I moved up on his shoulder he would surge a little and not let me by. He wasn't running for time, he was running to win, and he did just that, quite handily, in an ordinary time of 4:13.8 to my more ordinary 4:14.5.

After a brief cool down I plopped belly-down on the infield grass, buried my face in my arms and wept: the second time in my freshman year that Berkeley made me cry.

Brook Thomas noticed me on the grass, jogged over and in a voice dripping with disapproval, said: "Get up off the ground." I sprang to my feet hurling profanities, ready to duke it out with our Cross Country team captain if that's what he wanted. Seeing me on my feet again, Brook rolled his eyes and waved his hand at me in disgust, then returned to whatever business he was about before he butted into mine. Brook's humor and intelligence I admired, but I also often thought he took his senior responsibilities much too seriously sometimes. Then again, maybe I should have taken my blubbering elsewhere than on the Stadium grass. I wasn't ashamed of crying. Old-school stoicism wasn't my style. I had shed the tears of a warrior who had met a painful defeat. But once Brook left and I looked around and saw no one watching or caring one way or the other, I dried my tears, jogged over to my sweats, pulled them on, and finished my cool-down, and would never cry over a footrace again. @ @

The Big Meet was fantastic in '69, just not for me. Through the Largesse of Large, Al Sanford overcame winter illnesses to win his third consecutive Big Meet Mile (in 4:09.8), a feat never before accomplished in the seventy-five-year history of the rivalry. Earlier in the year he had run the fifth-fastest Mile in school history, 4:04.6, in a nasty shoving match in Eugene against Oregon that featured Duncan's disqualification, even though Dunc was simply retaliating for being pushed himself. The Javelin-hurling Southpaw Tom Colby unfurled an electrifying school-record 265-foot, eight-inch spear chuck that seemed to hover in the air forever; slick Rick Tipton from Silver City, New Mexico, the future conference high hurdle champion (13.9), crushed the hurdles field with "Indian" war paint slathered on his cheeks; and Team Captain T.C. Jones, our 280-pound black Prince Lightfoot and former J.C. state champion from Laney College in Oakland, uncorked a 58-foot, 1½-inch PR to win the Shot-Put on his final toss, then improvised an "Indian" war dance that drove me and our other teammates wild. "Heap Big Heave" was the headline over T.C.'s photo in the "Buck Club Bulletin," a booster publication that ballyhooed a day on which the Indians prevailed, 87-67, avenging defeats over the previous two seasons. The cumulative record of the oldest Track & Field rivalry west of the Mississippi: Stanford 39, Cal 34, with two ties and two years off for World War Two.

Two days later, on May 4th, Stanford's Board of Trustees voted to end all chemical and biological warfare research on-campus. Unfortunately they also voted to sell S.R.I., effectively wiping their hands of the entire issue of classified off-campus research – a Pyrrhic victory for the anti-war movement that seemed in hindsight to be the best we could have hoped for under the circumstances. America's military presence in Southeast Asia reached an all-time peak that month: 546,400 pairs of boots on the ground – while our Onitsuka Tigers continued to cover the hills and synthetic surfaces on and around the former horse farm of Governor Leland Stanford Sr., the old Robber Baron himself. @ @

Six days after the SRI vote, on May 10th – coincidentally the one-hundredth anniversary of the day that Leland Stanford drove the ceremonial Golden Spike to complete the First Transcontinental Railroad on the backs of Chinese slave laborers who helped make his fortune and eventually finance the construction of our university – I had my first taste of a big-time track carnival under the lights at the West Coast Relays in Fresno. Since I had failed to secure a Two-Mile qualifying time in the S.C. meet, the Coaches had entered me in the 5,000 meters. But after assessing my Achilles woes, a balky knee and that ongoing chest cold that caused me to miss three more days of training that week, they figured out something else for me to do: I would run the third leg on the Varsity Two-Mile relay team, a race which would give me all the competition I could handle in the incredible 90-degree heat and high humidity that lingered into the early evening. I took the baton under the lights from my fellow freshman Dave Whiteing (1:55.2), dragged myself through a pedestrian second leg in 1:55.5, and handed off to junior Kermit Sweetwyne (1:56.5), who gave it to senior Bob Anchondo, who anchored us home with a 1:54.8 in his last collegiate race. We had hoped to break 7:40, which would have earned us an invitation to the L.A. Coliseum Relays on June 6th, but we ended up fifth in 7:42.0, far behind Villanova's winning quartet, which ran a sparkling 7:18.5, just three seconds off the world mark held by a Soviet All-Star team.

I wandered the infield afterwards in a brown leather cowboy hat, wishing I could have a reason to feel cocky instead of vaguely sorrowful for the way my season had just petered out. There would be no Junior A.A.U. races for me that summer, because such things didn't exist in those days, at least as far as I knew. Instead I wandered the infield in a brown leather cowboy hat, thinking there were few feelings in Track & Field as grim as getting waxed in a huge, anonymous relay festival in the early summer heat of the San Joaquin Valley.

I watched from the infield while the Olympic Black Power rebel and 200-Meter bronze medalist John Carlos prepared his self-described "blazing" speed by hanging out in the stands until the 100-Yard Dash was called, at which point he trotted down the stadium steps, leapt over the railing, and did a little light stretching. An impressive figure at six-three and over 200 pounds, Carlos would win the 100, the 220 and anchor the winning 4x110 relay at the N.C.A.A. meet in Knoxville that year to end the season as the number-one 100-Meter runner in the world. That night in Fresno he produced a surge at sixty yards that provoked the loudest gasps I had ever heard at a track meet, and his time – 9.1 – tied the world record. Twenty seconds after the race, Carlos was striding across the infield not ten feet away from me.

"I got you in nine-flat, John," I shouted, holding up my stopwatch as if that proved it.

"I know what I ran," he screamed at me, flailing his arms and spinning angrily away. He had just heard (erroneously) that the wind was slightly over the legal limit, denying him the WR tie. I would have been pissed off, too.

Later that evening I saw Villanova's Marty Liquori, a college sophomore only seven months older than I was who had anchored the Wildcat's winning Two-Mile relay team that night, standing in the middle of a crowd of well-wishers and autograph seekers. I had just competed in the same race as history's first teenage Olympic finalist in the Metric Mile, shortly to be named the world's top miler in 1969. When the crowd thinned out I decided to talk to him, but what came out of my mouth was the very definition of lame. "This heat's really something, isn't it?" Liquori looked at me, his eyes widened, and with a startled expression, darted away. I have been told many times since that Liquori is a decent guy, but I am most amazed now, looking back, at how empowered I felt, inserting myself among the Track & Field headliners of the day. Only a year had passed since my claim to fame had been being the eighth-fastest High School Miler in the State of Texas. And now I was at a legendary track carnival, talking to Track Immortals, soon to reach on my own for a limitless sky. @ @

Our team had a respectable showing in Fresno – a fourth-place finish in the Mile Relay pushed us up to eighth out of twenty-five schools and teams, lodged between New Mexico and the University of Kansas, the latter the winner of the N.C.A.A. Indoor track title earlier that year. Afterwards we descended on a Fresno smorgasbord, where I challenged T.C. Jones, our Team Captain, to an eating contest, one on one. T.C. was almost twice my size and could bench-press a quarter of a ton. He had PR'ed in the Shot that day: 58-feet, 5-inches, the second farthest throw in school history, surpassing by five-eighths of an inch the effort of another Team Captain, Otis Chandler, currently publisher and part owner of the *L.A. Times*. The only reason T.C. never threw the 16-pound implement any farther was because his hands weren't much bigger than mine. Earlier that year he had made it through one football practice, after which he lost his heart (and his lunch) and never put on pads again, because he just didn't like hitting people that much. With his bubbly laugh, T.C. was a six-year-old and an old soul fused in a solid block of muscle. He was also Payt's man – Jordan's chosen Captain, since there was no democracy on our team (or in the U.S.), only a pretense of one.

"So T.C., tell me why you let Payt appoint you Captain without a team vote? Why didn't you tell him that he should have given your teammates a chance to say if we even wanted you?"

"Oh, now, Bob, stop it, Coach Jordan's fond of you. Don't go be makin' trouble, or I'll have to sit on you..."

With our gentleman's wager on, T.C. and I matched each other plate for plate for over an hour, but our contest ended in a draw, because we had to board the team bus home. @ @

I rode the shotgun bench all the way back to Palo Alto with Olympic Marathoner and future long-time *Sports Illustrated* Track & Field writer Kenny Moore, who was hitching a ride with us back to Palo Alto to be with his wife Bobbi, a Stanford undergrad who happened to be in my Sociology class. An Oregon graduate and recent Stanford Law School dropout who was 14th in the Marathon in Mexico City, Kenny competed for the Army now – I never had the guts to ask him why. I admired Kenny (who later established himself as the best writer on Track & Field and distance running ever), and was humbled by his willingness to talk with me for hours on that ride home, our faces lit by the flickering headlights of passing cars. He claimed not to be in top shape, but had performed decently that day in the Steeple; his image clearing the water jump just behind the race's eventual winner would make the cover of *Track & Field News*. He was also six months away from producing an American Record 2:13:28 Marathon on a famously fast course in Fukuoka, Japan. That night on the bus he talked about an idea he would elaborate a half-dozen years later at the funeral of a noted Oregon distance runner who died young. I would do Moore an injustice, attempting to recreate what he said, but the gist of it was that running was a "service," something we did for each other; each of us contributing to the creation of a culture that becomes the foundation for other people's aspirations as well as our own. I can't say I fully grasped what he was saying at the time. I was taken by the idea that teams were about the interplay of the individual and the group –

"– 'the strength of the wolf is the pack,' I always say. But there's an ingredient you're under-estimating, in my freshman opinion. I love the inspiration my teammates give me, and hopefully what I do can inspire other people. But at the end of the day it's the individual who pays the price of greatness or mediocrity or failure – isn't it? 'Service' isn't going to help anybody climb that mountain. An athlete has to have a big ego to do big things, doesn't he?"

I would reflect on this conversation often during an enforced two-week lay-off due to my bum knee, on doctor's orders. I knew that Kenny hadn't shared every thought he had about why people run and train and race, but this notion of service interested me in ways I wasn't prepared to acknowledge just yet. As focused as I was on my own self-improvement – as self-involved as I could be – all of my effort was linked to my identity as a Stanford Jock. It wasn't just that Stanford was my family school, although that was a part of it; it was also because I loved being part of a team that pushed me forward through pain, stress and the existential challenge laid on us by a world haunted by death. We were all interconnected, it was true. Maybe that was all Kenny was saying and nothing more.

The times were fostering social responsibility: early that summer I helped to coordinate a Boys Club of America track practice for disadvantaged Black East Palo Alto kids on the old cinder track at Angell Field – still the only time in my life I ever coached high hurdles. One of the (printed) signatories on my Boys Club "Certificate of Appreciation" was Richard M. Nixon, cheering on the Boys Club at the same time that he was shipping tens of thousands of "boys" into the quagmire of Southeast Asia through the Oakland Induction Center.

I had attended a non-violent rally earlier that spring that ended when police chased several hundred of us with tear-gas canisters and clubs. This was by some reckonings the day that had marked the escalation of anti-war activism from peaceful protest to confrontation. @ @

The mid-peninsula's anti-war crusade heated up on May 16th, six days after the Fresno Relays, when five hundred demonstrators, most of them students, brought traffic to a standstill on Page Mill Road outside the Stanford Research Institute offices, where scientists continued to conduct classified war research. I showed up after an unofficial track practice in time to see the picket signs – "SRI Kills" and "Pax not Pox," the latter referring to the viral smallpox weapon that S.R.I. reportedly had in development here – then to watch the demonstration turn into a police riot: one hundred and fifty cops moving in on a non-violent marchers with tear gas and clubs, a melee that ended with more than $20,000 in damage inflicted on S.R.I. buildings, along with many bruised heads and ninety-three arrests. This kind of aggressive action against the war effort was in order now, but I wasn't convinced that getting your head bashed in by the cops was the best way to halt war-related research at Stanford. It was becoming clearer to me and many other people who thought harder than I did about such things that the transformation of Stanford University from the respected regional institution it had been in my grandfather and parents' era into one of the great universities in the nation had occurred largely because of extensive partnering as a Research & Development center for America's ever-burgeoning Cold War military-industrial complex.

Stanford, Middle Earth of my family's aspirations for me and my own image of myself, was built on the foundation of a war machine currently waging an illegal, immoral land war in Asia. Talk about being brought up "schizophrenic:" the reality of my family's university's complicity in the War was something I could hardly begin to make sense of, but it hovered in the back of everything anyway. @ @

With Track done for the year and summer break approaching, I didn't think it was a big deal to participate in an old school Beta pledge event. I accompanied my pledge class to a denuded hillside behind campus, where we were ordered to strip naked and sprint up a steep hill, stopping along the way at four aluminum buckets, where we dipped a tall paper cup into some god-awful rum-tequila-pineapple juice concoction, and chugged it down. A game of nude tackle football followed, during which I earned serious style points for an open-field tackle of a galloping Varsity Defensive End twice my size. Afterwards we were ordered back into clothes and into vehicles for a squealing drive down to Lake Lag, where we stripped down to our underwear in front of dozens of sunbathers and dove head-first into the icy waters.

The shock of the cold did me in. I managed to haul myself back up on the wooden deck and apparently passed out there. Two dreamless hours later I was awakened in pitch-darkness by a strange woman standing over me, gently tapping my shoulder. The Beta bros had noticed that I hadn't returned from the lake and sent her back to drive me home to Branner. I woke up the next morning up with a five-star hangover, but I probably should have considered myself lucky: a drunken brother from Zeta Psi would drown in Lake Lag in 1987.

Despite my denials, I was apparently quite capable of behaving like a knuckle-headed frat rat, even if the "undercurrent of hipness" was what I wanted to be part of.

I had recently sprouted a small goatee that I thought looked pretty sharp, but which was still a no-no as far as Jordan was concerned. That team vote taken in January, declaring unequivocally that hair be a matter of personal choice, had been unilaterally voided by our Head Coach, who apparently had only allowed the vote to take place because he thought he would carry the day and have a cover story for the installation of "rules" he was going to put in place anyway. I made a point of avoiding Jordan, which wasn't that hard because school was almost out. You may doubt my ability to survive on a team run by this man, but I saw no contradiction between working on Payton's Farm and my own political and cultural engagements. But I did know enough to keep my distance, just as I kept my distance from the painful realities of Stanford's participation in the War. I could work around our Head Coach. I could work with him, too, if I had to. I was a warrior – an Indian! – who had succeeded until season's end despite two heavy chest colds, an injured tendon under my right buttocks, achy knees, chronic tight calves and brittle Achilles tendons that kept me from running on pavement or asphalt. My Achilles tendons had been "iffy" all year. When I tweaked them they would swell up and squeak for a week or two, and I would limp slightly when I ran. Some days I wasn't able to run at all, just ice my ankles in Dave's training room and hope for the best.

My physical problems all stemmed, I was convinced, from a more fundamental issue: I had been diagnosed with a forward displacement of my fifth lumbar vertebra when I was fourteen, and the faulty vertebrae had been surgically fused to my fourth. This didn't inhibit motion, but which did make me over-protective of my lower back, which in turn caused my hamstrings to over-develop in relation to my quads, which led to tight calves and my Achilles being a regular problem.

One day that spring I casually mentioned to Coach Clark that I might want to try steeple-chasing one day. He stared at me for half a second – me, leaping over five 36-inch-high rock-solid barriers and a water jump for eight laps? – and gave his decision: "Forget about it."

My back was the reason I was fragile, but my back didn't explain my end-of-year fade-out. I was quite aware that Coach Moultrie's prediction in the *Examiner* that I "was really going to get down there" before the season was over had not come to pass. I was passed over for Frosh MVP. That honor went to my friend Mark Haight, an accomplished high school runner from Evansville, Illinois who competed in both hurdle races, the Quarter-Mile and the Mile Relay, scoring more points than I did. I also hadn't qualified for Nationals in Knoxville, like Cliff West did. Cliff would run the Mile in 4:07.0, one spot ahead of senior Allen Sanford in 4:09.7; neither would make the famous Final in which Marty Liquori became the first American Miler in four years to beat Jim Ryun, the World Record-holder and reigning Olympic Silver Medalist, in an N.C.A.A. Meet Record 3:57.7. (When Ryun declined to double in the Three-Mile later that day, he cost Kansas a national title.) Our Varsity failed to score a point that June – no Stanford All-Americans this year. Maybe I could run in that meet, a year or two down the road? It didn't seem impossible. My prospects looked bright. I had gone from the High School All-Nobody Team to college freshman star. Hard training had revealed a significant talent that had pushed me to the lintel of the national stage. Much to my family's pleasure, I had also made the Dean's List all three quarters: achievements that measured up to my highest expectations. @ @

Back in San Clemente, President Nixon had moved in next door to my grandparents. Well, not quite, but Tricky Dick had recently purchased an estate only a few miles away from my grandparents' place, and dubbed it "La Casa Pacifica" (the House of Peace.) The world would come to know it as the Western White House. Visitors to this formerly-sleepy beach town over the next few years would range from Leonid Brezhnev and Frank Sinatra to anti-war protestors at La Casa's front gate. I was already into heavy road work in San Clemente when a Buck Club Bulletin arrived in the mail, dated July 3rd. Breezing through an article about Stanford Track & Field, I came across this: "...*Coe, who figures to be one of the greatest distance runners ever to attend the Farm...*" I never showed this clip to my family, not even my Dad. I sometimes thought that my grandparents understood my Left-leaning politics better than my investment of so much time and energy in a "minor" sport. My grandfather came right out and said so in a letter that year: "You'd be better off playing a sport that might help you professionally, like golf or tennis." But I had just had the best year of freshman distance running in Stanford school history, so "figuring" me for greatness was not so far off-the-wall.

Another piece of Stanford mail arrived in San Clemente in mid-July, a week after the Buck Club Bulletin: a letter addressed to all Track & Field men. Mine included a hand-written note from Coach Jordan that filled me with complicated emotions: "Bob," he wrote (that was still not my name), "you don't have to prove anything to anyone, but yourself. You have great potential as an athlete and a <u>man!</u>"

I pretended to be cynical about this praise from a Head Coach I did not entirely respect – especially that underlined "<u>man</u>." What in the world did *that* mean, coming from someone like Jordan? But the truth was that his admiration also filled me with pride and wonder. At that moment there was nothing I wanted to be more than Ron Clarke's "mate," Coach Clark's prodigy, and Jordan's "baby-faced assassin." On that particular field of dreams, Payton Jordan and I saw eye to eye. I wanted to be the greatest distance runner ever to attend The Farm, and I figured that all I needed to do to reach this goal was to keep putting in the miles, and everything else would take care of itself. @ @ @

"THE STRENGTH OF THE WOLF IS THE PACK"

My original plan for the summer of '69 was to move to Oahu in the Hawaiian Islands and live on rice and fish with Duncan and Stanford hurdler Tom Kommers (a future Berkeley physicist who would die shortly after his thirtieth birthday.) Dunc claimed that we could all find lucrative work in construction. "We'll train twice a day, make a lot of money, and never take off our shorts and running shoes," he wrote in one of the only letters I ever got from Dunc. This scheme didn't pan out, like most things didn't between Duncan and me, but that was cool, because I had a back-up plan: with the benefits of altitude training amply demonstrated by East African runners in Mexico City, I decided to spend my summer getting high in the mountains. I also needed to make money for school. So Coach Clark helped me land a job as a camp counselor in Plumas County, near the dot-on-the-map town of Portola, California. The pay would be only $50 a week, plus room, board and laundry, but after putting in a few weeks of training and lounging around San Clemente, I was ready to return to the Bay Area, board the "California Zephyr" in Oakland, and travel up the Feather River Canyon deep into the Sierra Nevadas north of Lake Tahoe, for my gainful summer employment at Walton's Grizzly Lodge. @ @

For eight weeks in the mountains I ran before breakfast along a narrow shoulder of dirt at the edge of two-lane blacktop, a steady diet of ten-mile runs at 6:00 a.m., building aerobic strength through the thin, silent, pine-scented air, wearing my almost-year-old Tigers, a jock and a pair of nylon shorts. Fifty-five hundred feet wasn't high enough to significantly increase my red blood cell count, which was why distance runners went to altitude, but Grizzly Lodge was higher than Boulder, Colorado, which some people considered a distance-running Mecca. A couple of thousand feet higher would have been better, but this was the best I could do and still pull a paycheck. I was in charge of "hiking" – taking kids out in search of old mines, bird nests and wrecked buildings in pine-needle-covered forests. We climbed Beckwourth Peak (7,218 feet), went crawfishing using orange peels as bait, and swam daily in the camp's private lake, where I also managed beach sports and a pack of unruly, energetic ten-year-olds. I even taught archery, which I only knew about from books, and thankfully there were no injuries to report. I had four younger brothers, so spending time with kids felt natural, even if I was sleep-starved on only eight hours a night, and sometimes less, and feeling isolated, too. On the first of my one day off a week, a fellow counselor and I paid a visit to the Mustang Ranch, the legendary brothel in the Nevada desert, where we checked out the scantily-clad ladies but did not partake.

Three weeks into the job, which ran from June 24th to August 24th, I lay in hot mud near an undeveloped therapeutic hot springs just over the Nevada border – land said to be owned by Althea Gibson, the first African-American female or male to win a Grand Slam tennis tournament. Her springs were surrounded by run-down trailers housing the halt and lame, none of whom paid a dime to be there, after Gibson had refused numerous offers to develop the property, preferring that it would continue to be used by the poor and destitute.

This was where my fellow counselors and I lay in the mud, sharing a six-pack and staring up into a cloudless sky at the spangled Milky Way and a luminous moon where an astronaut who lived three blocks away from my parents took one small step for a man, one giant leap for mankind. Sunday July 20th, 1969: "The Eagle has landed," declared our family's neighbor (and former Eagle Scout) Neil Armstrong on our tinny transistor radio in a Nevada mud flat. (NASA had asked Bill Anders to pilot the Lunar Landing Module, but after his experience on Apollo 8, thanks but no thanks. There may have been other reasons Bill declined, but Buzz Aldrin became the second man to walk on the moon.) Being a camp counselor in the Sierras was a novel experience, but one that soon wore as thin as the air. @ @

"I'm sick of running by myself over the same three trails in the heat without enough sleep," I wrote my folks after a month. But I stuck it out. My morning runs always ended with a tough half-mile uphill of several hundred feet, which at five thousand feet were as tough as you cared to make them. On our one day off I continued to hang out with the two other counselors who smoked weed, one of whom let me drive his Triumph convertible around Sierra Nevada mountain curves, probably faster than I should have, but what a gas.

News of an orgy that did not take credit cards reached me over a Grizzly Lodge sausage & scrambled breakfast one morning in mid-August: four hundred thousand hippies had just concluded what some people were calling the biggest event of my generation: three days of peace love and happiness on Yasgur's Farm, near Woodstock, New York. *Time, Life* and *Newsweek* fell all over themselves in praise of hippies. My assumption had always been that any depiction of the counterculture in mass media was phony by definition. Still, it interested me that some of the biggest national organs had decided that piping out a generous word or two about pot-smoking, skinny-dipping freakazoids was good for the circulation.

Nearing the end of my eight weeks at Camp Grizzly, I decided it needed a long-distance race, so I created one: a 500-yard haul from the "Essex" tack house near the horse stables all the way up the dirt driveway to the main lodge. After the age-group competitions were over, and there were some exciting ones, everyone lined the road for the first "exhibition run" of my career. Most of the course was a slight incline up, and I will attest that those last hundred yards hurt pretty good. The "Essex Run," which was the name I gave it, is still being contested under the name I gave it, more than forty years later.

I left the mountains strong, traveled to San Francisco, headed home to Houston, then journeyed north to "Champ City," the Hick Elysium known as Nacogdoches, Texas, where my old Clear Creek teammate John Walker went to school. A year ahead of me at Creek, the national "Postal" champion as a junior at Homestead High School in the mid-peninsula, John had produced a 4:06 mile that spring for Stephen F. Austin State College. Four days of training in the stifling heat and humidity of Nacogdoches while crashing in a rowdy Jock dorm made me count my lucky charms that I was on The Farm, but I still managed to log four straight 90-mile weeks in Texas before returning to Palo Alto. On my second day back I hooked up with senior Chuck Menz for an easy time trial on our old 4.2 mile course. Chuck, who along with Greg had inherited Brook Thomas' old job as editor of our entertaining summer newsletter, reported on our "breathless [21:48], according to Bob Coe's Trix Rabbit watch (Mickey Mouse can't hack it anymore.)" It was true: my Disney Chronometer had died and been replaced by a wristwatch faced with a cartoon breakfast cereal rabbit.

My wholesome summer had left me in great shape, with ten pounds of new muscle on my still-slender frame: a lean clean running machine without my spring goatee, gratefully looking forward to moving into Beta Theta Pi, where I would soon discover that "the re-invention of frat houses for hippies" remained very much a work-in-progress. @ @

Not long after pledging Beta last spring, I had attended an old school "Luau" in the backyard of a Beta from upscale Atherton, an affluent community just north of campus. To this afternoon bacchanalia for Pledges, upperclassmen and young alumni I brought a blind date, a very pretty Gunn High School senior my suitemate Zac set me up with. We smoked a joint along the side of the house and were lying belly-down on the Dichondra – John Lennon and Yoko Ono were doing a "Bed-In" for peace at the Amsterdam Hilton, turning their honeymoon into an antiwar event – listening to Steppenwolf's latest and watching several large and rowdy upperclassmen I didn't know, probably football players although each wore a flowered sarong, dipping their bamboo cups into plastic trashcans filled with some god-awful Brewsinski, and chugging it down. Suddenly Beta senior George Buehler loomed over us, reeling like a drunken Colossus. Brother George was a future "All-Century Farm Team" starter at middle guard and more recent recipient of a Pac-8 Defensive Player of the Week award for his performance in the losing effort against U.S.C. (He had also put the Shot that spring for the first time since high school, reaching 52 feet at the Easter Relays in April.) Buehler was about to embark on a nine-year pro career on the greatest Offensive Line in N.F.L. History, playing alongside Jim Otto, Art Shell and Gene Upshaw under Coach John Madden. Brother George would be the only one not inducted into the N.F.L. Hall of Fame, and deserves to be. But at the Beta Luau that day Brother George shook his fists at the sky and bellowed at my date, *"Gimme a kiss!"* Then he squatted down and delivered a stout slap to her behind. I leapt to my feet to defend her honor... Did you believe that for half a second? The better part of valor was to let all six feet, three inches and 250 pounds of Brother George become distracted and wander off to some other mess, which was what happened. An hour later I drove my date back to her parent's house in the '62 Chevy Impala Wagon my sister and I still shared, and never saw her again.

Skip later insisted that Brother George wasn't a jerk, just drunk, and didn't really think he owned Pledges' dates. But events like this made me wonder what I was getting into, signing on with these people. Where was the "undercurrent of hipness" in this sea of barbarity? Where was Skip's Theory in Praxis? My only comfort came from the knowledge that the Betas I cared about had known better than show up at the "Luau," starting with my official Big Brother Willy Wauters. Willy was a reason to like the Betas. Two weeks earlier, word had come down that pledges were to make their Big Brothers a Luau drinking cup out of bamboo and wax. I had protested roundly: "I'm not making you some fucking bamboo cup, Willy! Come *on*, man!"

"I hear you, bro," Willy said, rolling his eyes. "Forget about it. Don't sweat the small stuff." During my freshman year Willy had been the undergrad who dressed up in a costume to play "Oski the Bear" and prance around the dock at the Big Game bonfire rally at Lake Lagunita as an object of comic abuse. (Years later Willy would re-invent himself as an Episcopal Priest, working alongside Chicano fieldworkers and in barrio parishes in California, and later as head of chapel at his former elite Eastern prep boarding school, where he would be nominated for a New Jersey bishopric... *Yes, the times they were a-changing...*) @ @

Brother George was a Dinosaur from the late Jurassic compared to his classmate Dick Roth, a Beta God and Olympic Gold Medalist I met only once, on the lawn of the oval driveway outside the Beta House on 557 Mayfield Avenue, one golden dusk my freshman year. Dick Roth was the 1964 Tokyo Olympian stricken with appendicitis shortly before his final in the 400-Meter IM, the most grueling race in the pool, which he was favored to win. Prepped for surgery, he kept refusing the operation until his parents arrived and gave their consent to forego. Seventeen-year-old Dick got himself to the Natatorium for his heat and later won the Final, breaking the world record by three seconds, and only then was rushed away on a gurney to have his appendix removed in the States two weeks later. (When I had my own appendix out in 2003, my surgeon would recount this story about my fraternity brother without any prompting from me.) With serious good looks, long blonde hair and a raffish grin (not to mention serious family money), Roth was like some latter-day Errol Flynn, a suitable image for the bad boy of the swimming world, thrown off the Santa Clara Swim Club team for admitting to his long-time coach George Haines that he smoked dope. He was supposed to be away for a short time only, but Roth quit swimming entirely before the Mexico City games and joined a hippie commune for a while. (Later in life he would run a large chain of natural food stores in Santa Barbara, work on a half-million acre ranch in Elko County, Nevada for a decade, and go on to manage and facilitate workshops for a leadership center while writing a book on menopause entitled *No, It's Not Hot In Here*. By 2012 he was living in Park City, Utah, retired from what he described as a "company that develops renewable power plants for utilities," and doing the Sunday crossword puzzles.) *The times they were a changin'* indeed.

But maybe some things weren't changing much at all: I wasn't immune to the Beta's old-fashioned, Big-Man-on-Campus glamour, Sixties style. Among other things, there were some really good-looking guys at the Beta House that fall, among all the swimmers and football players and assorted Jocks — so many that when a San Francisco casting director needed to find a young hunk to show up in bed in a film with 28-year-old Katharine Ross, who had co-starred that year with Robert Redford and Paul Newman in *Butch Cassidy and the Sundance Kid,* this casting director went shopping on Mayfield. (The agent chose Dave Stevenson, a double science major from the State of Washington; forty years later Dave would be on the faculty of the Stanford Medical Center, an expert on neo-natal medicine.) I admit I wrote this home: "About the only aspect of being a fraternity brother that hasn't changed is that being a Beta still cuts a lot of mustard with women." But furthering my stunted ability to cut mustard was not the reason I pledged the Beta House. My deeper motivation was to further develop my recent friendships with two Jocks in the class just ahead of mine, neither of whom bought into the whole rah-rah thing, but who were both amazing athletes who wanted to become writers one day. @ @

My obsession with my athletic development did not mean I did not closely follow other athletes in other sports aspiring to greatness. Becoming a fan of certain people was not a difficult thing to do on The Farm in the fall of '69. Three Stanford Jocks performed feats of such kinesthetic grace and power that I might not have believed them possible, if I hadn't seen them with my own two eyes. The first was Jim Plunkett in pads, dropping back in the pocket, throwing a rope to a wide receiver in full stride forty yards downfield, and hitting him between the numbers. His Center John Sande claimed that Plunkett could throw a football so hard, it whistled. After #16 helped skunk Washington State that fall, 49-Zip, Cougar Head Coach Jim Sweeney called him "the best college football player I've ever seen." The second feat I saw but could barely believe was freshman tennis phenom

Roscoe Tanner slapping a blink-and-you'll-miss-it 130 mile-per-hour practice serve – with a wooden racket. (I saw him do it through a chain-link fence.) Tanner would lose the N.C.A.A. Championship Final that year to another freshman, U.C.L.A.'s Jimmy Connors, but later won an Australian Open and became a Wimbledon finalist and the hardest server in the pro game.

The third athlete I saw do things that made me rub my eyes was my fellow Beta John Ferris, doing the Butterfly. John wasn't an especially imposing physical specimen – barely six feet and 165 pounds – but with his powerful limbs and a hydro-dynamic barrel chest he could arc into a pool barely making a ripple – "diving into a hole in the water" was how he described it to me, taking a steeper, deeper angle than other swimmers – then perform a few underwater dolphin kicks before surfacing to weave over-and-under the water with all the velocity and liquid grace of a frisky Killer Whale. Adopted by the rest of the team, John's start – and his flip turn, too – would be taught in countless swim clinics until Head Coach Jim Gaughran would claim decades later that there wasn't a swimmer in the world who didn't use John's innovation, meaning John had "revolutionized swimming starts." Only weeks before becoming a Stanford freshman, John had broken the world record in the 200-Meter Fly, set just thirty-five days earlier by his former eight-year-old "sleepover" guest and long-time rival Mark Spitz, who re-claimed the WR thirty-nine days later. (It speaks volumes about our era, compared to the present one, to realize that Ferris showed up at his freshman dorm with a world record in an Olympic event, but only half a ride.) Ferris – everybody called him that – sometimes seemed more aquatic than terrestrial, but out of the water he was a funny, never-in-a-hurry German-Irish-Catholic kid, the son of a successful Sacramento insurance agent and one of seven kids, same as I was. His good looks and teasing sense of humor helped make John catnip for women: his high school sweetheart was Barbie Benton, currently Hugh Hefner's main squeeze, who appeared on the cover of *Playboy* in July. I had heard rumors from many different sources that the rooftop of the American dorm in Mexico City had been a scene of nightly orgies, but John swore he never partook – although after his world record in Tokyo at the World University Games in 1967, a beautiful stranger had approached him to inquire, "Would you like to try for another world record?" Ferris left that on the table, too, but did write about another out-of-body experience he had in Tokyo for a Stanford creative writing class. I was always a good audience for any and all first-hand stories from international competition. @ @

"I hadn't swum a stroke in four weeks when I dove into that pool," John told me over beers at a Beta House party, sharing swimming stories he didn't usually retail. "I came up from my dive to take my first stroke and I wasn't in my body anymore, Robert! I was two inches above myself and two inches ahead. When I touched the last wall I wasn't even breathing hard. But bam – World Record, Bob! I could have taken a five-minute rest and done it faster, because by then I was warmed up. It just shows how over-trained we were at Arden Hills…" His old swim club coach Sherm Chavoor had led the American women in Mexico with an un-modulated philosophy – "More Laps, Better Swimmer" – that helped turn the team into an unstoppable force, winning over half the aquatic medals at the '68 Games. Ferris told me with some chagrin: "I was one of Sherm's original guinea pigs."

Ferris also shared his version of passing out on the Mexico City medal stand of the 200-IM, a new Olympic event that year. The overwhelming favorite Charlie Hickcox surprisingly beat Ferris to the wall on the opening Butterfly leg, but John was still in second after the Back; on the Breast he was passed by his fellow Stanford Beta Greg Buckingham and the University of Michigan Wolverine from Peru, Juan Bello, but John's ferocious freestyle leg pushed him past Bello for the American sweep. The combination of the thin air and his predilection for fainting after hard swims anyway was why the whole world watched him swoon to "The Star-Spangled Banner." ("I faint sometimes after workouts," he told me. "It's not a big deal.") Four days later he had a strategy firmly in place for defeating Mark Spitz, the world-record holder and prohibitive favorite, who had beaten John in their last five 200-Flys by coming from behind. Another American had beaten Spitz in the 100-Meter Fly in Mexico by letting him lead, then out-kicking him, so John held back in the 200-Final until the halfway point, where he was more-or-less where he wanted to be, although slightly ahead of Spitz. The problem was that he was also next to last. The only man in the pool to negative split – swim the second half of his race faster than the first – John still finished a half-body length behind his good friend Carl Robie, the four-time world-record holder and U.S. Team Captain, who won the Gold in a time that John had surpassed many times in workouts at the team's high-altitude training camp in Colorado Springs. Ferris was left holding another Bronze, after being picked to Silver behind the swimmer who (in John's opinion) had choked like a two-dollar whore.

"Spitz was a real dick about it," John said, referring to his victory in the N.C.A.A. 200-Yard Butterfly in Spitz' home pool in Indianapolis, the spring after Mexico. His 1:49.6 made him the first person to swim the distance in under a minute and fifty seconds. "Spitz comes racing down from the stands, pretending he's there to congratulate me, when really it's to show everybody that the only reason I won was because he hadn't swum." Our conversation that night was unusual because when Ferris and I hung out, which wasn't often, we almost never talked sports, although both of us never missed a football game unless we had to; instead we talked about books and fiction-writing. Based on the few things of his I'd read, John was already the best letter writer I had ever come across, as well as the author of several short stories that struck me (in my still very limited experience) as early intimations of genius.

Ferris had spent his post-Olympic, national title spring living on the second floor of the Beta House, sharing a spacious deck above the front portico with his next-door neighbor, the Maui surfer and Backstroker Fred Haywood: tall, male-model handsome, and blonde – or green-thatched, like some Dr. Seuss character, thanks to the pool chlorine. A former national A.A.U. champion from the Santa Clara Swim Club and a teammate of Spitz's in high school. Fred had led the 100-Meter Back at the Olympic Trials with barely 20 meters to go when a previously-undiagnosed "atrial flutter" tumbled him back into seventh, denying him a trip to Mexico City. In an era of legendary Backstrokers Charlie Hickcox, Gary Hall Sr. and Mitch Ivey, Fred won the N.C.A.A. 100-Yard Back the same year Ferris won the 200-Fly, upsetting Hickcox, World Swimmer of the Year in '68. Fred and Ferris also famously toked up every night before bed during their prodigious post-Olympic seasons, providing more proof (if you still needed any) that smoking weed did not impede excellence in athletic performance. Early that fall Fred and I would go over the mountains to surf in Santa Cruz, accompanied by another Beta swimmer from Papua, New Guinea. And well in the future, in 1983, Fred Haywood would set a world windsurfing speed record of 30.82 knots in the waters off Hawaii, employing a carbon wing instead of a mast. @ @

The second Beta Jock I wanted to get to know better had introduced himself to me at Track practice that spring, shortly after the S.C. Two-Mile, by wrestling me to the infield grass, like a playful older brother would. Sophomore Jim Kauffman was actually barely four months older and twenty pounds heavier than I was and, but he was already being touted as the most versatile Stanford athlete of his era: a freshman basketball defensive specialist, a Track & Field Freshman MVP, a rugby hero, and most visibly the starting free safety on the Stanford football team, as well as its punt and kickoff returner, totaling 454 yards on 37 touches in his recent sophomore season. Jim was on The Farm on a double ride, competing in fall football and spring Track & Field, where he ran the Quarter and the 220 and did all the Jumps: Long, Triple, and High. His sophomore exploits had concluded with a 23-foot, 10-inch Long Jump PR and a 48.3 split on the Mile Relay team at the West Coast Relays in Fresno. "Kauf" – everybody called him that – exemplified the difference between speed and quickness: his 100-yard time was somewhere short of national caliber – "only" 9.8, which wasn't exactly crawling – but Kauf on a football field was "quick as a tick," as his Defensive Back and Track Coach Bill Moultrie liked to say. Kauf had that essential kick returner's ability to make the first man miss. Watching him "break ankles" with a football in his hands was electrifying. He was a phantom sprite who could make eighty thousand people gasp out loud. Unfortunately he had three Achilles Heels: first and foremost, he was a little too fearless; which wasn't always wise when your second problem is that you're the smallest player on the field. And thirdly, he was near-sighted. Not Mister Magoo near-sighted – as a sophomore he had returned a punt 49 yards to set up a TD against U.C.L.A. – but by his junior year it had become sufficiently iffy as to whether Kauf would catch the ball or not that Coaches decided to relieve him of punt return duties, freeing him to lead an excellent defensive backfield in interceptions, with four.

Jim was lucky to be playing at all: a year earlier he had trashed his shoulder attempting an open-field tackle of O.J. Simpson, who was considerably faster (a 9.4 100-yard man) and also out-weighed Jim by fifty pounds. "We were facemask to facemask in a pile at one point and the Juice says, 'Nice hit, brother,'" Kauf told me, adding (with a wink), "I took it easy on him after that…" Shoulder surgery would leave Kauf with a nasty knife scar courtesy of O.J. – not the only person who would be wounded thusly – but O.J. would also keep Kauf out of the Draft, after the team doctor wrote a letter to the Selective Service saying this man should be tagged "4F." Along with his amazing athleticism and a distinct facial resemblance to Johnny Depp (noted in hindsight, of course), the thing about Jim Kauffman was who he was: smart, fun-loving, full of good cheer and utterly unimpressed with himself, although I was sure he knew he could charm the birds from the trees. He was also an engaging writer: a future Rhodes scholarship nominee, Kauf had a natural breeziness on the page that reminded me of another former punt returner, this one for the Columbia freshman football team of 1940: Jack Kerouac. I was already a frequent visitor at Jim's family home up the peninsula in Millbrae, where father Herb and mother Caroline kept an open house for Kauf's Stanford friends. The cowboy hat I had worn on the infield of the West Coast Relays was the property of "Herbie the Hat," a Stanford Ph.D. and San Francisco State English Professor known far and wide for his outstanding collection of brims. John Ferris was another frequent visitor at the Kauffman family home. He and Kauf, both juniors now, were good friends and certified campus heroes – in John's case, an international superstar – while I was only a sophomore wannabe in a "minor" sport. I knew I was far more interested in them than they were in me. But I had pledged the Beta House anyway, in anticipation of gaining better acquaintance with the Stoner Jocks of Beta Theta Pi. @ @

Imagine my disappointment when I returned to campus ten days early to help with some house painting and repairs at 557 Mayfield, to discover that Kauf had already absconded to live with other Betas at a "Picker's Hut," the former home of Mexican field workers, surrounded by acres of walnut trees in nearby Portola Valley. Ferris would linger at the Beta House for another quarter only. But I decided to look on the bright side: once school started I would be only a Hop, Step and Jump from the Student Union, the Post Office and White Plaza. Campus opposition to the war was nearly universal by the fall of '69. Even the Beta House would organize, sending brothers out to canvas neighborhoods in the evenings, distributing pamphlets and drumming up support for the first Vietnam Moratorium Day on October 15th. I would attend most of the big demonstrations, but with the drama over S.R.I. in the rear view mirror, I wasn't looking for any more bandstands to jump up on. The previous spring I had declared a major in Political Science, before learning I only got a B-plus in my freshman "Introduction to Political Science" course: not a great start to a major in those days of grade inflation. So many classes interested me that quarter that I enrolled in 22 units, one and one-half times the usual work load. I took French each morning at 9 a.m. (the bane of my existence); American Public Policy in Poly Sci; a Stanford Workshop on Political and Social Issues (SWOPSI) course, "Disarmament Diplomacy," taught by Wolfgang Panofsky, Director of the Stanford Linear Accelerator, where scientists were studying everything from the workings of sub-atomic particles to the nature of the cosmos; and classes in Ethics (Pass-Fail) and Classic Greek and Roman Literature, the latter a core course for the "Humanities Special Program," which would have me reading all of Homer and Virgil (in translation, of course) with commentary provided thrice weekly by a wonderfully absent-minded, cigarette-addicted, post-retirement age Classics professor from Duke who had gone on archaeological digs in Lebanon in the Twenties. I dug all of my classes. I attended a few mid-day "Nooners" – campus-wide keg parties at "the Butt Hutt," as house denizens sometimes called the place – and I showed up for every home football game when the team wasn't racing. Otherwise I trained, with an ardor that left no doubt where my deepest passion lay. @ @

Another cross country season kicked off with our traditional, informal workout in Foothill Park, where we had run the previous November. On a gorgeous midday in wilderness we ran along winding red dirt trails past towering Oaks and red Madrone. One stretch of trail was an eight-hundred-foot climb in a half-mile that froze your thighs with toxic sludge, producing the kind of pain that made you want to scream out loud, and finally do just that.

Standing at the top of the mountain, bent over, crying out in pain, clutching kneecaps and sucking wind, I found breath to say: "All the ancients proclaim… a necessary relationship… between sacrifice… and bliss!"

Don, Chuck and Arv looked at me, their chests heaving, like – wha?

"We're here, guys!" I cried out again. "We're… *faaan*-tastic…"

It was too early in the year to get as pumped up and rah-rah as I seemed to be, but I couldn't help myself. We had reasons for dreaming big. Last year's N.C.A.A. cross country runner-up was back with a core of returning upperclassmen, and that wasn't even counting Duncan Macdonald, who was still enrolled in school but not running a lot. Illnesses? Grades? A recurrence of his Achilles miseries? Training on his own to prepare for spring track? I wasn't privileged to know. My freshman pal Jack Lawson ran that day, and was in the parking lot with us for our lift back to campus. Jack had spent the summer working in the sweltering heat of a Modesto cannery, which meant he had come back to school in considerably less than stellar shape.

"It was hard work, but I was making fifteen dollars an hour, Robert."

"You really couldn't train more, Jack?"

"I had to earn money, man! This school's expensive, in case you haven't noticed…" At moments like this one, I knew how lucky I was. Without the extra earnings, Jack's family probably wouldn't have sent him back to campus at all. He was gloomy about his situation, but I had to agree there was nothing he could have done differently.

Arvid looked stronger than before – still skinny, but more filled out. Chuck Menz and I had our Trix Rabbit Time Trial, so I knew Chuck was ready to go. Don Kardong had missed spring track at a Stanford overseas campus, and was still rounding into shape; last year's MVP, Greg Brock was back for his final season of Cross on The Farm, but not yet in top shape, having succumbed to repeated bouts of tonsillitis that led to his tonsils' removal and his track season's premature end after the Oregon meet last spring. ("It is that time of year," Brock had written in one of our early Fall newsletters, "when the leaves fall from the trees and certain young men, who want to avoid raking them, begin to run…") This meant that three of the five scorers on last year's runner-up team were back, with Brook Thomas and Al Sanford lost to graduation, although Brook was still around, planning to train with us to compete in Track as a fifth-year Senior while not incidentally preserving his student Draft deferment. Large had been sufficiently worried about the Selective Service System sending his ass as a grunt to Vietnam that he had enlisted at a Marine Reserve boot camp in San Diego, where as "Private Large" he would win a prestigious American Spirit Medal for having the best overall record in physical and mental tests of all Marine recruits in basic training in the nation. A rumor reached my ears that he had also set an all-time Marine Corps record for the Mile under a full pack and in boots – a rumor I was willing to believe, knowing how strong Al was. These successes and his Stanford background made him the target of abuse from a sadistic Drill Instructor. Al wrote Brook about it, and Brook wrote back that Al needed to stand up for his rights; somehow the Drill Sergeant got hold of one of these letters and forced Al to read it aloud to the whole platoon. When Brook heard about this, he had his father contact their

U.S. Senator from Maryland, Joseph Tydings, which led to investigators being sent to the base, but Al and others were too intimidated to describe their abuse and nothing was done about it. When his six-month reserve duty ended, Al would return to the Bay Area with an honorable discharge and recurring nightmares. Not a word of this surprised me, but it still made me so furious I wanted to spit. That a great guy like Al Sanford had been sent to hell and back in the uniform of his country was beyond despicable to me. The drill sergeant eventually did receive disciplinary action, while I would continue to be glad that my Student Deferment was in order, or I would have become a future Draft Dodger seriously plotting his escape to Canada. @ @

As always on college teams, there were freshmen, new arrivals eligible for Varsity competition now. Among the newcomers were some very good Milers: Brian Mittelstaedt, an outstanding high school middle-distance guy from Mt. Tahoma, Washington, greeted at his freshman dormitory by the smell of marijuana; and Decker Underwood, the California State Mile Champion (in 4:12.1) whose campus recruitment visit I had hosted the previous spring.

Decker and I hit it off from the start. He had been an outstanding age-group tennis player before settling on track, where he ran with a low-slung stride that reminded me of a sixteen-cylinder Jaguar, only running on biofuel. Decker and his South Torrance High School teammate, Pole Vaulter Steve Smith, had won a third-place team trophy at the California State Track & Field Championship for the distance-running powerhouse that had also produced Jeff Marsee, the Trojan runner who had out-raced Brook, Brock and me in the S.C. dual meet last spring, and our own classmate George Watson. (Steve Smith would go on to become the first man to vault 18 feet indoors and the first to vault 17 feet off a skateboard, after stripping off his psychedelic warm-up sweats.) Some South Torrance athletes trained on psychoactive Morning Glory seeds, and Decker had ingested a handful on his graduation night, which left him shredded for the Golden West Mile in Sacramento, where he finished sixth in 4:16.0. Decker was a Freak, in other words, although he didn't get stoned much anymore to guard against a paranoid streak; rather he was into all sorts of esoterica in those early days of my own countercultural evolution: Deck introduced me to Buddhist Sutras, which became important to me; he introduced me to the Velvet Underground – the Andy Warhol album with the "smokable" banana on the cover – and the New York underground band The Fugs, who performed such countercultural ditties as "Yes, I Like Boobs a Lot" and "I Like Marijuana!" Decker turned me on to William S. Burroughs' *Naked Lunch*, which would become a bathroom staple for decades. Decker was also fast and strong - fast enough as a Papoose to help us throttle Ducks, pound Cougars, shuck Huskies, slap Trojans, and wrestle some Bruins and Golden Bears to the ground. Our long runs became soul-to-soul conversations in mysterioso overdrive – detailed discussions of the nature of Dharma and what it meant to psych-in and dial up your best performance when it mattered most. We were Vision Questers, real-time conspirators in whatever it took to lift us to a Higher Ground. @ @

A few days after classes began that fall, we ran through the hills behind campus one afternoon, silent for minutes.

"They run…"

"Who runs, Deckerhead?" Decker had this annoying habit of taking weird conversational leaps into the void, although I liked them sometimes, too.

'Monks run… in the Hiei mountains… How do you … pronounce that?"

"What the hell are you talking about?"

"The 'Hiei' mountains… five peaks above Kyoto… Buddhist 'Marathon' monks run… like… twenty-five-thousand miles… through the mountains… in handmade sandals… white robes… over seven years… famous blue raincoats… Sincerely… L. Cohen…"

We had reached the crest of a hill high above campus. Stanford stretched out below us in all its glory: golden light glinted off the barrel tiles, the view backed by the ever-amazing cloudbanks above the San

Francisco Bay. It was an astonishing vista, but not one we stopped to admire. The sun was setting and we still had a few miles left to run. Decker was having dinner with me that night at the Beta House. God Herself could only guess what Stella was cooking for us, but if you paid your board at the Butt Hutt, you ate what she put on the table.

"Since 1885..." Deck said on a speedier downhill, "only a few dozen... 'Marathon monks...' survived this ritual... dating back to... the Eighth Century..."

Cruising now over a flat, rock-strewn trail that would tweak my Achilles if I wasn't careful, I let Decker continue: "A few monks finished it twice... Monks... who didn't... were expected to take their own lives... either by hanging... or disembowelment."

"Tough call... I don't know which –"

"– for three years... pilgrims rise at midnight... to pray... then run... twenty miles... around Mount Hiei... stopping 250 times... for prayer... Do this... for one hundred days... They run... with candles sometimes... prayer books... various... munchies... Next.... two years... more running... two hundred days... Winter comes... do temple chores and... and rest... Then the most difficult trial... your fifth year..." Decker was airing it out a little now on a stretch of dirt in a kind of bowl near the Dish. I had to find a gear to keep up with him. "Monks... 'gyojas'... sit... chant for nine days... no food... only water... and... and sleep... They call it 'doiri...' – not sure... how to... pronounce that... It means... 'entering the temple...'"

"Let's not race," I said, breathing harder.

"Sixth year..." Deck cried out loudly, lengthening his stride when I pushed up alongside him. "Every day... a hundred days... ultra-Marathon distances... daily... In seventh year... fifty miles a day... for a hundred days... Then 20 miles... a hundred more days... then you go... back to the temple ..."

"Would you stop? Decker! Wait!"

He was ten feet ahead of me, and I had to push harder than I wanted to, but I caught him. There was nothing to do but catch up –with yourself and with everybody else. We were "Gyojas," too, however you pronounced it. We were in the temple, too. @ @

The Brothers of Beta Theta Pi gathered for a team photograph on a chilly morning that fall in the middle of Arastradero Road, close to the furthest-most point of my favorite road run and not far from Zott's, a roadside watering hole from my parent's era. Twenty-five years later I would see the photograph we took that day still bolted to the wall behind a new pool table in the old Beta Chapter Room, and recall that I had only recently traded in my freshman "Preppie Look" for a short-lived "Austin Powers" phase: in the photograph I wear a tight-fitting, long-sleeved, horizontally-striped brown-and-orange cotton turtle neck shirt; a pair of beige hounds-tooth bellbottoms with a big flowered patch on the seat (you can't see it in the photograph); a three-inch-wide leather belt with a double-pronged buckle; and mid-calf buckled boots. My curly Prince Valiant haircut was flat-out mod. The fringy bangs were not quite Sonny Bono, but definitely "*Groovy, baby!*"

The picture snapped, we piled back into our cars and returned to the Beta House, where my third-floor single – my first single room in college – I had painted deep purple and covered with rock posters and a large purple-and-green poster of a naked woman viewed from behind, sitting on her heels, holding her long dark hair aside to expose a long, elegant spine. Incense smoke curled up on either side of her. I burned incense, too, sometimes, in front of my plaster-of-Paris Buddha, under a ceiling blacklight that caught the Day-Glo on my Jefferson Airplane at Winterland poster. I thought my room was very cool, and spent a lot of time there that quarter, reading and writing at my small desk before heading out to class or another workout, mornings and afternoons, alone or with the team. Occasionally I was ordered to sleep on the third-floor "Pledge Porch," but even there I would wake up shortly before dawn, pull on this year's Stanford G.I. Tigers and head out for my morning run – sometimes to the golf course, but mostly along my personally-designed 4.7-mile morning tour of campus, which I had created to take me almost entirely on dirt and grass, to spare my knees the pounding and my Achilles the wear. @ @

I loved my morning run that fall. I was almost always completely alone at that hour (years before half the student body jogged) and generally shirtless, because the cool air woke me up and kept me moving.

Every step of that trail is etched on my medulla oblongata: first down to Stanford Avenue on the southern edge of campus, then northeast until I reached El Camino, where I hung a left, looped around the Stadium, then returned to the Beta House across the heart of campus. After 28 to 32 minutes of effort, depending on how good (or bad) I felt, I would be trotting up the circular driveway on Mayfield, strolling under the seven slender green columns of the Beta portico, and minutes later be standing under a shower head, praying for hot water. Our leaky bathrooms were located over the kitchen, explaining the in-house outbreak of typhoid fever the previous spring. This guilty plumbing had supposedly been repaired, although no one seemed quite sure if it had or not, but enough sensible people seemed to think that the plumbing was fixed so I chose to believe it was true. My quick shower over, I would dress in my room and hustle downstairs to order breakfast from Stella, our ancient cook, who had somehow avoided the sack after the typhoid outbreak. When your order was ready, she would shriek from the kitchen in ear-shattering decibels: "French *TOOOOAST!* SCRAAAAAM-buld! *Baaaaay*-KUN! *PAAAAAAN*-cakes!" Straight out of a Warner Brothers cartoon. Two or three brothers would grin at each other across the table before returning to their meals, the green pages of the *San Francisco Examiner,* or perhaps their conversation with a "little sister" still in her bathrobe. The Beta House had groupies, several of whom would end up wives. After breakfast, I would head upstairs to study or off to class, feeling righteous, as if dues had been paid.

And that was how my days started in the fall of '69. @ @

The confrontation about my haircut was coming; I just didn't know when it would go down. As our October 3rd intra-squad time-trial approached, I could see Coach Clark getting up-tight around me. My hair wasn't *that* long, and I thought it looked pretty sharp. But the day before the time-trial, Coach told me to cut it, or I couldn't suit up.

"You know Coach Jordan's feelings about this, Robert. The hair has got to go." I was sure Coach Clark didn't give a rat's ass about my hair, nor did he enjoy pawning off Jordan's rules on us. But the Coaches held all the cards. If I wanted to compete, go along; I decided not to fight this one with cold steel. Thinking what a load of crap, I borrowed a pair of scissors at the Beta House and trimmed my curls off my collar. I kept it longish over my ears, but when Coach Clark saw me the next day he said nothing and let me run in the intra-squad tune-up. Five of us tied for first on our 4.2-mile course, side-by-side and feeling strong. Not wanting to risk it, I cut off a little more hair that night, and no one said a word about that trim, either. @ @

Our first official meet of 1969 was on Saturday morning, October 11th, over Sacramento State's newly-lengthened 4.5-mile course. The site of my freshman breakthrough had another overnight rainstorm that once again left it a soggy mess, but this year there was also wind, which hadn't been a factor the year before. Nevertheless as I approached the starting line my nerves gave way to a state of grace. With supreme confidence in my conditioning – get fit and the mental part often tends to take care of itself – I took off like the Alpha Dog in my first Varsity race. Leading the field from the get-go was not something I had planned do, and running in front into a headwind was probably not the brightest idea around. But it energized me to be out in front alone.

Still leading everybody into the maze of thickets along the river, I suddenly found myself at an unmarked fork in the dark trail twenty-five feet ahead of me. There was no sign indicating which fork to take, and no official to show me the way. So I took the advice of Yogi Berra – "When you come to a fork in the road, take it" and spontaneously veered Left, leading at least twenty runners down the wrong path before a Sac State runner who knew the course took the rest of the field down the right way. That fork turned out to be the trailhead of a loop, which meant that the two groups of runners – the one I led, and the correct one – had to squeeze by one another on a narrow, sandy path through thick brush. Bumping shoulders and elbows, I banged knees with somebody hard enough to leave a bruise.

Shaken by a debacle I had caused, I was passed in the final mile by the eventual winner, Gary Tuttle of Humboldt State, a two-time N.C.A.A. Division II Steeplechase Champ running that day for the L.A. Striders. (Tuttle would go on to become a three-time member of the U.S. World Cross-Country Team, as well as a runner-up in the Boston Marathon in the impossibly faraway year 1985.) I didn't even finish second; that honor fell to Cal Junior and All-American Three-Miler Bob Waldon, who came through twenty seconds ahead of me. Learning about the confusion on the course, race officials huddled and eventually concluded that since we had all run the same distance and no one had been there to show me the way, I would not be disqualified.

"Wow, thanks a bunch," I muttered to Decker, who was a lucky 13th in his Varsity debut – not a bad showing at all. Jack came through a few seconds behind Decker, in 18th. Stanford's scoring five all made the top nine: my third-place; Brock's fifth, eleven seconds behind me; Menz close behind Brock in sixth, Kardong seventh; and Arvid ninth. Nineteen seconds separated our five scoring runners – a fantastic spread – while our top seven came within thirty-three seconds of one another, which in some ways was even more impressive for our threadbare squad. Last year's N.C.A.A. runner-up team had won the meet by a single point; last year's number three team, U.S.C., ducked us this year, but we crushed those who didn't shy away: Stanford 25; Cal 96; Nevada-Reno 109; Chico State 115; San Diego State 128; Sac State and others farther back. Farm cross country was a powerhouse.

And I was Stanford's Top Man. @ @

Coach Clark decided to introduce a new ritual that Monday afternoon: he gathered us all in the locker room before our workout and opened a box of new white cotton running singlets, each with the word "STANFORD" and a Number printed on it, in red.

"We're going to start wearing workout jerseys reflecting where everyone finished the week before," said Coach. "'Number One' this week goes to Bob Coe." Coach tossed me my singlet, accompanied by my teammate's embarrassed golf clap. I knew they had my back and they knew I had theirs, but I still think we were all a little unnerved by the introduction of hierarchy on a team whose egalitarianism had functioned so beautifully without one. We didn't need visual aids to remind ourselves of where we finished, because we all knew. But Coach wanted to try this, so Greg, Chuck, Don, Arvid, Decker, and Jack silently accepted their singlets as well. I pulled my white Number One over my head and tried to appear nonchalant about it, knowing that this benchmark was one to savor for only a moment, because it was only one rung on a much higher ladder. And yet I silently vowed to keep this cheap piece of cotton labeled "Stanford #1" for as long as I could, through a dual-meet autumn march against U.S.C., U.C.L.A. and Cal, and beyond that, too, if we could manage. @ @

That Friday our crew flew south to race against three schools, including another powerhouse squad from S.C. We would race in the hometown I had left when I was fifteen, on an odd, serpentine course in Long Beach's Recreation Park: six-miles plus 149-yards of four roughly one-mile loops, one of which we would run three times. Except for one slight rise and descent, the course was flat as a pancake, all either grass or barren dirt, which meant that a fast pace was likely. Cal Poly and Pepperdine would join in, too – four schools in our race would mean almost thirty runners – but only the Trojans posed a challenge.

As the *Stanford Daily* noted on the day we left: "Against S.C., Stanford will be making its first run of the year on a six-mile course, and Coach Clark, not venturing to predict a winner, says, 'At that distance it's a question of who can stand the gruel.'" The afternoon before the race we ran a loop or two at the park before checking into the Golden Sails Motel on Pacific Coast Highway. As soon as I was in my room I phoned a friend from my old life: a girl I had been "in love" with, in the way one loves someone in elementary school, but we had always been friends, too. A sophomore now at Long Beach State, she lived only two miles from the course, but said she couldn't make it, and didn't have time to get together that evening, either. So I went with the team to see *Belle de Jour* and *A Man and a Woman* at a nearby art cinema in Seal Beach, then followed everyone to early bed ... *to dream about the course we looked at and would race along that morning... This dream race had no beginning or end, only a grueling middle over short devil grass and bald patches of dirt... wild exertion... I let no one by me... no one passes... I cannot find the finish line... where is it? Where am I? How much farther do I have to go...?*

From the crack of the starter's pistol the morning race was dominated by U.S.C. freshman phenom Freddie Ritcherson. Freddie had finished third in the Two-Mile at the California High School State Championship meet where Decker won the Mile, then surprised a lot of people by winning the Golden West Two-Mile in a quick 8:56.4. A scrappy Black kid from Salesian High School in L.A., Freddie was closer to my age than to his classmates, but he had followed up his Golden West triumph with a sixth-place in the A.A.U. six-mile track championship, a considerable achievement for someone barely out of high school. Ritcherson followed this up with the greatest summer of off-track distance running in American schoolboy history: on July 26th he became the first prep athlete to break 12 miles in the One Hour Run; a few weeks later he broke the high school record in the Marathon with a 2-hour, 23-minute clocking. And back in December 1968, he had run ten miles in 49:19, which would still be the American schoolboy record forty-five years later.

I was fine with Freddie doing the work in front while I hung at the back of the lead pack for the first three miles or so, at which point Freddie decided to leave us all behind. I took out after him and soon it was just Freddie and me, him leading and me on his shoulder. At the 4½-mile mark, running up the slight incline on the course, I felt him slow slightly. I probably should have remained content to "sit on him," since I had confidence that I could out-kick this long-distance specialist over the final quarter-mile. But perhaps unwisely I raced on instinct, which told me to take the lead. This was an awkward place and time to try to pass unless I was ready to smoke Fred, which I wasn't. A quarter-mile later we were still side by side along a narrow path between a cyclone fence and a school building, completely out of the view of spectators. This was where Freddie decided to re-take the lead. I wouldn't give it to him. He pushed harder. I pushed back. And in a moment we were in a balls-out, shoulder-to-shoulder sprint, which lasted eighty yards or so.

"To hell with *this,*" I told myself, or thought to that effect. "This is way too early in the race to be pushing *this* hard. If Freddie wants the lead this badly, he can have it." So I took my foot off the pedal, and Freddie resumed the driver's seat. My thoughts ran on, more-or-less thusly: "I'll catch you on the back end, Fred." The problem was that I was hurting from our mid-race sprint, and with no fans or spectators in sight to urge me on and my teammates some unknown distance behind me – and me having never felt this alone in a race in my college career – I let Freddie go. In the parlance of distance runners: Freddie broke me. Then he gapped me. Then he dropped me.

My thoughts ran on, although not this coherently: "It's going to be a long season... You had a tough effort in Sacramento last week... You weren't sharp in workouts. Settle for second... It's not so bad... If we win, nobody will give a damn." Letting these ruminations rattle around my consciousness and passing them off as sound strategic thinking, I coasted alone for the next half-mile or so, running well within myself – and gathering strength, as it turned out, because near the end of a race that would culminate on a quarter-mile all-weather track, a challenger emerged: S.C.'s Rick Muth, the former Santa Ana J.C. runner who had beaten Arv on the track in the Two-Mile last March, was at my heels. Jolted awake, I instantly discovered reserves of energy I hadn't known I had. In a heartbeat I was on my toes and sprinting, making up fantastic ground on Fred – flying around the track like a Miler, narrowing the distance – keeping my breathing quiet in hopes of catching the race leader dozing. I could see Freddie just ahead now, loping along comfortably, thinking he had this thing in the bag – until some knowledgeable S.C. fans noticed I was closing fast.

"Move it, Freddie!" they shouted. "Here comes *Coe!*"

How thrilling, to hear myself objectified as a competitor! That Freddie knew who *"Coe"* was! When Ritcherson turned his head around, his eyes widened. Then he turned back around and began a kick of his own. I continued to gain on him, but in the end I ran out of race: I lost by two seconds – maybe ten feet – behind Freddie's course record 30:33.0, both of us under the old record. (Fred would round off his stellar freshman year in the distant spring with a fourth-place finish in the N.C.A.A. Six-Mile on the track, won by Frank Shorter of Yale in a time of 27:57.5.) My teammates were closer behind then I knew: all of us were within twenty seconds of one another: Don was fifth, just six seconds back; Arv, Greg and Chuck in seventh, eighth and ninth, respectively. All finished ahead of S.C.'s third man. Jack, our sixth runner, was 15th, 40 seconds behind me; Decker's wheels fell off over the last mile and he ended up a minute and a half behind the leaders.

Once again, course management issues: Freddie and I had apparently looped clockwise around the track when we should have looped counter-clockwise at some point. "But because the distances were equal," the *Daily* later reported, "it didn't shuffle the finish." The meet belonged to us over last year's third-place team at Nationals, 31-45.

Last year's runner-up had lost its two top guys to graduation, but as the *Daily* claimed, this year's team was "a force to be reckoned with." And though I had been beaten twice, I was still Stanford's Top Man. @ @

Decker and I celebrated at his family home in the foothills of the Palos Verdes Peninsula. Decker's father Bob Underwood, Class of '38, was a former Captain of the Stanford tennis team, now a successful insurance agent who donated the equivalent of Decker's athletic scholarship to the Buck Club, Stanford's alumni booster organization. Cal Berkeley had offered Decker an enormous package – tuition, room, board, laundry expenses, and a host of other perks – but like me, Decker had never doubted where he would go to college. Mr. Underwood's bull session that night all about the Don Budge-Bobby Riggs era in his game kept us entertained throughout the meal: "Oh sure, Mickey

Rooney played at our tennis club *all* the time! What a pest *he* was! Big movie star! *Ha!* A bunch of us grabbed him one time and held him upside down over a toilet bowl and flushed. You know – gave him a Swirly? You boys ever do that? *Ha!* ... Bobby Riggs: now Bobby was *always* good... What a hustler! Any time there was money on the table, Bobby found a way... Can I pour you some more wine there, Bob? Of course I can..." Those World War Two-era Dads like Decker's and mine really did enjoy a good time.

In the morning Deck and I headed out early for what we hoped would be an easy fifteen miles in the Palos Verdes Hills. With my mistrust of asphalt we kept the pace slow on rolling streets with dramatic ocean vistas and got lost. Our fifteen miles ended up closer to eighteen, but it was okay. Running near my boyhood home, the feel of the fresh ocean air kissing my skin, felt both familiar and refreshing, even though it left my knees stiff and aching afterwards.

"Life is good," I said as we gimped down the steps to his hillside house, sore as bandits. "Although I do need to drum up more of a winning attitude over six miles than I demonstrated yesterday. I also need to race smarter, you know? I'm too willing to run within my limits over six miles, instead of past them..."

"Go Indians," Underwood said in the "dead" voice he sometimes used to indicate irony, especially around subjects like our disgraced mascot. Decker's sense of humor was at least as dark as mine. But I was un-ironically and fully aware that I was beginning to deliver on the promise held out for me at the end of my freshman year. I had reached base camp in my assault on the Big Rock Candy Mountain. Whether or not I would deliver on my potential was, as in all things having to do with running, something only time and hard work would reveal. @ @

The Cross-Country meet at Sacramento State prevented us from attending the football game of the year in the L.A. Coliseum against fourth-ranked U.S.C., a week after a gut-wrenching non-conference loss to Purdue, 36-35. Clarence Davis, O.J.'s replacement at Tailback, wasn't a huge downgrade, but the key players in the game were the

Trojans' so-called "Wild Bunch" defense, arguably the best in school history. (In 2002 S.C. would erect god-awful statues of the Wild Bunch in front of Heritage Hall: five defensive linemen looking like "Gumbys" in football uniforms, only cast in bronze.) "Dump... the... Plunk... Dump... the.... Plunk," the Coliseum home crowd chanted, and most of the 82,812 in attendance saw Plunkett spend a good amount of the game on the seat of his pants. Yet his 67-yard pass completion to J.C. transfer Randy "the Rabbit" Vataha set up Steve Horowitz's 37-yard field goal, leaving the score 24-23 Stanford with only 1:03 left on the clock. The sixteenth-ranked Indians looked to be on the verge of finally beating S.C. But then the Trojan offense lived up to their reputation as the "Cardiac Kids" by driving 68 yards in 55 seconds, making several long pass completions, and converting successfully more than once on fourth down. With no time left on the clock, S.C.'s 34-yard field goal attempt split the uprights for yet another last-second S.C. win and Stanford loss, same as last year. (If you can bear to look at it, you can still see that kick and watch our team's reaction today on youtube.com: some players sprawl face down, weeping into the grass and pounding the turf in frustration.) Center John Sande declared it to be the only time in his life that he ever cried after a football game. Many Indian fans in the stands wept, too. Thousands remained in their seats for ten minutes after the final gun, absorbing what would be our only conference loss, but one that kept us from the Rose Bowl. Decades later, Stanford alumnae would still be talking about that day in the Coliseum. Plunkett would call this 26-24 defeat – after losing 27-26 on a last-second field goal the year before – the most disappointing loss of his college career. "The football gods weren't on our side," Plunkett said. I was so disappointed I was almost glad I was racing in Sacramento and couldn't travel south for the game. All the same, with the core of this football team intact, we knew we weren't done. I was not alone, nor were we the first, in thinking this thought: play out the season. We'll get 'em next year. @ @ @

"NUMBER 73 AMONG THE 100 GREATEST TRACK & FIELD AND CROSS COUNTRY COMPETITIONS OF THE TWENTIETH CENTURY"

I was in bed in my room at the Beta House one Sunday morning, reading my tattered paperback *Aeneid,* when one of the house football-players – the same guy who had given me my first "hack" with a paddle as my reward for being named "Model Pledge of the Week" the week before, leaving no love lost between the two of us – strolled into my tiny quarters with a towel wrapped around his waist, otherwise naked and dripping from the shower.

"Your Coach is on the phone," he said. Then he turned around and strolled out the way he had come, leaving a puddle behind.

I dashed down to the ground-floor closet. Coach Clark was calling.

"Robert. You've been named a 'Stanford Athlete of the Week.' There's a Buck Club Breakfast tomorrow morning. Can you make it to the Hyatt early?"

"As long as it's after my morning run."

"That shouldn't be a problem. I'll pick you up at the Beta House at eight."

Stanford's alumni booster organization convened its weekly Monday morning event in a red & gold dining room at the Hyatt on El Camino in Palo Alto to honor that week's gridiron hero or maybe two. In this case my fellow honoree was a defensive player I didn't know who had starred in Stanford's Seven-TDs-to-Zip shellacking of Washington State in our Stadium, a defensive performance matching the second lowest total yardage for an opponent in school history: 109. This weekly fall Buck Club breakfast was mostly a celebration of football, but did sometimes throw a bone to a minor sport, just to provide a little variation over the bacon & eggs.

The M.C. that morning as always was Stanford Information Director Bob Murphy, the "Voice of the Indians" since 1964 – a larger-than-life character with a silver tongue to go with a reputation (among the hipper athletes) as a blowhard who parsed, praised and dismissed as he pleased, while remaining essentially clueless about anything outside his ken, which was basically football, baseball, swimming, and golf.

"Stand up, Bobby. There he is, folks: Bobby Coe, the top Indian runner in an outstanding cross country victory over the Trojans on Saturday." A smattering of applause from the potbellied crowd, eager to get back to matters of pigskin but perhaps slightly curious, too. "Bob finished second... Over six miles, correct? Now tell us, Bobby, because we are curious (yellow): how many miles do you fellows run in a week, say?"

"Right now? Well – maybe – about... seventy or eighty miles?

"*A week???*" Murph gagged. "What in the world?!? I'm lucky if I can make it to the bathroom in time!" Murph proceeded into what felt like a full minute of stand-up about his flabbergasted disbelief regarding the miles we ran and what we put ourselves through as distance runners. He was like some drunken clown in an Irish pub. And boy did his mugging play! Jowly Buck Clubbers emitted howls of derisive laughter, slapped thighs in hilarity. Or at least that was how I saw and felt and heard it. I lacked the maturity or presence of mind to produce a comeback on the order of: "Yeah, Murph, we *DO* run seventy or eighty miles a week! And sometimes more! And sometimes I think it's not enough!" Instead I just stood there tongue-tied, my cheeks burning, while Murph – an Old School Icon for many in the Stanford athletic community – produced more wisecracks at a sophomore's expense.

Finally he said, "Well – you've been a good sport, Bob. Come on up here and accept your brand-new, red-and-silver Buck Club necktie!"

I politely avoided shaking Murph's out-stretched hand, took the boxed tie and returned to my seat. That necktie would end up stuffed in the back drawer of a dresser, seeing as how one of my goals in life was never to have to wear one of those things except at funerals and weddings, and only then if someone asked me to.

Coach Clark and I finished our bacon & eggs and headed back to his car, when I finally spoke my mind.

"Could you believe that, Coach? Murph was working the room at our expense! I can't believe I was invited to this event to be honored, and I end up going home feeling like I've been disrespected! Was I put in my place back there, or what? Am I wrong about what just happened? They were *laughing* at us, Coach!"

That's when I noticed that Coach Clark wasn't just mad; he was livid. Red-faced, spitting angry. The maddest I had ever seen him.

"If I needed an illustration of how cross country is a stepchild in the Stanford Athletic Department, I just got it," he muttered through clenched teeth, adjusting his rear view mirror while tearing in reverse out of the Hyatt parking spot. "Although I really don't think I did…"

My first impulse was to make him feel better. "Coach, maybe Murph honestly doesn't believe we train as much as we do! People really don't know, do they…" This was years before the running boom of the late Seventies. The New York City Marathon didn't even exist. The first one, the following year, would have a field of fifty-five. @ @

At the workout on the golf course that afternoon, I told my teammates all about what had gone down at the Buck Club Breakfast.

"When I told Murph how many miles we run a week, he acted as if he'd just swallowed his teeth!"

"What an a-hole," remarked Brock.

"A Wanker," said Duncan.

"Doesn't he know how cool it is to be a distance runner?" Kardong deadpanned – joking, sort of.

"My guess," said Menz, "is that Murph subscribes to the old high school adage that if you're not big enough or strong enough or fast enough to play a *real* sport –"

"– you run cross country," we all said in unison, which at least gave us something to laugh about.

There was no getting around it. We were Nerds. But we weren't ridiculous. We were one equal temper of heroic hearts. Okay, maybe we were ridiculous. But there was no law against a parcel of geeks like us tackling a sport as obsessively, compulsively punishing as long-distance running. *Sports Illustrated's* Kenny Moore would write about our "endemic Stanford wackiness," and that was how we rolled: workouts with Brock, Kardong and Macdonald couldn't help but be high-spirited productions worthy of a Restoration Comedy (sort of), with lots of good-natured teasing and mutual support. Duncan did not feel ready to race with us yet, but he was showing up for workouts with his professional-grade Donald Duck impression, which never failed to have us almost splitting our sides with laughter: *"Boy o boy o boy let's get this party started… We got some tree-tirties t' run… get outta my way…"*

Our weekly routine was the same as last year's: Mondays we ran four to five one-mile loops at race pace on the golf course; Tuesday, 24 x 330s in sets of six on the soccer fields, sets separated by a mile jog; Wednesday, a long run; Thursday, six to eight searing Thousands on the soccer fields. For shits & giggles I started showing up on Tuesdays in a red Speedo and worn-out Stanford water polo earpiece.

"Hey guys, what's happening?" I asked, jogging up to where we were stretching, wearing my red banana hammock and Rocky the Flying Squirrel water polo head gear.

"If it's the pool you're looking for," Don remarked, "you've come to the wrong practice."

"I don't see a pool around here," Duncan said, "but he's got shoes on, so he might as well run with us."

"Robert told me this *was* water polo practice!" Decker said.

"Come on, jump in, the water's fine!" Brock cried. "Anyone care to get in a workout today?"

It was early performance art, I guess you might say, or a self-conscious cultivation of my hotdog reputation. But none of my teammates had any issue with it, as far as I ever heard, and Coach Clark didn't, either. This was not a liberty I took because I was the team's top man. Showing up dressed like a water polo player at cross-country practice had nothing to do with how extraordinary I thought I was, or how ordinary, either. I was just having a goof to amuse myself and my teammates, during a time when everybody was entitled to express their own uniqueness in a free-spirited atmosphere of creative celebration and fun. (Or something like that.) Anyone who worked as hard as we did could do his or her own thing, too, and nobody would stop you, unless it involved long hair and Coach Jordan.

Coach Clark, with stopwatch and clipboard, didn't look at me any differently as we jogged to the line for twenty-four 330s: four sets of six.

"Ready... *go*..."

That was what we lived for: our team, our workouts, and our races. As far as all of us were concerned, the Non-Believers could kiss us where the sun don't shine. @ @

After dismantling the Trojans in Long Beach, we faced U.C.L.A. next on a beautiful 70-degree morning on our home course. This would be our third tough race in three weeks, and second in a row over six miles. Two weeks earlier the Bruins had destroyed a Golden Bears team that Cal's Head Coach was calling the best in school history, 20-41, meaning all five Bruins finished ahead of Cal's second man.

We knew U.C.L.A. would come out gunning for us, and they did. Seven Little Indians came through the first mile between 4:47 and 4:49, a quick opening split, but all five scoring Bruins were right there, too, racing with a pack-like aggressiveness we had not encountered before. Something else was new at the Mile Mark: a half-dozen members of the Stanford Band, instrumentation determined by whoever had been willing to drag himself out of bed on Saturday morning to fire up some ad hoc version of the school Fight Song to urge us forward. To my harried harrier's ears, this slightly hung-over ensemble sounded sweetly, endearingly pathetic, but even a cosmic jolt of school spirit didn't help me: I felt sluggish from the start, and ran just behind the front pack with my eyes half-closed – hypnotizing myself to maintain a pace that didn't feel comfortable at all. Seeing Coach Clark notice my no-doubt stressed expression let me know he knew I wasn't feeling it today, but it didn't matter. We had to hang in there together, our teams a mingled phalanx of red & white, blue & gold, thundering down the underpass below Junipero Serra Boulevard, then up and down the steep hills on the south side of the course, and back under Junipero Serra.

At Mile Four our top five men were still together – me, Kretz, Menz, Brock and Kardong all passed through at 20:04 to 20:06, our fast pace slowed by those tough back-course climbs. But all five pesky Bruins were still with us. An argument could be made that this morning the "W" would go to the team that wanted it more. By Mile Five, Stanford's wheels were wobbling. Lawson and Underwood had disappeared, but looking around I saw that Brock was gone, too. (He had fallen back twenty seconds in the fourth mile alone.) Kardong was suddenly nowhere to be seen, either, far behind us, suffering the first of many side stitches that would plague his racing career for years to come. With three-quarters of a mile left, the pack was down to three Indians – Arvid, Chuck and me – and all five Bruins. This was when Arvid Kretz – skinny-as-a-stick-of-macaroni Arvid Kretz – took over a cross country race for the first time in his college career. I covered his move, but barely, advancing into second through no agency but will.

Stanford was now 1-2, but I was seriously close to maxing as we scrambled over the final bunker. I had a clear view of the finish line, a hundred and fifty yards ahead of us. Seeing a finish line always invigorated me, so I gutted by Arvid and took the lead in the race for the first time all day. Only one hundred and thirty yards to victory! Ahead of me a half-dozen Band members leap to their feet and snatch up their battered trumpets, tarnished baritones and a single garish trombone to launch into the most raggedy-ass cover of "The William Tell Overture" I had ever heard in my life. For me this was not a moment rich in satiric possibility, and yet with a hundred yards to go and my reputation as a kicker on the line, I thought I had the U.C.L.A.-Stanford cross-country meet of 1970 in the bag.

A blue and gold uniform streaked past on my right.

U.C.L.A.'s sub-nine-minute Two-Miler Ron Fister, sixth in the Indian-Bruin dual meet the year before, made it to the finish line first that day, two seconds ahead of me. I had closed my last mile in 4:43, but it wasn't enough. Arv and Chuck broke 30 minutes, too, in third and fourth, respectively. Our fourth man, Jack, scored for the Varsity for the first time, finishing ninth in a course PR 30:14. Brock, our fifth scorer, had a serious off day in 10th, while Kardong struggled home with his side stich in 12th, just behind Decker, our two non-scorers in the team competition. Our top four finishers had their best performances of the year, but three guys under 30:00 wasn't enough, as U.C.L.A. grabbed first, fifth, sixth, seventh and eighth spots, and in a "stunning" upset, as the *Daily* noted, beat us by a point. The Blue & Gold hooted and shouted and slapped each other's palms. On our home course. Rubbing salt in the wound of a defeated adversary wasn't very classy or respectful, I thought. It pissed me off, actually. What hurt even more was seeing how crestfallen Coach Clark was after his first dual meet loss on The Farm.

"The bubble broke a little," Coach would tell the *Daily*, speaking for all of us. "It will take more to win conference than we thought."

I had done better than the best I could. I had performed far over my head. But the fact remained that if I had fought off Fister over those final 100 yards and nipped him at the tape, we would have carried a day that saw our football team come from behind to tie #6 U.C.L.A. 20-20 – another away game against an undefeated team, like the S.C. match-up that ended with our unforgettable last-second loss in the Coliseum. We would have come away with a win if the Bruins had not blocked a chip shot field goal with four seconds left on the clock. @ @

One week after this tough defeat Stanford cross-country destroyed a much-diminished San Jose State squad, 15-46, with Menz, Lawson, Kardong, Brock and me crossed the line together on the Spartans' 4.1-mile home course in San Jose's Coyote Park. The following Saturday, November 8th, we pounded the injury-riddled Golden Bears, 17-44, our 4.2-mile course. Cal's Bob Waldon took out the pace with a quick 4:40 first mile, but Chuck and Don finished tied for first in a quick 20:05.6, ten seconds off the school record. Brock was third in 20:21, and I was fourth in 20:25, humping it to the line just ahead of Waldon one second behind, with Cliff West four seconds behind him. These are the only races of my sophomore season I do not recall, and I know why: the first race didn't matter, and the "Big Cross Country Meet" against Berkeley was too depressing to recall.

Not a terrible performance, but our fifth hard race in a little more than a month had tapped me out. That would be a tough schedule for a mature runner, much less kids like us. (The Pac-8, as Coach Clark told us, was "a special kind of meat-grinder.") Olympic-caliber athletes try to run no more than three hard 10Ks a year, but college runners don't run to maximize their potential, they run to score points for their schools. And yet dive deep into the well once or twice too often, which you necessarily do when you race hard over long distances, you will eventually reach a point where the well may well be dry. A team with more runners than ours would have had the luxury of funneling people in and out of competitions, so that some could rest while others raced. But like last year's N.C.A.A. runner-up team, we only had five guys good enough to compete in the big races; our sixth and seventh men were too far back to have an impact. And after these seven runners, we didn't have anybody even close. The fact was that my nineteen-year-old body was bushed and maxing, but tough luck: our next meet, the weekend after Cal, would be the first Pacific-8 Cross-Country Championship, a six-mile race against the top teams on the Pacific coast, on our home Golf Course. The timing for me personally couldn't have been worse for another reason: the week before the Conference Championship was also Hell Week at Beta Theta Pi. @ @

My pledge class had done the best it could to downplay fraternal hi-jinks: for our "Pledge Prank" we discussed kidnapping two upperclassmen and putting them on a plane to Reno; snatching, stripping and handcuffing somebody to "The Claw," the fountain sculpture in White Plaza; or adding chemicals to Stella's orange juice so that everybody's pee would turn blue, or their faces purple, which was supposedly do-able. In the end we stole the distributor caps from everybody's cars and hid them in a place where we knew people would find them right away. The house Rah-Rahs decided we weren't taking this Pledge thing seriously enough, so like panicked parents trying to convince their ten-year-olds about the existence of Santa Claus, they invented a transparently-cockamamie story about some dude from Beta Theta Pi's National organization – from Alabama, no less – who was supposedly coming around to inspect the Stanford chapter from top to bottom, meaning that "hippie freaks" like me and a few others might end up costing the House its national accreditation. Each member of our pledge class, which included football and water polo players along with Mark Shelley, the Olympic alternate swimmer I knew from Branner, had to step into the chapter room in front of blinding lights to sing a tune of our own selection for this straight-arrow 'Bama guest.

For this travesty I dusted off my squirreliest faux-operatic counter-tenor to perform from Franco Zeffirelli's recent film *Romeo and Juliet: "What is a youth?* (I sang) *Impetuous fire/ What is a maid? Ice and desire/ The world wags on /A rose will bloom/ It then will fade/ So does a youth/ So do-uh-uh-uh-oes the fair-est maid…"* The response – dumbstruck silence – was exactly what I had been gunning for. My warbling complete, I wheeled around and without another word exited the room.

164

"Roberto!" Big Brother Willy cried afterwards. "Your boy castrato dropped us in our tracks!"

"Yeah, and I believe in the Tooth Fairy, too," I fired back while reaching out to slap his congratulatory paw. "This entire thing is so obviously a *scam*, Willy! With all the responsibilities I have towards the cross country team this week, the last thing I need is all this fraternity... *bullshit!*"

But no such luck: at 2 a.m. the Monday before the Saturday Conference Championship, four Old School upperclassmen came bursting into my room, screaming "Get up, Pledge!"

Instantly wide awake, I sat up in bed and screamed back at them: "No way! Kick me out of this fucking place if you want to, but this is the week of the Pac-8's! Now get out of my room, because I need my fucking *sleep!*"

I knew from the looks on their faces that they hadn't expected such a psychotic reaction. I also thought they empathized; they were Jocks, too, after all. To my surprise, they left without further commotion and after conferring in the morning with others in the Old Guard, sent one of their hipper emissaries to propose a compromise.

"We're going to cut you some slack, Bob. There's only one thing you can't miss. One dead-of-night thing: 'The Ceremony of the Dead Dog.'"

"*Noooo...*"

"It's the oldest ritual in the Beta tradition! One late night! That's all! You'll miss an hour's sleep at most..."

Two days later at two in the morning, a half-dozen upperclassmen descended on my room in numbers that rendered resistance futile. They slipped a pillowcase over my head, clamped fists around my arms and half-hoisted me downstairs and out of the house, where I was thrown into the backseat of a car that went squealing off into the black night. Ten minutes later, at an undisclosed location high in the cool, dusty hills behind campus, my hood was removed and there stood the entire Beta membership, including a few older guys I had never seen before, solemnly gathered around a large, freshly-dug hole, in the bottom of which lay a recently-deceased canine, breed unknown – a Mutt obtained in a manner I was not privileged to know. (Years later I would learn that during a U.C.L.A. Beta ceremony a cocker spaniel puppy had its throat slit by Nixon's future Chief of Staff and most trusted aid and guard dog, Bob Haldeman. True story.) A hoary Beta handbook was thrust into my hands, from which I read by flashlight some mumbo-jumbo about the late dog and the Beta bros and a grand tradition etc. The most sacred ritual in the Beta canon was like a parody from the *National Lampoon,* an as-yet unpublished magazine created by a group of *Harvard Lampoon* alumni; whose first issue would come out in April. When the moment arrived for the brothers to bury the pooch, I grabbed a shovel and enthusiastically helped, because the sooner we got this poor dog interred, the sooner I could get back to sleep.

It turned out I was also not exempted from the "Pledge Olympics," M.C.'ed by Willy, one of the sweetest guys on the planet but thoroughly hammered that night and wearing only a jockstrap filled with strawberry jam. The third-floor linoleum had been slimed with some sort of cleaning product, which each Pledge was expected to breaststroke across and did, until one of our number, Ted Bleymaier – the last Starting Quarterback in the history of Stanford freshman football and a born-again Christian (the Betas took all kinds) – lost a contact lens, burned his cornea, and ended up in the Stanford Infirmary. This was when our pledge class rose up and in one voice announced that this stupid hazing business would stop, now. My classmates and I didn't think of ourselves as "fraternity brothers" except as a joke. Basically we were a bunch of guys who lived together because we wanted to. Our taste of the piss-poor priorities and rancid group-think of Greek tradition inspired our vow to make a revolution at Beta Theta Pi's Lambda Sigma Chapter next fall, when we were the "brothers" in charge. @ @

The first-ever Pac-8 Cross-Country Championship convened on

Saturday, November 15th, 1969, one day after Apollo 12 lifted off for the Moon to land five days later on the northwest rim of Surveyor Crater, 600 feet away from *Surveyor III,* an unmanned spacecraft that had set down on the spot two and a half years earlier. A little more than two weeks before, an S.R.I. computer scientist with a Department of Defense contract had sat down at a computer terminal in Menlo Park and received a message from another computer at U.C.L.A. – an event that many people would later consider the birth of the Internet.

I was so awestruck warming up I could barely look around. I stole only the briefest of glances at Washington State red-shirt senior Gerry Lindgren, taking in the black horn-rimmed glasses, jug ears, skin as white as a vampire's over spidery blue veins, and zero body fat on a five-six, 119-pound frame. At age twenty-three Lindgren was already considered by many to be the greatest American distance runner who ever lived, with Native American Billy Mills, the 10K Gold Medalist at the Tokyo Olympiad, his only serious competitor. The "Spokane Sparrow" – third son and "lost child" of an alcoholic father, bullied at school for his squeaky voice and wimpy appearance – had grown up a freak of nature and nurture, with inner demons and no psychological boundaries when it came to training and racing. Rumors persisted that in high school Lindgren had sometimes climbed out of bed in the middle of the night to run ten miles (probably true); also that he once trained 350 miles a week for six straight weeks (almost certainly untrue). "The pain and agony is the accomplishment," he later wrote, but running set Gerry free. As a high school senior in the summer of '64 he had defeated Russia's unbeaten 10K runners in the U.S.-Soviet Dual Meet at the L.A. Coliseum, causing Robert F. Kennedy, still emotionally labile six months after his brother's death, to be teary-eyed as he shook the winner's hand, calling it "a great victory for America." This kid still in high school went on to crush Mills in the '64 U.S. Olympic Trials, but a sprained ankle in Tokyo meant that he finished only ninth in the famous race in which his rival Mills took the Gold.

And only then did Gerry go away to college. By the end of his freshman year he had tied Mills over six miles – the distance we were covering today – in a world-record 27:11.6, faster than the existing world record in the 10,000-Meter Olympic distance, based on conversion tables, meaning we would be racing today against a former world-record holder at the distance, also the N.C.A.A. cross country champion in 1966 and 1967 and a three-time track champion at both Three and Six Miles. Lindgren had dropped out his junior year to prepare for Mexico City, but had trouble adjusting to altitude and an injured Achilles, which limited him to fifth in the 10K and fourth in the 5K Trials, keeping him off the U.S. team. I stole only one more glance and oh my god: Lindgren had thighs like a Marvel comic character! I imagined him a hundred yards ahead of everyone and sprinting like a madman. *Look! Up in the sky! It's a bird! It's a plane! It's…. Super-Nerd!*

An instant later another runner jogged into view, along with three or four of his fellow Oregon Ducks in their day-glow yellow and green uniforms. Steve Prefontaine gave off a glow like a piece of jagged glass. He looked like Super-Boy – *who could change the course of mighty rivers, bend steel in his bare hands...* I had the courage to glance only once more at this sensational freshman prancing narcissistically, his long silken hair bouncing, but one glance was enough to convince me that every report I had heard about our sport's newest superstar was true: "Pre," as he was universally known, was one obnoxious little prick. Humility is the natural state of distance runners because our sport is so fundamentally humbling, even for the most gifted of us, but Pre had chucked the "natural" state of distance running into a cocked hat. Oregon Head Coach Bill Bowerman reportedly called him "Rube" because he hailed from the bad-ass blue-collar town of Coos Bay, Oregon, where he could have gotten into drugs, according to his older sister. (I had heard he was into pot anyway.) But instead of becoming a big-time druggie, Pre became the American high school Two-Mile record-holder and had competed in Europe over the previous summer. He was eight months younger than I was and almost exactly my height and weight, as I instantly noticed; he should never have thought he could man up against a former world-record holder and Olympian five years his senior. But in Pre's college debut at the N.C.A.A. District 8 Northern

Division Championships at Oregon State's Avery Park in Corvallis two weeks earlier, he had shocked the American distance-running world by destroying Lindgren by over twenty-seven seconds and smashing the course mark, set by Oregon State's 1968 Olympian Tracy Smith, by over half a minute. Rumors were that Lindgren had been coming back from an ankle injury that day, so there could be little doubt that he would be gunning for payback today. I also had no doubt that Prefontaine thought he could run Lindgren into the ground a second time. Today's race was shaping up to be a clash of Northwesterners with balls the size of Nebraska – two men who never entertained a thought of losing, except to inspire themselves to feats of endurance that few other Americans could manage, collegiate or otherwise.

All of my nemeses were there that day: Cliff West and Bob Waldon from Cal; Freddie Ritcherson from S.C.; U.C.L.A's Ron Fister; and my old teammate at Clear Creek High School, Mike McClendon. Mike had been undefeated as a sixteen-year-old high school senior and the national "Postal" champ, running 14:00.0 for Three Miles. Recruited to Oregon, he had already set a freshman school Three-Mile record (13:57.8) that Pre would obliterate in a few months. But at the District 8 championship meet two weeks earlier, Mike had surprised everyone by being Oregon's second man in his and Pre's first Varsity race. My father was on the golf course that day, too, in the Bay Area on business, preparing to watch me compete in a college uniform for the first time. And there I was, running my sixth hard distance race in thirty-five days. But I had no doubt what I would do that morning: I would leave everything I had on that Bermuda grass. The Conference Championship was Do or Die, and Death was not an option. @ @

I had never smelled blood in the water before a race, but in the seconds before the gun sounded that day, there was blood in the water, no doubt about it. I didn't feel like I was at start of a footrace with all eight Pacific Conference schools strung across the starting line. I felt like I was about to take a running leap off a very high cliff.

The gun sounded and Pre and Lindgren exploded off the line as if fired from cannons. I couldn't believe what I was seeing: Super-Nerd and Super-Boy, sprinting like they were competing over a quarter-mile, not six – veering out of their way to collide and bounce off one another, then move in to collide again – arms entangled, elbows jabbing! They were like a pair of battling wolves! Under normal circumstances this would have earned them both a DQ (disqualification), but today's race was anything but normal. A gauntlet had been flung. I had no choice, and none of us did: we launched ourselves after the pair, me sprinting on my toes like a Quarter-Miler, hoping that when the dust settled I would find myself at least among the top ten behind this pair of macho lunatics. I felt the pace slow at the half-mile mark, but far in the distance Pre and Lindgren continued at a near-suicidal clip: later I heard it claimed that they went through the mile in 4:18, but Brock – a borderline savant in recalling splits – was close enough to hear their time called out ahead of him: 4:23. Gerry Lindgren was famous for this kind of insane early speed: he went out in 4:14 in his American Record Three-Mile (12:53.3) in 1966. But today's race wasn't merely suicidal; Lindgren and Pre were each flirting with their own "death" in order to cause the agonized torture and demise of their opponent. Pre later claimed the pace was his doing: "I felt I had to go fast from the start because Gerry is fast," he said, which makes no sense, but there you are. Over forty years later Lindgren would remember the day somewhat differently: "The week before this race [sic] Pre beat me good in our dual meet [sic]. That was the first time he ever got the best of me and his head was HUGE! I took off extremely fast just to try and intimidate him (that always worked) but at the mile he caught me and even took over the lead. NOBODY had done that to me before. They always let me go!" I cannot attest to the truth of either version, but I know I crossed the mile mark with the co-leaders at least eighty yards ahead of me, in 10th or 11th place, and Coach Clark shouting out my split time as I raced past: "Four-thirty-three, *THIRTY-FOUR...*"

This was one of those "uh-oh" moment that every distance runner dreads to the depths of his soul – one of those horrible instants of recognition that every instinct in your body tries to protect you against.

Eighteen months earlier my best all-out Mile on a flat track was 4:25; our team had almost never run a training mile under 4:45. But I had just run my first mile of six in *4:34*, which meant I would be spending the next five miles dealing with the oxygen debt incurred in this opening savage folly. The first Pac-8 Cross-Country Championship was guaranteed to be a "gut race" now. And this was what Pre said he wanted: "Most people run a race to see who is fastest," he would remark some years later. "I run a race to see who has the most guts, who can punish himself into exhausting pace, and then at the end, punish himself even more... I'm going to work so that it's a pure guts race at the end, and if it is, I am the only one who can win it."

What Pre may or may not have realized was that in the guts department, Gerry Lindgren was every bit his equal.

I, meanwhile, encountered a second problem besides the insane pace: I didn't have a clue as to the whereabouts of a single teammate (although photographs show that Greg and Chuck were not far behind me, and Don and Decker close, too.) The field had strung out wildly. Coach Clark's imperative at last year's N.C.A.A. meet – that we get together and run as a pack – had been blasted to smithereens. @ @

My memories of the next twenty-five minutes are fragmentary. Photographs show me wearing a desperate expression that disturbs me to this day, still in the chase pack at two miles, just behind Brock and S.C.'s Ritcherson and shoulder-to-shoulder with McClendon of Oregon. On most cross country circuits, your place at Mile Two is fairly indicative of where you should end up, barring a major collapse or major surge. But I vaguely recall Washington State freshman Mark Hiefield (Pre's primary high school rival) easing by me not long after Mile Three. Just before the short, steep downhill at three and a half miles, leading to the base of our monster two-hundred-yard-long uphill climb on the Par Three 16th fairway, my old high school teammate McClendon passed me without so much as a "Suck it up, friend." The second pack, including Brock and Ritcherson and Jeff Marsee of S.C., had already dropped me at this point. Coming off the top of the monster hill, which was as far away from the finish line as our course took us, I was so trashed I could barely put one foot in front of the other. I am not exaggerating: I could barely move my legs, and yet I had two miles to go. I wasn't competing anymore. I was only trying to survive. I recovered a little on the long descent towards Junipero Serra, but midway down I could only watch as Cliff West went smoothly past me. The first Pac-8 Cross-Country Championship had turned into a Death March — again, exactly what Prefontaine wanted. Years later I would come across a quote of his quite apropos of that day we shared: "The best pace is a suicide pace and today is a good day to die." Actually this is a fairly dumb remark, unless you can maintain your early speed *without* dying. Pre's foolhardiness about pace was already pointing him towards his do-or-die, all-or-nothing, out-of-the-medals fourth-place finish in the 1972 Olympic 5,000-Meters in Munich. @ @

Two hundred yards ahead of an outstanding field, Pre and Lindgren were locked in a duel that ESPN later ranked seventy-third among the hundred greatest Track & Field and cross country competitions of the twentieth century. Running silently with visible effort, Pre was not the most beautiful runner in the world, but he was extremely efficient, and no one worked harder than he did. (Despite having a scoliosis similar to mine, Pre would never miss a single workout in college, including during a nasty case of strep.) Lindgren's teammate Wayne Ristau later wrote that Gerry ran "using his familiar loud breathing technique that sounded like a cross between heavy breathing and a whistle." Lindgren later (mis?)remembered: "I took off and had a big lead [sic] going up the first big hill at Stanford on their golf course. Near the top of the hill there was Pre going ahead of me and I had to catch him going down the hill. Through the whole race I'd sprint to try to get ahead of him and he would sprint with me every darn time." Other more reliable accounts claim that Lindgren dominated the downslopes while Pre commanded the hills. They averaged a less-then-searing 4:50 per mile after their psychotic first one, but as a feat of intestinal fortitude, this race must have been a marvel to behold.

A Stanford freshman Dolly later claimed she heard Pre turn to

Lindgren at the five mile mark and say, "Do you want to tie?" Lindgren supposedly gasped back, "I'm not sure I can make it." At the small rise 130 yards from the finish – the spot where I had briefly taken the lead against U.C.L.A. – Pre gained a half-step on a dying Lindgren and tried to cut him off from the finish line. Lindgren later claimed (and photographic evidence supports him) that Pre kept pushing him into the crowd to his left, with the smaller man pushing back. They crossed the finish this way after an ordinary last mile in 4:46, Pre pushing Lindgren left, their shoulders touching and arms entangled like clawing animals, each with the same expression of exhausted surrender and their inverted hawk-moon mouths agape. But the more experienced Lindgren was leaning forward, half-raising his hands to break the tape. Those inches made all the difference. The race was close enough to be called a tie at first, and a myth is extant that a Polaroid was examined, but in the end officials gave Lindgren the nod. To this day conference records still list the winner as the Cougar from Pullman. @ @

The editor of *Track and Field News* for three decades, Garry Hill, would call the Pac-8 Cross Country Championship of 1969 "the single greatest foot race I ever saw." Coach Jordan would call it "the best cross-country race ever run in the West." In coming years it would frequently be cited as the last great American distance-running competition of the Sixties. Nine days later, "[running] scared," Lindgren would decisively defeat Pre at the N.C.A.A. Championship to take his 11th individual collegiate title, and a short time later graduate and soon become "schizophrenic," or so it was claimed. By 1980 Lindgren would abandon his wife and children, leaving behind a note that read "get a divorce, sell the business," then disappear off the face of the earth, only to turn up years later in Hawaii, running road races under an assumed name. The Seventies would belong to Pre, who would break every American distance-running record from 2,000 meters to 10,000 meters and single-handedly transform his sport, shattering its nerdy stereotype and replacing it with his Ali-size ego, a new showmanship and even sex appeal. Pre's bold courage would become one of the touchstones of the coming running boom, with the final spin on the legend being his tragic death at the age of twenty-four, James Dean style, legally drunk and suffocated under his flipped sports car on a roadside in the southeast hills of Eugene. Decades later, Track & Field's greatest legend since Jesse Owens would become the subject of two feature films, the best of them *Without Limits* (1998), written by Kenny Moore, directed by the great Robert Towne, and produced by the actor Tom Cruise, who would want to play Pre, but by the time the film was financed Cruise was too old.

And what of your author on that overcast morning of November 14th? While Pre and Lindgren covered our hilly six miles in 28:32.4, obliterating the course record by 1:14, I crossed the finish line [see cover of book] slightly over a minute behind them, one of eighteen runners under the old course record, in 29:33.0 – my PR by 21 seconds, but surpassed by (among others) Greg Brock, who in a masterpiece of "peaking" – gearing his training for championship season – closed his final mile in 4:38 and finished fifth, in a school record 29:08, just behind Oregon's Steve Savage, a future Olympian and the N.C.A.A. steeplechase runner-up the previous spring, and Washington State's Rick Riley, another great eastern Washington runner whose interscholastic Two-Mile record Pre had broken earlier that year. U.S.C.'s Ritcherson, who had beaten me by two seconds a month earlier, was seventh; McClendon, tenth; Cliff West, thirteenth in 29:22, with his little brother Cornel in attendance. Oregon State junior Spencer Lyman, winner of the seventh Equinox Marathon in Fairbanks, Alaska two months earlier, finished just ahead of me, after having stalked me for virtually the entire race.

And I came in fifteenth. Buried. In fifteenth place.

Wandering around afterwards thoroughly broken and trashed, I found Brock near the finish line, looking a lot fresher than I felt.

"I trained through every meet," he said before I could say a word. "I was running two-a-days on Fridays while the rest of you guys were taking it easy!"

I had never known Brock to be an asshole about anything, and that's not how I heard his words now. I simply acknowledged the apparent truth of what he said with a brief nod and headed off to run my cool-down alone. I felt no resentment whatsoever about Greg's boasting, if that's even what it was, after the best race of his career. He had shared an important lesson with me about "training through" early season meets so you can show up when it counted most. I had apparently scuttled my chances of performing well at Conference for the gratification of holding on to that "Stanford #1" jersey through our dual meet season.

Decker showed up huge that day, too, finishing just two seconds behind me and obliterating my freshman school record by almost a minute and a half. *Brock & Decker! Two Industrious Tools! Talk about psyching-in...* Kardong, our fourth man, came through just ahead of U.C.L.A.'s Ron Fister, in eighteenth place with a course PR 29:41, as disappointed with his performance as I was with mine, such that years later he wouldn't remember this race at all. Stanford's fifth scorer Jack Lawson ran a so-so 30:27 in 32nd. Chuck Menz, who had been with Brock and me at two miles, dragged himself across 35th, fifty seconds off his course best, while Arvid, who was also with us early despite being bothered by tendonitis in one of his hips, went totally tits up, finishing next to last in 32:34. Our 86 points nipped S.C. (90) and avenged our loss to U.C.L.A. (94), but Northwest powerhouses Oregon and Washington State finished one-two, 46-63. And third wouldn't be good enough. It wouldn't matter to the Athletic Department that the two teams that had beaten us in this "spectacular" race (Coach Clark) were two of the best teams in the country: there would be no return to the N.C.A.A. Championship Cross-Country meet for last year's national runner-up. A "force to be reckoned with" in the early season would be shut down for the rest of the year – collateral damage of the two greatest American distance runners of the age. My disappointment felt even keener because my father was there to see it. "You saw it, Dad," I told him, once I had composed myself enough to talk. "Lindgren and Pre blew everyone else's race out of the water..." @ @

I would have plenty of time to brood over what I had and had not accomplished in my sophomore cross-country season. I was wrong to be so hard on myself for my performance, but it was how I felt at the time. "The Baby-Faced Assassin," the Buck Club "Athlete of the Week," the cocky sophomore who showed up at workouts wearing a water polo uniform, had failed to show up on Game Day. Averaging 4:55 miles over a hilly six-mile course was nothing to sneeze at, and I had beaten some very good runners: Oregon's Norm Trerise, third in the N.C.A.A. Three-Mile the previous spring and a 3:59.1 Miler in the coming one, finished 39 seconds behind me after collapsing at the top of the long hill. But our Coaches were under-impressed by what I had done: they named Brock the Team MVP, although he had only beaten me twice all year, including at the one meet of the season that apparently truly mattered.

The Athletic Department sent Brock alone to Van Cortlandt Park for the N.C.A.A. championship, where he would avenge his conference loss to Rick Riley and Steve Savage and finish ninth in a field of 254 runners, earning All-American honors for a second straight season. Five foreign runners from the University of Texas at El Paso (four of them freshmen) took the team title over favored Villanova and the University of Oregon, the latter hard-hit by a nasty flu but led by Pre in third, soundly beaten by Lindgren and Mike Ryan from the Air Force Academy, last year's titlist while Lindgren took time out for the Olympics (and a transfer student from Stanford, where he had struggled academically as a freshman in Brook and Big Al's class.) My ex- teammate McClendon became All-American, too, in fifteenth.

A full Stanford team should have been there. @ @

That same Saturday, November 23rd – three days after the Indians of All Tribes (IAT) occupied Alcatraz Island, not to be evicted by the U.S. government until June 1971; also the day that an undefeated Stanford-of-the-East team scored 16 points in the final 42 seconds to tie an unbeaten and un-tied Yale squad, inspiring the immortal *Harvard*

Crimson headline, "Harvard Beats Yale 29-29" – I joined a near sell-out crowd of 80,000 at Stanford Stadium to witness one of the greatest and certainly most thrilling Big Games in the long history of the rivalry: a 29-28 come-from-behind Stanford victory behind two Plunkett's TD arrows, a career-high 381 yards in the air and 409 yards total offense. Plunkett ended his junior year and first All-Pac-8 Conference season with 197 completions in 336 attempts and two conference records – 2,673 passing yards and 20 aerial TDs – while the team finished 7-2-1, ranked 19th in the nation. This may have been the best Stanford football team in all the years I was there. Only three plays kept the '69 Stanford Indians from having a perfect season: Purdue's successful two-point conversion in that 36-35 loss in Lafayette; any of the successfully fourth-down conversions on S.C.'s final drive in the Coliseum; and the last-minute blocked field goal in the U.C.L.A. tie.

Could have been, should have been, wasn't. Isn't that nine-tenths of the story of sport? @ @

Nine days after the Big Game, I was sitting on the gummy brown leather sofa in front of the Beta chapter room's color TV, watching a woman pulling numbers from a barrel for Uncle Sam's Selective Service System. The U.S. government in its wisdom had decided to dismantle the "II-S" student deferment system and hand each Draft-eligible male born between the years 1944 and 1950 a number, from 1 to 366. (Some wag had dubbed it "Washington Roulette.") I had written a few letters to doctors to see if I could be graded 4-F because of my lumbar fusion, but the point was moot: my lottery number was 147, and the Army would only draft to 125 that year. In one Stanford residence, a student whose birthdate came up Number One threw his chair through the TV screen. I was out of the Draft forever – news that provided a measure of relief but little comfort in the wake of November 12th reports that in March 1968, nearly five hundred un-armed Vietnamese civilians had been massacred by American G.I.s in the village of My Lai, South Vietnam. This put everything in a different light. Showing up for a cross country workout dressed like a water polo player wasn't really far-out after all. Stanford students always seemed to find a way out of the Draft, often with help: the Athletic Department had a doctor in Atherton who produced letters to Selective Service for specific start athletes (only), declaring them medically unfit for duty. My only Farm friend who went on to be drafted ended up working in the K-9 Corps in West Germany. @ @

The Saturday after the Lottery – a foggy day in the low sixties – Decker wheeled his new motorcycle up the driveway at 557 Mayfield to offer me a ride on the back to hear the Rolling Stones play a free concert at the Altamont Raceway in the East Bay.

"Hop on, man! It's gonna be a gas! Free concert!"

"Sounds great, Deck, but I gotta run Woodside today …"

I put in my thirteen miles while Decker drove his bike between miles of cars clogging the highway into Altamont, where "all normalcy and control had gone – there was no nothing," as Mick Jagger inelegantly told the media. Decker was too far back in the crowd to see the Hell's Angel knife a gun-wielding troublemaker at the foot of the stage. That same month the fifty thousandth American serviceman was killed in Southeast Asia – news that made me want to puke. When the final stats were tallied, 11,465 of the 58,282 U.S. KIA in Southeast Asia would be in their teens – a stat ignoring *3.8 million* Vietnamese dead, including two million civilians, in an American war driven by the metrics of body counts and kill boards. *My country t'is of thee…*

With cross country season over, I decided to let my hair grow longer – it had been over my ears a little at the Conference meet – and re-sprout the small goatee and sideburns I had summoned last spring after track season ended. News of my countercultural visage must have reached the ears of the U.S. Olympic Coach, because he summoned me to his office for what almost immediately felt like an intervention.

"You have to look like an *athlete*, Bobby!" Coach Jordan told me, leaning across his desk and gazing imploringly into my eyes. It was as if he could see his Fair Haired Boy lurching on to the shoals of the counterculture, and was desperate to avert The Horror. Jordan actually believed that short, neat hair meant you embodied wholesome All-American values, which of course was a total crock.

"This," Jordan said, waving his hand at me, "is not the image you want to project in a Stanford uniform!"

"But I'm not wearing a Stanford uniform right now, Coach!"

Jordan jerked his head back as if I had slapped his face. Then he turned all pouty on me, as if I had hurt his feelers, and our meeting petered out soon after. I hadn't meant to be smart-alecky, only that I literally wasn't wearing a Stanford uniform at the time, because we were between seasons. Once track started I would go along with Jordan's stupid rule and follickly conform, and I never told him I wouldn't. Oregon Coach Bill Bowerman (who didn't spend WWII stateside, like our *Life* magazine cover boy, and who negotiated the surrender of a German army in Italy) reportedly told his team that that no one could grow his hair any longer than his dick. But the larger spectacle of Stanford's Head Coach lecturing me – *me* – about the pride of wearing a Stanford uniform wasn't surprising, but it was flat-out insulting anyway. The only thing that should have mattered to Coach Jordan was how I behaved, which was wholly-heartedly like a committed Stanford Jock. How was it possible for anyone to think otherwise? Didn't Jordan know me at all? My hair was an expression of how I felt apart from Track & Field, where I had a life, too. But this carried no weight with Jordan, who was more interested in what his Fair-Haired Boy represented than in who I was, because what I represented he could dictate and control. And because wasn't rushing out to a barber shop, I had become some sort of heretic, or at least the object of an abject concern that needed to be addressed, intervened upon and managed.

Battles over hair were taking place all across America in those days, but I would bet dollars to donuts I was the only youth in the country told to get a haircut by the Head Coach of the U.S. Olympic Team and an Apollo Astronaut preparing to fly around the Moon. I made no promises to Coach Jordan that day, preferring to leave matters hanging on the earth-shattering issue of my haircut. A more important drama had been unfolding since winter quarter of my freshman year: whether or not I would elect to spend the first two quarters of 1970 at a Stanford campus in Europe. @ @

Stanford offered undergrads means to study aboard for six months by operating a half-dozen European campuses that charged the same tuition and room-and-board you would pay in Palo Alto. Javelin Thrower Tom Colby's third-place finish at the N.C.A.A.'s in 1968 had qualified him for the U.S. Olympic Trials, but he chose to go to a Stanford overseas campus instead. (Today he's a Professor of Pathology at the Mayo Clinic.) Al Sanford had gone to Stanford-in-Italy, in Florence; Brook Thomas chose Stanford-in-Britain, as had Don Kardong, living and studying at Harlaxton, a forbidding early 19th-century manor house in Lincolnshire, well north of London or any other major urban center, although Don was able to spend his second quarter in the newer, more fanciful Stanford-in-Britain campus, Cliveden House in Buckinghamshire, twenty-five miles due west of London. My sister – a senior Psychology major now – had spent her last two sophomore quarters at Harlaxton and the summer traveling on the continent with her boyfriend, a former Stanford Half-Miler from Large and Brook's class. When I was fourteen my grandparents had taken my sister and me on a month-long trip to England, Germany, Italy and France, a few months after our sister's death. Europe had been a romance in my family for as long as I could remember. The notion that I would skip the intellectual, cultural and spiritual betterments of Europe to compete as a college athlete was so remote from our family values that I never presented the option to any of my family members in quite that way, because I knew it wouldn't fly. But I also knew that going abroad would mean sacrificing my sophomore track season, and I was ambivalent about doing that, to say the least.

While I footed Arastradero, my grandparents were footing the bills. My retired grandfather had a handsome pension, but would always claim that his stipend as founding editor of *The California Freemason* magazine was what paid for my room and board, one-third of my tuition, and a $25 monthly allowance. (The Masonic Lodge of California was paying my way through college. Go figure that one out.) My grandparents urged me to seize this opportunity, and offered to pay all my additional expenses for travel in the summer after school let out, just as they had for my sister. My father had a different take on the matter: maybe he was remembering what the United States Olympic Coach had said about me in the *San Francisco Examiner*, but my Dad thought the decision should be mine, of course, but that I would have plenty of time to see Europe and rarely such an exciting opportunity to compete as a college athlete. The Pac-8 Meet must have impressed him. I thought about enrolling at the campus in France where I could work on my only foreign language skill, but Tours was by all reports a dull, provincial town, and focusing on French wasn't what I wanted to do anyway. So I decided that if I went anywhere, it would be to live in a castle on the Thames and trip into London whenever I felt the urge.

Intense ambivalence produced indecision: I intentionally missed the first Cliveden orientation the previous spring, and in late May was told I couldn't skip another, and also that my name had already been moved down the waiting list. To preserve the Stanford-in-Britain option I registered for classes, thinking I could still drop out once I made up my mind. For a time I thought about attending during the summer and fall quarters, instead of during winter-spring, which would mean I would miss cross country, but not Track. "Cross country is a high-pressure drag compared to track," I wrote my folks, thinking again about the long, grueling season just past. "This is a really tough call." @ @

Eventually I made an appointment to discuss my dilemma with Coach Clark. A part of me wanted him to come right out and ask me to stay; I would have been susceptible to that approach. Instead I sat at his desk and he tipped back in the visitor's chair to offer a much more subtle and measured argument, one contoured for and pertinent to me.

"Your background is solid, Robert. Your speed has improved significantly from last year. You've matured a lot. You were barely shaving when you got to campus. We'll need you to run a lot of Half-Miles this spring, because that's where we need people. But Coach

Jordan and I think you're fully capable of running a 3:57 Mile this spring." That was what my Coach told me. No Stanford runner had ever run Under Four. But not just Under Four; Coaches Clark and Jordan thought I could run *3:57*. I instantly remembered that 3:57.7 was Marty Liquori's N.C.A.A. Meet record. These words, coming from a man not given to rash predictions – I had never heard him make one – were mind-blowing. This estimation of my potential in the near future had to be inflated – used as a tool to persuade me not to leave the country. But the way Coach explained it, it didn't sound implausible.

"You ran 4:09 in a gale as a freshman. Your six-mile time is over a minute faster now. If you can manage to run a 3:57 Mile at the age of twenty, I think you would have a legitimate reason to think about making an Olympic team one day."

"Wow" was all the response I could muster. This was so much more than I could have ever imagined back when I first broke five minutes as a high school sophomore. I thought that he had to be inflating my promise. This couldn't be realistic. A 3:57 Mile, six months from now? Coach had to be just trying to get me not to leave. Or was he acknowledging a middle-distance guy who was also excelling at longer-distances, meaning that his potential really couldn't be circumscribed?

I left Coach Clark's office that day still not sure what to do. @ @

Another factor pressed into my decision-making process: burn-out raised its ugly head. Not long after my talk with Coach Clark, Kardong and I went out together for an informal interval session on the golf course, where he kicked my butt through six half-mile reps.

"You burned me, Don," I panted afterwards. "No gas... in the tank... I'm broken... by that damned... cross country... season..."

Don looked at me with one part sympathy and two parts wish-I-could-help-but-I-can't. Cross country had kicked my ass and stolen my spirit, but I knew it was only temporary. Of course my spirit would return. I even knew what I needed to do: back off for a while, run a couple of easy fifty-mile weeks, and listen for my body to tell me when to resume hard training. But after the debacle of the Pac-8 Cross Country Championship and my unpleasant meeting with our Head Coach, I may not have been thinking straight. I still can't tell you what I should have done, so I certainly couldn't have done it at the time.

In the end the decision made itself, as tough decisions often seemed to. On December 5th I opened my mailbox (6005) at the Stanford Post Office and found there the official letter notifying me that I had been activated for Stanford-in-Britain. In the moment I read it I decided to go. Pre wouldn't have done it, but I did. I would spend the next two quarters abroad and the summer traveling on the continent, as my sister had done. I was well aware I was stepping off the high road my Coaches had laid out for me, but only for six months or so. Running was part of my educational experience, but travel was, too. I was only nineteen, heading off to Europe on my own, knowing I would have a blast, but also that I would return in shape, ready to compete in Stanford cross country in the fall of '70 and Track in the spring of '71.

In the course of this history, if you have ever wanted to say I wasn't serious enough or committed enough to reach the potential held out for me, now would be the time. But I had hard roads to travel that would take me far, far away from everything I had ever known before. As I wrote my grandparents shortly before my departure: "Herman Hesse said it this way: 'The hardest road to travel is the road into yourself.'" The cliché of a hippie quoting Hesse as he heads off to Europe for the close of the Sixties is mildly painful to me now. Maybe it was selfish on my part, not to stay in Palo Alto and use my running talent for the well-being of my teammates, my Coach, and my school. But I had the rest of my life to think about, not just my brief time as a Stanford Jock. My grandparents' belief that travel was broadening was reason enough for me to look forward to six months abroad, especially since my foundational belief remained unchanged: I was entitled to as much experience as I could possibly devour. @ @ @

GIMME SHELTER

Our Stanford-in-Britain group landed at Heathrow on December 30th and boarded chartered busses to the castle overlooking the Thames Valley, which was to be our home until June. Photographs had failed to do justice to the spectacle of what was Cliveden House, a sixteenth-century Italianate stone palace on 368 acres of National Trust Gardens and woodland in Buckinghamshire. Eighteenth- and nineteenth-century fires had almost totally destroyed the place, but a rebuilt palace was purchased in 1893 by America's richest citizen, William Waldorf Astor, who gifted the estate to his son, the second Viscount Astor, and his American-born wife Nancy, who went on to become Britain's first woman MP and hostess of the so-called "Cliveden Set," Hitler's best friends in England, aside from some of the Windsors themselves. In the early years of World War Two Lord Astor had donated this wonderland and all of its contents, its 18th-century clock tower, extensive gardens and grounds to the Trust, from which Stanford had rented the place the year before. The contrast with Harlaxton Manor, the gloomy old Stanford-in-Britain where Kardong, Al Sanford and my sister went to school, couldn't have been starker. The writer Harold Nicholson, visiting Cliveden in the Thirties, had claimed that "to live here… would be like living on the stage of the Scala theatre in Milan."

As a student from sunny California, I saw the place a little differently. While I acknowledged the gorgeous setting, what I mostly felt was the

184

damp cold that permeated every nook and cranny of the place in that bone-chilling winter, not to mention the wretched English food. Male students crammed in the extensive servant's quarters, where my roommates were Stanford's All-Pac-8 football Center and frosh discus thrower Jon Sande, a straight-arrow who I would barely get to know at all, and a nasty right-wing intellectual – a rarity in the student body in those days – who I came actively to loathe. Academic classes were convened in the main building, taught by a self-contained faculty either imported from Palo Alto or hired locally. The nearest contact with any civilization other than our own was Feather's, a pub a mile away at the foot of Cliveden's long pebbled driveway, reached past "The Fountain of Love," a fancy set atop a giant cockleshell of Siena marble. Limited access to public transportation completed the sense that we were living inside a hermetically-sealed pleasure dome, far removed from English life. Cliveden made "The Farm's" traditional aloofness from its neighborhood surroundings seem positively warm and cuddly.

Many if not most of our group embraced our isolation – Cliveden was, after all, reputed by no less an authority than John Dryden, the 17th-century English poet laureate of the Restoration, to be "all for women, painting, rhyming, drinking." But I skipped our in-house New Year's Eve festivity to take the forty-minute train ride and hop a Tube to say farewell to the Sixties at a Times Square-type revel outside St. Paul's Cathedral. Freed from training for the first time since my sophomore year in high school, I embraced high hippiedom: on my second visit to London I visited King's Road, where I bought a pair of tie-green dyed crushed velvet pants and two see-through Indian shirts at a head shop I came across. Soon I was haunting the shockingly-inexpensive theaters of the West End, seeing two or more plays a week, from the musical *Hair* to Laurence Olivier in *Merchant of Venice* for two shillings (24 cents) in the Upper Balcony at the Old Vic, south of the Thames. I also saw John & Yoko cruising through Piccadilly in their psychedelic-painted Rolls Royce, free of charge. A few weeks into our stay I ventured west with a classmate to the city of Bath, where I met a red-haired witch, or so she claimed at closing time, and brought me back to her coven. Before leaving town I discovered a nineteenth-century-era antique costume shop, where I purchased myself a royal blue Regency mid-calf overcoat, worthy of Bath's own Beau Brummell. With lavish fox fur trim and fake silver braids and buckles, that coat ended up worn to town exactly never, but I liked having it around. @ @

We had our Castle on the Thames, our costumes, our gardens, our music; the only ingredient missing from our post-Sixties bacchanal was remedied when an amazing woman in our group – the first openly-homosexual person I had ever met, at a time when homosexual behavior was illegal and classified as a psychiatric disorder that could be treated and "cured" – scored a pound of some primo blonde Lebanese hash from a wholesale dealer in the West End. (Note that the "Beat Revolution" was almost entirely the construction of "Jocks," "Queers," "Weirdos," and various hybrids thereof.) After our team score, half of our group spent the next few days exploring the nooks and crannies of our hippie Xanadu, perusing the more-or-less unusable hard covers in the ancient Astor Library or lounging on a great hall sofa the size of two king-size beds, which fronted our grand, usually-unlit fireplace. I could see cliques forming, but I wasn't becoming part of one. There were people in my group I liked, but it was soon apparent that I wasn't going to make a single fast friend. Maybe I seemed weird, doing my exhibitionistic tabletop dancing at the basement pub parties. (Describing it that way, I definitely must have seemed weird.) I was a lone wolf without my pack. As for me and Farm women: I had never had a "date" with one. Being a distance runner was of no help in this, with Title IX, prohibiting gender discrimination in school sports, still two years away. Stanford didn't recruit women or offer them athletic scholarships, and intercollegiate competitions were scarce. I was not immune to infatuation, and would soon develop a mild crush on a classmate (who decades later would run for Mayor of Denver), until the day came when I realized she was taking modest steps to avoid me.

That was the day I said to hell with it and started going into London alone – even skipping classes to catch Cliveden's daily van to nearby Taplow, hopping the ten-bob rail to Paddington Station, jumping on the Tube and surfacing wherever I pleased.

On one of these London expeditions early in our stay, I brought along my running gear in a rucksack, changed in a restroom stall of the Charing Cross Tube Station, stuffed my street clothes into a locker and headed out for a lark around Westminster and St. James Park, past Buckingham Palace to Green Park, then all around Hyde Park: a slow, easy lark that lasted almost an hour. "[Afterwards] I took a sponge bath in the sink," I wrote my grandparents – "the Irish attendant thought I was a bum and let me save the 6d. I admit I looked like one – turtleneck sweater, ragged Levis and boots. Also I'm tired of combing my hair, so I'm letting it just grow as it will. I've got curls all over my head, just like when I was a baby! Ahhh!"

Nature Boy soon got to know every pothole in the trails that laced our square mile of National Trust Gardens, and even ventured sometimes down "the rabbit hole," as we dubbed the steep grade hedged by brambles, leading down to one of the loveliest stretches of the entire Thames, the Cliveden Reach, by the cottage where Christine Keeler had shacked up with a Russian spy while also having sex with Britain's Minister of Defense, Lord Profumo, up in the Big House. (The scandal nearly brought down the Macmillan government in 1963.) But I soon found the frigid weather not at all to my liking, and possibly a factor in a strain I developed at the top of my right quadriceps, almost in the groin, which made it painful to lift my knee high, which in turn made it impossible to run fast at all. I tried to run on the equestrian trails between English hedgerows outside Cliveden's grounds, but all of them were frozen and pockmarked by horses' hooves, which forced you to pay extra attention to every step you took, not something you wanted to do when you were trying to run hard. So I took a stab at the narrow, shoulder-less roads of Buckinghamshire, but Lorries barreling by made me feel like I was taking my life in my hands, and asphalt had never been my friend. So with a subtle blend of false bravado, envy and denial, I wrote Decker: "Running isn't everything." Since I couldn't run the way I wanted to run, I decided to have more high hippie adventures, only on the continent this time. @ @

On our first school-sponsored junket in early February to Paris, I ditched our group and hitchhiked alone with my backpack and sleeping bag through the Loire Valley to the Stanford campus in Tour, planning to hang out for a few days with a (Black) high jumper and classmate who had leapt an impressive 6'8" our freshman year. The scene in Tours was basically students sitting on their beds in darkened rooms day and night, obliterated on hash, plus the city was as boring as everyone said it was, so after two days I hit the road again with the bizarre notion of hitchhiking into the Swiss Alps in the dead of winter. I lucked into a ride with a trucker who took me more than 200 miles to Lyons, where I got cocky and thought I'd try to make Geneva by nightfall. I ended up caught in a snowstorm halfway into the mountains. I walked for miles in the freezing dark until I reached a pitch-black village, found a small hotel and knocked on the door. The woman who answered told me they had a room for me, but that the kitchen was closed for the night. My teenage self immediately burst into tears, at which point this woman took me in and served me a huge tureen of warm potato soup, two baguettes and three oranges, and I ate everything but the rinds. Then she showed me my room, where I slept with the window open, sweating under the warmest Swiss duvet.

The next morning I hitched to the most bourgeois town in Europe and was soon hitching out of town around Lake Geneva, which was how I met two fellow hitchhikers, young women my age heading home to Lugano from a jazz festival in Basel. I joined them thumbs out on the side of the road until we scored a ride with a German tourist over the St. Gotthard Pass, the highest in Switzerland, in the dead of winter and a blinding February snowstorm. On the Italian side the sky over the Alps was cloudless and we found a hotel on the side of a mountain and slept there – me on a divan at the foot of their double bed. We arrived in Lugano the following day. I spent the next five days there with the family of Maria Pia, a blue-eyed, flaxen-haired, nineteen-year-old Italian-Swiss, sharing their dinner table, speaking only French, our one common language, sleeping in the bedroom of her absent brother, a six-six Forward on the Swiss National Basketball team (Pia was five-four), and exploring the exciting Lugano jazz scene at night. Eventually we traveled to Milano and spent two nights in a small hotel: two teenagers in love, sweet, ardent, and time-stamped.

We said farewell on a Milano street corner, where I jumped a trolley to the train station. I had never known anything as beautiful and intimate as the closeness we shared, which was probably why I didn't know how to value it. I might have been making plans to bring Pia back to Maidenhead, or plotting her travel to Palo Alto, or at least thinking about how to return to Lugano as soon as possible. But I had no money, even if I had the intention. Was I just another American cad, a frat-boy Lothario "picking up chicks" in Europe? No. Pia was better than that. She was also more than an Italian-Swiss factory-worker's daughter who had fallen for a privileged middle-class American teenager from an elite private university. Pia was cool. Pia was jazz. Pia understood the liminal. Our paths had crossed for a time on our very different roads and wouldn't cross again. @ @

I don't remember much about my trip back through Switzerland, with brief stops in Interlaken, Bern and Basel, or the train from Stuttgart to Amsterdam, or my ferry ride across the Channel and the final train and jitney to Cliveden, where people were wondering where the hell I was. Two of my Professors told me they were unhappy about me skipping two weeks of winter classes. I didn't sweat it. I would pull a B-plus in Econ One with minimal work; scribbled desultory remarks about "Appeasement in Europe, 1932-39," in a house rich in its history; and composed ten drafts of an overly-ambitious and poorly-thought-out paper on Wordsworth, Keats and Coleridge's conception of death, which contributed to my getting a B-minus for a course on the Romantic Poets, mostly because Professor Anne Mellor thought I had skipped too many classes, although secretly I thought she had more of an issue with my preference for Wordsworth's "remembered glory" over her beloved William Blake's innocent and fiery visions. I didn't give a poor grade a thought. Freed from external constraints (like a 3:57 Mile), I wanted to have more adventures in my flea market motley, believing, or struggling to believe, that the street politics of everyday breathing would somehow change the world. The earth belonged to countercultural athletes of the spirit – or was it that the future could wait? Or was the future was ours already, because the future was Now? "Ah, the halcyon days of youth," my grandmother wrote on a postcard from California, although she was privately fretting (according to one of my cousins) that I was "having sex." I *was* having sex, and sex was having me. The distance runner had tasted something carnal, caramel and unconscious, listened to Neil Young's "Cinnamon Girl" – "*...a dreamer of pictures/I run in the night/I see us together/chasing the moonlight/My Cinnamon Girl...*" – and thought I was that runner now.

I joined a group of Cliveden students who were meeting regularly to discuss the work of Krishnamurti, a Hindu sage, which steered some of us into the practice of Transcendental Meditation (TM), which I learned after one afternoon of training in London. For twenty minutes twice a day I sat with eyes closed, silently repeating my mantra, provided free of charge by disciples of Maharishi Mahesh Yogi, the Hindu teacher the Beatles and Donovan had tracked down in India not long ago. The magical symbiosis of sex and Eastern religion, the cultural distractions of London, and Cliveden's abundant hashish moved me off the Dean's List, but my major distraction was my lust for travel. For Easter Break I purchased a $21 one-way plane ticket not to fly over the Alps, but to sun-kissed Iberia for Semana Santa.

"I'm running every day now," I wrote home. "My injured upper thigh is mending, slowly but surely. I'll run every day in Spain, too." @ @

On an easy lope through the streets of Madrid, near the Prado late Palm Sunday morning, I got lost on back streets and entered a small square just as a crowd emerged from a modest church. At least a dozen *Generalissimos* appeared, strutting in their white starched uniforms, rows of colorful medals splayed across their chests. I noticed their deferential body language towards a melancholy older man in a long gray trench coat. I was not ten feet away from him when I realized that this man was the Spanish dictator Francisco Franco, who had ruled Spain with an iron fist for decades and owed his office to Adolf Hitler.

I recognized him from the coins in my pocket. We even made eye contact. Franco studied me for a few seconds, lifted a corner of his mouth in a sort of acknowledgement, then took a deep French inhale on a filterless cigarette and turned wearily away. I turned around and ran hard back to my hotel, checked out and took the next bus to Toledo, where I had a second tough training session in the late afternoon on the steep medieval stone stairs that laced that hilltop town – an irresistible, thigh-burning workout. In bed unaltered by any substance I had a vision of the Virgin Mary on a white cloud in a corner of my hotel room ceiling. Her robe was a rich El Greco blue. (Francisco Franco and the Virgin Mary on the same day? Quite a dream to have during Semana Santa in El Greco's home town.) The following day I took a grueling overnight bus ride to dusty Ciudad Real in central Iberia, where on a blazing Ash Wednesday I watched as *penitentes* dragged massive stones through the streets and others lashed their bodies bloody with shattered canes (giving back to me one of the original meanings of *"make it hurt…"*) Another all-night train (on which I slept) carried me to Málaga, from which tourist trap (or so it seemed to me then) I hitchhiked further south, all the way to the coastal town of Torremolinos, a former hippie colony on the Costa del Sol recently over-run by northern European tourists. The chilly beaches shrouded in overcast might have made me consider hauling myself away from hippiedom on the road, but on the contrary, I grabbed a bus to continue east along the southern portion of the Costa Blanca. @ @

In a village halfway to Almeria, our bus stopped to let us stretch our legs and I discovered a bar that sold tiny milkshakes in plastic containers. I hadn't had a milkshake since I couldn't remember when, so I chugged down one. Delicious. I wanted another, but first I stepped outside to make sure the bus hadn't left. Then I dashed back in to chug down seconds. By the time I got back to the street the bus was leaving the curb. Instantly reborn as a runner (and wearing my Stanford-issue Tigers), I took off as fast as I could run, committed to catching that bus if it meant destroying my Achilles tendons for a week. But as I raced around a corner I saw the bus was already far ahead of me and moving at a fast clip – next stop, Almeria. My wallet and passport were in my pockets, but my backpack and all of my travel possessions – my road life– had just left town without me.

I walked a mile until I reached the countryside, and started hitchhiking. The sky started drizzling, and night fell. It was pouring rain and pitch dark before a car stopped. The driver who leaned across his bench to let me in was American, a Harvard dropout, as it turned out, from an urban studies program in Sweden, taking a break from academics and bunking with an AWOL American G.I. who had been expected back at his base outside Frankfurt three weeks earlier.

"You're not getting any further tonight," Tom told me. "Come stay with us. But first I have an errand I need to run."

We drove to a nearby field where he handed me a machete and the two of us climbed out and began hacking away at someone's sugar cane field, surrounded by crackling lightning and booming thunder. We tossed the wet cane in the trunk of his car and found our way back to his white stucco cottage in an ocean-side village where the storm had ended.

"I've got to figure out if I'm going back or not pretty soon, cuz after thirty days I'll be officially considered a deserter," the A.W.O.L. G.I. told me as he served us dinner.

"Bummer," I told him.

"Tell me about it. This war is shit, man. I've had lots of buddies killed, wounded – maimed for life! No way I'm putting on that uniform again."

"I hear you, brother…"

We talked about the war and over a glowing bowl of Moroccan hash they hauled out guitars and we sang songs we had in common until midnight, when they said goodnight and I crawled into a hammock they had strung for me across the middle of the candle-lit living room.

I woke up Easter morning to the sounds of The Beatles' "Abbey Road" on their tinny hi-fi. I dressed and went for a walk under a luminous blue sky in a picture postcard village in Andalusia... *"Here comes the sun... It's alright..."* Returning with a half-dozen brown hen's eggs and a loaf of bread I bought from a toothless crone on the corner, I found the AWOL G.I. boiling water on a hot plate.

"I was a distance runner, too!" said Tom, the AWOL Harvard student. "At Boston Latin! I'm telling you, there are miles of dirt roads down in the flatlands that are perfect for training! You can run for miles down there! On soft dirt! If you want to move in with us, I'll loan you my car, you can go check it out."

This was the closest I ever came in my countercultural rambles to bail on Stanford and go it alone. I had already been thinking about dropping out for a year to find a job in Washington, D.C. and write two 20,000-word theses for a double major in Poly Sci and the Humanities Special Program: an idea that had not gone over well in San Clemente or El Lago. I had also floated another, not-entirely dissimilar notion of dropping out of school entirely "so that I can train myself for the Olympics." But this idea of dropping out *right now* and remaining in Franco's Spain, training mainly on the plain for the next three months, then returning to Palo Alto in time for my sister's June wedding to the Stanford Half-Miler and spending the rest of the summer on campus working out with my old high school buddy John Walker, who had run another 4:06 Mile that spring for Stephen F. Austin State and had written me about wanting to come back to the Bay Area to train – this idea was a new one. I seriously considered it.

What foiled my pipe dream was the fact that my backpack and all of my things were either lost or waiting for me at a bus station in Almeria. So I bade farewell to my new friends and hiked up to the road. @ @

Within five minutes I was picked up by a newly-married American couple and a twenty-six-year-old second-grade schoolteacher from Oregon with a teaching job in Seville, enjoying vacation rounds on the beaches of southern Spain. They invited me to come with them, but first they took me in their battered Fiat all the way to the bus station in

Almeria, where my backpack rested untouched on the carousel. Then we turned around and drove back in the direction we came from, with wild Moroccan music playing on the radio until we reached Cartagena, where we spent the night in a cheap hotel. After breakfast we went for a drive and with the brilliant lack of design that often characterized hippies traveling in Europe in those days, stumbled upon a warm saltwater bay known as Mar Menor, separated from the Mediterranean by a spit of land called La Manga, or "The Sandbar."

We lived naked on La Manga for the next three days: two couples making love in the warm Mediterranean and on blankets concealed between lavish dunes. "This is what I came to Europe for!" Cathy cried to the wind, and I felt the same. One cool morning I put on my Tigers and ran buck naked along La Manga for four miles, turned around and ran back, without seeing another soul.

This idyllic portion of my Iberian holiday, which included regular two-a-day workouts, were cut short by a scary run-in with Franco's Guardia Civil, federal police, during a shopping expedition to town – an event that shook up my traveling companions enough to inspire their immediate return to Seville. So we said our farewells on the side of the road and two minutes later I was in the back seat of a Mercedes convertible with three German tourists who took me all the way to Alicante and Annette, a United Nations translator I had sat next to on my flight from Gatwick. I spent five days with the Lovely English Rose (without running a step), getting thrown out of our first hotel for too much noise. At the end of five days her Mum came to visit from England, took a shine to me and invited me to come along to Marrakesh, Morocco, where hippies were being busted literally by the hundreds in North Africa. I wanted no part of a Moroccan jail. Annette waited with me on a ticket line for six hours until I got the last ticket on a ferry to Ibiza. We said goodbye on the pier. She had never concealed the fact that she was going back to her junkie boyfriend in Manchester. Back at Cliveden I would write the Lovely English Rose, but her Iberian Boy Toy in the Sexual Revolution never heard back.

My twentieth birthday celebration was on that overnight ferry to Ibiza, leaving behind my teen years with three new friends I met on the boat: Bob, a cheerful hippie from San Luis Obispo who traveled with his guitar, his beautiful Danish girlfriend whom he called Sweetpea, and Mel, a mysterious American Naval deserter who always wore a long black cape with many hidden compartments filled with potent Black Nepalese Hash. We lived together on Ibiza, the four of us, for four days in a German-built hotel with all the hot water you could ever want (a luxury in Spain in 1970 – I did my laundry in the tub) for one American dollar a night. I wanted to resume training there, but I never found a surface that wasn't either stones or asphalt, so I gave up. On the afternoon the Beatles broke up (Paul was leaving the band), I traveled by hydrofoil to the nearby island of Formentera, where I met American hippies living in caves, battling lice and malnutrition. The next morning I opened my eyes and Mel was holding another burning chillum pipe for my morning hit of his Nepalese Black. By dinnertime I was so wasted I had no idea where I was or who I was with, except there was this dead lobster who wouldn't stop staring at me. When I woke up in the morning with Mel hovering over me for yet another "Wake & Bake," I realized I had to pull myself off this island in the Mediterranean (said to be the home of the sirens and sea-nymphs who sought to lure Ulysses from his ship in Homer's *Odyssey)* and caught the next boat to Barcelona, a direct flight to Gatwick, then an assortment of public transports to Cliveden House, arriving ten days late for the start of spring quarter. In another day the administration would have contacted Interpol, since I had not told anyone where I was going for spring break. Good thing they didn't call, because back home in the States there would have been hell to pay. @ @

Track & Field was in full swing in Palo Alto. I got all the gory details from ten letters teammates had written me while I was in Spain. This was how bad things were: the Stanford University Varsity finished second to De Anza Community College in a tri-meet with Santa Ana J.C. In a dual meet against Occidental, officials robbed Kardong of a victory in a Half-Mile he won by a yard. In the Mile against the feisty

Ducks in Eugene, elbows flew again as Duncan, seeking to avenge his DQ in the Mile the year before, put up a valiant fight before losing, as Al Sanford had the previous year, in a PR 4:06.7. Coach Jordan attempted to kick Jim Kauffman off the team for showing up weeks late after rugby season – an effort Jordan made largely because he knew that Jim wasn't one of his "boys" and didn't respect him at all, or so Kauf believed. Not one to be denied his rights (and also to "stick it" to the Paytriot), Kauf circulated a petition signed by a number of many top Stanford athletes and most of the coaches in the Athletic Department to pressure Jordan into letting him suit up. Eventually Jordan relented, with the stipulation that Kauf play no more rugby. Kauf went out and raced against U.C.L.A. and got his clock cleaned by the great Quarter-Miler Wayne Collett down in L.A. – rugby had removed the "pop" from his legs. That same night his close friends Wade Killefer ("Killer") and Jack Schultz ("Schultzy") called Jim in Palo Alto, informing him that they were at the Santa Barbara rugby tourney with a team in trouble after a rash of injuries.

"'Kauf,' they said, 'we need you to come down tomorrow to play in the finals!'" (Jim told me this story years later.) "We've got injuries and we need you!' 'I can't,' I told them, ' I just promised Jordan I'd play no more rugby.' Pause... 'Kauf, we need you'... Longer pause... 'Oh-kay, I'll be down in the morning." So at the crack of dawn, [Kauf's future wife] Priscilla and I drive down to Santa Barbara. We win the game, which made us the 'unofficial' National Champs that year, as we had been the year before and would be the year after, winning the Tourney in dominating fashion and me ending my best year as a rugger. But towards the end of that game I was running with the ball and felt a pop in my knee... nobody even hit me... it just went – a fate destiny dished back at me, I supposed at the time! The assistant trainer Scotty checked it out and said yep, you've torn your cartilage. Shit... what am I gonna tell the Paytriot? Even more, I had scored a try in the game, so we had to hunt down the *San Francisco Chronicle* writer who was covering it to ask him not to use my name in the paper or I'd be busted for sure. We were sitting there flummoxed, when Scotty out of the blue said, 'Al

Green,' or some such generic name. 'Use that name,' he told the *Chronicle* reporter. 'There's always some "Al Green" back-up on any team.' We all looked at each other dumbfounded and then roared with delight… and it was done." Kauf could still sprint, but the injury to his take-off leg meant he would never Long Jump again. "Jimmy Kauffman is in pretty good shape," Paytriot would tell the *Menlo Times* on March 31st. "He's been working out twice a day. He's a tough kid." What "Jimmy" told Coach Jordan was that he hurt his knee racing Collett, the future Olympic Silver Medalist in the Munich 400.

And where was the Baby-Faced Assassin through all this? In Europe chasing after his bliss, on a wild vacation from his "real" life – a hitchhiker now, but hoping to be a running champion later. @ @

The seventh manned Apollo mission launched from Cape Kennedy on April 11th: a projected lunar landing mission that had to be aborted two days later when an oxygen tank exploded, crippling the service module upon which the Command Module depended. Despite limited power, freezing cold, a shortage of drinking water and a critical jury-rig of the carbon dioxide removal system, the three-man crew of Apollo 13 made it safely back to Earth on April 17th – around the time that I was wondering if I would ever make it back again. My spring studies were more interesting than my winter ones. I wrote a paper for Econ 116 – "Postwar Europe" – about the prospects for a common European currency and guestimated thirty years, which turned out to be almost on the Euro. I also read a book that changed my life. I had known for a long time that fiction can create alternative worlds, but until I read James Joyce's *Ulysses* in Professor Rob Polhemus' "Twentieth-Century British Comic Fiction" class, I had never realized that fiction could reinvent the world we live in now. I couldn't have explained to you precisely what I meant by that – I was still working it out in my head – but the experience of *Ulysses* took me into an alternate universe – a place where language, experience, and creation commingled and where I could imagine a world made new. Revolution, in other words, could be found in the pages of book. I asked a fellow tourist to snap a picture of me sitting on a plinth in the ruins of Kenilworth Castle, clutching my tattered copy of *Ulysses* to my chest.

A paper I wrote for Rob's class was about "Nighttown," the Red Light district in Joyce's Dublin, sealed it for me: *Ulysses,* and soon the novel in general, had become windows into my joys and my estrangements. I felt as if I had found an academic direction, and maybe even a scholarly vocation. Something other than running, politics, sex, drugs, and rock & roll had finally reached equal footing in my inner world. Two other Stanford runners would take Joyce to heart as well: Brook Thomas's doctoral dissertation at U.C. Santa Barbara would be entitled "James Joyce's *Ulysses*: A Book of Many Happy Returns," and Don Kardong would christen his 7.46 mile road race in Spokane, Washington "The Lilac Bloomsday Run," after the single day – June 16th, 1904 – when the fictional Leopold Bloom roamed Dublin in Joyce's 1922 masterpiece. By the Eighties, Bloomsday would be one of the largest timed foot race in the world, building on another tradition of the Emerald Isle: Joyce was said to be an avid distance runner himself. As he claimed, "running through space elates one." @ @

I had done just enough training in Spain to want to try to do something I had wanted to do since arriving in Faire Albion. I wrote my grandparents at length about my trip to the Crystal Palace, an international Track Mecca south of London: *'I joined the London Athletic Club who sponsored the meet, and they got me into the 5,000 meters on Saturday (that's 188 yards over three miles.) There were several Olympians running and many good runners. It was raining but they had an all-weather track. Before the race the announcer said, 'We have a new competitor not listed on your program, No. 26, Robert Coe, of Stanford University, U.S.A.' I'm afraid I let down Uncle Sam, but I am in sickening shape and running 15:28 is OK for someone in my condition, I guess. I was getting the ovation they always give stragglers when the announcer (from the L.A.C., which was glad to get a 4:09 Miler, no matter what his condition) said, 'We must apologize to our American visitor. He is from California and probably not used to this rain.' Finishing 22nd, with 2,000 people in the stands: Egad! But I'm running for a club now, with two meets a week to choose from, and am training harder, hoping to rush back into shape. On April 29th there's a mile and a half-mile race I could enter, and on May 16th, a national championship. As a student I am eligible, because it's being run at Oxford…"*

These races never happened, at least not for me. Before we left for a second field trip – to Amsterdam this time – black news rained like ash: apparently Nixon and Kissinger had been waging secret war in Cambodia since March. American B-52s had been pulverizing a neutral nation, causing hundreds of thousands of civilian deaths. Violent protests, sit-ins and arrests followed almost immediately on college campuses coast to coast, including on The Farm. In the heat of these demonstrations, the May 4th shooting deaths by National Guardsmen of student demonstrators at Kent State (and later on May 15th by police at Jackson State in Mississippi) sent some protestors into a frenzied rage. Eighty thousand dollars' worth of windows were shattered by demonstrators on the Stanford campus, and National Guardsmen were called in on more than one occasion. Friends of mine, including some true innocent bystanders, were assaulted with tear gas. The prediction of our ex-Student Body President Dennis Hayes my freshman year had finally come to pass: the Stanford campus was one of 442 American institutions of higher learning that closed its doors for the rest of the school year, although finals would eventually resume on The Farm on a limited scale.

In May, 1970, global anti-war sentiment was peaking. @ @

The depth of our outrage about America's grotesque, misbegotten war as well as our military presence around the planet, wherever our armed forces slept, is difficult to fathom and almost impossible to evoke if you weren't there at the time. The anger was public and political, but it was personal, too. It touched every aspect of who we were. I didn't hate America in May 1970, but I hated much of its works. In my journal and letters home I meditated on the authoritarian structure and logic of a system that never seemed to address human justice and human rights and only seemed interested in the exercise of power: "The natural self is tied to the chair, like Bobby Seale, bound and gagged [at the trial of the Chicago Seven]," I wrote in a letter home so despairing I never mailed it. "I fluctuate between intense depression and short periods of happiness… There is no reason to go back to America now except that every place is the same… Track filled this void before – I could go back to that, and probably will…" "Meaning" was what I was searching for, whether I realized it or not, and running now felt like nothing more than a big plug I had used to fill the meaningless void in the center of myself. A J.V. runner reported Coach Jordan's response to the campus crisis: "Before the S.C. meet he called a team meeting in the locker room, where he stood in front of a blackboard with a crude color drawing of an American flag fluttering on a flagpole with a 'paytriotic' slogan scrawled beneath it, and commenced this grand homily meant to inspire everybody to do their best at the meet on Saturday. How was 'running for the flag' supposed to make us faster?" my friend Chuck Dyer rhetorically asked me. "It was pretty ridiculous, if you ask me." Jordan's old-fashioned, flag-waving style of patriotism couldn't begin to cover this disaster.

Running was part of everything anyway. Lawson, Underwood, The Hulk and I had had spent hours contemplating the metaphysical absurdity of an activity that was, as The Hulk rightly claimed and I generally agreed, largely an existential pursuit. But this existential quest was only one side of the coin. The dialectic at the heart of all competitive sports – the essential meaninglessness of competitive play, combined with its positive ability to nurture and sustain a community of like-minded souls, which was the dualism Kenny Moore had expounded to me on the bus home from Fresno freshman year – didn't cross my mind as often as it might have that spring. Separated from my pack, I became obsessed with distance running's ultimate lack of any real human value, compared to other forms of endeavor I might have pursued. Running seemed to me then like little more than an escape from a world exploding all around us, and I was not sure if escape was what I needed to be doing at that moment, not when I could be confronting the world in some manner that made more sense, after Transcendental Meditation faded off the menu. I speculated in still another unsent letter to my grandparents that "the most powerful question of every young person's life right now is what you're running away from, and what you're running towards." This was the question I had faced my freshman year: were distance runners in flight from something much more important, evading some greater responsibility we should address? It wasn't just the nature of our sport and my separation from my pack that had driven me into my head like this. It was the times themselves. Many of my teammates still home were having feelings close to mine. Jack, who hadn't written for two months, sent a postcard in May mentioning that he was "depressed." Mark Haight dropped a note about feeling "low." The silence of The Hulk, who had written at least one insulting letter a month during my first quarter at Cliveden, was the most eloquent communication of all.

"Youth in America feels cut off and impotent," my unsent letter concluded. "We leave for Amsterdam on Saturday..." @ @

While my Cliveden group tromped dutifully through the Van Gogh and the Rijksmuseum, I escaped for daily runs over cobblestoned streets, festooned bridges and dank canals, hoping to find some new vest pocket park with winding trails. Wandering this countercultural paradise, I never knew who or what I might come across. Adventures seemed to be everywhere. I purchased a worn-out, fur-length grey rabbit fur coat second-hand at an Amsterdam flea market for twenty-five cents American and wore it to the rococo hash bars, where one afternoon a stoned Dutch hippie passed me a bowl of yogurt and pineapple, saying, "Take! Eat! This is the food... *of the Gods!"*

"Thanks! Don't mind if I do!" I replied, since I enjoyed playing the American Buffoon when I felt I was being treated like an idiot. A lot of the stupider hippie folklore left me cold. People talking about "Atlantis" as if it was a real place? Please... Then one day I was strolling across a square when I spied a tall blonde Swedish hippie wading towards me across a fountain, smiling, wearing nothing but a pair of panties, a white fringed leather vest and a daisy behind her ear. We got to talking – she was tripping on Acid – and I ended up leaving our Stanford hotel and crashing with Britta at her youth hostel-cum-hippie-house-party for a couple of nights. After she returned to

Stockholm I hooked up (platonically) with Elly and Gail, two earnest young American Zionists in blue jeans, semi-transparent peasant blouses and no bras, who it turned out were leaving that day to hitchhike to Jerusalem, or so they claimed with straight faces.

"You're hitchhiking to Israel? Far-out! Let's go!" I went back to my hotel, grabbed my backpack, and off we went to catch what would need to be a series of rides to the Holy Land. We weren't far into West Germany – a nation that filled them with fear and loathing – when my traveling companions discovered my views on the Palestinian Question, which were not entirely on the side of a nation they idealized, but which I considered an oppressor. "Palestine is a Third World country fighting for its nationhood, just like post-Colonial Vietnam!" I told them. "I also have issues with any state dominated by a single religion. The nation of Israel should have 'many rooms,' to paraphrase Jesus Christ, who was Jewish, too, as you well know..." We argued until sleep overtook us, huddled in a carrot field outside Dusseldorf – me wedged between the two Zionists in my rabbit fur coat, without my sleeping bag, which I had left at Cliveden House.

I woke up at dawn under a drizzling sky to find Elly and Gail gone already, leaving behind two closely hand-written pages detailing just how wrong I was on the Palestinian Question, and that they couldn't possibly hitchhike to Jerusalem with an anti-Semite. I was no more anti-Semitic than my rabbit fur coat, but I was glad they had left anyway, since this obviously wouldn't have worked out.

This misadventure should have been my wake-up call, but I over-slept.

My Stanford group had already returned to Cliveden, meaning there was no reason to go back to Amsterdam. So I strapped on my backpack and hitchhiked down the autobahn to Frankfurt and from there to the hilltop Stanford-in-Germany campus in Beutelsbach, where I spent a couple of days with the ex-girlfriend of one of my track teammates. (She said they were exes, although I was never sure.) After another night in a field outside Heidelberg, and another, according to a letter home, "on the floor of a bus in Lausanne, Switzerland with some

French horticulturalists," although I have no memory of this whatsoever, I staged an intervention on myself, and with ten dollars of my own and another twenty borrowed from a different friend in Beutelsbach, returned to Cliveden to finish sophomore year. @ @

Four p.m., another high tea. My classmates and I laid down our books and flung our Frisbees at the sky, which was falling. *"Gimme shelter,"* sang Mick Jagger. I lived in a rainbow of disarray.

It wasn't a functional crack-up I was in the middle of, but there were days when I felt as if my old personhood – my earlier, American self – had dissolved into molecules, revealing this person "Robert Coe" to be nothing more than a construction fabricated by family, culture and society and foisted on me since birth, while the "real" me lay buried deep inside, still struggling to get out. The Greater Houston Optimist Club "Boy of the Month" for February 1968, who once figured to be "one of the greatest distance runners ever to attend the Farm," was moving on to a newly-liberated plane. The Chambers Brothers echoed in my ears: "My soul... has been *psychedelicized...*" I re-read *Ulysses* as Holy Writ, a second time and a third, along with concordances and explicating texts. I took breaks from my studies to lounge on a sunlit Cliveden lawn in front of a flower bed of yellow daisies, bare-chested, wildly healthy in my tie-dyed green bellbottoms, my long brown curls tumbling past his shoulders, my face shrouded in a beard – I have the photograph to prove it. Sometimes I climbed a nearby garden trellis to break into the off-limits Astor pool, where Christine Keeler skinny-dipped, Lord Profumo snapped a towel at her lovely bare bottom, and the Macmillan government nearly toppled. On one stoned visit I stripped in a light rain and dove naked to the bottom of the unheated pool to gaze up at the soft raindrops pelting the surface, thinking *"Man, you been a naughty boy, you let your face grow long..."*

Then one day I noticed that I could sprint full-speed after a thrown Frisbee. My upper thigh had mended. With no internal debate whatsoever I put myself back into training twice a day, running the trails on the Cliveden grounds that by now bored me silly.

I never did show up for that meet in Oxford, where I would have only embarrassed myself. On May 16th, championship day, I hitchhiked instead to Stratford-on-Avon to see the Royal Shakespeare Company production of *Measure for Measure* and spend the night in a Warwickshire field, snug in my rabbit fur coat. I started a novel and got four pages into Chapter One, wrote toe-scrunching songs on a guitar badly played, and discussed Krishnamurti at length with the Cliveden group, pondering his warnings about the Poisons of Desire. One evening we listened to a brilliant tape-recorded lecture delivered at Stanford's Dinkelspiel Auditorium that spring by the LSD experimenter and defrocked Harvard Professor Richard Alpert, describing his passage to India and his reinvention as Baba Ram Das.

"Be Here Now," Ram Dass told us, and we listened closely. That was what I knew I wanted to do. I wanted to Be… Here… Now… Only on the Roads… Putting in the Miles… @ @

[]On a Stanford campus where the Administration summoned the police thirteen times that spring, an All-Beta swim quartet of Butterflyer Ferris, Backstroker Haywood, freshman Breaststroker Brian Job – each a past or future N.C.A.A. individual champion – together with a very good freestyler, Steve Carey, set a new American collegiate record in the 400-yard Medley Relay (3:24.99.) Greg Brock and Don Kardong had crossed the finish line together in a school record 8:45.2 for Two Miles, but the team didn't manage to win a single dual meet all season and got hammered in the Big Meet, 95-59, in front of five thousand fans in Berkeley. It was an exciting meet at points anyway, I was told in letters, highlighted by Cal's 4x110 relay team, the future N.C.A.A. champion, turning a scintillating 39.7, still the meet record forty years later. Three runners tied in the Quarter in 48.5, and not even a Polaroid could determine the winner, which in the end went to the Cal guy, who got the nod over Kauf. The Mile was a thriller, too, with Cliff West out-leaning Duncan at the tape, both in 4:05.6 (Duncan's PR) and Kardong a step behind both in a PR 4:06.0.

More news from the Track: in the conference championship at

U.C.L.A., Pre won the Three in 13:27.8, with Kardong fourth in 13:37.4, just missing Brock's school mark of 13:36.4, and Greg just behind in 13:41.4. Brock would close his college career with a third school record, 29:02.6 over Six Miles, although his dismal 13th-place finish at the N.C.A.A. Championship – his last collegiate race – must have been a major disappointment. Redshirt senior Brook Thomas tied Harry McCalla's school record in the Steeplechase with an 8:59.6 fourth-place finish at Conference, qualifying him for the N.C.A.As, where he would make the Final and finish 11th. And Duncan Macdonald had run a Mile in 3:59.6

3:59.6. I didn't learn about this feat until two weeks after it happened, in a back issue of the *Daily* someone had tossed across a Cliveden dining table. Last year's disqualification after the shoving match in Eugene had lit a fire under Duncan, or so Coach Clark claimed. Overcoming illnesses, academic issues and balky Achilles, Duncan had delivered on his massive potential with a monster six-second PR at the Pac-8 Conference Championship, trailing only Washington State's Rick Riley and Oregon's Roscoe Divine while becoming the first Stanford Miler to run the distance in under four minutes, and only the thirty-third American. This was the high point in the meet for our team, which finished last, after a sixth-place finish the year before. Dunc would tank at N.C.A.A. championship, finishing eighth in his heat in 4:09.8 and not advancing to the Final, but for his sub-four Mile my envy was surpassed only by my awe. Pre would go sub-four for the first time, too, in early June, running 3:57.4 at the Oregon Twilight meet, followed by five current and former Ducks, all under 4:01.8. Would the two of us have been measuring strides down the final straightaway? It seemed far-fetched, but no one would ever know. And now I was heeding John Lennon's advice on *Let It Be*, the album that broke up the Beatles: *"Get back, JoJo... get back to where you once belonged."*

Only not just yet: one day after my last final exam – June 13th, 1970 – I boarded a ferry across the Channel and spent a few days at Stanford-in-Germany again before meeting up with my cousin and her boyfriend in Amsterdam, where they were picking up a new VW Microbus direct from the factory. Their plan was to tour the continent, driving through Yugoslavia and as far south as Greece. My plan was to travel with them, and log some serious miles along the way. @ @

We headed east across the Netherlands into West Germany and across East Germany to West Berlin, where we found a camping spot in the parking lot of the 90,000-seat Olympiastadion, site of Hitler's XI Olympiad. Temperatures soared into the mid-nineties on our first day there, but I still scaled the stadium's cyclone fencing, just as I had on my first day at Stanford, to run in the vast Olympic bowl.

I was completely alone – no one, no guards in sight – inside one of the great stage sets of the twentieth century, where Jesse Owens, tenth child of black sharecroppers, had given the lie to Aryan supremacy and Hitler's fantasies of a "Master Race" in the Berlin Games of 1936. I laced up a new pair of racing flats I had purchased in Amsterdam and stepped on the newly-resurfaced track. This was the fastest surface I had ever set foot on. I had to do hard intervals. So with the ghosts of eighty thousand screaming Nazis in my ears and my thoughts on Payton Jordan's old friend, Jesse Owens, I ran over my head: eight 400 meters in 60 seconds flat, each rep followed by a ninety-second one-lap dog trot. Swimming afterwards in an ice-cold pool the size of four football fields, with the heads of four hundred people bobbing around me, I told myself there was no way I should have been able to do 8 x 400 meters in 60 seconds with a quick recovery on my first day of interval training in eight months – especially in that heat. But it was what I had done. Robert, I told myself, you have some serious catching-up to do... You are not there yet... But you... are... coming... *back*... But there was still more of Europe to see.

As we drove south along the Rhine a few days later, I told my cousin and her boyfriend to drop me off twelve miles from the campground where we would spend the night. I ran along the edge of a narrow, heavily-trafficked road with an eighty-foot vertical drop a foot away and every bend of the Rhine revealing some incredible vista of storybook castles or enormous restaurant patio thronged with tourists and locals, pumping out recordings of Beethoven and Wagner loud enough to echo across the blue river to green mountains vaulting to the sky. Two hours of running – the distance turned out to be closer to 18 miles than 12 – brought me to our cozy campsite, where I showered and though seriously stiff and sore prepared a stew on our tiny butane stove. I slept outside that night in my cozy sleeping bag, gazing up at spangled Rheingold sky. Watching that shimmering lattice of stars and blackness, I had the "noetic" sense that the sky overhead was disclosing an objective truth about reality: that the ever-changing vastness of space is always with us, which indeed it was, and is today.

The next day we found a secluded parking spot in one of the world's largest urban parks, Munich's 1.7-square-mile Englischer Garten. I abandoned the upper bunk in the VW's pop-up roof to give my cousin and her boyfriend some privacy and spent the night in the bushes nearby. I woke up at midnight with the black sky raining cats and dogs and a river flowing through my orange plastic tube-tent. I woke up in the morning soaked to the skin and feeling like some German forest creature, set out for a ninety-minute morning tour of the park, sticking for the most part to the firmer trails around the meadows. In some places the Englischer Garten looked untended, as if nature had taken back a huge swath of the city. At one point I entered what I dubbed a "Magic Meadow," a vast stretch of near-wilderness in the middle of the largest city in Bavaria. Venturing on to city streets, more than one motorist leaned out their windows, banged on the sides of their car, and bellowed encouragement in words I didn't understand. The Munich Olympiad was still two years away, but citizenry seemed eager for opening day. And judging from the miles I was covering and the attention I was getting, I looked like a serious runner again. @ @

On July 4th we met the financial backers of my European adventure – our grandparents – in Vienna as planned. My nomadic visage, shoulder-length hair and shaggy goatee announced what everyone already knew: that I had replaced my cousin Larry as the family rebel. (He had run off to Hawaii to surf.) My grandfather had hoped I would visit Moscow during the summer, to see how the other half lived, but he had to know I hated the Soviet Union, end of story. That I was a young man of twenty with much promise was still assumed, but my grandparents also considered me naïve, impulsive and unrealistic, which made my college years especially crucial to the man I would become. I disagreed with their interpretations, but I was still happy to see the founders of my feast, because I loved them and I knew they loved me. My Grandfather wanted to celebrate Independence Day at the Sacher Hotel over a plateful of "Sacher Tortes," which he had been raving about since he first tasted them almost twenty years ago, in 1951. The Sacher Maitre'd took one look at my long brown ringlets and my cousin's boyfriend's blonde mop top and wouldn't let us in the door, even after we borrowed neckties. We had to find another place to celebrate the Fourth and speak at length about events on The Farm, where the rise in campus violence and the disruptions and school closure in May had led to President Kenneth Pitzer's abrupt resignation, effective September 1st, after only nineteen months in office. Pitzer had hosted my sister's graduation ceremonies only weeks before, which my grandparents had of course attended.

"Pitzer's June 25th letter to university trustees," I said, pulling an old *Stanford Daily* from my backpack, "cited... here it is... 'trends have made it increasingly difficult to obtain the very broad and active support from all those groups who together are responsible for the well-being of the university.' Just as well," I concluded, tossing the paper aside. "Since his first day on campus, when a bunch of Black student radicals invaded his office and he refused to talk to them, we've known that Pitzer couldn't handle the job...." My grandparents had little to say about any of this. What was happening in the big wide world out there seemed beyond the control of any of us. @ @

After another day or two in Austria's capital, my grandparents and our fifteen-year-old cousin who had accompanied them (she was a few years away from going to Stanford, too) and my traveling cousin and her boyfriend went our three separate ways. I had decided not to go on to Yugoslavia and Greece, as we had originally discussed. Instead I stayed in Vienna for one more day, crashing with friends at Stanford-in-Austria and logging fifteen miles in two workouts through crowded Viennese streets and parks. I never did cross paths with Pre, a frat boy, too, by the way: a Pike, Pi Kappa Alpha. Two days after I left England he had made the cover of *Sports Illustrated* ("Only 19 but blessed with speed, stamina and a canny coach") and had headed out to compete on the European circuit, where on July 9th in Stuttgart he would set an American Junior Record in the 5,000 meters (13:39.4) that would last more than forty years. And if you believed the rumors I heard, he was also sharing his bed nightly with two or three different girls, and probably having sex with them, too. Pre was on a course to demolish the old high-school image of distance runners as people who couldn't make it in another sport, but I think our generation did it with him: a hippie entrepreneur I had met over Easter in Torremolinos had offered me a summer job DJ'ing in a discothèque on Sardinia, and I gave this some serious thought, but in the end I boarded an un-air-conditioned charter train from Vienna on July 8th and spent the night on a train to Amsterdam discussing D.H. Lawrence and Gunter Grass with two London School of Economics students and rock music with three beautiful young Austrian women we met, until all of us lowered the chairs in the cabin and slept together in one big bed. (One couple quietly made love in the darkness to the thunder of wheels.) From Amsterdam I boarded a ferry to Dover, then two trains and a lorry hitchhike back to Cliveden House, where I crashed with some new arrivals I knew from home for two weeks, eating the lousy food for free this time, and training twice a day around Cliveden's grounds and farther afield sometimes, on equestrian paths past fifteenth-century country churches, until my blessed flight home on July 23rd. @ @

My transatlantic, transcontinental non-stop TWA from London to Oakland was postponed three times due to mechanical failures. When we finally took off one of the only passengers left on our 747 – one of the first, and my first time flying on one – was another returning Stanford student, a Chicano kid from an East Bay barrio who had picked up a seriously-manic Cockney accent after spending a year working as a grave digger in Brighton. Also on board: an all-girl rock band that had just spent the summer touring Europe as the opening act for Three Dog Night: dead-ringers for Mick Jagger, Michelle Phillips and Cass Elliot, respectively, together with a kick-ass Native American drummer who refilled our champagne glasses with both fists, howling "One for the Spider Woman!" Drinks were on the house for the flight as a thank-you for our patience with the many delays. We were barely over Shannon before the stewards and stewardesses were as schnockered as we were. In fact they were the parties that suggested a game of Trans-Atlantic Tag.

"You're it, Robert!" shouted the prettiest stewardess, flinging her shoes at me and taking off at 35,000 feet, sprinting as fast as her lovely slender legs would carry her.

"Look out!" I shouted. "I am about to set a new World Record for the Mile-High Dash! I will run the length of this 747 in 3.14159 seconds give or take a decimal point!" And that was more-or-less exactly what I did, sprinting full-tilt boogie down an aisle in what probably was a World Record for covering the length of a 747 bound from Europe across the Atlantic and North America. I got in at least a dozen training circuits around the long aisles before I lay down on some empty seats for a nap. When I woke up a few hours later a strong smell of hash was emanating from one of the closed lavatories. That had to be José and the Band smoking the last of their stashes. I knew from that smell that customs would be a bitch, and I was right: José (the Mexican kid, naturally) had the lining of his coat torn to shreds by the Customs Pigs, while I was patted down in a manner less than friendly.

"Take it easy!" I told my Customs Inspector. "If I was 'holding,' do you think I'd come through dressed like this?" I had costumed myself for my American re-entry in a see-through Indian shirt, tie-dyed flowered bellbottoms, Frye boots, and a pseudo-Native American headband to hold back brown curls swirling past my shoulders, matching the untrimmed beard that covered my neck. Watching the Customs Pig paw past my rabbit fur coat, my bells and necklaces, my Regency jacket, and all the rest of my high hippie regalia from my six months abroad, I had the satisfaction of knowing he would be bitterly disappointed.

"You're clean," he snarled at last, clearly unhappy that he couldn't bend me over the table for a body-cavity search, which by the way almost happened to me once, going from Switzerland into Germany, but the Customs guy changed his mind.

"And José was clean, too. Now point us towards the bus to Palo Alto. Or on second thought, we'll find it ourselves..." Exiting through automatic glass doors I spun around at the last moment and flipped off the Customs guy with both hands. The youth who had been too embarrassed to talk back at a Buck Club Breakfast had left the building. And now a changed young man was coming home. @ @

Riding that bus down the Bayshore Freeway to Stanford, soaking up the bright mid-peninsula greenery and elated to be back, I knew that Europe had broadened me, and flattened me, too. And now I was Camus's Stranger with a Cardiovascular System, coming back through the Looking Glass to re-join the Family of Man. At Cliveden some of us had studied Krishnamurti on the importance of transcending desire, but that day on the Bayshore I decided Krishnamurti was wrong. Not desiring anything was a sign of depression; what got people into trouble were the things they desired, not the act of desiring. My desire was to return to my former life as a Stanford distance runner, which made perfect sense to me, spiritually, psychically, in every which way, because running was the most solid shelter I had from the existential storm that was the world. Training for racing over long distances would once again become my refuge; would once again become the enigma into which I poured all of my loneliness and confusion, my love of drama and community, my desire to excel and my love of teams. In Europe I'd had just about as much experience as I could readily devour, at least for a while. Returning to The Farm was my great leap into paradox: I felt like I had no choice but to become a Stanford Jock again, and all the choice in the world.

"Gimme Shelter..." *For Stanford I Will...* @ @ @

RUNNING MAN

Home is where they have to take you in, so I hailed a cab from the bus stop in Palo Alto straight to the Beta House. The place looked deserted in mid-summer. Its big blue front door was wide open to the elements and its entry hall strewn with leaves, but electricity was on, so I located an empty second-floor room with a firm mattress and an old electric frying pan and was in the middle of cooking my first American meal in seven months when a very large white Chow suddenly appeared and without giving me so much as a glance leapt over my hotplate and out the open window. I leaned over the windowsill, expecting to see a dead canine splattered on our front porch, but instead saw a live one sprinting up Mayfield Avenue. That dog turned out to belong to fellow squatters, two pretty summer students from San Luis Obispo who had stumbled on an empty frat house and moved in, then enrolled in a federal food stamp program to feed themselves. For my part I needed a job, and by the end of the week I had one: Official Mouse Custodian of the Stanford Medical Center, charged with changing the sawdust after washing the cages of literally thousands of white mice four days a week from 10:30 to 4:00 p.m. I would develop an almost primal affection for these pitiful creatures, living detritus of oncology experiments, bulbous with bunches of pink tumors, like vascular grapes. For this noble chore I was paid $2.31 an hour. The Federal minimum wage in those days was $1.45, and $2.31 could buy you a pound of coffee and four gallons of gas. The $55 a week I took home at the Medical Center was $5 a week more than I had made at Grizzly Lodge the previous summer. I would have made a little better money DJ'ing in Sardinia, but I was better off training here. @ @

For the next six weeks before fall classes started, I cleaned mouse shit, ate, slept, and ran. On workdays I would get up late, make it to the hospital, get back to the Beta House, change into my workout gear, and hit the roads, then dine on the squatters' Food Stamps and hang out with them for a while before going to bed, so I could wake up in the morning and do it all over again. My new life was un-textured but laser-focused. I wasn't even reading much, despite my new-found love of novels that could change the world – only *The Collected Works of Franz Kafka* and a novella, *Been Down So Long It Looks Like Up to Me*, by Joan Baez's late brother-in-law Richard Farina. My mouse custodial duties required being on my feet six hours a day, so on my four work days a week I limited my training to one long road run, usually but not exclusively after work, depending on what time I went to bed the night before. The three days a week I wasn't at the hospital I added a morning run. I could regularly complete the moderately-hilly 10.5-mile Arastradero loop in the 57- to 58-minute range: more than ten miles at about 5:30 pace, which wasn't so taxing that I couldn't do something close to the same thing the next day. On some workouts, cruising along and barely breathing hard, I felt as if I was out for a fun run through the Eucalypti. I *drank* Arastradero that late July and August. I could hardly remember a time when I didn't have an appetite for long hard road runs. Once or twice a week I pushed farther: 13, 14, 15 miles. I skipped workouts, too, occasionally, if I felt I needed more rest, and took it easier on rare days when I needed more recovery. My mileage for those six weeks held steady in the high 80-to-low-90 miles-a-week range. All of them were unrecorded except in memory.

Different thought processes fueled my training now. Since my sophomore year in high school I had kept training logs and thought it foolish not to, but going forward I kept no records at all. I wanted my body to tell me how far and fast to run, not some pre-ordained plan. I still wanted to "Train, not Strain," but at deeper levels than I had previously imagined. My running became a kind of meditation-in-action, freeing me from outside distractions and constraints. My "Natural Self" was in training now, traveling across the earth placidly amidst the noise & haste in last year's Onitsuka Tigers, a jock and shorts – no socks and or shirt, ever. What I sought was that energized, energizing state that runners call "The Zone," where running feels effortless and free, and it astonished me how often I found my Runner's High that summer, under brutal sun and drenching rain, it made no difference to me. I was no longer the naïve nineteen-year-old who had minded ten-year-olds in the Sierra Nevadas the summer before. I wasn't Coach Clark's prodigy or Jordan's "baby-faced assassin" anymore, either. I wished I could be really pretentious about it and say I was an "Artist," like Steve Prefontaine said about himself. But I was doing what I needed to do to run faster. Those six weeks at the Beta House were my Spartan Boot Camp. I had made myself Other. I had become Elemental. I was Running Man.

Midway through my pre-school lockdown I decided to test my new approach at a Saturday all-comers meets at the College of San Mateo, halfway up the peninsula to San Francisco. Minutes before the Mile Relay I hooked up with three other runners on the infield and became the third runner who give the baton to anchorman Norbert Payton, a former Washington State sprinter who would run a world-leading, wind-aided 9.9 100 Meters two years later. I split a PR 50.5, barely two seconds slower than the time that won The Big Meet open Quarter that spring. *Sports Illustrated* had claimed that Pre had lowered his best Quarter from 51 to 49 seconds since his freshman year, but Kenny Moore later wrote that Pre never broke 50, and none of our distance crew had, either, except Duncan, back in high school. And I had just run 50.5. This was not crazy fast but it wasn't slow, and I had done it in the middle of my summer base work, without any speed training since Berlin. To see if I could go faster, I ran a second Quarter from a standing start in 51.5, then followed it with a 4:24 Mile, just for the workout. America's current national record holder in the Marathon,

Stanford grad Ryan Hall, can't break 53 over 400-Meters. I probably had 48-second quarter speed, fast enough in those days to be a top 5,000-Meter runner and a decent Miler, if that's what I chose to try.

Those fast Quarters renewed my confidence that my approach to training was working. I was in the best shape of my life.

Two days before school started I made my final preparation for cross country: I borrowed a pair of scissors from one of the Beta squatters, cut my long hair and shaved my beard. I did keep some curls over my ears, along with a moustache and muttonchops, because I knew this wouldn't keep me from getting into uniform. Newly-shorn, I went out and ran Woodside: thirteen miles. Then I met a friend of a friend in White Plaza and gave him five bucks in exchange for a little purple pill to "drop" (as we said in those days.) "The Doors of Perception" had opened so wide on the Stanford campus that I was no longer afraid to walk through them. Then I walked to Frost Amphitheater to hear the Grateful Dead open for Miles Davis. *Thirteen miles... then one Miles...* I have a photo of myself that day, seated Indian-style on Frost's grassy knoll with some friends, bare-chested and deeply-tanned. I am wearing red running shorts, sockless Tigers, and a beaded necklace with a cowbell (more cowbell!) My head bowed in meditation as the Dead played for everybody, and Miles played only for himself. Miles was in his funky electric jazz fusion stage then... *Bitches Brew* had come out in April... He stood upstage with his back to the audience the whole time, playing only for himself... As a cross-country runner tripping on Mescaline, I understood both the Dead and Miles' perspectives: *for the strength of the wolf is the pack, and the strength of the pack is the wolf...* @ @

Two days later I was at the Stanford Medical Center. A Doctor was listening to my chest. He had his stethoscope pressed to my chest and fingers resting lightly my wrist. He looked up at me in alarm.

"You have a resting pulse of 35!"

"I'm a distance runner!"

"Ah!" he replied with his face relaxing. "Would you mind if I brought in some people to listen to this?" He thumped my chest with a heavy forefinger.

Within minutes I was surrounded by a half-dozen white-coated physicians taking turns listening to the highly-efficient heart of a highly-trained Mammal. Having a cardiovascular system fit enough to be admired by residents at the Stanford Medical Center ought to have given me more of a thrill than it did, but in those days I was thinking of running as a reaction against any overly-rational, technologically-obsessed worldview you had out there. I wasn't some lab creature, like the rodents I cared for at the Oncology Lab. I was a Human Aspirant, striving body and soul for higher ground. But paradox abounds: I was also looking forward to the on-the-clock, gut-check, non-hippy-dippy training and fierce competitions that lay just ahead of us. @ @

The first teammate back from the summer, the day before our traditional semi-official kick-off run at San Gregorio Beach, was Decker Underwood. We hugged and levitated, lifting each other off our feet and off the ground, like characters in an R. Crumb comic.

"Bob Coe!"

"Deck-uh my man!"

"Missed you, dude!"

"Missed you, too!"

"Uhh! So great you're back!"

"So great to *be* back! Look at you, Deck-uh! Lookin' *psychedelicized!* Workin' that Southern Cal hippie beach *thang!* With the shock of red hair? Cleft on the side like a 'fro? Madras shorts, t-shirt, sandals – you look *fit*, brothuh! But you know you're gonna have to cut off that hair if you wanna run for Stanford U…" I had read in the *Daily* at Cliveden about Decker's 4:10.2 Mile against Oregon: a PR faster than the old freshman mark, but not as fast as mine. He had finished within spitting distance of Don and Dunc: *Duncan, Don 'n' Decker… The D-Men… The 3-D's…* We piled into my old '62 Chevy Impala station wagon with the mushy shocks – mine alone now, since my sister had graduated, married the Indian Half-Miler the next day and moved to L.A., where he would go to Med School– and set out over the coastal range, planning to grab a bite somewhere, snag a spot on the beach, unroll our sleeping bags, stare at the sunset and crash & burn for the night before joining the team for our annual beach workout in the morning.

We woke up in a lovely misty fog breaking with the morning light to discover we had spent the night ten feet upwind from the rotting corpse of a four-hundred-pound sea lion crawling with maggots. The air around us felt soft, sweetening our lungs. The mist had burned off entirely by the time we hit the road for another glorious day on the lamb. We got ourselves to the San Gregorio parking lot ahead of the rest, stripped down to birthday suits and set off around the corner of a cliff for a short warm-up on the nude beach, just to stretch our legs.

The Stanford van was pulling into a parking spot as Decker and I ran up to greet the team. For my teammates' first sight of me since Europe, I was wearing my Tigers. Otherwise I was as naked as the day I was born.

"Hey guys! Hey Coach! How zit hangin'? Great t' see you! How were your summers? How was the drive over?"

Decker and I couldn't stop laughing at the freshmen looking away in embarrassment. The upper classmen who knew us just grinned, shook their heads resignedly, and slapped our extended palms.

"Couple o' weenies," quipped Kardong, going Old School on our asses.

"Where are your titty tassels?" said Duncan. He had re-grown his moustache over the summer, and looked in good shape. Duncan had run a sub-four Minute Mile last spring! I still couldn't get over it.

Coach Clark took one look at his top two returning veterans from last year's Conference meet and yielded a weary smile. He looked the same as he had nine months before and if anything, even more patient.

"Pre runs nude sometimes," I said to everybody, adding "true" while I trotted with Decker over to my wagon to grab our jocks and shorts for the workout. I could feel my heart fluttering in my chest. I couldn't stop grinning. I wanted everybody to know I was back, and that they should get as pumped as I felt. I wanted them to know that I may have become a Hippie Freak, but I was definitely On the Bus.

"Hey guys!" I called out to my teammates, who were sitting on the runner of the van, changing their shoes. "Our year!"

"Home from the Wilderness!" Decker said, goofing on something I had told him on the drive over the mountains. "Back from *Europe!*"

"Listen up, everybody. Today's workout will be five or six miles down by the edge of the water. Keep it easy this morning. Go out for twenty minutes, then turn around and come back. Everyone clear?"

"Clear as Tahoe, Coach…" And with these instructions we gathered and plodded off through the thick sand to the harder stretches along the water's edge, on the side away from the nude beach. Running in sand I never enjoyed, but training day at San Gregorio was a team tradition, so I took part. I couldn't believe how fantastic it felt to be back on the Stanford cross country team. I didn't feel like I was bringing it all back home. I almost felt – almost – like I had never left. Our returning veterans were phenomenal: Sub-Four Miler Macdonald, not yet known for racing further distances, but getting ready to try; Kardong, fourth in the Three Mile on the track at Nationals last spring; Kretz, who was nearly as fast as Don was; Underwood, who had finished just two seconds behind me at the Conference Championship last year; and finally me, who had never lost a Varsity cross country race to any of these guys, except once, when Don beat me in last year's Cal meet. This was the most formidable cross-country crew in Stanford school history. But unfortunately we were just five, like our N.C.A.A. runner-up team in '68. We would once again face the challenge of keeping our tiny pack together, but even so we had legitimate reasons to believe we were a contender for a national cross-country title. @ @

The first meet of 1970 was contested in the late morning of October 10th, a few weeks into the school year: the Sacramento State Invitational, the scene of my freshman breakthrough and sophomore screw-up and third-place finish the year before.

Everyone arrived at the locker room in time to meet the van – everyone except Decker. What was he doing, keeping us all waiting? As the minutes passed I began to get a bad feeling about this. This wasn't like Decker. This wasn't like Decker at all. We finally drove to his on-campus trailer and received shocking news: the previous night Decker had given the motorcycle he had driven to Altamont too much gas while hopping on, and side-swiped a parked car.

We arrived in time to see him emerging from his trailer on crutches, his right knee encased in a thick brace, an expression of pain, bafflement and embarrassment on his face. He was off to see his orthopedist again. Major surgery was already in the offing. Our eyes didn't meet, because Decker wouldn't look at us. The team made the drive to Sacramento in dead silence. Personally I couldn't begin to process this, not with our season opener that day asking for everything I had.

The course at Sac State that morning was bone dry, hard and dusty where it had been deep in mud the two previous autumns. We joined a throng of one hundred and fifty Varsity runners cascading out of Hornet football stadium, lofting ourselves over the bank of the levee and through the thick brambles and sandy trails along the American River. Kardong, Kretz and I were part of the lead pack that emerged from the long stretch of sandy river bottom, soared back over the levee and began the approach to the stadium. (If Duncan raced that day, I have no memory of it.) I did not plan to do what I did next, and not more than three seconds passed between the thought and the deed, but I was feeling my oats, running well within myself well into the second half of the race. So without giving it a second thought, except that we had maybe a half-mile to go, I decided to put this race to bed.

"Let's go, Stanford," I cried, and surged into the lead. I was half-expecting or at least hoping my teammates would follow. Within seconds I was alone... I thought... *Hmmm... that should not have been that easy...* A full minute must have passed before it dawned on me that I might have made a terrible mistake. For starters, I wasn't actually perfectly sure how far away from the finish line I was, just like I wasn't freshman year. Only this time I was running alone, far ahead of the Varsity pack, not seeing or hearing a soul down a long stretch of dry road and rock behind the stadium. This was the wildest, weirdest, most violent sensation I had ever had in a footrace: to have one hundred and fifty people following me in hot pursuit, and not a single one, or even a single spectator, reaching my senses. Hundreds of fans were hanging on the outcome of this competition I was leading, but all I was aware of were my screaming thoughts and burning body, wracked in a hyperbolic void. How much farther did I have to run? A quarter-mile? A half-mile? *What?* What if I tied up? How many people would come flying by me? Two, like last year? Ten? Fifty? How long could I take this pain? Panicking, red-lining, dreading the appearance of the infamous "wall," where body systems crash and running stops, I pushed on in a state of blind terror, focusing all of my will and effort on preserving my form and cadence and listening for what would surely be footfalls coming from behind... It wasn't until I rounded the corner of the stadium and knew for sure where I was – about forty-five seconds from the finish, if that – that I stole a glance behind me.

And there was Don, at least sixty yards back. He was as alone as I was.

I broke the winner's tape that day and saw white light. I swear I did. I didn't black out, I *whited* out. Apollo Thirteen had landed!

As I staggered down the finishing chute my vision returned. I turned around and saw Coach Clark not six feet away from me, staring at me in slack-jawed disbelief. No one had expected a dominant performance from me in my first race back from Europe.

I was only twenty years old. @ @

Kardong's spring had been highlighted by an All-American fourth-place finish in the N.C.A.A. Three-Mile Final in Des Moines. This was the same place he had taken in the conference meet, but this time he ran 13:28.0, eight seconds faster than Brock's old school mark and faster than Lindgren's old meet record, but trailing Pre, Gary Bjorklund and Dick Buerkle, future Olympians all. This was the race dramatized in the 1998 film *Without Limits,* in which Pre had badly cut his foot the night before the race during imaginative sex with an Iowa gymnast. According to people who were there, Pre had had a run-in with a bolt on the diving board at his team motel, but Kenny Moore and director Robert Towne should be forgiven for altering this small fact, because even the most out-sized myths can sometimes use a little fluffing. Doctors told Pre not to compete, but the freshman had run anyway with twelve stitches in his foot, scorching the last half-mile in 2:00.4 to put the kibosh on rumors that he had no kick. He later claimed his foot only hurt during his final sprint to the finish line that assured Oregon a tie for a national team title with B.Y.U. and Kansas.

Kardong would finish eleven seconds behind me that day in Sacramento. The next three finishers were all recent college grads, running for the six-year-old West Valley Track Club, the Bay Area's hub for distance runners. In third place, more than a half minute behind me, came twenty-five-year-old Bill Clark, a 4:06 Miler who had finished second in the 1968 Boston Marathon and won the sea-level U.S. Olympic trial semi-finals over 10,000 Meters that same year. Five seconds behind Clark came Rich Delgado, who six weeks earlier had broken a legendary course record in finishing second in the oldest trail race in America, the 7.4 mile Dipsea Race from Mill Valley to Stinson Beach; fifteen seconds behind Delgado, in fifth place, the thirty-year-old Colombian Olympian Alvaro Mejia, tenth in the Mexico City 10,000-Meters and just six months away from winning the Boston Marathon. Sixth place went to our Bernie Lahde (was he coming around at last?); seventh, to Mark Covert, the national junior college record holder over six miles, whose last day off from running was July 20, 1968, before beginning a daily streak of running that would last for exactly forty-five years. In eighth place, our Arvid Kretz; in ninth, Bill "Mad Dog" Scobey, fifteen months away from a world-class 2:15:21

Marathon and two years away from setting an American Record over 50 kilometers; and in tenth, Duwayne Ray, a 4:02 Miler and the 1969 Division II National Mile Champ at Chico State. (Our fifth man, in 16th place, was sophomore Bob Geisler, who I barely knew.)

Later that month the West Valley Track Club newsletter, in applauding my victory, would claim (incorrectly) that I had won the Sac State Invitational the year before: "[Coe] seems to thrive on tough courses and this is a real toughie." Thank you, Sacramento! – the city where my great-grandfather, the President of the California State Fair, had built the largest agricultural fair in the world! Button-holing a course official after the race, I discovered the origin of my mistake: unbeknownst to me, or maybe even us, the course had been lengthened from 4.5 miles to 4.8 miles that year. This meant that I had made my move not from a half-mile out; but closer to a mile. But as can sometimes happen, a tactical blunder proved to be visionary strategy: I had stolen a race from the top distance runners in Northern California with a decisive mid-race surge, a classic weapon in the racing arsenals of international veterans like Ron Clarke and Gerry Lindgren. Although in my case I had surged by mistake, in my first serious race in over ten months.

"That was a great move, Robert," Kardong told me as we ran our cool-down. "I wish I could have gone with you!"

"You don't know the half of it, Don!" I told him how badly I had miscalculated the finish line.

"I don't care," Kardong replied. "That was still a sweet move…" @ @

There would be no ceremony of the #1 singlet in the locker room on Monday afternoon. Teammates had told Coach that they found last year's ritual demeaning, and I had no problem with this, since I had always thought it was a little corny (and I had hung on to last year's jersey anyway.) Assessing my performance in Sacramento, I wondered if I was at the start of a monster cross-country season. As a team we had kicked butts and taken names, too, winning handily for the third year in a row. But my larger concern was the season-ending injury of my best friend. The brutality of something like this was hard to fathom. It was like the figurative death of a teammate, since it was a certainty that Decker wouldn't be returning this year, not even for Track. No more running in the "Hiei Mountains" for Deck, at least for a while, and possibly ever. We would hang out a fair bit that fall, Decker a casualty on pain-killers, his knee propped on an ottoman. His doctors waited until after the S.C. football game to perform a surgery that left him with a nasty scar shaped like a question mark. His doctors told him he would never run again, but Decker would prove them wrong, working his way back and even jumping into a Varsity race or two. But multiple comebacks would be cut short by recurring ankle sprains. Coach Clark would let him keep his athletic scholarship, but in the end he would surrender that, too. The former California State High School Mile Champion never ran a full season in a Stanford uniform again.

What sort of parable was this? Were we Hippie Jocks tempting fate with our risk-taking hubris? What was Decker doing anyway, riding a Hog? My family never let me anywhere near one of those things. Had this been an accident waiting to happen? Did we really think we could soar towards the sun on our wax wings, and not tumble from the highest heavens back to earth? I think we probably did. We sometimes acted like we were demi-gods, when we were truly mortal clay. @ @

Europe had changed me. I had stripped down to Nothingness abroad, and now I was returning in a condition of absurdity and paradox: choosing to run, even as running was choosing me. I had tripped naked on the beaches of the Costa Blanca, had visions, and reveled in Art and in Literature. Music was a kind of glue, but not enough to hold the times together. Friendships and athletics were the more steadfast truths, it seemed to me, along with our studies. But Stanford had changed, too, while I was gone. Running north from the locker room to Arastradero or one of our golf course workouts, we crossed a campus where the counterculture had triumphed. No one's colors ran dry in the fall of 1970. The Farm was a cosmic carnival unfurling across a landscape recently traumatized by its closing over the atrocities in Cambodia and the massacres at Kent State in Ohio and Jackson State in Mississippi. Long hair, paisley and loose-fitting clothing were everywhere you turned, and you wore them, too. Recreational drug use took place openly on lawns, sidewalks and in dormitories. In White Plaza and even in fraternity houses, at parties and lecture halls on the Quad, you smelled the sweet scent of marijuana, looked around and speculated on the source and the ingenuity involved in firing up a joint or pipe without being seen or caught, and usually learning that the magic smoke was simply drifting through an open window, blown by a breeze from who knew where. Rock music and the scent of pot and patchouli drifted through the air like sunlight. Posters on campus-wide kiosks advertised rock shows, peace marches, Be-Ins, and musical groups, and every kind of countercultural sound, from folk and bluegrass to rock was performed almost daily in White Plaza, where hippie entrepreneurs set up tables to sell tie-dyed clothes, knitwear, hand-made jewelry and organic baked goods. All of these were expressions of a new mid-peninsula economy in formation, as well as of all sorts of new social and political arrangements, all of it shadowed and compromised by the obscenity of War in Southeast Asia.

And yet for all the color and exuberance on display, the anger and the despair that had darkened campus the previous May had not entirely abated. Cambodian Spring had fractured the solidarity of the peace movement, sowing fertile ground for extremism, including of the violent sort. A month earlier a home-made bomb had exploded at the University of Wisconsin at Madison in protest against the university's research involvements with the military, killing a man and injuring three others. National polls showed that majority of Americans wanted us out of Southeast Asia, but millions of law-abiding citizens were having trouble making common cause with a "Peace" Movement that many people thought had become a shelter for violence. Many committed radicals didn't know what to do to stop the War except either bust up the place or move their politics from the public sphere into their private lives. This was what I was doing when I formally changed my major from political science to the Humanities Special Program. The most powerful thing any of us could do now was to stick together in any way we could through that ragged year 1970, through this never-ending war, under governments we mistrusted and loathed.

A plan was afoot for a while to move into a house off-campus with Duncan, but plans never seemed to materialize between Dunc and me. Kauf, Ferris and several other friends and strangers had taken over a six-bedroom ranch home estate in Portola Valley, where there was no room a for me, although I would attend many hilltop pool parties there over the fall, enjoying the mid-peninsula weather and a country-club atmosphere with a great crew of athletes and sybarites who rented this estate for a song. Among Kauf and Ferris's housemates was a former State high school wrestling champion I got to know a little: his nickname was "Baggins" for his Hobbit-like stature. "Bags" could sit around the pool in Portola Valley for hours making his three-string mandolin sing like a lyre. Steve Harvey was also an inspired director of experimental theater – an interest that my running life kept me from pursuing at all. Between workouts and studies, there was little room in my schedule – or my head – for much else. So without even a glint of a fantasy of anywhere better place to live, I transitioned seamlessly from summertime squatter to full-time fall renter at the Beta House. @ @

The Butt Hutt had changed significantly while I was gone, like everything else had. The "Old Guard" was vanquished entirely, and many of the "brothers" in my class – the ones who had vowed to make a Revolution this year – were gone, too. The house had fallen almost entirely into the hands of the latest round of "Pledges," sophomores for whom the frat boy jargon and "Bro" routines were as ludicrous as they were to me. Hoary traditions were vanishing everywhere on campus in 1970: there was no home-coming bonfire and pep rally in Lake Lagunita that fall, cancelled permanently due to environmental concerns. No more Ram's Head Gaieties, either – an old-fashioned musical-theater tradition dating back over sixty years. As recently as a year ago the Beta House had Pledge Pranks, Pledge Olympics, a Pledge Porch, Pledge "hacks" and "little sisters," but these were no longer part of the repertoire. Hell Week was banished, too, along with creepy ceremonies involving dead dogs. The only traditions that survived at the Beta House did so wholly in realms of the invisible – in mystical playgrounds not far from the rest of the whole countercultural guacamole, on a campus roiling with hatred of war, anger at authority, and discontent with anything at all Republican or Mainstream.

My new third-floor room at the Beta House was a suite, thanks to an adjoining empty room overlooking the volleyball court. Sophomore swimmer Brian Job lived directly across the hall. At age sixteen Brian had won a Bronze Medal in the 200-Meter Breaststroke in Mexico City, and barely two weeks before we met he had shattered the world record in the 200-Meter Breaststroke by more than two seconds at a meet in L.A., concluding a freshman year in which he lowered an American mark every time he swam in a meet. Job, who pronounced his last name like the Old Testament sufferer, swam with a drive that seemed like destiny, given that he was built like a frog, with a short upper body, long lean legs, radically hyper-extended knees, and weird feet that splayed out at 180-degree angles. Two days after his world-record 200-Meters and just before school started, *Sports Illustrated* had run a lengthy profile of Brian, "The Impatience of Mrs. Job," detailing his childhood abuse at the hands of the ultimate poolside mother. When he broke the American record in the 100-Meter Breast, the reigning Olympic Gold Medalist in that event had looked up at him from his Silver podium spot and said, "You are crazy to swim that fast!" Later in life Brian would appear crazy to a lot of people, but when I knew him he was on his way to becoming Stanford's first dominant national swim champion, winning five individual titles over the next three years, while also completing a double engineering major (Electrical and Mechanical) that led to a Harvard M.B.A. and a life in early Silicon Valley start-ups.

"My dream is to put the breaststroke world records out of reach forever," Brian told me that fall as he passed me his red plastic bong, much like the one Olympic Gold Medalist Dick Roth had used two years earlier to turn on Stanford's new Swim Captain, Beta senior Fred Haywood, for the first time. There would be many an evening that quarter when I would loll on Job's king-size waterbed and watch his enormous tropical fish tank. And when I grew tired of that would amble down to the rabbit hutch of Brent "Stony" Berk, eighth in the 400 Free in Mexico, whose nickname said it all. Along with these Aquatic Betas came Terrestrial Newbies, among them gridiron mammal Eric Cross, a fleet-footed sophomore wide receiver who would score on a 61-yard punt return in Stanford's opening day upset of fourth-ranked Arkansas in Fayetteville. During an "away" win against Washington State that fall, Eric would be cruising down the sidelines towards a sure TD when a drunken fan stumbled down from the stands to attempt an open field tackle. Eric pancaked the dude to complete his 24-yard score. Coach Ralston was the one who sounded cocky afterwards, boasting to the press that the intruder had landed the Cougar's "hardest hit of the day," but Eric was cooler about it: "The guy wanted a thrill," he told one journalist, sounding a bit like James Bond tugging at his cuffs, "and I didn't want to disappoint him." Police arrested the intruder; Cougar yell leaders passed porkpie hats through the home stands, collecting bail money for their "Twelfth Man," who would receive a game ball at a campus-wide pep rally held in his honor.

One new Beta who became a good friend was Pat Moore, to my knowledge the only Varsity football player in Stanford history to also letter in Volleyball. Seeing a sophomore Strong Safety with thighs the size of tree trunks "dig" for a ball on the hardwood floor of Maples Pavilion was well worth the price of admission. "Pimo," as he was known, was not especially fast or even very big – maybe six feet and 190 pounds soaking wet – but he more than made up for it with power, poise, and the most under-rated athletic gift: sheer coordination. Pat would earn a reputation that fall one of the team's hardest hitters and surest tacklers – a stone-cold run-stopper, which he would perform with a grin that could define the term "rascally." One night he told me how he came to The Farm as a heavily-recruited Quarterback from Mira Costa High School in Manhattan Beach, the beach volleyball capital of the world. "S.C.'s coaches told me, 'Come here, you'll be starting Quarterback in a Rose Bowl Game one day," Pimo told me as he passed over this sweet little pipe he had, adding, "We'll see who plays there this year..." Pat had the arm and the smarts to be a

Division I QB, but not the big frame to run the pro set at Stanford, plus there were six other freshman Quarterbacks recruited that year. So Coaches had shifted him to Defense, and later to Linebacker. The funny thing about all this was that football and volleyball weren't even Pat's best sports. As a switch-hitting high-school baseball Catcher, Pimo had hit for average and power, and he could throw a rope from Home Plate to Second Base while standing on his knees. The Montreal Expos drafted him out of high school, but Pat chose Stanford – a wise move, not least because two years later the Expos would draft another Southland high school Catcher, the future Hall of Famer Gary Carter, who would have been coming up behind him. The only reason Pat didn't play baseball on The Farm was because in his one meeting with long-time Farm Baseball Head Coach Ray Young, the man said some things that Pat considered a serious turn-off, Young being one of those Old School "you-can-do-that-but-not-on-my-team" type Coaches, a style that never sat well with any of the Jocks I called friend. @ @

Brian Job had a double major to keep him busy, and Pimo was a Psych major and Spanish minor who read widely, but there were other Betas who didn't qualify as your classic scholar-athlete types or "countercultural athletes of the spirit," either. I wasn't one to believe that because a guy transferred from a Junior College it automatically meant he wasn't bright or academically engaged, yet many of the New Beta football recruits were definitely assisted by Sixties-style Admissions policies that had set aside the time-honored Stanford cliché of the well-rounded Straight-A student body president type that had bored everyone for decades, in order to admit the occasional B-plus student who happened to have performed on violin at Carnegie Hall, or the 1250 SAT guy who had solo'ed a fifteen-foot Lido to Hawaii or invented some new electronic gadget, or the J.C. grad with decent Math scores who weighed an eighth of a ton and could run a sub-five 40. New Betas of this ilk included "Hollywood" Roger Cowan, a sweet, handsome, future 14th Round Pittsburgh Steelers draft pick, currently second on the depth chart behind star Defensive End Dave Tipton.

"Hollywood!" I would cry, "what's shakin', son? Slip me some skin!"

Roger would extend a flat palm the size of a 2' x 6,' which I would slap, as hard as I could. Then I would offer him mine. Hollywood would rear back his mighty paw as if he meant to wallop me into next week, only to decelerate at the very last instant and ever-so-lightly, ever-so-delicately, touch my palm with the tippy-tip-tip of one forefinger. Why did this always crack us up so much? Maybe because Hollywood was twice my size. Hollywood Rog didn't have an unlikable bone in his body, but the fact remained that Stanford football was in cahoots with Admissions to deepen its engagement with a practice that other Pac-8 teams had done for years. Stanford couldn't have dreamt of making it to the Rose Bowl in Pasadena without a bunch of these J.C. guys. @ @

Another Junior College transfer at the Beta House that fall I'll call "D." An under-sized Italian-American linebacker and special teams wrecking ball who lived next door to Job and directly across the hall from me, D trashed his knee early in the season but was refusing surgery, preferring to play in pain (and on pain killers) rather than miss Jim Plunkett's final season. Rumor had it that D's summer job was running stolen cars between L.A. and The City for the Mob, which was an internship remote from most notions of Stanford "timber." He and his gorgeous opera-singing Italian-American girlfriend used to screw for hours on his king-size waterbed. I got used to her screaming at the top of her lungs, or at least learned to turn my radio up loud.

One night I heard a soft persistent knocking on my door. It was D. He was sweating profusely. His face twitched as he shifted his weight from one foot to the other. I had no idea what he was on, but he had to be on something.

"You roll a good join'?" he asked me.

D and his football buddies, so hosed they couldn't roll a decent joint, or even pronounce one? This I had to see... So I followed D across the hall, where a recently-installed blacklight cast a psychedelic glow that always reminded me of the Men's Room at Winterland.

Inside D's room was Stanford's entire starting Defensive Line, the soon-to-be legendary "Thunder Chickens" – a moniker dreamt up by Defensive Tackle Pete Lazetich, who grew up in Montana knowing a motorcycle gang with that name. "U.S.C.'s defense was 'The Wild Bunch,' so I thought Stanford's defense should have a nickname, too," Laz told the press in his unforgettable baritone machine-gun patter.

"With Plunkett and the offense setting all those records, we were getting tired of just being called 'the defensive line.' The 'Thunder Chickens' were wild and reckless and ran all over the place, just like we do." A future first team All-American and second-round draft pick of the San Diego Chargers, Laz was in D's room that night, along with his St. Bernard puppy Bruno, who he sometime brought to practice. Everybody but the dog was practically pissing themselves laughing at one of Laz's monologues from the moment I walked in the room. Dave Tipton, a J.C. transfer and future fourth-round draft pick of the New York Giants, six-year N.F.L. veteran and Stanford assistant coach, who I had never met before that night, was laughing so hard tears were rolling down his cheeks, reminding me (somehow) of another of Laz's explanation of the origin of the name Thunder Chickens: "Tipton looks like a big chicken the way he runs around flailing his arms."

Junior Larry Butler was present and un-accounted for, too: an un-heralded 232-pound DT who was quietly leading the team in tackles, because teams preferred to run at him rather than Laz. Butler would stuff an S.C. drive on Fourth and Goal at the six-inch line before heading off to play for a while in the Canadian Football League. The final Thunder Chicken in D's room that night was Greg Sampson, the gentle giant I used to have oatmeal breakfasts with at Branner Hall. At six-five and however-much-he-weighed, Sampson was not only the biggest man in the room, he was also reputed to be the fastest.

"So I gather you guys need some help," I announced, then planted myself on the wooden frame of D's waterbed and proceeding to roll licorice-flavored joint after licorice-flavored joint from a half pound of weed that D had dumped in a record turntable cover.

Rolling joints for the Thunder Chickens! – Yeah! Now there's a tale to tell the (grown-up) grandkids! It was a little weird they couldn't quite roll their own, given that these four future professional athletes (five, counting D) were all accomplished renegades, defying their Coach Ralston (with an assist from the team manager) by wearing – are you ready for this? – non-regulation white shoes on game day, among other sordid delinquencies. With the exception of D, all of them were members of the fraternity whose brothers had shaved David Harris's head three years before. And now the Delta Tau Delta Thunder Chickens were getting toasted at the Beta House, on their way to a possible date with destiny at the Granddaddy of all bowl games!

That Delts would leave their Animal House for the Stoner Jock Beta House to get high was no surprise, but any stoner on campus could have told you that if you needed to score weed, you could always do it at the Butt Hutt. I had no idea where D copped his lids, but there had been a house explosion of recreational drug use, much of it attributable to the presence of an incoming sportsman who for obvious reasons shall remain nameless but who had created one of the largest marijuana distribution networks on campus, working with an M.O. that involved sending multiple couriers across the Mexican border with five suitcases and returning (un-inspected) with six. In this manner he was moving twenty-five pounds of excellent field-grown Central American marijuana a week, which he hid in the basement of a house he bought for that purpose in South Palo Alto. Major bulk sales were never handled on premises, but some of the proceeds were used to help prop up the Beta House's precarious finances, overseen by a Harvard-educated Stanford Law School R.A. who liked to toke up, too, along with his live-in Wellesley girlfriend, a graduate student in Native American studies who I would develop a mild crush on. Drug money also enabled us to send checks to the Beta's national organization in Ohio, with the tacit understanding that the fraternity that had produced Ken Kesey, Bob Haldeman, and more U.S. Supreme Court Justices than any other (nine) would turn a blind eye to our hippie ways.

"And they never ask where the money's coming from?" I asked my friend, a short-haired Econ major with a mousy girlfriend. He certainly didn't look like a prototypical hippie pot dealer, which he wasn't anyway. (He has been out of the business now for decades.)

"They have no idea where the money's coming from," my friend replied, wearing his usual poker face. "And they also can't seem to think of a reason to look a gift horse in the mouth. They probably think we're just a bunch of Stanford trust fund kids…" Bulk sales also helped to underwrite the latest round of Butt Hutt Nooners, which featured a band that included the younger brother of the recently-graduated Beta Olympic Silver Medalist Greg Buckingham, along with a lead singer named Stevie Nicks. These two graduates of nearby Menlo-Atherton High School would go on to become the cornerstones of Fleetwood Mac, but for now Stevie and Lindsey Buckingham were the heart of the Butt Hutt House Band, playing great music on our front steps during campus-wide parties you could hear from a half-mile away. Everyone and anyone was welcome to show up, dance how they felt, smoke a doob, pump a keg, or just roll around on the grass.

Strangers were constantly wandering into the Beta House to borrow rooms (pot, sex and psychedelics only), which was cool, or at least I never heard anybody complain about it, or about much of anything, for that matter. Equal parts Frat Rat Nest and Hippie Crash Pad, the Butt Hutt was one of the epicenters of a desire to do something that no Stanford football team had managed since the 9-2 squad of 1951, the year after I was born. Jim Plunkett could have gone Number One in the N.F.L. Draft the year before, and thought about doing so because his Dad had passed away recently and his family needed money. But Plunk was on a mission for his teammates and the school that had backed him through his cancer scare. This would be the last chance for the Class of '71 to avenge those two heart-breaking losses to U.S.C. and make it to a Rose Bowl Game in Pasadena. @ @

The victory I had stolen in Sacramento started my year on the good foot. Hard work had brought me back at least to where I had been the year before. Only thing was, several teammates had improved significantly while I was gone. Duncan was stronger in workouts than I had ever seen him, although he still didn't feel ready to compete in cross country. Don had become our most formidable teammate, and Arvid was nearly as strong as Kardong was. So no more showing up for workouts in a Speedo and a water polo cap for one "Bobby Coe." No more "running-as-meditation," either. Keeping up with the Kretzes, Kardongs and Macdonalds proved to be a daily challenge.

Training hard seemed harder now. There had been no team newsletters that summer, or none that I ever saw, only scuttlebutt about guys being ready to go. Brock, our two-time MVP, had been lost to graduation, and so was Chuck Menz. Jack Lawson, our fifth man at conference last year, was gone as well – not running anymore, I didn't know why, since my last contact with my freshman roustabout had been his letter to Cliveden months ago. I suspected he had de-commissioned himself over some combination of money problems and the general bummer that the campus scene had become for many. The Oregon Miler, George Watson and The Hulk had each fallen by the wayside, too. Only Arvid, Bernie and I remained from the "strong" Class of '72, along with Dave Whiteing, our gifted but enigmatic Southern Californian Quarter-Miler and Half-Miler, who never seemed to work very hard or get very far, but who had scholarship offers from U.C.L.A. and Tennessee out of high school and dropped a 1:51 Half-Mile on the U.C.L.A. track the previous spring.

The Monday after Sacramento, Coach strolled over to our golf course stretching area with a little surprise. "Instead of our usual five-by-One Miles at race pace, we're doing six today."

"Great, Coach!" I called out. "No problem! We'll dial it in!"

The guys who didn't know me yet lifted their heads and looked around, like, *wha?* "Get me the phone number," I heard one of the freshmen mutter. This talkative Papoose had arrived on campus from the San Fernando Valley in Southern California, claiming to have logged 150-mile weeks all summer and free-associating about "Ionesco's Ice Plant," referring to the French Absurdist playwright and a common plant from the fig-marigold family.

"It's going to get us all! We'll be running down the road and it'll reach out its tentacles and… and… *arggghhhh!!"*

"What did you say your name was?" I had asked. "Bernstein, you say? You're gonna fit right in here, Neil!" But something akin to this eggplant thing must have happened to him, because after competing with the Varsity a few times he would vanish mid-season, re-surfacing a year later as a full-time Bay Area Peace activist before moving to Israel to live on a radical kibbutz. Another new freshman "Indian" arrived straight from the Res: a Navaho, one of twenty-two Native Americans admitted under Stanford's newly-expanded definition of the nation's minorities, who never uttered a word in my presence and was gone before the season started. Without major freshman contributors and with Decker lost for the year, Don, Duncan, Arvid and I would need to stay healthy and Bernie and Brian Mittelstaedt would need to step up if we were to have even a prayer of being sent Back East to Nationals, which would be at William & Mary College in Virginia that year.

Six one-mile reps at race pace or faster: okay, got it. Hard Days like this were what we lived for, or so we told ourselves. Hard days like this one grounded us, hurt us, stretched and challenged us. And that day would be a Hard Day I would remember well more than four decades later. We banged out the first Mile in 4:51, which wasn't that fast, but quicker than my best time as a high school sophomore, and quick (or so I thought) for what we were gunning for that day. Don, Duncan, Arv and I ran together on a mile loop that circled back around without quite closing, which left us with an easy three-minute jog from the finish back to the starting line. We prided ourselves on keeping moving between reps, even when we felt like walking or resting, because it made us physically stronger, and mentally tougher. Mile Two: 4:53, same grouping. I thought today would be tough, but it was dawning on me that today might be murderous. Mile Three: another 4:51 for the top guys; 4:52 for me. I let the leaders slip away a bit because I didn't feel comfortable pushing up front with them. Not on that rep, anyway.

"You okay?" Arvid asked as we trotted back to the line.

"Sweat freely, Arv!" This was one of Coach Ralston's favorite instructions to the football team and probably not what Arvid was expecting from me, but he smiled back like he knew what I was talking about, even though I wasn't sure I did. Those three-minute jogs between the reps were starting to feel like ninety seconds tops.

Mile Four took 4:54, with me just behind the lead group again. I was hurting, but close. *Suck it up, Robert...* Mile Five: 4:52 – or rather, Don, Dunc and Arv ran 4:52. I let them get away from me completely until my pride kicked in and I boosted the last 150 yards to come in significantly behind the lead pack in 4:57. Coach Clark looked at me funny, and I shrugged back. A half-minute before that extra (sixth) rep, Don thought to cheer me up a little: "I was in the training room the other day... and Dave overheard me telling someone... where I'm from... and he said... 'The only good thing that ever came out of Seattle... was the I-5...'"

I was grinning like a fool when we got to the starting line, where damned if Don, Duncan and Arv didn't decide to hammer that last Mile. I wasn't sure know how hard they were trying, but I was basically going all-out to finish close behind the trio in 4:46.

This was one killer workout – add up the times and it was close to a national collegiate record for six miles, although of course we had those three-minute jogs between each mile – and I think we all felt pretty good about it. "Train, don't strain" didn't mean we didn't take it to the wall sometimes. A tough workout like this one was a confidence builder, part of how we measured ourselves, and what we claimed to live for: to be beaten with clubs. (Pre: "Somebody might beat me, but they'll have to bleed to do it.") What had become clear to me was that despite my stolen victory in Sacramento, I was still playing catch-up after missing spring Track, and I was game to try. But some afternoons it was all I could do to get back to the Beta House for Stella's dinner, some light reading and an early bed. I was in a brave new world in the fall of '70. It was exciting to be there, even if our training had never been tougher, and it seemed that along with the dues every one of us paid to be part of this club, I was paying a surcharge for Europe. @ @

Don Kardong was named Team Captain that year. This matter was never put to a discussion or a vote, but I had no problem with it, because the decision was the right one – a no-brainer, although the position was largely honorary. All-American Kardong's new-found strength wasn't the biggest surprise; the continuing maturation and emergence of Arvid Kretz was. Arv had always had the smoothest, most effortless running style of us all, including Don and Dunc. But it was this skinny dude's imperviousness to pain that truly astounded me. Before going abroad I had thought I "owned" Arv, because he had never beaten me when I was at full strength and because my upside was probably higher than his. But in truth Kretz had never been far behind me – and more importantly, he never stopped working. Arv was a truly relentless runner. ("I do not run like a man running aimlessly." I Corinthians, 9:26.) Don told me he and Arv had come back from a hard eighteen-mile road run last spring – "and Arv goes into the weight room and pumps iron for half an hour! The guy's an animal. An animal!!" You can't appreciate this joke if you didn't know Arv, a Born-Again Christian and mild-mannered music major. He reportedly played Sax, but I thought his instrument was the Bassoon.

One Wednesday that fall Arv said, "Bob, I'm stuck for a place to practice tomorrow. Any chance I could use your room at the Beta House?"

"Arv, absolutely! We double-reed players need to stick together! ((I had told Arv that I used to play Oboe in my junior high school band. My musical high point: learning the melody line to "My Favorite Things.") "So come on over at three! That's when The Hulk's picking me up for a run... Consider yourself warned..." Our Team Trickster The Hulk had yet to run so much as a step for the Varsity, as far as I knew, but he continued to log almost as many miles as we did. Running was what held The Hulk together, as I suppose it held me together, too..

I was sitting Indian-style on my platform bed a little after three, enjoying Arv's surprisingly fluent allegro – I asked "That's Bach, isn't it?" and Arv dipped his head "yes" without missing a note – when in skulked The Hulkster, dressed for a long run. Seeing Arvid on his big Bassoon, The Hulk's face lit up with a fiendish delight.

"Arvid my Man! On Bass-*ooooon!* Roll over, Johan Sebastian, and give John Coltrane the *news!*" Hulk's purposefully-retarded patter and Arvid's loud playing began to attract Betas from other rooms, and soon there were enough people to fill my small space, a few of them joining in Hulk's loud teasing. This Philistine Gangbang was stupid and mean, but Arvid didn't miss a note: kept right on blowing, fingers flying over the stops. I had to give it up to my teammate: Baroque or Go-For-Broke, Arvid Kretz had guts to spare – or as Don Kardong would comment decades later, "Arv's as tough as a bucket of nails."

"Everybody! Out of my room! No, not you, Arv! You stay! Just pull the door shut behind you when you leave. Hulk, you and I are going for a run, now!"

I'd like to share a life lesson here, something I picked up in college: nothing earns respect like performance. You wouldn't catch me making fun of or under-estimating Arvid Kretz again – especially not during an additional Mile rep on Monday or a Thousand on Thursday, when it was all I could do to stay up with him as he cruised alongside Don with little visible effort, while I stayed back in the hurt locker, not coming out anytime soon. Maybe it was the individuals Stanford tended to attract, but our cross country team always had room for anybody with talent and the willingness to commit himself to excellence, including the likes of me. I guess I wasn't as special as I used to think I was. My teammates were an awesome bunch of guys. @ @

The Saturday after Sac State, the S.C. Trojans and the San Jose State Spartans journeyed north to challenge us on our home turf. Trojans, Spartans and Athenians lined up and away we went! The pace felt quick from the get-go. I struggled along just behind the lead pack, hanging tough until the four-mile mark on the long downhill, at which point I could only watch as Don, Arv and San Jose's Gary Hanson (90 seconds behind me at Sac State the week before) pulled steadily away. The *Daily* would publish my picture on the sports page on Monday, crossing the finish line in a time of 29:51, the same time that had won the U.C.L.A. meet my sophomore year, when I finished second. In the *Daily* picture I am wearing a very cool pair of green Italian racing spikes that Duncan had given me, since they never fit him right. My eyes are half-closed and mouth agape in the upside-down hawk moon that Pre and Lindgren had worn at the close of the '69 Pac-8 meet. I look relaxed and strong, but pain is etched on my face. Looking at this picture today reminds me how much that race hurt, much of the pain coming from holding off the Spartan visible just over my shoulder, but also because I was finishing behind two teammates for the second time in my college career. And then there was the *Daily* picture caption: "ONE-TWO FINISH – Don Kardong and Arvid Kretz are seen finishing together in last weekend's win over U.S.C. and San Jose State."

Wouldn't you know it? My first picture in the student newspaper came out mis-captioned. (Some stoned paste-up editor's handiwork, no doubt.) What they had meant to show was Don and Arv tying for first place in 29:31, two seconds faster than my Pac-8 PR and twenty seconds – more than 100 yards – ahead of me. I took what comfort I could from our team results: Stanford 24, U.S.C. 46, San Jose State 56. Coach gathered us for a brief pow-wow immediately after the race, and after distributing praise to Mittelstaedt and Macdonald, for finishing eighth and ninth, got to the heart of things.

"We have a tough re-match coming up next week against the Bruins in L.A.," Coach said. "They graduated four of their top five runners from the team that beat us last year, but they've had a major influx of J.C. talent that's left them potentially stronger than before. Last week their top two men both broke Berkeley's course record. They've also competed two more times this year than we have, so they have more of a racing edge, but we have more experience overall. This will be a major test of where we stand, fellows. So good work today. Let's keep it rolling." @ @

Yes, let's keep it rolling. This was shaping up to be my most challenging season yet, even tougher than the season before. I wasn't running badly, but since I was no longer our top man, I felt like I was. I was third man on one of the best college cross-country teams in the nation, and if Duncan ever stepped up the way we all knew he could, I could well become our fourth. I should have anticipated this, in fact. Kardong's good but not great cross-country season the year before could be attributed to his having spent spring track in England, as I had done. He and Arvid had fine spring track campaigns to build on. So "Be Patient." The important thing to remember was that talent doesn't go away. The important thing I had to do was to keep working and not get carried away by losing. The upcoming U.C.L.A. meet would be a good test for me and for the team, and we felt ready for the challenge. This would also be the first time my grandparents would see me race and their first glimpse of me since Europe, where the world had been blown wide open and I had seen eternity in a flower.

The Westwood side of my family turned out in force, despite their lack of serious interest in running or sports of any kind. My Grandfather brought along his Rolleicord and 16-mm Bolex movie camera to record what would become the only moving images I possess of my days as a college distance runner. Decades later, this footage of the Stanford-U.C.L.A. cross country dual meet of 1970 would be collected and stored in American Academy of Motion Picture Arts & Sciences, along with my grandfather's entire home movie collection, in museum-quality facilities in Hollywood. (You can't make this stuff up.) Seeing DVD images for the first time in decades, in the course of writing this book, I was astonished to see our names on the back of our red road singlets: "KARDONG," "KRETZ" and "COE" are legible across our backs and shoulders: a detail otherwise totally forgotten. (MACDONALD you never see, although he ran that day.) Underneath Don's name is a hand-made, safety-pinned name tag, reading "MYSTERY MAN." An L.A. newspaper had referred to him as the "Mystery Man" left uncounted at the close of the Westwood meet in '68, so Coach Clark's wife had made Don this humorous badge for race day in Westwood.

My grandfather's film reminds me of the cool, hazy ocean fog that lingered over the U.C.L.A. course that morning. It was a classic day for cross-country racing. I see Don and Coach grinning fiercely at one another for a moment, sharing some private joke, which reminds me of how Coach scrunched his nose when he laughed, and the skinny, nondescript ties and narrow-lapelled sports jackets to meets – more details otherwise quite forgotten. I see Arvid, behind Coach and Don, trip slightly while stripping off his warm-up pants; I see Mittelstaedt, Neil Bernstein and our seventh man, tall, blonde sophomore Peter Fitzmaurice. In a moment I walk into the frame, unaware that I am being filmed, carrying my sweats to the team pile, look over, see my grandfather, and do a double-take, then smile warmly into the camera.

I remember exactly what I was thinking at that moment: "Granddad and his Movie Camera." For my whole life, and my mother's, too, my grandfather had been taking pictures of us all. It was two minutes before race time, but I do not look at all annoyed by this small break in my concentration. My movements are relaxed and efficient. I look like a young man in his element, which I was. @ @

Stanford and U.C.L.A. harriers hover that day above a white chalk line. Smoke appears from the muzzle of the starter's gun (this is a silent film as A/V video cameras were barely getting started) and off we go in a pack. My grandfather was already failing at age seventy-two, so some of the images are shaky and un-centered, but he manages to catch a few seconds of me and a Bruin running shoulder-to-shoulder, leading the field through a first pass across the starting line, the rest of the field strung out close behind. (Although beaten by teammates last week, I was running in front because I felt like it, and because my family was watching.) I see Decker in civilian garb – he had flown south for the meet – pounding his crutches into the earth and shouting encouragement as we hurtle by. While the racers leave the soccer field for the tough half-mile climb on Sunset Boulevard, my grandfather takes pictures of my grandmother and her toy poodle, Pierre; my sister and her new husband, the ex-Stanford Half-Miler; my Aunt and Uncle and my two youngest first cousins: all of these images preserved in museum-quality archives at the Academy of Motion Picture Arts and

Sciences.

Far from the camera's eye, the racers are finishing our second pass up Sunset, arriving at the crest of a hill and a patch of dirt where Don and Arv commit a perfect execution of elementary cross-country strategy: they push hard just before the crest and just after it, taking psychological advantage of moments when competitors might be inclined to slack off after their arduous climb. I tried to go with them and in doing so separated myself from the rest of the field, but I couldn't keep up with Don and Arv and had to run on alone, unseen, pain-wracked, along a stretch of downhill grass on the far western edge of campus, still miles from the starting line. Cars rolled by on the street, drivers slowing down to stare at me, clueless that I was in the middle of a tough six-mile Pac-8 Conference dual-meet competition. As I watched Kardong and Kretz run round a corner out of sight, I had a stray thought about the great-grandfather I never knew, the late State Fair President and Trustee of the University of California who I was named after, and who was said to be most responsible for building the "Southern Campus" in West L.A. instead of Palos Verdes. Thank god he did, because the hills there would have been murderous.

The last images my grandfather took of the race show me covering the final twenty yards at a noticeably-slower tempo than when last seen. I finish seven seconds behind Don and fourteen behind Arvid, who won his first-ever intercollegiate cross-country race. My time over that tough 5.7-mile course (30:06) was ten seconds ahead of U.C.L.A.s Neil Sybert, one of the two Bruins who destroyed Cal's home course record two weeks before. All four of us broke the old course record set by Tarry Harrison of the Southern California Striders, who would run a super-fast Three-Mile at the A.A.U. Track Championship that spring. Duncan finished fifth, only thirteen seconds behind me. We hammered U.C.L.A. 21-34 on their home turf, a year after they squeaked past us by a single point on ours. "Stanford was not expected to defeat the Bruins by such a wide margin," the *Daily* later reported, "and the UCLA coach even expressed confidence before the meet. 'I feel that the top five runners on this year's team are as good as any top five I have had in the past,' claimed Coach Jim Bush. Even in defeat, the UCLA coach would not fault his runners. 'All our boys improved their times in this meet and one [Neil Sybert] broke our course record. Yet, we still were beaten in every way possible.'" The prize we took home to Palo Alto was not just our victory and revenge, but also our honor, which embraced our foes: we made a point of not doing an Indian war dance over how we had just pissed on their campfire, unlike the Bruins, who had desecrated our sacred burial ground with their celebration the year before.

My grandfather's film preserves a few seconds of my cool-down. I look stiff after our punishing race, but otherwise resemble one of those elite runners you see on TV. It astonishes me, all these years later, to be reminded of how physically adapted I was for racing long distances. After my cool-down I submitted to the usual family portraiture, squinting in the soft Southern California sunlight, the sweat on my face and body glistening like some rare oil. I was not overly-impressed with my third-place finish, even if I was under the old course record. But I was curious what my family's reaction would be. There appeared to be none. My brother-in-law, who was at U.C.L.A. Medical School now, had a few things to say, being a former Stanford runner himself, but nobody else said a word to me about what I had just done. They talked about other matters instead. I didn't let on how hurt I was by this non-response. It hurt me because I thought it implied: you didn't win; why are you bothering? I had beaten all the Bruins, just as I had defeated all of the Trojans the week before. On any given Saturday I probably could have out-raced any college distance runner in Southern California. But this wasn't on my mother's family's radar. Not the way Europe was. My grandfather didn't have an athletic bone in his body. Or maybe my West L.A. family just didn't know what to say. @ @

My father knew better – and my stepmother, too, who supported my running and thought I ran beautifully, although she could never bear to watch me compete. My father and I had never had a conversation about my aspirations in my sport, but I knew he knew I was within shouting distance of a Mile time that people had thought impossible back in the days when he spent a semester in medical school, just after my mother's death. My Dad had been a college athlete, too: a three-year letterman in the pool at Wesleyan, fifth in the 100-yard Back in the New England Championships his senior year. My mother had been an even better pool athlete. All my life I had read about her exploits, collected by my grandfather from local sports and metro sections and pasted into bulging scrapbooks. She had been a Southern California A.A.U. champion as a diver and as a breaststroker, trained by a former U.S. Olympian springboard specialist at the Los Angeles Athletic Club in Downtown L.A. She had also been a Junior Pacific Coast Fencing Champion, a fact my father didn't know about until he read their engagement notice in the *L.A. Times*. Early in their courtship he had thought to impress the co-ed he was dating by challenging her to a race in Lake Lag. He was surprised when he had to push to beat her. In one of the few conversations he and I ever had about my mother, he told me she had only survived her car accident for twelve hours because her heart had refused to stop beating. "You inherited your cardiovascular capabilities from her," he told me.

Sports were not deep in my family mythology, but I was no heretic. I inherited my Mitochondrial DNA from my mother. My will to run was in my heart, a part of who I was. "For Stanford I Will." @ @

Two more weeks of training on The Farm: Mondays on the Golf Course, Tuesdays on the soccer field, Wednesdays on the Roads, and Thursdays back on the soccer field for those punishing Thousands. We had been scheduled to compete in the Pacific A.A.U. Championships in San Francisco, but Coach gave us a bye. Cal was next, in Berkeley, and I was nearing the end of an easy seven-mile run the Friday before the Big Cross Country Meet, breezing along a dirt path that I almost never ran near the Leland Stanford Jr. Mausoleum, the tomb of our university's namesake who had died of typhoid fever at the age of fifteen, the summer before he was to have entered college, and whose death inspired his parents to build our school in their son's memory. I was thinking about where I might go for dinner that night and some reading I needed to finish over the weekend for my Humanities

Seminar – "Humanities and the Social Sciences."

Out of nowhere I felt a sharp pain in the inside of my right knee.

I ran another hundred yards, but the pain didn't go away.

I walked for a few seconds and shook out my legs. When I tried to resume running, my knee hurt so much I couldn't even jog. I had to walk back to the locker room. The next morning – the morning of the Big Cross Country Meet – I climbed out of bed and couldn't even bend my knee without a deep, dull ache or a searing, knife-like pain. I called Coach at his home phone with the news. Our conversation lasted twenty seconds.

The Cal meet went on without me – a close Stanford victory, with Don beating Cliff West by twenty seconds, followed by Bernie in third place and Mittelstaedt coming on strong in fifth. When my knee felt no better on Monday, Dave the Trainer set up a Wednesday office visit with Stanford's team orthopedist, Dr. Fred Behling from the Palo Alto Medical Clinic, who also worked with the San Francisco Forty-Niners (and later wrote the letter that kept Kauf out of the Draft.)

"It's tendonitis in a spot that won't take a shot of cortisone," Behling told me. "You're just going to have to ice it every day and wait until the pain goes away."

"When will I be able to run again?"

"Time will tell, not me. I'm sorry, son."

I went straight to Coach Clark's office with the news. We stared at one another for a second or two, then spoke of other things. We both knew that the timing of this injury couldn't be any worse. The biggest meet of the year, the only meet that mattered – the conference championship in Pullman, Washington – was barely thirteen days away.

I briefly asked myself again if my countercultural involvements had anything to do with this, and immediately decided no, at least not in any direct fashion. I had never missed a workout because I was stoned and I had never shown up at a workout stoned; I had run stoned a couple of times alone in England, and I didn't like it. It was true that our workouts had become daily tests of our mantra of "Train don't strain," and that this could be the result of trying too hard to catch up after my European hiatus. Every explanation I could think of – from "stuff happens" to some deeper underlying physical issue related to my lumbar fusion – passed through my mind. But in the end there was no explaining what had happened to me with any certainty at all.

I gave myself a few days of complete rest before phoning Coach to ask for a solo workout, just the two of us. The plan was to try some quick 330s on the soccer field grass. I went to the starting line after barely warming up. Coach held his clipboard in one hand and lifted his stopwatch with the other: "Ready... *go*..."

I didn't make it fifty yards. I walked back to where Coach stood, still with stopwatch in hand, having already made up my mind.

"I'll find a way to run, Coach. I'll be on the starting line in Pullman. Count on it."

Coach and I both knew but declined to state the obvious: if I didn't show up for the Conference Meet, our hugely-talented but threadbare squad didn't have a prayer of making it back to Nationals. Short of death, there was no way I wouldn't be running in Pullman. Like D, I did not think I was being a hero. I was just being part of a team. @ @

November 14th, 1970 was the day a plane crashed in West Virginia, claiming the lives of thirty-seven members of the Marshall University "Thundering Herd" football team, eight members of the coaching staff, and twenty-five supporters. It was also the day our Cross-Country team woke up in an ice-box of a motel in eastern Washington State, in the heart of the ice-bound gloom of a barren, rolling plain swept by unremitting wind and cold and known as "The Palouse." "'The Curse of the Palouse,'" Northwest native Kardong told me in one of our freezing motel rooms. "This is where visiting football teams come to die." Stanford hadn't won a football game in Pullman since 1956, and hadn't won one there that year, either, because a suspected springtime arson had damaged the stadium sufficiently that the Stanford game against the Cougars had to be played in Spokane, where Eric Cross crushed the drunken civilian, Jim Plunkett broke the N.C.A.A. passing mark for career yardage, and the Indians destroyed Washington State, 63-16. A month later, temperatures in Pullman were close to freezing, and the howling sleet on the Washington State University Golf Course drilled through our nylon outerwear to the very marrow of our bones. We would be competing under conditions outrageous to contemplate on two legs, much less one. I had no business racing six miles that morning – no business except team business. I had to do some kind of warm-up, so I forced myself to run three hundred yards on the frozen, rock-hard turf, limping heavily. I had a strong hunch that the blustery cold (35 degrees at race time) would numb the pain soon enough. But pain was the least of my problems. Fifteen days of lost training was a far graver matter. This race in Pullman would be the toughest race of my life – not just physically but emotionally, because I knew I couldn't perform anywhere near the level of which I was capable.

Yet there I stood on the line and at the crack of the starter's pistol set off with the rest (sort of), running into a howling wind and driving, icy rain, which made me forget my knee almost immediately, even though my limp never went away. I remember almost nothing about this race except the pain, the hard sleet on my face, the numbness of my half-frozen limbs, and the deceptively-steep hills of glacial dust that never stopped coming. Seven months earlier almost to the day I had been running naked on a beach on the Costa Blanca – now *the Palouse?* Pre won handily in 30:11.7, a slow time in challenging weather for a teenager who had run the fastest Three-Mile in the world and the best by an American in two years when he won the N.C.A.A. Track Championship race in Iowa last June. Oregon State's Keith Munson was second, fifteen seconds behind. "I knew the course today, but it didn't make it easy," Pre told the press. "It was colder today [than at the Northern Division race earlier that year, when he ran twenty-five seconds faster on the same course] – too cold. My lungs are burning."

Don Kardong came through seventh in 31:19, over a minute behind

Pre, after another side ache claimed him mid-race. Arvid finished eighth in 31:27 and Duncan ninth in 31:28 – the first time Duncan ever showed up big at a distance longer than a Mile. I was Stanford's fourth man in 17th place, 27 seconds behind Duncan – somehow managing to defeat thirty Pac-8 runners, one second behind Pre's Oregon roommate Pat Tyson and U.C.L.A.'s Ruben Chappins, a two-time California State High School Two-Mile Champion who would finish third in this meet a year from now. Our fifth man was Bernie, in 25th, leaving us with 66 points, which was twenty points better than our third-place finish the year before. But Northwest powerhouses Oregon (43) and Washington State (58) were once again one-two, with us in our familiar third spot. Fortunately for my conscience, my bum knee wasn't what sunk us. If pigs could fly and I had beaten Pre, we still wouldn't have won the meet. If I had been healthy and run with our top trio, we still would have finished third, but by a single point. The only reason we were third was because I showed up. If I hadn't, Oregon State 13 points behind us would have grabbed the third spot, leaving us in fourth, meaning that I had taken a bullet to move our team up one notch, at the end of a very long season that had promised a great deal more. Early in the year U.S.C. and U.C.L.A. had been given shots at second and third in the Pac-8 behind Oregon, but with the exception of Stanford, California cratered in the frozen north: Washington finished fifth, leaving our three southern rivals to fill out the cellar, with Cliff West the top Golden Bear, buried in 37th. @ @

Attempting to disembark from our plane in San Francisco, I discovered my knee had frozen at a twenty-degree angle during the flight and wouldn't bear any weight. I was alternately hopping and hobbling down the airport terminal when Don and Arvid ducked under my arms and without a word began half-carrying me to baggage claim. Pogo-ing slowly down the long terminal hallway, we suddenly found ourselves face to face with Coach Jordan, who was standing not six feet away. He had accompanied us to Pullman, but out of respect for Coach Clark (I was guessing on this one, because I wasn't sure) he had never addressed us as a group.

"Hey, Coach," I said. I enunciated clearly. It was impossible that he didn't hear my hello. But he looked straight through me as if I wasn't there, turned and walked right on by.

"Wow," I muttered to Don and Arv. "No 'You ran tough, Bobby?'"

"Let it go," Kardong muttered, and we continued our gimp towards baggage claim.

As I thought about this snub later – and it was a snub – I decided that Coach Jordan had seen enough of me to know that I wasn't one of his "boys." Or maybe he snubbed me because if you don't show up on Championship Day, no matter what the reason, it's your fault. Or maybe he snubbed me because the Anointed One of two years ago was nothing now but a crippled loser. That sounded harsh, but the fact remained that one of Jordan's Indian Braves had just dragged his wounded knee six miles through a raging ice storm, and it didn't seem to matter to him. He beatified his "boys" who "taped it up" after a superficial spike wound and ran tough against a bunch of junior college scrubs, but that day at the airport he might have spared even a ray of his legendary sunshine to help us recover from our failed enterprise and shattered season. I knew I would never be able to disregard Jordan entirely, but I made a silent vow that day never to enjoy his admiration again. And yet I also knew, pathetic as it may sound, that underneath my anger and disdain I still wanted his approval as a validation of the runner I still hoped to become in the eyes of the world. @ @

The Athletic Department declined to send our cross-country team to Nationals for a second straight year, but Coach, Don and Arv did travel to Williamsburg, where Arvid tanked but Don produced the first great race of his early career, completing six miles over the flat-as-a-pancake Virginia course without a side stitch, just ten seconds behind Pre and two seconds behind future Irish Olympian Donal Walsh of Villanova. Don actually caught the Duck at four miles, where Pre glanced around, saw who it was, and brought the hammer down. Pre's first place finish (in 28:00 flat) led Oregon to an apparent 86-88 upset of Villanova, with pre-race favorite U.T.E.P. a distant third. The

University of Oregon team had already left for the airport when Villanova's fifth man, who had slipped and fallen in the chute, noticed that several runners who he knew he had beaten were listed ahead of him in the scoring. Villanova filed a protest and a determination was eventually made that Villanova's fifth runner had indeed finished 62nd, not 67th, giving the top spot to the Wildcats, 85-86: its fourth national championship in five years. Bowerman would file a protest of his own, but to no avail. (You can look it up: to this day Oregon claims they won that title on goducks.com.) Don would produce another great race five days later, finishing third in the A.A.U. Cross-Country Championship in Chicago behind two future Olympians, Frank Shorter and Jack Bachelor, post-collegiate training partners in Florida.

Running Man, meanwhile, lay stretched out on his bed at the Beta House, icing his knee and reading Thomas Hardy's *Jude the Obscure*. @ @ @

THE ROSE BOWL, STANFORD V. OHIO STATE, 1971

Coach Clark always told us "consistency is key," and my knee injury had stolen mine. I wrote my grandparents three days after Pullman, putting a hollow spin on my disaster: "I'm very tired of running, so the enforced layoff with this knee – it's really bad now – should be good. I'll be starting from scratch on my conditioning, though." And that was a big problem. Being unable to run was nothing less than a shocking affront to who I was. After surrendering my sophomore Track season to Europe, I might now be playing catch-up for the rest of my junior year! My college career could be three-quarters over before I had run even a step for Varsity Track! Bill Bowerman always told his runners that how they handled adversity would eventually correlate closely to their success or failure, and I believed this, too. What a champion does when he gets kicked in the teeth is step up his game. So like most Jocks who journeyed through the Home of Champions would have to do at some point in their time, I sidetracked myself into the Valley of the Shadow of Dave's Animal Kingdom.

That was what I had taken to calling the Training Room during my many visits there to ice my aching Achilles. Dave's Animal Kingdom had no staff of forty – that would be a twenty-first century innovation. The Stanford Training Room in 1970 was basically Dave and his assistant Scotty, a very cool guy who had come up with Kauf's "Al Green" alias at the Monterrey rugby tournament and saved Kauf from the ire of the Paytriot. Everybody liked Scotty, but Dave – Dave was another story. Ever since he decided to kiss my keister so I wouldn't rat him out to the Athletic Department for hitting me during my second week on campus, Dave's behavior towards me had seldom been anything less than respectful. I could have owned Dave, and I think we both knew it. But I also needed him to get me running again, right now, so I continued to consider us square.

On my first day in rehab Dave gave me my orders above the roar of his Jacuzzis: "Injured runners put on weight!! So if you don't want to turn into a big fat pig, cut back on your eating, Coe!! Otherwise I want you here every afternoon, five days a week, but only after you freeze your nuts off in the pool to keep your cardiovascular system –"

"But Dave, swimming in the pool is no *fun!* That water's so *cold!*

"Who's talking about *fun* here, Coe?" (Dave completely missed that I was making a joke.) "After the pool I want you here in my training room to ice your knee for an hour, then in my hot tub!! Got it?"

I shared Dave's oval bastion of tin often that late fall with a back-up 230-pound Defensive Tackle with a bad ankle and, as it happened, a major similar to mine.

"What are you reading?" he asked one afternoon.

"Samuel Richardson's *Clarissa!*" I waved the paperback above the rising steam. "For Dick Scowcroft's 'Introduction to the Novel' class!"

"You're takin' Skowcroft? I took Ian Watt's 'History of the Novel' last quarter! We didn't read *Clarissa,* but I dug *Tom Jones.* Henry Fielding and Richardson had this rivalry thing goin', didn't they?"

"So I hear! I'm reading dozens of novels this quarter! I'm making up my own major in the Humanities Special Program! I call it 'The Modern Novel!' Which is kind of an oxymoron, right? Like 'Military Intelligence?'"

"Or 'Jumbo Shrimp!" the hurt DT chuckled heartily.

"I mean there's no such thing as an 'Ancient Novel,' right?" Except

251

maybe *The Odyssey*... By having this major means I get to cherry-pick courses in the English, French, German, and Slavic language departments – in translation, of course – which is perfect," I said, thinking how pleasant it was to spiel another Jock who cared about this stuff, "because I'm mostly interested in the Continental Novel –"

"You! "Up! Out of the tub! Not you, Coe. The chubby one. Yes, you! Up. Out. Time for treatment." I had seen Dave's "water therapy" before. Dave would order a football player twice his size to strip and step into a tile shower so that all five-feet, four-inches of Dave (or however short he was) could aim an ice-cold, rock-hard jet of water on the player's injured parts, while the victim gripped the pipes in agony. Kidneys, Buttocks and Hamstrings were his favorite targets.

"Dave's Closet of Horrors!" I shouted above the roar of Dave's jet and the Jacuzzi. I know Dave heard me because he rolled his eyes, delicately re-crossed his nymph-like ankles and ever-so-casually re-trained his powerful jet on the Gluteus Maximus of my DT friend, who grabbed a section of pipe and tried not to scream out loud. I shouted louder: "I ask you, Dave, what is a runner who can't run, or a football player who can't hit people? I'll tell you what they are, Dave! They're lost souls! And so they come to you! To Stanford's Shaman Healer!"

"Shut the fuck up Coe," growled Dave, who spent half his life annoyed, a third being an asshole, and the rest taking care of Stanford Jocks in any fashion he deemed appropriate.

"Here in the Land of Broken Toys!" my DT friend yelled over his shoulder. "Hey Dave! Watch the nuts!"

"Dave! I thought you said he had a bad ankle?"

"Stay out of this, Coe! This guy's banged up all over..." With swelling annoyance: "Why don't you just mind your own fucking business!"

"Oh Dave, you're nothing but a big... blustery..." I was about to say "bully," or maybe "baby," but cut myself short. I would give Dave this much: the man was wholly committed to his work. And yet regardless of the race of the victim, Dave with his water cannon always reminded me of Sheriff "Bull" Connor of Birmingham, Alabama, assaulting black demonstrators with a fire hose. I knew this wasn't fair, but I didn't mind being unfair to Dave the Trainer. @ @

Spending as much time in the training room as I did, I got to watch Dave run Dave's Ticket Scam. Football players would drop by and hand over their player comps, which Dave would funnel to wealthy alumni in a manner I never discovered. Never kept written records, or at least I never saw a scrap of paper; did it all by memory, like a good numbers runner. The best seats in the L.A. Coliseum could go for fifty dollars a pop, serious coin in those days. I couldn't count the number of times I saw Dave dig into his starched white pants, pull out a wad of twenties, lick his thumb and start forking cash into players' open palms.

"You gave me four tickets, right? Here's your two hundred," Dave would say, counting off crisp new bills. If the N.C.A.A. ever got wind of this little scam, sanctions would have ended Stanford's best shot at a Rose Bowl Game since 1952, when the Tribe played in the first-ever nationally-televised college football game. Dave's Ticket Scam might have effected Plunkett's N.C.A.A. total offense record and his potential Heisman Trophy-winning season, a candidacy which "Voice of the Indians" Bob Murphy would later brag about spending only $179 to promote, while Ole Miss cranked out bumper stickers, handbills, recordings of "The Ballad of Archie Who" and an "Archie" doll to promote the candidacy of their QB, Archie Manning, and the Notre Dame Athletic Department had their candidate Joe Theismann change the pronunciation of his name from *THEEZ*-man to abet his HIZE-man cause. Dave's Ticket Scam would probably not have cost Plunkett his school-record 96-yard scoring bomb to J.C. Transfer Randy Vataha against Washington State, but it would not have mattered as much without the Rose Bowl at stake. Dave should not be given all the blame, or all the credit, either, for providing this financial service for friends of mine, even if it was against "The Rules," because whose "Rules" were we talking about here? The N.C.A.A.'s, but not our Athletic Department's, which had to have known about Dave's Ticket Scam, or Dave wouldn't have risked his job. What was actually more interesting than Dave's rinky-dink little kickback to players and a handful of incidents in which the Athletic Department rescued athletes in trouble with The Law – like the time some Delts got caught ripping off a black lawn jockey from the local Hyatt, or a certain Beta football star got caught red-handed with a warehouse full of property stolen from the university food service, or the Atherton physician the Athletic Department kept on tap to write letters to the Selective Service to keep its stars out of the Draft (non-college kids had no such recourse) – Stanford ran a more-or-less squeaky-clean athletic program.

To the best of my knowledge, Performance Enhancing Drugs had not yet touched Stanford's athletic programs at all. PEDs were new in the lexicon of sports. Olympic drug testing was employed for the first time in Mexico City, where Coach Jordan had been a vocal and sincere opponent of drug use (an honest-to-god believer in those "precious bodily fluids.") But testing methods were crude, and rumors of abuse by major U.S. stars were rampant, although without any hard evidence to back them up. Stanford Quarter-Miler Jim Ward, Jordan's 1968 Track Team Captain, would claim that all six runners who finished ahead of him in the N.C.A.A. 400-Meter Championship Final in '67 were doping, and that his friends at U.S.C. and U.C.L.A. were given PEDs like candy in training room dispensaries. Maybe there were scenes at Stanford that I didn't know about, but in an era that introduced a number of innovative approaches to training, encompassing not only drugs but also the human potential movement, I saw evidence of neither in Dave's Animal Kingdom – and if there was any other serious monkey business going on, I was pretty sure I would have heard about it. Except for Scotty, the Stanford Training Room was about as retrograde a place as you could find on campus in 1970.

I was also a tool to keep athletes in their place, as training rooms had been for generations. Ralston didn't like players injured, but he also didn't like long hair, so when shaggy All-Conference Offensive Tackle Steve Jubb hurt his ankle playing rugby in the off-season, Dave refused to treat him until he shed his offending locks. A smart way to treat the person defending your Heisman Trophy Candidate's blind side, don't you think? There was no denying that Dave was a douche, but when all was said and done he and Scotty did have a knack for getting people back in the Game. Or as Dave so eloquently informed an ailing linebacker he suspected of malingering: "Get the fuck up and go to practice! You can't make the club if you're in the tub!!" @ @

I followed Dave in everything. I "froze my nuts off" swimming in the team outdoor pool for an hour a day – definitely not fun – then sat becalmed in the roiling waters of Dave's Jacuzzi before icing my knee at either Dave's Animal Kingdom or the Butt Hutt. Six weeks later, almost to the day, I woke up one morning and poof: my joint was better. I could run totally free of discomfort, as if nothing had happened to me at all. On my third day back into running, I showed up for my first official workout in the Stadium since freshman year and almost before anyone knew I was there went through a quarter-mile in 51-flat on a 500-yard time trial. That was the fastest 440 I had ever run from a standing start, and I had maintained the pace another 60 yards.

"Holy Catfish, Coach!" I exclaimed to Coach Clark. "How do you figure? I barely run at all for two months – don't run a step for six weeks, other than Pullman – then I train for three days and run a Quarter in 51-flat? And keep right on going for another sixty yards? What's with that???"

"You've clearly done all the right things," said Coach, who stared at his stopwatch for several seconds, as surprised by my time as I was.

A week later, shortly after my last final exam and just before the Christmas holiday, I woke up with a low-grade fever and fatigue so intense I could barely stand. Feeling the swollen glands in my neck, I feared the worst. Dragging myself to the Health Center, I had my self-diagnosis confirmed: I had Mononucleosis! Kissing Disease! The same illness that had caught up with Jim Ryun before the '68 Olympics!

I got myself to the airport that afternoon and flew to LAX, headed south to San Clemente and slept for seventeen straight hours in my grandparent's guest room. When I woke up I phoned Coach Clark with the bad news. Then I phoned Decker.

"Can you believe this, Deck? Recovering from Mono can take months! What did I do to deserve this?"

"Whoa whoa whoa... Wrong question, Robert! You didn't call me to talk about what you *deserve*, did you?"

"You're right, Decker! Wrong question –"

"The wheels of karma are constantly turning –!"

"But still, I worked so hard and sacrificed so much to get back! How can I help feeling that the gods must be angry?"

"The *gods?* I don't think the gods give a rat's ass what happens to us..."

I didn't entirely agree with that last remark, but I took his point. I had no choice but to lash myself to the mast (like Odysseus did) and stay the course, whether the gods cared a fig or not. I had been inhaling fat Russian novels that fall quarter, from Dostoevsky to Pasternak. Finishing *The Brothers Karamazov* at the Beta House, where I still lived, too lazy or pre-occupied to take steps to move elsewhere, I went back to page one and started over. But I didn't have to inhale fat Russian novels to know that "Stuff Happens." What else can you say when the fickle finger of fate pokes you in the eye? I had never thought that life was meant to unfold according to some grand design, or that every disaster could be averted – some things *can* be prevented, but I had no idea what I could have done to prevent Mono, since I didn't know how, when or where I got it. All I knew was that my junior year was now ass over tea kettle, and what kept running through my head were a couple of songs: first Donovan's "Season of the Witch," because I was the *"rabbit running in the ditch."* And also Albert King's great "Born Under a Bad Sign," in Cream's version from their "Wheels of Fire" album: *"If it wasn't for bad luck, I wouldn't have no luck at all..."* @ @

Great things were happening in the Stanford Athletic Department, just not to me. If you cared about college football, you had to be fascinated by the Stanford Indians of 1970. Head Coach Ralston had refined a pro-style passing game at a time when practically every college team in the country still used an option offense. From that opening road win against fourth-ranked Arkansas – the only football contest I remember discussing with Coach Clark, both of us laughing ourselves silly about the moment on TV when workhorse fullback Hillary Shockley (three TDs, 119 yards) had to be lifted off the turf by his teammates following his 43-yard touchdown run in the tropical heat of Fayetteville – the brilliance of Stanford's football team helped us forget, however temporarily, the horrific War in Southeast Asia and its violent opposition, and me to ignore that I couldn't run a step. Interest in things like Fifties-style bonfires and pep rallies had declined to a point where Stanford's yearbook had been cancelled due to a lack of buyers, but our football team let us pretend we were having a Norman Rockwell college experience after all. Not that the team saw it that way: before the Arkansas game Ralston had sent in a troop of professional incentive builders "to psyche us up," according to back-up Thunder Chicken Tim McClure, in an interview/article ghost-written for one of the last issues of *Look* Magazine. The team's response: demand that the trip home include a stop in Las Vegas! (The Coaches and Athletic Department reportedly agreed, but the stopover never happened.)

Stanford held a 27-7 halftime lead over the #4 Razorbacks in a nationally-televised spectacle when our Band took the field to play a medley of songs by the Beach Boys, led by drum major Geordie Lawry in an underwater mask, fins and snorkel. Jan & Dean's "The Little Old Lady from Pasadena" named the town where we wanted to go on New Year's Day. A game that started as a blow-out would end a close one – Indians 34, Razorbacks 28, with Beta Mike Simone's game-saving tackle to shut down the comeback – but ABC commentator Bud Wilkinson, legendary ex-Coach of the Oklahoma Sooners teams of the Fifties, claimed that Jim Plunkett had just done "the greatest job of Quarterbacking I've ever seen." Plunkett wasn't brilliant every weekend: three weeks later against Purdue he threw five interceptions, fumbled once and was sacked five times in a humiliating 24-16 loss to which Kauf contributed. After Purdue missed a 47-yard field goal attempt, he fielded the short kick at the fifteen-yard line but somehow managed to get himself thrown out of the back of the end zone by Purdue wide receiver Darryl Stingley, who would go on to play for the New England Patriots and end up a quadriplegic after a vicious hit by Ohio State alumni and Strong Safety Jack "The Assassin" Tatum.

"My rugby instincts fired up and I almost kicked it out of the end zone," Kauf told me later. Luckily this safety and non-conference defeat didn't count at all towards a Rose Bowl appearance. As always for the Athenians, the road to Pasadena went through the University of Southern California and the topless towers of Ilium.

The Trojan-Indian Wars of the past two years had both ended with game-winning S.C. field goals in the final seconds, but hopes ran sky-high this year, despite the thrashing by Purdue and the fact that U.S.C., the "Cardiac Kids" and "The Wild Bunch," were even better this year than they the year before. The Saturday Stanford man-handled Arkansas, S.C. opened its fall campaign by destroying the last segregated University of Alabama football team, 42-21, in a game played in Tuscaloosa that would be widely credited with leading directly to the de-segregation of the entire Southeast Conference, which is to say it changed the South itself. Some people rank the S.C.-'Bama game of 1970 as a watershed on a par with Jackie Robinson de-segregating Major League Baseball. Crimson Tide Head Coach Bear Bryant claimed many years later, "Sam Cunningham did more for integration at Alabama than anybody else. He was a black running back for Southern Cal [and a great shot putter, too.] Came down here and ran all over my skinny little white boys. Scored three touchdowns." This Trojan team that had swamped the Tide was the unit that the Indians would have to overcome to reach the shores of Pasadena. The scout S.C. sent to watch the Purdue match-up was so underwhelmed that he didn't even file a game report. What he didn't realize was that Ralston had held out five starters to be ready for the ultimate Trojan War against a team that hadn't lost a regular season game since 1967, and which by the time we played them will have tied national powerhouse Nebraska on the Cornhusker's home field in Lincoln, 21-21. @ @

Saturday October 10th – the day I won that cross country race in Sacramento, so I wasn't present – eighty-six thousand people filed into Stanford Stadium, the largest home crowd since 1935 and the second largest in history, despite the bomb threat phoned in by callers who identified themselves as the Marin County cell of The Weathermen. Addressing the sell-out crowd over the P.A. system, Stanford's new President and former Provost Richard "Dick" Lyman, Pitzer's replacement that summer, declared that "blackmail and threats must not be allowed to paralyze a nation or an institution. If it once becomes established that such tactics can succeed, we shall have magnified enormously the capacity of a malicious few to sabotage society. We have decided, therefore, that the game will continue as scheduled. By your presence here you are indicating that you feel the same." "Bigger than the Rose Bowl" was the *San Francisco Examiner* headline, particularly for those seniors who had stayed on campus all summer to work out together in preparation for this afternoon. The core of the team, including Plunkett, Tight End Bob Moore ("B.M."), Strong Safety Jack Schultz, and Wide Receiver Jack Lasater, came from poor or middle-class families, and had wondered how they would fit in at a university with so many wealthy classmates. Moore was walking down the ramp into the stadium with tears streaming down his face when Schultzy, the team's Co-Captain (with Plunkett), saw him and burst into tears, too. Our guys were there to play as if their lives depended on it, while the Trojans, who hadn't lost to the Indians since 1957 – twelve straight victories, including those two last-second field goals – would be taking the field with 99% of all the confidence in the world.

The game went our way from the beginning. On our second possession Plunkett hit Moore (a future Fifth Round Draft Choice of the Oakland Raiders) in full stride on a sideline pattern for a 50-yard touchdown reception. A second quarter 47-yard punt return by Beta Eric Cross, followed by a 14-yard run by running back Jackie Brown (winner of the Big Meet 100 and second-place finisher in the 220 our freshman year), setting up his two-yard TD plunge, left the score Stanford 14, U.S.C. Zip. The Trojans mounted a comeback late in the half, but junior linebacker Jeff Siemon made two huge defensive plays, one killing an S.C. drive at the Stanford One. Making up for his gaffe against Purdue, Kauf made another stop on 4th and Goal, a photo of which appeared in the *San Francisco Chronicle* the next day. Like my win in Sacramento, his tackle was a fluke, as Kauf tripped over the man he was supposed to block and knifed between the legs of Trojan QB Jimmy Jones, who earlier that season had become the first black Quarterback ever to grace the cover of *Sports Illustrated.*

Chants of "Beat S.C., Beat S.C." echoed at Halftime between the sunny and the shady sides of the stadium – between students and alumni – but the third quarter began with a commanding 74-yard Trojan march that made it Stanford 14, S.C. 7. We came back with an 89-yard drive, which featured four Plunkett completions and ended with another short plunge from Jackie Brown, putting us up 21-7. But with four minutes left in the Fourth, Jones fired a 17-yard TD pass that trimmed the Indian lead to 21-14. The game was then in the hands of the Stanford offense, either to burn the clock or score again. One Plunkett pass was tipped and nearly intercepted before B.M. grabbed it to put the team within field-goal range. Horowitz iced the kick, and that's where the show ended. We had finally beaten U.S.C., 24-14, a team left so disheartened by its loss that lowly Cal beat them later that season. Coupled with Oregon's 41-40 upset over U.C.L.A. the same day, our guys only had to beat Washington State and the Bruins on the road (check), Oregon State at home (check), and finally a University of Washington team in Stanford Stadium, smothering Husky Quarterback Sonny Sixkiller, a "real" Indian and the top-ranked statistical passer in the country that year, by sacking him six times and intercepting him four times in a thrilling 29-22 victory. I heard from friends that the jubilation in our locker room knew no bounds, especially among those seniors who had fought for three years for this day to come. @ @

With the Rose Bowl in the bag, our guys went out and dogged it against a mediocre Air Force team in Colorado Springs, losing 31-14 and setting up yet another afterthought in Stanford's first Rose Bowl season in eighteen years: the Big Game of 1970. I was in the stands in

Berkeley that day, bad knee and all, a week after the Pac-8 Cross-Country Championship and well before catching Mono. I breathed the sweet-scented pot smoke that wafted on Zephyrus breezes through the visitor's section while Stanford's madcap band poured into Memorial Stadium, led by a stripper who band members had recruited during a drunken bender in a San Francisco topless bar the night before. Watching the Mondrian-Meets-Crazy-Horse-bedecked Dollies stride to midfield with The Axe, that immortal implement awarded to the winner of the Big Game since before my parent's time, I bonded and soared with hundreds of thousands of students past and present, present and not – my grandfather, parents, aunts, uncles, a sister and a brother-in-law – filling my lungs with the once-a-year "Big Game" rant, inspired by Aristophanes' *The Frogs* (Brekekekek croax croax): *"Give 'em the Axe the Axe the Axe/ Give 'em the Axe the Axe the Axe/ Give 'em the Axe, give 'em the Axe, give 'em the Axe – where? Right in the neck the neck the neck/ right in the neck the neck the neck/ right in the neck, right in the neck, right in the neck –* there!"

"Is that the greatest cheer in college football or what?" I asked Decker, wiping away the tears of joy that streaked my cheeks. (Seriously, I was that much of a geek.) "Did you know that cheer dates from 1899?"

"But it's also a bit psychotic, don't you think?" Deck screamed back at me. "'You want our god-damned Axe? Come and get it, suckers! We'll give it to you – right in your *neck!!!*'" Psychotic violence advocated (tongue-in-cheek, sort of) for four generations or more was amusing until some of our sideline boosters prematurely fired our team's victory cannon, sending the ramrod straight into the Cal rooting section, injuring a fan and resulting in the Pac-8 conference banning all pyrotechnics the following year. Stanford's halftime show was highlighted by the unscripted appearance of a member of a Berkeley anarchist group known as the People's Athletic Committee, who stormed the field boldly waving a Vietnamese National Liberation Front flag in protest of the fact that they had not been given free admission to the game. Stanford Band members and various police officers restrained the long-haired fellow, who was cheered lustily by

Cal supporters as cops escorted him from the stadium. The Dollies recruited the Stanford Lacrosse team to patrol the sidelines with their sticks, snagging water balloons chucked at our cheerleaders by the boorish, golden-bearish crowd. Once again, it appeared that our guys were so relieved to finally be going to the Rose Bowl that they didn't feel like playing hard. Cal had an ordinary 5-5 record that year, despite the S.C. win, but damned if they didn't beat us in the Big Game, 22-14. It was Plunkett's only career loss to Stanford's traditional rival, who reclaimed The Axe from that year's Pac-8 conference champion. @ @

This Big Game debacle, coupled with the Air Force fiasco the week before, set up the following New Year's Day scenario: the undefeated Ohio State Buckeyes – not just a good team but quite possibly "The Team of the Decade:" an old-fashioned, four-yards-and-a-cloud-of-dust Big Ten throwback to the Fifties if there ever was one, coached by the infamous tyrant and Drill Master Woody Hayes, a close personal friend of the "Whittier College Poets" ex-third-string guard Richard M. Nixon (who claimed that Hayes' support helped him carry Ohio in the '60 election against John F. Kennedy) – a coach who had publically declared "hippies" to be a threat to the future of the nation – versus Leland Stanford Junior University and its toe-jam-football-playing gang of countercultural wastrels, under-sized pot smokers, acid heads and Thunder Chickens, coached by an accredited Dale Carnegie instructor, led by the son of blind Mexican-Americans, and cheered on by a controversial racial mascot hotly contested to wide publicity by Native American groups, then with the whole meshugas skewered by a Marching Band of Weenies and their wild-and-woolly halftime show!

What could possibly be any better than this? Sure, Stanford fielded its fair share of Campus-Crusade-for-Christ types, too, including 235-pound consensus All-American middle linebacker Jeff Siemon, a seek-and-destroy missile bound for N.F.L. glory and the College Football Hall of Fame. Siemon wasn't one of the pushier ones; there wasn't a player on our team who didn't have total respect for Jeff Siemon. But Stanford vs. O.S.U. still shaped up to be an epic battle of aerial hip vs. ground-grinding square – the Sixties versus the Fifties, if you will, with the

Good Guys (us) the 19-point Underdogs, and deserving to be, as far as Vegas was concerned. Some O.S.U. players sweetened the pot by complaining to the media about having to play a 12th-ranked, 8-3 team with an unexceptional defense (don't tell the Thunder Chickens that), a one-dimensional offense and a two-game losing streak at Bowl time. They should have looked on the bright side: the Indian-Buckeye match-up wasn't a deal breaker for their national championship aspirations. Even a squeaker would set them up for the unofficial national title, especially if Notre Dame upset top-ranked Texas in the Cotton Bowl earlier on New Year's Day (which would indeed happen.) For all the bravado the Buckeyes were feeding the press, I knew they had to be feeling under pressure. I liked that we were Underdogs, because I knew our guys believed that on any given Saturday we could defeat any college football team in America. And the less The Ohio State University understood this, the better off we would be. @ @

Mononucleosis was the worst. I moped around San Clemente, nursing dark thoughts, sleeping a lot and trying to read for school, but mostly just feeling sorry for myself and devastated by this turns of events. How much more misfortune could I take? After willingly surrendering two-thirds of my sophomore year, I now had my entire junior year in jeopardy. I had survived Europe to triumph at Sac State – or had I survived Europe? I asked myself again if my hard left turn into the counterculture left me more vulnerable to illness and injury. Had I been running with scissors? Only Time would reveal the truth of this matter, but I couldn't stop myself from wondering if going overseas and losing my sophomore track season had been a mistake after all.

I felt sufficiently recovered after a week (and certified non-contagious by my doctor) to phone Pat Moore and see if I could drop by for a visit. The Stanford Rose Bowl team was staying at the Edgewater Hyatt in my old hometown of Long Beach – "The Edgie," Mom used to call it, close to Long Beach State College campus where our team was holding a final week of two-a-day practices and drill. (Ohio State, meanwhile, was hunkered down in a Christian monastery in rooms that contained, as one player later recalled, "a bed, a Bible and a toilet.")

"Yeah, sure, come up, hang out," Pimo told me. "You can have fun for all of us…" Apparently Ralston's two-a-day practices were wearing on people's nerves. The two season-ending losses had convinced their Head Coach that his team needed to return to basics, and so he had installed a boot camp environment at the Edgie. The players disagreed, and the tension was not doing anyone any good.

Entering the hotel parking lot I drove by the glistening row of brand-new luxury Chrysler convertibles parked outside for the use of players, courtesy of one of the game's TV sponsors; Pat had already told me that Ralston wasn't letting anybody drive one. I knocked on his door shortly after the team dinner and hung out for a while with him and his roommate, starting slot receiver Demea Washington, a former Pasadena high school star taking a break that night from his hot new love affair with the first-ever Black Rose Bowl Princess. We smoked a joint in their room and headed out in my station wagon to see some forgettable foreign flick in an art house cinema down the road in Seal Beach. We didn't get back to their room until well after Ralston's curfew, which neither Pat nor Demea seemed especially concerned about, as there were no bed checks in the 1971 Stanford Rose Bowl Camp. As with most things at Stanford, including un-proctored exams for the general student population, the football team ran on the Honor System. Overnight guests were strictly *verboten*, too, of course, but I didn't want to drive almost all the way to San Diego County at close to midnight, so Pimo and Demea said sure, of course, grab a blanket and crash on the sofa for the night, it's cool. So that's what I did.

They were long gone for morning practice by the time I woke up. I was strolling naked towards the bathroom and thinking about the easy run I wanted to try that afternoon in San Clemente. When I passed a mirror I did a double take. My stomach was covered with a bright red rash. Within seconds I was dressed, opening the door with my elbows and racing to my station wagon for the drive to San Clemente, where a Doctor confirmed my self-diagnosis: I had just brought a case of German Measles into the Stanford Rose Bowl camp. @ @

If this was a fiction instead of an account of actual events, this incident might be viewed as a metaphor, alerting the reader to the misguided life the protagonist was leading, for which he was about to reap the whirlwind. The punishment for this risky behavior of an overnight visit in the Rose Bowl Camp – i.e., my unwillingness to live by rules and the clean power of positive thinking – was to be the destruction of Stanford's football team, one week before the 57th Rose Bowl Game. I spent the next several days in bed, tossing and turning in a state of barely-suppressed hysteria. My doctor had told me that measles are infectious before you see the rash; that the virus can spread through respiration and linger in a room for more than an hour; that measles can be contracted from two hundred yards away. And Pimo, Demea and I had smoked a joint together! I was sure my doctor would have claimed that you couldn't die a thousand deaths from German Measles, but I begged to differ. My own misfortune was a mere bagatelle compared to the anxiety I felt for our football team. I may have single-handedly doomed Stanford's first Rose Bowl shot in eighteen years! – carved myself a permanent niche in the Stanford Hall of Shame! – screwed the pooch *and* Norman Rockwell! – stolen the prize our seniors had worked for their entire college careers! – ruined what Jim Plunkett had postponed his entry into the college draft to achieve – and handed the victory by default to the Bed, Bible & Toilet Gang from the Buckeye State!

I phoned Pat every night, hoping he wouldn't hear how stressed I was.

"Hey, we're fine, everything's cool," Pimo would say night after night. "Except these two-a-day practices are for the birds..." There was no reason to reveal to them that I had brought an infectious disease to the Edgie, because Pat and Demea would either get sick or not; no need for them to worry about it, too, or get pissed off at me, which would have not been fair, although it would have been understandable. Call me a coward if you want, but if I kept my mouth shut about this, nobody would ever attribute the Rose Bowl Measles Outbreak of 1971 to me. And what was I guilty of? Breaking a rule established to avoid a situation like this one was the obvious answer. But other people broke rules, too: Coach Jordan advised lying on a form to the N.C.A.A., and Dave ran an illegal player ticket scam out of the training room, to give only two examples. Breaking an honor code we had no hand in writing was something some students did, which I suppose made it common in every sense of the word. Everybody broke "The Rules," except for my parents and grandparents, who never seemed to.

I asked myself more than once what this act of "risk-taking hubris" (as I once characterized Decker on his unseemly Hog) should be asked to symbolize in the pilgrim's progress of my athletic career. I was sure I wasn't a virus in the Athletic Department; I just had one. Eventually I decided that my measles was nothing more than one of those nightmares the universe churns up every once in a while to keep itself entertained, and us humans on our toes – because as you probably have guessed already, nobody got sick, and I was off the hook, without a reprimand. After taking a bullet in Pullman; I had just dodged one in Long Beach. What is the more powerful symbolism here: that my rule-breaking had almost destroyed Stanford's Rose Bowl chances, or that I had gotten away with it scot-free? You choose, because I prefer not to have to make up my mind. @ @

As for those two-a-day practices that Pimo and everybody kept bitching about: the issue came to a head one morning not long after my departure when the players gathered in the locker room before practice and decided that since they were going to be playing in a Rose Bowl Game in less than a week, so by god they were going to have some *fun*. So no more morning workouts! *"Boy-cott Prac-tice, Boy-cott Prac-tice!"* I don't know if anybody actually chanted that, but the instinct behind a Sixties-style "People's Revolt" had reached the football team at last.

When news reached the practice field that the team wasn't coming out, P.R. Flak Bob Murphy stayed to do damage control with the media, making up some cockamamie excuse about why the team wasn't out there, while Ralston hurried to the locker room to find out what the heck was going on here. My friends on the team always told me that Ralston was a "plastic man," which he was – a self-proclaimed "nut on self-improvement, self-imagery," like Payton Jordan; also like Payt, Ralston claimed to care deeply about his "boys" while churning out "Rules" for them like there was no tomorrow, which was why he seemed generally more respected than loved. (Seven years later, Ralston would lose his head coaching job with the Denver Broncos of the N.F.L. after a players vote of no-confidence, despite having just led the team to a franchise record 9-5 season.) I never did find out who said what to whom that morning, but I did learn that Co-Captains Plunk and Schultzy, Demea and Linebacker Ron Kadziel (aka "Baby Cakes," who lived with Kauf and Ferris up in Portola Valley) were the point guys who spoke to Ralston. Plunkett would tell the press that he thought their Head Coach had taken too much personal responsibility for the team schneid against Air Force and Cal because of some questionable third-and-one play calls he made, and as a result was over-reacting. Red-Shirt back-up QB Don Bunce put it in simpler terms: "The demands were to make this as enjoyable as possible!"

I gave it up big-time to John Ralston. He grumbled loudly at first – in some versions of the story he threatened to resign on the spot – but in the end he surprised everybody by acceding to his team's demands. No more morning workouts. He also arranged team excursions to Marineland, in addition to the usual Disneyland junket shared with Ohio State. The curfew was pushed back 30 minutes, too. Some guys even climbed into those new Chrysler convertibles. Ralston demonstrated that he truly believed trust was a two-way street. But he must surely have also realized that if his team didn't deliver on game day, after he counted on them to do it their way and not his, he might be out of a job. But look at it from another angle: maybe those two-a-days served a purpose, toughening the team for Game Day, and now the players got to feel they owned their preparation, too. And so the stage was set! The stars aligned! There would be not an Indian on the field who wasn't convinced that we could slay Goliath! The Buckeyes, meanwhile – a team that hadn't lost a game in two years or a Rose Bowl game in fifty – continued to grind out two-a-day practices without a sense of humor to save themselves. @ @

I showed up in Pasadena three days before kick-off, recovered more or less from Tendonitis, Mononucleosis, and German Measles, and ready to party where the winds of freedom blew me. I skipped the Parade (Squares-ville!), so I was not among the million people lining the streets and sidewalks of Pasadena, or the fifty million people reportedly watching the Rose Parade on television while the Stanford Band ambled all five-and-one-half miles in their wacky outfits, stopping to kiss innocent bystanders, collect free beer and toke on joints when they were offered, which they were. Otherwise I availed myself of every Rose Bowl party that sounded even remotely promising; invaded I-don't-remember-how-many-motel-rooms for I-don't-know-how-many-let's-raid-the-mini-bar escapades; hooked rides with strangers from one Pasadena mansion to the next one; showed up in jeans and a t-shirt for formal balls hosted by last year's debutantes in taffeta gowns ringed with sequined holsters and vodka Jell-O shots; spent time in the family home of Pasadena Beta Steve Biegenzahn ("Biegs," a future Marine Corps JAG and L.A. bankruptcy attorney, because like I keep saying the Betas took all kinds); and crashed on a sofa, a lumpy pull-out and one luxurious king-size bed, respectively, without ever knowing where I would lay my Head on the night to follow. I don't remember many more specifics about those three days and nights in Pasadena, which means (thank you Robin Williams) I must have had a really good time.

But the excitement and fun that had turned the City of Pasadena into one giant tailgate party paled beside the excitement Decker and I felt as we filed into the Rose Bowl on Saturday with our eight-dollar tickets, joining 103,837 other fans to watch good friends – Kauf, Pimo, many others – compete as 13-point underdogs (now) in a nationally-televised spectacle (with play-by-play by Curt Gowdy, voice of the Boston Red Sox) against a team some people called the greatest college football unit of the past ten years. @ @

Ohio State took the 2:00 p.m. opening kick, but their drive fizzled on the Stanford 41. For our first offensive play from scrimmage I trained my binoculars on my old Cliveden roommate Jon Sande, the second-team All-American Center I had slept alongside for most of my six months in England. Forty pounds heavier after chowing down on his Mom's steaks in Reno all summer, Sande lined up across from Ohio State's All-Everything Outland Trophy-winning Nose Tackle Jim Stillwagon, a match-up considered key to our prospects. I was astounded to see Sande perform a "center pull" on the first play, acting as a lead blocker on a reverse. He would end up driven ten yards downfield by one of his own teammates, but in the meantime Wide Receiver Eric Cross, my game-breaking Beta Bro, ripped off a 41-yard end around all the way down to the Buckeye 18! Our "one-dimensional" offense followed this bit of trickery with a TD air strike to B.M. that was called back for illegal procedure. Ralston's ginned-up game plan included all sorts of gizmos and gadgets that O.S.U. hadn't seen on film: on our third play from scrimmage, Plunkett surprised the entire Ohio State defense with a Quarterback Draw up the middle for 12 yards, which was followed by a Jackie Brown four-yard touchdown scamper and Holy Cow! – after just five minutes of play and our fourth touch of the game: Stanford 7, O.S.U. Zip! Our second possession ended with a 37-yard Steve Horowitz field goal: Incredible! Ten-Zip! But Ohio State's powerful offense would soon be marching up and down the field with scarifying ease. Two TD plunges by All-American halfback John Brockington left it 14-10 Buckeyes at Halftime. It would have been worse without the 20-yard Field Goal attempt blocked by our DB and future long-time Dallas Cowboy Benny Barnes. @ @

At the start of the halftime show, drum major Geordie Lawry drove on to the field on a tricycle, tipped it over (a bit ripped off from Arte Johnson and *Laugh-In)*, and stripped off his yellow raincoat to reveal a Baby New Year costume, a huge safety-pinned diaper and a "1971" sash. The Band also introduced Arthur P. Barnes' recent arrangement of the English band Free's 1970 hit "All Right Now," which would become Stanford's *de facto* fight song for the next forty years and counting. But the mood in our locker room was darkened by the knowledge that O.S.U. had outscored opponents 90-9 in the Third Quarter that season. Buckeye QB Rex Kern had been running the Wishbone with shocking efficiency, rushing for 99 yards in the first half all by himself, with big John Brockington adding another 117. Tim McClure's *Look* article claimed that some of our players gobbled "greenies" at the Half – amphetamines, without the knowledge or approval of Coaches or Trainers – in part because they figured Ohio State players were doing the same. My informants would tell me that only a small number of guys "beaned up," and McClure would claim that this part of his story hadn't been meant for publication anyway. He would also claim that Stanford Football had become a high pressure, win-at-all-costs "business." But so was Cross Country, and I say if you can't stand the heat, get out of the kitchen, cuz people want to cook.

The third quarter did not produce a Buckeye blowout. The teams traded field goals, including Horowitz's Rose Bowl record 48-yarder, leaving the score 17-13 O.S.U. as the fourth quarter commenced. From there the game had two turning points: one on Defense, one on Offense, for each team. When a 74-yard Buckeye drive stalled on the Stanford 20, Coach Hayes elected to go for it on Fourth Down rather than take the easy field goal. Our coaches gambled that the Buckeyes would send Brockington right; Brockington went right. Cakes made first contact, four other guys jumped in, and Pimo launched himself across the top of the red jerseys, stopping the Buckeye dead in his tracks: First Down, Indians! Our offensive turning point came directly in front of Decker and me in the stands: a spectacular 35-yard over-the-shoulder catch by All-American Bob Moore – a reception that so infuriated Coach Hayes that he dubbed it "The Mad Dog Catch," as in: "That Mad Dog Catch should never have happened!"

"That 'mad-dog' pass was almost serendipity," Plunkett later recalled. "In the huddle, I told Bob Moore to stay in and block. But as I was walking to the line, I said to Bob, 'You better go out.' I just felt I might need him. I dropped back and was running out of time. So I rolled to my right to give myself more time. I saw him roll to the right side. He was six-three, so I put the ball up high. And he went up and made a great catch between numbers of defenders." Moore's snag led to Jackie Brown's second one-yard scoring plunge of the game, and with the extra point good, the score was Stanford 20, Ohio State 17. Safety Jack

Schultz choked off the Buckeye's drive for the lead with a diving interception of a Kern pass, then Plunkett drove a stake through the Buckeyes' heart with a ten-yard scoring strike to future New England Patriot wide receiver Randy "The Rabbit" Vataha – aka "The Human Flea" for his diminutive size and uncanny cutting ability. @ @

The strength of the Indian was the Tribe, and the strength of the Tribe was the Indian! All four quarters saw outstanding performances all up and down the Stanford line. Slot Receiver Demea Washington, my training camp host *("Pass me that joint, brother")* had the game of his life in his hometown in front of his Rose Bowl Princess, making six grabs for 80 yards, after having only 15 catches all year. My dog Pimo stuffed a Buckeye for no gain on another late fourth-and-short-yardage situation at midfield – take that, O.S.U. Strong Safety Jack "The Assassin" Tatum, watching from a sideline! Coach Ralston gave John Sande help blocking the Outland Trophy Winner in the first half, but not in the second, because on play after play the Ohio State great appeared to be fired from a cannon – against a brick wall. Our bend-but-don't-break defense was one of many keys to the game: the Thunder Chickens (who fired up my licorice-flavored joints at the Beta House) made huge plays all over the field, led by senior Dave Tipton (12 tackles); born-again Middle Linebacker Jeff Siemon was the best defensive player on either team, finishing with a game-high 15 tackles. Whoever heard of a team rushing for 364 yards and scoring only 17 points? I hadn't until that day in Pasadena. Even the Dollies were heroic, dodging a barrage of horse chestnut seeds ("buckeyes") thrown by ungentlemanly rival fans. But the difference-maker in the game was its MVP, the U.P.I., *Sporting News* and *Sport Magazine* College Player of the Year and one of the greatest offensive players in the history of college football, senior Jim Plunkett, who finished the day 20 for 30 for 215 yards with one TD and no picks. Ralston's game plan had been masterful – the gadget plays aside, Ohio State had never seen an offense built around the pass before – but Plunkett also called at least 25 audibles, according to Ralston's count. Some observers would describe this as the afternoon Stanford unveiled for the nation (pre-Bill

Walsh, the putative inventor) what became known as the West Coast Offense, which would come to dominate the National Football League. The efforts of Buckeye QB Kern were heroic – he rushed twenty times for 129 yards – but Hayes finally benched him, partly because of his inability to get the ball in the end zone, but also because our "unexceptional" defense had beaten the crap out of him all day.

A mist was drifting over the field, as over a battlefield. With only a few minutes left and the score holding at 27-17, Stanford fans began to move down from the stands until only the Dollies and Prince Lightfoot stood between us and our demi-gods. All of us were waiting for the moment when we could flood the gridiron. We knew something almost miraculous was happening: our deepest fantasy realized by virtue of careful planning, pure improvisation, loads of dedication and hard work, and no small measure of luck. Thousands of us pressed almost to the sidelines until the final gun sounded, which was when we sprinted on to the field, leaping, dancing, screaming, and thrusting fists in the air! In the college equivalent of Joe Namath and the New York Jets' upset of the 17-point-favorite Baltimore Colts in the Super Bowl two years before, the 13-point Underdogs had prevailed against the old-fashioned college football "Team of the Decade," 27-17! @ @

The Incomparable Leland Stanford Junior University Marching Band joined the student body on the field for a victory concert. As a writer for *Rolling Stone* later noted: "It's hard for anyone raised on rock to imagine that a band could sound this loud without thousands of watts of amplification." The concert concluded at dusk with band leader Arthur P. Barnes' gorgeous rendition of the "Star Spangled Banner," featuring a single trumpet playing the first half of the song, joined midway by soft woodwinds and tubas before the full power of the brass sweeps in on the final verse. The joy I felt personally was especially sweet, and not because the Buckeyes would probably have beaten us nine times out of ten, as Plunkett himself conceded decades later; and not because Ohio State's Head Coach was in the loser's locker room spraying the press corps with spittle – literally foaming at the mouth over his team's upset, which meant the loss of a certain national championship that went instead to the once-tied (by U.S.C!) Nebraska Cornhuskers, after Notre Dame had upset top-ranked Texas earlier that day. Talk about excuses: decades later some Buckeye players would claim that they had been "off topic" that day in Pasadena because they so deeply resented their control freak Coach's insistence that they bypass most of the Rose Bowl festivities to focus on practice. Woody Hayes would be fired not soon enough for slugging an opposing player on the field in the '78 Gator Bowl.

The scale of the victory mattered, but the day was especially sweet for me personally because Stanford's first Rose Bowl win in thirty years unequivocally demonstrated something that outsiders might not have understood the way I did. I wasn't thinking that a bunch of hippies had taken down the Ohio State Buckeyes. I was thinking that a Dionysian spirit had worked in harmony with a Puritanical work ethic to produce a phenomenal Rose Bowl victory. And I was thinking that a *team* had won this game – a team that included all kinds of folk, from Born Again Christians to countercultural types who supposedly lacked the discipline to succeed at this level of college sports. This *inclusiveness* – this embrace of people unlike yourself who shared common goals and practices, which was the notion that inspired much of our politics, too – this *inclusiveness* was the soul and spirit of the Sixties' cultural revolution, and it was what Stanford's football team embodied. And it was how the Sixties upended the Fifties, and the Winds of Freedom had pancaked Woody Hayes! And I must not fail to mention the reported sightings of football players driving those "borrowed" Chrysler Rose Bowl convertibles around campus for weeks after the game, although these reports were only hearsay to my ears, so I can neither confirm them nor provide you with a firm denial. @ @ @

DEVIL-TAKES-THE-HINDMOST

The Rose Bowl was for me the highlight of a holiday that was mostly low lights. My season-ending knee trauma in early November, followed by Mono only days after my knee had healed, topped off by German Measles: that was one tough Trifecta. Missing State Meet my senior year in high school didn't hold a candle to what I went through in the winter of 1970-71. This was the most difficult period I had ever experienced as an athlete. My rise as a runner, even after my hiatus in the wilderness of Europe, had seemed so inexorable, it was difficult to grasp now that it had been so grievously slowed – my career momentum, interrupted by Europe, had in fact become completely stalled, and no amount of visits to Dave's Animal Kingdom would get me that lost time back. I briefly considered quitting running altogether, and wrote my grandparents about it. My grandfather's reply surprised me: "I was a little sad to hear that you are giving up running," he wrote, "you put so much store in it. It does take a lot of your time however. I was always in hope that you would do something with debating and dramatics, fields in which you have a great deal of talent." He was hopeful that I might become involved in something else, but I was changing my mind a lot in those days, and my family was used to it.

Shell had recently transferred my father from Texas to the Amsterdam front office on a one-year assignment, and I looked forward to visiting there over the summer, but my folks asked me not to come. They never came out and said why ("It's not a good time") but I thought they worried that my countercultural ways might influence my three younger brothers who still lived at home. Some of the concern may have stemmed from the fact that I had never kept entirely quiet about my countercultural escapades, helping no doubt to open what was referred to in those days as "The Generation Gap." I had even told them that I smoked marijuana occasionally. On December 6th I wrote the people paying one-third of my college tuition and all of my room & board: "First of all, the facts. Contrary to what you may think, marijuana use is rampant in colleges throughout the country, even in the South… I enclose a recent article from the S.F. *Examiner*, which notes that the number of Stanford undergraduates who have tried marijuana at least once has more than tripled in three years to 69%, and those are just the people who admit to it. Also that 'the use of marijuana by students of this university is becoming an accepted mode of social expression and this acceptance is not confined to members of the drug-using subculture itself…'" I wasn't content with simply telling my grandparents that I smoked weed every once in a while; I had to describe to them what it was like: "You've seemingly never heard music until you've heard it stoned. You feel like you're missing nothing – although of course you always come down in the end…"

This sounded sophomoric to me even at the time, and trying to convince a retired Los Angeles County Superior Court Judge about the righteousness of firing up some really cool Michoacán was probably a losing battle to begin with. But I continued to want to explain myself to the people I loved, who happened to be living in a different country than the one I was living in then.

My grandparents were far from foaming at the mouth (like Coach Hayes) about my decision to major in the Humanities Special Program, but they did consider it a serious misstep in what they had hoped would be a useful career. My grandparents were far from Philistines: my grandfather had published essays on Mozart and Shakespeare and my grandmother read widely and played classical piano at concert level on her Steinway Baby Grand. They just wanted me to study something "practical," like Economics, or Political Science – practicality being a shibboleth in our family, even if I didn't appear to be getting behind it. And they also knew not to protest my major too strenuously, because my grades were excellent (after my felony in Europe) and it wouldn't prevent me from applying to law school one day. The drama for countless young Americans like myself, whether we were athletes or not, was that we were leaving the destinies and futures and roadmaps laid down for us by our families in order to drop out of the mainstream by the hundreds of thousands. This was not an easy thing to do when bonds of love were involved.

Our disagreements came to a head with my grandparents over a Christmas holiday dinner at a restaurant in San Clemente. During a heated discussion about the myths and realities of American life, my grandfather let slip a question that in hindsight shocked me, but one that had probably been on his mind for quite some time.

"Well," he asked, "what do you think of *me?*"

"You did what you had to do," I blurted, "and I'm doing what I think is necessary from my point of view." The years have only deepened my shame about how I answered my grandfather that night. Even before returning to campus after the greatest Rose Bowl weekend ever, I felt conscience-stricken about how disrespectfully I had spoken to a man who had lived an honorable, even estimable life, and who was giving me the gift of a Stanford education to boot – a New Deal Democrat who had written the definitive work on California Probate Practice and opposed the War as I did, but who also didn't care for civil disobedience, or incivility, either. I thought about apologizing to him – I knew he hadn't given up his hopes for the grandson named after his father – but in the end I decided that what was done was done. A cultural revolution was in progress. Millions of American families were watching their kids' ambitions change with complicated emotions. Family disagreements were inevitable. And so I coldly resolved to continue extracting myself from my family's expectations of me, to focus on literature, and to snatch back what was left of my athletic year from the maw of injury, illness and disaster. @ @

Returning to training after Mono was tough. No one told me, presumably because no one knew, what recovering from Mono would entail, or in fact gave me any information about it at all. I was running on my own, running just a little, hoping to keep my competitive spirits tamped down and my mileage low. But I didn't feel like myself. My arguments with my loving grandparents weighed on me. In that first week back on campus I visited Coach Clark to provide him with an update: "Sometimes it feels like I'm running under water, Coach. Like I've got some kind of – some kind of – metabolic *blockage*... I *reach* for it, but I can't turn it on!"

"That's what you should expect when you're recovering from a glandular fever," Coach said. "Just take it easy, Robert. Let yourself come around when your body feels ready."

His calm was reassuring. Plus I knew he was right. What I always needed to work on was patience. I told myself that of course I would find a way to train hard and race again. I had too much going for me, too much talent and pride and dedication, for good things not to happen for me sooner rather than later. @ @

So my mileage stayed light and my effort low until mid-January, when a couple of decent road runs filled me with the irrational exuberance that is every athlete's occasional bedfellow. After less than three weeks of training in the previous three months, I called Coach Clark to see if he could get me entered in the *San Francisco Examiner* All-American Indoor Mile at the Cow Palace in Daly City, twenty miles north of us and a few miles south of The City.

"There will be a world-class field there, Robert. I'm not sure I can get you in. But give me a few days…"

A few days later: "They said your best time isn't fast enough" – my best Mile was still that freshman 4:09.5 at the Easter Relays in '69 – "but if you want, they'll let you run in the Devil-Take-the-Hindmost Mile."

"Great! Get me in!"

"Are you sure you want to do this, Robert?"

"Why shouldn't I want to do it? Is it my fitness level? – "

"No, it's just that – well, a Devil-Take-the-Hindmost can be kind of a *circus*…" A Devil-Take-the-Hindmost Mile is indoor track's version of a novelty act, a twisted Musical Chairs: with eleven laps to a Mile on a 160-yard track, participants were typically given four or five "free" laps, after which whomever was in last place at the end of lap six, seven, eight, and so on, must step off the track. Usually only two or three runners cross the finish line, so a runner's goal was not to be yanked off the boards – after which, may the best man win. The parallels with *They Shoot Horses, Don't They?* – the recent film about "Marathon" dancers trying to stay on a dance floor in the middle of the Great Depression – were probably obvious to everyone but me. @ @

The *San Francisco Examiner* All-American Indoor Meet on January 24th, 1971 was held at the Cow Palace, the former site of the California State Livestock Pavilion and current home of the San Francisco Warriors of the N.B.A. A sell-out crowd was on hand, more than 13,000 track fans – not quite a Rose Bowl-size gathering, but more spectators than had ever attended any meet I was part of. The huge arena was electric with bright flags and shattering colors on my first visit to the Cow Palace, where I would come back a year later for a George McGovern campaign rally and to hear Stevie Wonder open for the Rolling Stones. That night's Track & Field meet would resemble a coronation, which was part of why I wasn't in the Open Mile: Jim Ryun, the outdoor world-record holder (3:51.1) and my high school idol, would be running his first competitive Mile race since July 1969, when he faced off against Martin Liquori in the A.A.U. Championship and walked off the track after two laps, in the middle of what he later described as a "mental breakdown." In the interim he had accepted Jesus Christ as his personal Lord and Savior, and now he was back from the tomb of a premature retirement. But before he could run his first race as a Jesus Freak, I was jogging to the start of the Devil-Take-the-Hindmost Mile.

The gun sounded and away we went, me and a bunch of Junior College scrubs turning tight circles around the Cow Palace's stone-age wooden boards. From Lap One, everything felt wrong. I knew we weren't running that fast, but I was barely hanging on at the back of the pack. At Lap Six or whenever it was time to begin snatching runners off the boards, I had to move up, but I could barely find the pedal, much less the metal. I was dead last with one circuit remaining and knew I had to punch it. I gave it everything I had, but still ended up the last runner 160 yards short of a finish line I probably would have crossed in my best high school time. I knew I was Hindmost, but every instinct in my body rebelled against leaving a race. I had almost finished the curve when two meet officials appeared on the boards, blocking my way – Ye Shall Not Pass! – while a third came at me from behind, grabbed my hips and literally spun me in a 360 off the boards. I was like some gate crasher at a charity ball, or a crazed fan pursuing a celebrity. A circus? This was Grand Guignol! This was a Punch & Judy Show, and exactly what Coach Clark had hoped I would avoid!

But it was too late. A once-proud Champion had just made a total ass of himself in front of thirteen thousand people, or so I thought at the time. I couldn't face Coach, my teammates, anyone. I cooled down for a long time in the Cow Palace corridors, peeking out only to watch six-foot-two, 168-pound Jim Ryun, still in the pink & gray of the University of Kansas, run the Open Mile. Ryun had recovered from the Mono he contracted in late May 1968 in time to Silver in the Olympic 1,500-Meters in mid-October, running two seconds faster than he had thought possible. His race in the Cow Palace would be a Turkey Trot, because all of the top Milers of the era had ducked the race. Ryun led the first few slow laps, at which point our own Duncan Macdonald took over for him, and slowed the pace even further. After four and a half more laps of this nonsense, Ryun lowered the boom and sprinted the final three laps, his arms pumping in that metronomic motion I had copied as a freshman, clearly feeling good about it, a huge grin plastered across his face. Ryun broke the tape to a standing ovation in 4:04.4. Duncan finished second, 40 yards back in 4:10.2; Washington State's Rick Reilly, who had gone sub-four in the same Conference

Championship race that Duncan did, was third, in 4:13.5; Arvid Kretz, last in 4:14.4. (I wished I had been there.)

Four weeks later in San Diego, Ryun would set his first world indoor mark, a 3:56.4 Mile. Later that night at the Cow Palace, Shot-Putter Al Feuerbach – he of the unruly Fu Manchu – would establish a new world indoor standard, heaving the 16-pound implement 68' 11".

And all I wanted to do was hide my head in shame. @ @

I sat in a backseat of Coach Clark's station wagon down the Bayshore Freeway home to campus, not talking to anybody.

In the parking lot on our way to the locker room, Coach angled up to me and we finally spoke.

"What a mistake, Coach. I should have known I wasn't ready. I felt like a total idiot out there. Like some kind of Cow Palace... *rodeo clown...*"

I could tell from the look on Coach Clark's face that he was sharing my mistake, for letting me do what I wanted.

"You're still coming back from Mono, Robert. You have to be patient. That was also only your second race indoors – "

"The boards weren't the problem, Coach! Something's wrong with me... Something's not right... Something is seriously *wrong...* "

"Be Patient" and "Listen to Your Body:" always good advice. Practical advice, too, because for every Low there will be a High, and vice versa. Go, Zen. But I still needed to know: be patient for what? How would I know when I was ready to train hard and race again?

The next day I went to UGLY and researched some articles about Jim Ryun's battle with Mono. I was surprised by how conservatively his doctors had approached his getting better. He took a full three weeks off before resuming any training, and ran only every other day for the next three months, at the end of which he produced a 3:55.9 Mile. Then he trained for two days with the third day off for the two months leading up to his spectacular run in Mexico City. Ryun's doctor told *SI* that Mono "is one of those things you are never certain about. You must wait and see. And hope." 1968 N.C.A.A. Mile Champ Dave Patrick of Villanova claimed that "if you start to run again too soon, it takes longer to get over it." That I had rushed back into racing as soon as it felt possible had apparently produced a predictable result.

I brooded over my possible courses of action all that day and the next without finding a single one that made me happy. The simple fact was that this was all too much. Family fights, a light course load but an honors thesis hanging over my head: there was a lot on my plate that quarter. A long perspective was not something many of us carried around in our pockets in the winter of 1970-71.

On Monday morning I went to Coach Clark's office and exhaled.

"I think it's in the best interests of everybody if I left the team for a while. I should go off on my own to see if I can get my act together."

If Coach Clark had come right out and asked, I probably would have stuck around. Instead he listened to me closely and when I finished, said, "You do what you need to do, Robert. You know you're always welcome back." I walked out of the track office and headed first to the Beta House, where I lay down on the brown leather sofa in the living room, opened a book and tried to read. Eventually I set the book aside and stared at the ceiling. Notwithstanding my earlier letter to my grandparents about maybe quitting, I still couldn't believe that I had actually just done it. I described my situation in a semi-coherent letter to my grandparents dated January 30th: "I've decided to stop running. I just can't devote the mental energy to it. The time I have. But it's too hard to make those sacrifices..." I was putting the best face on quitting. But it's an uneasy time when long-held dreams are broken.

Ten days later, the world learned that the U.S. had invaded Laos. @ @

News of this illegal escalation of the war and the American rape of another impoverished Southeast Asian nation mobilized hundreds of thousands of students coast-to-coast for action for the first time since last year's Cambodian spring. On the day the news of Laos broke – February 10th, 1971 – the *Daily* also ran a long article about how the

Stanford Research Institute had successfully co-opted the Computer Center, an institution that wasn't as innocuous as it sounded. Early video games were in development, along with some of the first software written for distribution independent of hardware; early computer music and artificial intelligence experiments were in progress as well. But so, apparently, were plans for an amphibious invasion of North Vietnam. The idea that the War was literally being both conceptualized and actively engineered on campus enraged hundreds of students, including me. I wasn't part of the latest "slew of irresponsible rebels" who broke the lock on the front door of the Computer Center, but I did participate in the "mill-in" that lasted several hours until a Tact Squad of eighty County Sheriffs arrived. I ran from police clubs, along with hundreds of other students, for the second time in my life. I saw fleeing demonstrators pummeled and bloodied. At one point I hurtled a fallen body to avoid a clubbing of my own. A friend from Jordan House, an on-campus co-op residence where I sometimes dined, left the demonstration and returned in a ski mask to cold-cock a (helmeted) County Sheriff with a two-by-four.

Whether you were a Jock or not didn't matter. It was time to interfere with our university's involvement with our nation's despicable war. Those of us who participated in this purportedly "illegal" action were supposedly incited by Stanford English Professor H. Bruce Franklin, one of several speakers at a White Plaza rally earlier that day who had supported a strike at a number of campus facilities, including the Computer Center. It was increasingly difficult to miss this vaguely-Maoist, crypto-Stalinist Herman Melville scholar who almost single-handedly was hijacking the Stanford Peace Movement before our eyes. As a member of the Bay Area chapter of the Revolutionary Union and more recently of an armed revolutionary group called "Venceremos" – Spanish for "We Will Prevail," said to be the battle cry of Che Guevara – Franklin had made himself the public face of campus demonstrations as well as myriad acts of borderline legality, including the incitement of more than one demonstration that turned violent. My grandparents worried that I might be falling under Franklin's "spell," which actually offended me a little. "No way am I jumping on Franklin's bandwagon," I wrote them. "In fact I viscerally dislike the man, who among other things I consider manipulative and intellectually dishonest..." Nevertheless the idea that H. Bruce Franklin had somehow incited the Computer Center action would set in motion events that ultimately led to his becoming the first tenured professor to be fired from an American university in more than a century. @ @

"I have not been 'incited' by Franklin, nor has anyone I know," I told Decker as we loitered together in White Plaza, half-listening to one of Franklin's over-amplified rallies that winter. "We don't need his self-serving rhetoric to want to end the war. Forget Bruce Franklin. Decker, tell me something: what serious person thinks there's going to be a political revolution? In this country? In the United States? An overthrow of the federal government?'"

"'The Revolution Will Not Be Televised,'" Decker said, quoting "The Last Poets," a proto-rap group whose recordings we loved. ("Whitey's on the Moon" was another great poem of Gil Scott-Heron's.) This "un-televised" revolution was something different than "the whole world is watching," or the revolution Franklin spouted off about. It was related but ultimately different from the revolution to be found in the pages of a book. What The Last Poets said was that real change, true revolution, would not happen in the phony glare of consumption and publicity. The un-televised Revolution wouldn't be just political; it would be informed by politics, but it would be personal, and in time cultural (or countercultural), and over a long duration it could gather enough momentum and power to change everything, including our politics, and even our sports. This was what I thought at the time, when I thought about such things. But I also recognized that political revolution and the violent rhetoric that Bruce Franklin used to drive it carried an emotional appeal for at least some opponents of the war.

"Venceremos" was doing some good things off-campus, like organizing a drop-in medical facility and drug clinic, defending and educating "political prisoners," and setting up legal defense funds for anti-war activists. But the return of violent demonstrations on campuses across the country would also reinvigorate the national backlash against the counterculture and anti-war activism generally, assisting Richard M. Nixon in claiming the existence of a "Silent Majority" in support of his duplicitous "Peace With Honor" that seemed no closer to ending the war than when he took office. @ @

Surrounded by these sorrows and distractions, these triumphs and fiascos, I stepped out of the shower at the Beta House one morning that winter and practically killed myself slipping on the ooze on the bottom of the stall. Five months of disgust spilled out of me.

"Who *cleans* these god-damned bathrooms? I've lived here for months, I don't even know!"

"You askin' me, bro?" said one of the newer Brothers, a vague-looking water polo player who was trying to shave in a mirror D had shattered with his forehead on a bad mescaline trip not long ago. (The Betas always included lots of water polo players, who I thought were among the toughest athletes on campus. While I was shivering in some under-heated classroom on the Quad in January, these dudes were trying to drown each other in Lake Lag.)

"Look at these toilets!" I raved on. "Does anyone *ever* clean these things? Look at this – there's – there's *algae* growing in the urinals! It's like somebody's experiment in *horticulture!* We're lucky we don't have another typhoid epidemic, like the one in '69! Plus the *noise* in this place! People coming, going, playing tackle football in the halls, eating mushrooms, dropping 'Windowpane...'"

"It's the same fucked-up place it's always been, bro," my bathroom companion, lazily returning to a hard-to-reach spot under the wing of his nose.

The grossness of the Beta House had gotten to me finally. And yet some of the old animal magnetism and BMOC glamour still clung to the place. "Cutting the mustard" brought me a casual friend for a couple of weeks that winter. She was one of the most beautiful women

I had ever seen on campus, and she tumbled into bed with me one night, only to spend the next week quizzing me about running.

"What's it like, maintaining the sort of dedication it takes to be a good distance runner? How do you focus so much time and energy on running when you're also in school? Isn't a lot of long-distance running painful? What inspires you to do this? Is it your teammates? Trying to improve? What? What? *What?*" I am probably exaggerating a little – in fact I'm sure I am – but I truly did not understand why she was interested in me. A weird thought intervened: her former boyfriend was an old teammate of mine. Had he painted me out to be some kind of star? This had to be a preposterous fantasy, right? That this gorgeous former Hawaiian bikini model, a blonde, blue-eyed sophomore, who was also fiercely smart, was some kind of cross-country *groupie?* We'd came a long way since *The Graduate*, baby. The idea swelled into a strange form of romantic paranoia. It just seemed too bizarre that she had sought me out for this intimate sharing, only to quiz me about being a Jock.

"Your psychology fascinates me," she replied, when I asked her about it, which I did. "High-performance psychology fascinates me."

"My *psychology* fascinates you? I'm a distance runner! You should be talking to a Rose Bowl football player! You're like the Polish actress who sleeps with the screenwriter!"

She wasn't the least offended by my tacky joke; in fact she laughed at it. Women at Stanford were taking possession of their sexuality with the same freedom men were. A lot more sexual experimentation was happening on campus than before I left for Europe. But my uneasiness about my new friend's motives eventually took the air out of her and me, and we just kind of moved on (Years later, when I learned that she was a successful psychiatrist with a thriving practice, I would wish I had gotten over myself and gotten to know her better.) @ @

One slip in the shower wasn't what pushed me out of the Beta House, rather a constellation of fuck-ups. Ferris, Haywood, Kauf, Willy, Pimo

285

and many others who had lived there over the years remained great people in my book, but almost all of them had flown the Butt Hutt years ago. The night that convinced me I had to get a life elsewhere was the night D shot a home movie of one of the Thunder Chickens screwing a Townie on D's king-size waterbed. Hot lights had been set up all over D's room, and fifteen Betas were hiding on the Portico, peeking through the windows as the Thunder Chicken's naked ass plunged up and down between the legs of this faceless woman.

"What's that noise?" the woman kept asking.

"Come on, it's nothing," said D's friend.

"Why's it so bright in here? Can't we turn the lights down?"

"No, I like it like this. Come on baby…" The Devil took the Hindmost: once she realized what was going on, she shoved D's friend away, cursed him out, threw on her clothes, and stormed out the door.

Pandemonium on the Portico! D, shaking his fists at the sky, shrieked "this is the greatest day of my life!!" (Another Beta, the son of the sitting Republican Lieutenant Governor of Pennsylvania, would go on to become a leading Bay area lawyer in the field of sexual harassment, but not because of this.) I didn't waste a breath condemning the indefensible, and I won't now. I simply told myself that the Beta House had failed "to marry the exuberance of fraternal hi-jinks to countercultural extremities," as Brother Skip had spun it psychedelically back in the spring of '69. Smoking dope and gobbling psychoactive drugs had become just another thing for frat boys who wanted to get fucked up, despite the best intentions of high-minded stoners like Skip and me, not to mention budding gurus like Dick Roth.

A month into winter quarter I moved out of the Butt Hutt and into a room in a 1890s-era house in College Terrace, a five-minute walk from campus, where I wouldn't have to deal with constant noise and filth and could clear my head and focus on what I needed to do to pull myself out of the mess my junior season had become. The Lambda Sigma Chapter of Beta Theta Pi, meanwhile – one of Stanford's original fraternities, founded with the school in 1894 – would muck along until 1997, when some combination of infractions I don't have the heart to relate resulted in its being barred from campus. Future generations with other Greek letters would have to figure out how to make fraternities more civil places, because the Sixties had come and gone on The Farm, and a Frat House remained a Frat House after all. I still had friends who lived there and who I would visit every so often, but my days as an active Beta were over and done. @ @

Quitting running haunted me. It weighed on me, too. I couldn't comprehend how I could be walking away from a commitment that had owned me for years. "Nice not to have to run every day," I wrote my grandparents in early February. "Might go out for a 'jog' later…" That morning I ran my usual 4.7 mile "jog" around campus – easy to do because my new residence was on the edge of the trail. (I had taken notice of this before I took the place.) I put no pressure on myself to run hard or fast, and it felt pretty good. When I did it again the next morning, it felt natural to pick up the pace a little. When it still felt good, I said to hell with it and ran Arastradero. I was sore the next day but went for another long run and felt good again, once I loosened up. In another ten days I could run Arastradero – eleven miles from my new place – in a little more than an hour. By the second week of March, I was trying some light intervals on the soccer field. I let Coach Clark know that I was back in training, and began to hope, as preposterous as it would have sounded only weeks before, that I might manage to pick up some of the pieces of my junior season after all.

Our dual meet season was in progress, but I did not want to rush back into competition. If I was to be anywhere close to competitive in the Half and Mile, which seemed the best events for me, I would need to do fast intervals on the track. And I would need to do them alone. So twice a week I did what I had done on my first day on campus, only under cover of darkness: I scaled the barbwire fence enclosing Stanford Stadium and ran private workouts, at least on those evenings when the sky was cloudless and the moon was more than half full, because otherwise it was too dark to see. Running these ghostly reps in moonlight, pacing alone in the 85,000-seat bowl where our football team had knocked off S.C. last fall, and hearing no sounds except my own breath and footfalls, were among the most memorable intervals I ever ran in college. The drama of my solitude brought out the best in me, as it had in Berlin eleven months before, only here there was silvery moonlight to run through, not ninety-degree heat. Monday nights I would run ladders: a 660 at 1:30 pace, jog a 660; a 440 in a minute, followed by a quarter-mile jog; then a 220 in 28 seconds, and jog a 220; then do the quarter-mile segment again, then the 660 again, and repeat the entire series this way two more times. I had rarely done hard intervals alone before, and hadn't known I could. Almost two years had passed since I trained consistently on a track, and yet this was what I had always thought training for track was since high school. Only now Cat Stevens ran through my head. *"I'm being followed by a Moonshadow... Moonshadow, moonshadow... And if I ever lose my legs... I won't moan and I won't beg... And if I ever lose my legs... I won't have to run no more..."* Afterwards I would trot back to College Terrace, shower, have a hot meal and usually tumble into bed – and as I closed my eyes come back to myself for the first time since my Spartan summer after Europe and my abbreviated cross-country season the previous fall. @ @

I was staying away from the team until I got my act together, but I still heard news about Stanford Track & Field. The highlight of the Stanford-Oregon dual meet in Eugene was Steve Prefontaine's Three-Mile victory in a PR 13:01.6, an Oregon school record, Hayward Field record, and the fastest time in the world so far that year – although Pre was reportedly disappointed that he fell eight seconds short of Lindgren's American mark. Kardong's Log, Star Date April 3rd, 1971: "Meet with UO, got the dukie kicked out of us in everything but hurdles, PV, TJ. Ran 13:34.4 behind Pre at 13:01.6 and Arv at 13:31.9. Feel good and depressed." Jordan was quoted in the Eugene papers as saying that the team he had brought north "was the best dual meet team in all my years here," but on the flight home to San Francisco he told Dave Whiteing that this was the last year he was bringing a full squad up to Hayward Field if all it meant was another Indian massacre.

The score against Oregon had been close to that of the U.C.L.A.-Stanford dual meet score earlier that year – Bruins 108, Indians 37 – although I don't remember hearing this at the time, since we didn't tend to talk much about scores, for reasons that should be obvious.

Four days after Eugene, Jim Kauffman took me and a female friend from the Jordan House co-op to celebrate my twenty-first birthday at a winery in Palo Alto, and afterwards to a campus screening of a Ukrainian film, *Shadows of Our Ancestors.* This was why we missed Nixon's televised address informing the American people that the stories of atrocities emanating from Southeast Asia shouldn't be used to disparage the noble work of the over two and one-half million men and women in uniform who blah blah blah. The following morning, another police riot off campus: thirty hours after the Black United Front, the Black Liberation Front, Venceremos and the Latin Alliance occupied administrative offices at the Stanford Medical Center to protest the firing of a Black custodian, the cops smashed through a glass door with a battering ram, leaving thirteen officers and two dozen protestors injured in the melee. I happened to be at the Beta House when a half-dozen activists came racing up the front steps out of breath, insisting that we all had to rush away to join the righteous anti-police action. I thought about following them, but I didn't know what I was prepared to do, or what the thing was about, really. So I was not even a spectator of this cop violence, and barely of a world gone insane once more. I was too busy reading books and trying to be a Jock again.

After three more weeks of solid training – seven weeks into my comeback – I felt fit enough to give Coach Clark a call.

"Could I have a time trial –"

Coach replied before I could finish my sentence. "I'll set something up for you. Be down at the Stadium tomorrow at 3:30."

Two minutes later I did what I knew I knew I had to do: I borrowed scissors from a housemate and cut my latest growth of curls. @ @

My audition for the Track Team took place on another perfect mid-peninsula afternoon, Monday, April 26th, 1971. Coach Clark thought a 1320 was just the thing for me: a three-lap time trial. After we discussed the pace I thought I could handle, he arranged for a pair of rabbits: Kardong would take me through my first lap and a half; Macdonald, my second. With old friends and teammates on the infield screaming encouragement (I don't remember Jordan being there), these two future Olympians helped me hit my targets: a 61-second first lap; a 62-second second lap. On lap three people ran down the back straightaway, roaring in our ears: *"Goooooo!!!"* I pushed across the finish line and jogged on to the infield. I recovered almost immediately.

Coach Clark walked up to me and without reading from his watch said: "3:03-flat, Robert. Your last quarter was 60-flat." This was short of national caliber, but it was a presentable start for my year, and as such prompted the only occasion in my college career in which I raised my fists to the heavens and unleashed a primal scream: *"Yessssss!"* I even ran a mock victory lap to the loud guffaws and low fives of teammates who were still lining the oval. My biggest compliment of the afternoon: "I don't think I could have run that fast today." "That's a load of crap, Duncan," I replied, "but nice of you to say so anyway."

Ten minutes later, leaving the Stadium for an easy five miles to close my day, I was thinking this: how sweet to the soul is desire accomplished! Coach had just informed me that I would be on the flight to Seattle on Friday for our dual meet against the University of Washington Huskies. My experience as a Stanford Jock underwent a serious upgrade five miles over crystal-blue Crater Lake in Central Oregon, then at our motel overlooking Lake Washington, with views of Mt. Rainier, the Olympic Mountains and the downtown skyline of Seattle as well as our next-day venue, Husky Stadium, where I would soon be pacing my very first Varsity Mile against Arvid Kretz and a trio of panting Huskies. I thought I was on the way back, and now I would have to prove it. @ @

Arvid had pushed the pace from the start, probably because he knew that if he didn't and it came down to a kicker's race, he might well lose.

Arv was having a very good Track season that spring: his 13:31.9 Three-Mile in Eugene was faster than Kardong's season's best, faster than Brock's old school mark, and only a few ticks behind the school record Don had set at the N.C.A.A.s last year. With that effort Kretz had finally entered the national conversation. He had also run a 4:07 Time Trial earlier that year, and now I was twelve feet behind him on the final back straightaway, when two Huskies suddenly appeared on my shoulder, pressing to get by. Urged on by teammates screaming *go-go-go* (I'll never forget them) I held off our opponents until I cleared the last curve and entered the final straightaway. Mission accomplished: Stanford would go one-two. So I set my sights on Arvid, ten feet ahead of me and sprinting for all he was worth.

We were shoulder to shoulder at the tape.

We used to razz Arv at workouts for practicing his "lean" – the lunge you make to break the tape just ahead of an opponent. Well, that day in Seattle Kretz beat me with one. We were both given the same time: 4:10 flat – a half-second slower than my freshman PR, but still the second fastest Mile of my life. And I had negative-split – running my last half-mile faster than my first, and my last lap in 61 seconds. Just beyond the finish line Arvid and I hugged: "Great race, Arv!" "You, too, Bob!" Then we stepped off the track and the meet resumed. (The Northern California Track & Field Association would name Arvid Athlete of the Year at the end of our junior season.) I wasn't overjoyed with my 4:10 Mile, but I was pleased. This was something more to build on. I only wished we had more season ahead, instead of just one more dual meet, against Cal. As I ran my cool-down I became the recipient of loud congratulations from teammates – partly to welcome me back, but as one teammate later confided, also because "nobody's seen a Stanford runner produce a finishing kick in weeks." @ @

On campus the following Monday felt like my first day in the spring of freshman year: the same nervous bladder, the jolts of adrenalin, the general excitement about my first official Stanford Track practice in almost two years, not counting that 500-yard time trial just before

Mono struck me down. It was astonishing to think that only now, at the end of my junior year, was I arriving at the Stadium to train as a Varsity team member – mind-boggling that it had taken me this long to leave behind the fractured worlds of war and alienation and strife and settle into what had been my dream as an eager freshman who tore his running shorts climbing over the fence to break into this very same track where I would be training today. And only now was I trotting down the stadium ramp a few minutes before the 3:30 start, fully aware that I was finally joining a program that had been my dream ever since I first thought about running for the school.

No team warm-up was in progress, because apparently Jordan's team didn't have one, so I wasn't sure where to go. I saw sprinters on their patch of grass, stretching or resting; field men in another; weight men had their spot, too. The energy was casual to the point of lethargy. Okay, things will pick up later… I jogged down to where Don Kardong was stretching, alone near the long jump pit.

"Don, what's up?" I said. "Where's Coach?" We both knew I meant Coach Clark, although Coach Jordan was nowhere in sight, either.

"Not here yet," Kardong replied. "Ignore everything, keep your head down and stick with us."

Don stood up, brushed the sand from his hands, and the two of us set off for an easy mile around the well-worn grass and brown dirt just inside our Tartan track. Arvid joined us on our second lap, then a few more of our guys. It felt like the start of a cross-country workout, which was fine with me. We had almost finished warming up when one of the sprinters came jogging up alongside me, twisting his bare torso in my direction, clearly dying to talk and thrilled to have a kindred spirit Back on the Bus, or so he reasonably imagined. @ @

Chuck was how we knew him then, but he would become known around the world as Charlie Francis. He was Canada's reigning 100-Meter sprint champion and one of the only Canadians of his era to out-race his countryman, Olympic Bronze Medalist Harry Jerome, but

292

having only a so-so senior year on The Farm, running some 9.5's over 100-Yards. Training on his own in the summer, he would blaze a 10.1 100-Meters, one of the fastest times in the world, at the Canadian Pan-Am Games trials in Vancouver. Considering that forty years later only one runner of European descent has broken ten seconds, Chuck's time remains impressive – and if Stanford rules then had allowed marks made over the summer after graduation to count towards the Athletic Department's record book, as they do today, Charlie Francis would still be easily the fastest man in school history in 2015. Chuck would end his so-so senior year as the fifth-ranked 100-Meter runner in the world, and a year later become a Canadian Olympian in Munich, where an injury would take him out in a Quarter-Final. He would later testify that he had not known about performance-enhancing drugs until 1973, two years before the IOC banned anabolic steroids, when he took five milligrams of Dianabol daily for three weeks and repeated as Canada's 100-Meter champion. By the Nineteen-Eighties, Charlie Francis would be recognized as possibly the most knowledgeable sprint coach in the world, guiding athletes to 250 Canadian records, 32 world records and nine Olympic medals, achievements dwarfing those of his college coach. But Chuck's greatest notoriety would come at the 1988 Summer Games in Seoul, where a sprinter he coached since age fifteen year shattered the world record over 100-Meters and won the Gold only to be stripped of both in the most famous drug scandal in Olympic history. Charlie would provide historic testimony to Canada's doping council about a sport that he (and others) claimed was dominated by "enhanced" athletes, remarking: "There is a level playing field out there, just not the one you know." The "real" playing field was one where everyone "juiced," which was why Charlie had done it, too – not as a substitute for hard training, but as "an essential ingredient within a complex recipe." As a participant in a vicious cycle of drug abuse, our Chuck Francis would go on to become the most reviled Track Coach in Olympic history.

"Nice Mile in Seattle, Bobby!" Chuck called out on my first afternoon back. "Train on your own for seven weeks, then drop a four-ten-flat?

That's a good start for you! You want to hear what 'Payt' has in mind for the sprinters today?" And before I could tell Chuck whether I wanted to hear what "Payt" – a name he always spat out in a tone of withering sarcasm – had in mind or not, Chuck was describing in full detail the workout "Payt" had planned for him, which Chuck considered the most asinine thing he had ever been asked to do in his life. "This is mid-season we're talking about, Bobby!" he said, looking at me bug-eyed as we jogged along. "I'm telling you, man, it's *insane!!*"

I didn't know enough about sprint training to know whether Coach Jordan's workout that day was "insane" or not, but I did know that Chuck could be so arrogant and obnoxious about our Head Coach that a lot of people avoided him. I liked Chuck, because he was not only the smartest athlete I ever met at Stanford, he was one of the smartest *people* – a pragmatist and a technocrat more interested in finding ways to do things better than in doing "the right thing." (Another teammate of ours, sprinter Kevin McNair, made his own study of kinesiology and in his first year as Head Coach of Track & Field and cross country at Occidental College, won the 1978 N.C.A.A. Division III championships in both.) You may think I'm exaggerating Francis' loathing of "Payt" – he wouldn't even grant Jordan the honorific "Coach," preferring "pompous ass" and "buffoon" – but to exaggerate his hatred of Jordan would be impossible. Chuck knew about my run-ins with our mutual nemesis, which was why he was welcoming me back so heartily on my first afternoon. It was evil of me to wave a red flag under Chuck's nose, but baiting him was fun.

"I have friends who call Coach Ralston a 'plastic man,'" I said. (Coach Jordan was still nowhere in sight.) "What does that make 'Payt?'"

"'The Man in the Empty Track Suit?' The Emperor's New Clothes? Come on, Bobby, you tell me…"

Coach Clark had arrived. Our distance crew was about to begin the day's workout – twenty reps of a Quarter-Mile, the ideal interval for Mile training. But before I could leave Chuck grabbed my arm.

"One more thing: so Stanford hasn't beaten U. S.C. in a dual meet since 1933, right? This would suggest that the problem is systemic – it's structural! But this year 'Payt' pushes his chalkboard into the middle of the locker room to illustrate for us 'boys' – mathematically, mind you – how if certain of us surpassed our lifetime bests, then we could manage to score just enough points to defeat the Trojans on our date with destiny in the Stadium, or some shit like that. But then somebody goes – and I swear it wasn't me – somebody goes, 'Hey Coach! You added wrong. We still lose by ten points.' Jordan checked his arithmetic – and promptly changed the subject!"

We had a nice chuckle over that. "What about Jordan's 'Chalk Talk' in the locker room before the S.C. meet last year?"

"You mean that 'paytriotic' speech in front of the color chalk drawing of 'Old Glory?' That was hilarious, too. But what was funny this year wasn't his bad arithmetic. That was a mistake anybody could have made. What was funny was Payt thinking that half the team could pull off a PR on the same day! You don't just pull a PR out of your ass, Bobby, do you? You gear your training, you peak, you taper – right? But I guess that's not 'The Way of Payt,' is it. With Payt it all just happens with a sprinkling of inspirational fairy dust! Anyway – go join your workout. Have a good one... Talk soon..."

Some readers might think it was above the pay grade of a bunch of smart-aleck undergrads to take the measure of the most successful Track & Field Coach in Olympic history. But we had come to The Farm to learn to think for ourselves, and many of us were doing just that with a rigor inflamed by the anti-authoritarianism of the times, and influenced, too, by the misconduct, lies and betrayals of our national leadership, no doubt. Plus we had Jordan's own Assistant Coach for sprinters, Bill Moultrie, on our side. The first Black Coach at Stanford in any sport, recruited a few years earlier from Ravenswood High School in East Palo Alto, had taken me aside on the infield during the S.C. Track Meet my freshman year – *me*, a freshman, with the meet still in progress – to rail at length about Jordan's old-fashioned training and his intolerance of the differences between people. Moultrie bolted The Farm a few years later, eventually to become Head Coach at Howard, where he produced 71 All-Americans and ended his twenty-five-year career in the Track & Field Coaches Hall of Fame. @ @

We smart-alecky undergraduates had all kinds of evidence that our Head Coach was no longer the great coach he had been at Oxy, or that the world of Track & Field seemed to think he was. The number of All-Americans attributed to Coach Jordan in his years on The Farm was one measure of his achievements there. To be "All-American" in those days required a top-six finish at the N.C.A.A. championship, which meant that around three hundred All-American awards were handed out annually. In his twenty-three years at Stanford, Jordan would be credited with coaching 25 athletes to 29 All-American honors, but at least two dozen college Track & Field coaches and programs nationwide produced numbers far in excess of the roughly one top-six national performance that Jordan managed annually on The Farm. Producing All-Americans should not be the sole measure of a college coach's success, but Jordan's head count was decidedly middle of the road, and certainly no great shakes for a program that presented itself as among the elite. How, then, did we account for Jordan's triumph with an Olympic team that set six world records, after setting another four in the Trials? Several prominent Olympians testified to the inspiration Jordan had provided them in Mexico City, but all of them had gotten to the Games without Jordan's help. The most successful Track & Field college coach in American history, Arkansas's John McDonnell, who would lead 185 Hogs to 652 All-American performances during his thirty years in Fayetteville, would describe an Olympic Head Coach as "basically a baby sitter. Make sure they get to the track in time for their event. They all have their personal coaches."

Jordan's lack of openness to recent developments in techniques and training methods wasn't just eye-opening, it was shocking. Here were his thoughts on Dick Fosbury, his Gold Medal Olympic High Jumper and pioneer of "The Fosbury Flop," which sent high jumpers over the bar on their backs into a soft-cushioned high-jump pit: "Kids imitate champions. But if they try to imitate Fosbury, he will wipe out an entire generation of high-jumpers because they will all have broken necks!" Some people thought Jordan was joking when he made this comment, since no one in their right mind would flop into an old-fashioned sawdust pit, but Stanford had the modern, cushioned kind, where Jordan continued to coach the Western Roll while the rest of the world learned to "Flop" without any greater incidence of injury than before. There were also his views on strength training: a free-spirited Stanford football player named Terry Albritton would finish second in the Pac-8 Shot Put as a freshman in the mid-Seventies before dropping out of school, disillusioned by the violence of the gridiron and Jordan's resistance to his introduction of new training techniques from behind the Iron Curtain. Terry would work out on his own for a year, transfer to the University of Hawaii, and as a mere twenty-one-year-old college junior set a new shot put World Record of 71' 8½". Months later Hawaii dropped its Track & Field program entirely, and Albritton returned to Stanford to continue his education and win an N.C.A.A. Shot Put title in 1977, with a throw four feet short of his lifetime best.

In the sprints, supposedly Jordan's strong suit, our Head Coach could represent with his 1967 Quarter-Mile Relay team, which set a world record in a race contested in the U.S. and the British Commonwealth. But I preferred to trust the critique of Chuck Francis, an also-ran under Jordan, who coaching himself would become the fifth-best 100-Meter man in the world that very year; also Jordan's assistant for sprinters, Bill Moultrie, who wasn't given the freedom to run his own program the way Coach Clark was. As for middle- and long-distance training, I knew something about myself. I knew that Coach Jordan was aware of training methods around the world, and had even corresponded for a time with distance guru Arthur ("Train Don't Strain") Lydiard. I knew that Jordan and his proxy Coach Barland had helped bring a trio of Stanford Milers close to four minutes in the early Sixties, and that Jordan's Occidental teams had produced world records in the Two-Mile and the Distance Medley Relays (my events), as well as a Silver Medalist in the Metric Mile at the Helsinki Olympics, Tom McMillan, who missed the Gold by one-tenth of a second. But Kenny Moore, who had observed Jordan and Jerry Barland's program first-hand while attending Stanford Law School, would sum up their approach succinctly in a book published many years later: "Daily intervals and unquestioning faith – the cycle repeated by abused runners everywhere." In Moore's 2006 biography of Bill Bowerman, "the great guru of track coaches," as *SI* called Bowerman in the spring of 1970, Kenny would recount a letter he wrote to his former coach at the University of Oregon, who had also served as Payton Jordan's assistant for distance runners and who done the actual organizing of the '68 Olympic training center at Lake Tahoe; in it he shared a little of what Jordan and Barland were up to on The Farm. "As a Coach," Bowerman replied, "my heart is always divided between pity for the men they wreck and scorn for how easy they are to beat." Jordan did have admirers among his coaching brethren, including fellow glad-handers Jim Bush at U.C.L.A. and Vern Wolfe at U.S.C., whose teams annihilated Jordan's on an annual basis. But Moore would claim that Bowerman was so turned off by Jordan's training philosophies that he never minded running up the score against Jordan's teams, something he never did against W.S.U.'s Jack Mooberry or Cal's Brutus Hamilton.

What Moore termed "abuse" had ended when Marshall Clark arrived; we weren't being "wrecked" by anybody. We practiced a "Tao" of training – not a term Coach ever used, I made it up. We did intervals and long runs and had hard days and easier days, all of it built on a foundation of lots & lots of *miles*. As someone who planned to compete at distances ranging from the Half-Mile to Six, I was certain – along with Lydiard, Bowerman, and most masters of these events – that aerobic strength was key. And the best way to build aerobic strength was through "The Long Run." Long Runs had certainly been crucial to the breakthrough I had experienced since high school, transforming me from a so-so high school runner into the runner I became. Over-distance training was a staple i of elite distance runners all around the globe. But in Jordan's 1968 book *Champions in the Making: Quality Training for Track and Field* (note the use of the word "Quality") he paid lip service to the Long Run literally one time, when he mentioned in passing that during fall cross-country "certain amounts of long, continuous (marathon type) runs are invaluable" – but only as foundation work, because "in the development of superior endurance in long distance and cross-country running, the pace in training should be equal or be slightly faster than race pace." There it was, in black & white: "quality" intervals were Jordan's (and Barland's) preferred M.O. for building middle- and long-distance racing champions. This was a notion about as far from "Train Don't Strain" as you could possibly travel. Distance coaches and runners should not ignore "quality," but Coach Clark did not expect us to kill ourselves running intervals on an almost daily basis, the way Barland had. Balanced moderation was our ticket to ride: a Taoist blend of speed days and slower days, hard days and easier days, work and recovery. That was Coach Clark's recipe, and we cooked it together. Jordan probably preferred "quality" over "quantity" because it had worked for durable athletes with huge natural talent, like himself. Fortunately for us, Jordan's "quality" approach had become so irrelevant to what we actually did under Coach Clark that when Jordan's book came out my freshman year, I not only didn't read it, I didn't know it existed until thirty-five-years later, when I googled "Payton Jordan" and found used copies on Amazon.com. @ @

Even all these years later I can still feel Coach Jordan getting under my skin. I spent far too much time that spring of 1971 thinking about a coach who didn't even give us our workouts. Protesting as loudly and as often as I did, I knew I had to be conflicted about something, and was probably unable to face it. Maybe I resented that I still felt any pride at all in being one of his "favorites," as Coach Clark would remind me decades later – a resentment and pride mixed with chagrin that the distance runner he had tagged as "'the best long-distance prospect to enter Stanford since I've been here" was now a junior and had barely scratched the surface of his talent. But those weren't the core of my problems with our Head Coach. My problems stemmed from the absolute sway he had over us, and how he never seemed interested in engaging anyone with an open mind. Behind that plastic good cheer of his, that shiny optimism and hale fellow bonhomie – personal qualities so characteristic of Jordan's World War Two generation – all I could feel was his passive-aggressive will to control. I did not think our Head Coach loved losing meets week in and week out, but I did think that even more than wins, what Jordan wanted were more incoming freshmen to indoctrinate into "The Way of Payt," while simultaneously preserving his solid-gold excuse for why the resulting team were consistently on the wrong side of ordinary. I heard him trot out myself one morning in early April during an office visit to plot my comeback with Coach Clark. Jordan had emerged from his office – his Agoraphobe's Olympus – holding a letter from the Admissions Office detailing the composition of next year's entering class. He had his free hand plastered across his forehead, as if in disbelief. Looking up and seeing me, he shook his head sorrowfully.

"We just can't get the boys past Admissions, Bobby!"

Man, did I ever have to bite my tongue! First of all, what were us "boys" now, chopped liver? Jordan was consistently landing some of the top high school Track & Field athletes in the country, only to see them under-perform once they arrived. One of our top freshmen that spring was one of the greatest schoolboy sprinters America had ever produced: Kenny Curl had run a near-world-record 9.3 for 100-yards when he was just fifteen years old and been profiled in *Sports Illustrated* while a Houston, Texas high schooler. But he arrived on The Farm thirty pounds overweight, and despite Jordan's supposed expertise at motivating his "boys," Kenny still had ten pounds to shed and would manage only an ordinary 10-flat for 100-Yards that freshman year. Not all athletic failure should be laid at the feet of a coach; athletes have some responsibilities, too, but Kenny never did seem to keep a fire lit. The following season I would see him upset the world-record holder in the Quarter-Mile, U.C.L.A.'s John Smith, over 220-yards in the Stadium, but in a time he had run as a high school junior, and to the best of my knowledge that would be the highpoint of Kenny's Stanford career. Another high school superstar Jordan succeeded in recruiting was the youngest Track & Field Olympian in American history: Casey

Carrigan, a cheerful, good-looking sophomore who I would see often that spring, sitting on the grass near the pole vault pit, re-taping his poles. Casey was a self-taught vaulting genius who had qualified for the Mexico City Olympic team as a high school junior and briefly held the U.S. Trials record at 16' 6¾". As a senior he had vaulted 17-feet, 4¾ inches, a national schoolboy record that would climb only ten inches in the four decades that followed. Think about it: a high school Pole Vaulter, short of the world record by the length of his palm! Great things were expected from Casey on The Farm, where he had followed his two football-playing older brothers, but Mono caught him his freshman year, the season I was in Europe; even so, he cleared 16-feet to tie for fourth at Nationals, earning an All-American award. In the current season he had vaulted 16-7, but after a 15-feet, 6-inch clearance at Conference and three misses at 16-feet at Nationals, this son of a Washington State logging trucker would drop out of college for good – "not his cup of tea," according to the *Daily* – discouraged by illnesses, recurring injuries, and (by a few reports) the Payton Jordan regime. (Four years later Casey would stage a comeback and become the best Pole Vaulter in America and one of the best in the world, clearing 17-10¾, only not in a Stanford uniform – or the Emperor's New Clothes.)

"Sure Enough!" was one of the inspirational slogans Payt had framed on the locker room wall. Sure enough, Stanford's admission standards were as high as any Division I program in the nation; no doubt many athletes Jordan coveted failed to win acceptance. But sure enough, some of Jordan's difficulties he brought upon himself: rumors had persisted since my freshman year on the Athletic Council (Brook Thomas had heard them, too) that the Stanford Admissions Office was so turned off by Jordan's dicta about hair and appearance that they no longer accepted track athletes with borderline applications, a favor they had extended to other teams for years. Also note that Jordan had fewer scholarships to offer than the powerhouses, U.C.L.A., U.S.C. and Oregon; the PAC-8 wasn't a level playing field, leaving Jordan little room for mistakes. But mistakes were made, huge ones, and often: I saw scholarships awarded to athletes with little motivation to train and no accomplishments beyond a good mark or two, some of them possibly bogus. Jordan may well have become so frustrated not being able to get "boys past Admissions" that he had given up on the whole process. I didn't knock Jordan for wanting what every college coach wants: more talent. But the most important thing any college coach should be doing is nurturing the talent he has, which clearly involved more than an athlete's willingness to submit to "the Jordan Treatment." I thought blaming Admissions for why his teams weren't competitive was a big fat excuse and little more. The real problem was that Stanford Track & Field (with apologies to Pete Seeger) was "neck deep in the Big Muddy, and the Big Fool said to push on." @ @

Yet there were a few afternoons that spring when I would gaze across the infield and see Coach Jordan timing runners and encouraging field men – almost always with that Klieg Light smile on his face and a springy bounce in his slightly pigeon-toed stride – and try to cut the man some slack; try to think of him as a victim of changing times, trapped on the wrong side of history, unable to pass into a post-Sixties world. I would imagine that the trying times we lived in were what had caused so many of his athletes to come up short or be driven away. But then I would remember that Jordan was a national conservative icon, a half-step behind Bob Hope, John Wayne and Woody Hayes in the eyes of some people, and a man whose coaching style was perfectly congruent with his politics, and inseparable from who and what he was. We might dream of E-Massa-Payting ourselves from Massa Payt, kicking the Fifties off Stanford Track (as our football team had taken down Woody Hayes), and letting "the wind of freedom blow," but we all knew that Coach Jordan wasn't going anywhere. And we also knew why so few outsiders viewed our Head Coach the way we did. His sunny demeanor and youthful achievements was part of the Jordan brand. So was his record at Occidental and his 1965 N.C.A.A. "Coach of the Year" award. So was his (demonstrably untrue) claim that his teams were consistently among the top ten dual meet teams in the nation, when the only Pac-8 team Jordan ever beat with regularity was Cal. Remember our loss last year to De Anza Community College? But then there was his Mexico City triumph, one so complete that it could be argued that Jordan was the greatest Olympic baby sitter in history.

There was also the U.S.-U.S.S.R. Track & Field meet of 1962, which only came off because Stanford's then-Athletic Director had approached Jordan about arranging the fourth in a series of dual meets between the Cold War rivals, in order hopefully to erase a $100,000 department budget deficit. The 1960 U.S. Olympic Trials that Jordan had organized attracted a two-day crowd of 108,000, still the Trials attendance record over a half-century later, but this time Jordan pulled off an even bigger box office coup, attracting over 155,000 ticket-buyers for a two-day Soviet-U.S. competition whose primary reason for being wasn't to nurture understanding between Cold War superpowers, as the propagandists told us; it was to make a buck, and it did, eliminating the Athletic Department debt entirely. I didn't believe there was anything wrong with combining a noble cause and a handsome profit, but when Jordan told people that the U.S.-Soviet competition transcended politics and revealed our "common humanity" – well, if you believed that was all Jordan was up to, I would have tried to sell you the Dumbarton Bridge. Why else would our Coach show up at an official team meeting with a crude chalkboard drawing of an American flag, if he didn't think this show of "Paytriotism" would inspire his "boys" to great feats of athleticism in a time of national turmoil? Why else would he insist that we all look like Young Republicans, if not to demonstrate that we were everything those long-haired, left-wing, "anti-American" hippies were not?

The success of the Capitalists versus Commies Stanford Athletic Department Rescue Mission– a half-century later bleacherreport.com would call it "The Greatest Track Meet of All Time"– had to be another reason why Jordan never faced any repercussions over the consistently-poor performances of recent teams. The Athletic Department must not have cared about the numerous talented walk-ons and scholarship athletes who had under-performed or been driven away by Jordan's outdated training methods, his Paleolithic conservatism and the whole team vibe. I had to think that the Athletic

Department was either unaware of or didn't care about his letter-writing campaign to parents during the Pat Morrison affair, or how he had broken his word to his team about abiding by our vote on appearance. But – *basta!* As Duncan Macdonald would note decades later –"To call Coach Clark a positive influence is a gross understatement." I thanked my lucky stars every day that I was training under Coach Clark's practical, minimal guiding hand! @ @

From Payton Jordan to H. Bruce Franklin, from Richard Nixon to my own grandfather, I did battle authority. But I wasn't looking for a countercultural coach, or countercultural training. Our distance crew was its own counterculture. My freshman year, also Marshall Clark's first, the Athletic Department also hired Dan Millman, a young gymnastics coach from Berkeley who quickly brought Stanford teams to national prominence, training (among others) Steve Hug, a three-time N.C.A.A. All-Around Champion, two-time Olympian and the greatest American male gymnast of the era. Coach Millman would later write a semi-autobiographical novel, *Way of the Peaceful Warrior*, about an injured gymnast who meets a man at a gas station and dubs him "Socrates." This book would be far too much of a rip-off of Carlos Castaneda's *The Teachings of Don Juan: A Yaqui Way of Knowledge* to be of interest to me (although I would like the 2006 movie, with Nick Nolte as Socrates.) I much preferred our Coach's consistent, un-mystical, laid-back coaching style: tough-minded and mutually respectful.

In my freshman Sociology class I had read studies claiming that successful cultures in all walks of life are all built on a foundation of mutual respect, and we distance runners had it. This was why it still felt right to show up at the Stadium on those beautiful mid-peninsula afternoons to run workouts that were models of good judgment and high morale. Compared to the rest of the team we distance guys were the Hobbits of Middle Earth, a kick-ass Garage Band, the 101st Airborne! Our school record intermediate hurdler Randy White told Kardong that he so envied the freedom and camaraderie we shared that he wished he could run with us, too, and not under Coach Jordan. Chuck Francis and Kenny Moore admired our coach as well. I had flourished under his system – blossomed beyond all expectations! "Unity Through Diversity:" that was how the Native American 10K Gold Medalist Billy Mills explained what later became known as multiculturalism, but it also described what our distance crew felt like to me. (Or as a 2015 ad for Android phones would put it: "Be together, not the same.) Following your instincts and your values and letting differences flourish while focusing on common goals: that was a much better way to work together towards the attainment of great things than through any enforced conformity or rule-making. It was a better way to work in the macrocosmic world of people and politics, too, not just in the microcosm that was our distance running world. Coach Clark wanted us first and foremost to believe in each other, and he gave us leeway to be ourselves. This was part of the reason why I would have "run through a brick wall for that man," as Jack Kemp said of Coach Jordan back in the Fifties. The only time I ever heard Coach Clark enforce a "rule" was when the rule was Payt's. Our coach didn't have any "rules" because he didn't need any. (Confucius, Analects 2.3: "Lead the people with rules, and order them with punishments, and they will avoid punishments but be without shame. Lead the people with Virtue and order them with norms and they will have shame and order themselves.") Coach Clark wasn't our Sheriff, and he didn't try to be our Dad. He didn't come at us like a force of nature, behave like a fair-weather friend, or try to infantilize us just as we were becoming men. Coach Clark held out our potential to each one of us, along with means to realize it, and let us decide whether we wanted to go there or not.

Not a day passed with Coach Clark that felt like "his way or the highway." Our Coach worked from the point of view that there was "much we'll learn together;" Coach Jordan saw his job as bringing us around to his way of seeing the world. Jordan would tell anyone who would listen that working "together" made for better teams, but except for a handful of anomalies – his non-interference with Smith and Carlos in Mexico City and allowing us distance runners to pick our own Coach from a list he compiled, to name the only two things I can think of – "togetherness" to Jordan meant unquestioning obedience to his way of doing things. He had a libertarian streak, too, and a flair for the dramatic, which was probably why he hadn't intervened before Smith & Carlos raised their gloved fists on the Mexico City medal stand. But mostly Jordan prided himself on his ability to crawl inside the heads of his "boys" to could mold them into "Champions" in his own image, a persona born in sunny Southern California, where Midwestern actor-turned-Governor Reagan had come into his own, too. This was as far from "the strength of the Wolf is the Pack, and the strength of the Pack is the Wolf" as one could think to travel. @ @

Not everyone on the Track & Field team were like Chuck Francis and me, "nattering nabobs of negativism," to steal Vice President Spiro Agnew's term for the media covering the Nixon Administration. We had teammates who probably thought our points of view were over-the-top and unfair. But I would still argue that the vast majority of my teammates had issues with Jordan but kept them to themselves in order to show up at 3:30 p.m. and do the workout, shrugging off conditions that would only steal your energy and focus. Kardong's strategy – "Ignore everything" – and Brook Thomas' – "Tune It Out" – made sense to most people. But there were teammates on Jordan's wavelength, make no mistake about that. At least fourteen former Occidental and Stanford athletes had named or would name a son either "Payton" or "Jordan." Jordan was "the nicest man in the world," according to Darrin Nelson, Stanford's future N.C.A.A. football career record-holder for all-purpose yardage, who would compete for two years in Track & Field before tearing a hamstring long jumping and missing the entire '79 football season. Was Nelson simply fooled, or was he seeing facets I couldn't? One of our discus-throwers – another "Jordan guy" – was the only person I ever heard on campus talking about how we should take the gloves off and stop fighting like "pussies" in Vietnam. Steve Davis I could live without, but other Jordan acolytes I truly liked, like T.C Jones and Clint Ostrander, the former freshman Pole Vault record-holder (15'1"), whose son T.C. would be a starting QB on The Farm thirty-five years later.

The current Co-Captains were Jordan's picks, natch: High Hurdler Rick

Tipton, a hyper-competitive conference champion, Duncan's friend and a member of Delta Tau Delta. Many decades later Tipton would become involved in a real estate scam engineered by 1968 Team Captain Jim Ward and end up sentenced to eighteen months in federal prison for his part in swindling some two hundred investors, many of them senior retirees and at least one former teammate, out of millions. Before his own trial, Ward would co-author a book about Payton Jordan entitled *Champions for Life,* which among other things claimed that he was "a teacher of character development." As the mastermind of the real estate scam, Ward would get five years. The other '71 co-captain was Allen Meredith, a two-time N.C.A.A. Triple Jump finalist whose 52-foot 3-inch conference meet record would stand as the Stanford school record until 2014. After Meredith finished behind Jim Kauffman in the regional long jump competition that qualified people for the High School State championship, he had gone to Kauf on his knees: *"Please,* Jim! You're going to State in the Quarter! Drop out of the long jump and let me go! *I've worked so hard for this!"* Begging for something he hadn't earned, from someone who wasn't even a teammate? Kauf told him "no way," and that was the end of it.

"Al," I told him one afternoon at practice, "I see your hair's getting a little long on the sides there," fluttering my hands around my ears and grinning like a fool, so he would know I was joking. Al knew what I was up to, but being a good "company man" in every sense of the term, he smiled right back at me, although he was usually smiling.

"You're right, Bobby! I am due for a haircut!"

"Al, don't do it because of something *I* said! It's just that – well, a rule's a rule with Coach Jordan, right? But why do you think we should all have short hair? What's your opinion about that?"

Seeing I was getting in deep here, Meredith re-adjusted his game. "I think Coach thinks the best way for us to become a team is for all of us to conform to a single image and speak with a single voice!"

Once I stopped laughing, I said, "Al! I don't speak with a single voice to myself, much less everybody else!" This was when Meredith had the good sense to wave a hand at me and return to his previous business, which was all the attention I deserved in the middle of a workout anyway. Al must not have realized that he was talking to someone whose life had been changed by James Joyce's *Ulysses*. But at the end of the day, none of us were any different or better than anyone else was. If you worked on Payton's Farm, you did as you were told. @ @

I was watching that day as our discus thrower Steve Davis spun around the Stadium ring and unleashed a hard throw that looked slightly awry, although still inside the "legal" area, over fifty yards away. The Coaches had warned us many times about not stretching or running on the grass when the discus throwers worked – advised us to "pay attention" – "watch out" – "be careful." Davis had been nearly struck by a discus the year before, standing on the grass in a conversation next to Coach Jordan. This time Triple Jumper Rod Utley was jogging across the infield directly into the line of flight. I instantly measured in my mind Rod's forward speed and the discus' angle of descent and had a cry rising from my throat the instant the four-pound, seven-ounce implement struck Rod squarely on his right temple.

The "thunk" echoed around the Stadium.

I sprinted over and was among the first to reach him. I saw the gaping cleft in Rod's black skin; saw inches of his bone-white skull.

Jim Kauffman was kneeling beside him, speaking into his ear. "Lie still, Rod! Don't move! Lie still!" Kardong told me later he was sure Rod was dead. But Rod was not only alive, he was conscious, squirming his legs, repeating over and over, "I can't see! I can't *see!*"

A group of sprinters turned and raced up the stadium ramp to the Training Room to call an ambulance and fetch Dave's help. Coach Clark hovered over Rod's body, stricken with horror and disbelief. Beside himself, Davis drop-kicked his discus halfway across the football field. If Jordan was present, I have no memory of it.

Rod permanently lost vision in his right eye. He would drop out of school and file a lawsuit, with Jordan reportedly a co-defendant. (Two seasons later Rod would return to land a PR 50-foot, 4 ½-inch triple jump; his 50-foot-even leap would remain the freshman school mark for another twenty-four years.) It seemed important to me to point out that this accident wasn't entirely Jordan's fault, or Davis's, either.

"We're all to blame," I vented to anyone who would listen. "This is *our* team, isn't it? Why are we so passive, when this was an accident waiting to happen? We should have forced the Athletic Department to address this worker safety issue – we're Labor, aren't we?"

Stanford's Athletic Director was Chuck Taylor, one of the legendary "Wow Boys" on the undefeated 1940 Stanford football team, the Coach of the 1952 Indian Rose Bowl team, and someone I would never lay eyes on in my four years on campus. Taylor surely had the final say as to where our discus and javelin throwers practiced, and apparently Taylor believed there was nowhere better to do it than on the infield of a Stadium that Jordan once judged "the best of all worlds for every event." My thoughts about all of this would coalesce around the second "Earth Day" on April 22nd, an occasion marked by thousands of "consciousness-raising" events around the nation and a reprinting of the famous "Pogo" cartoon in newspapers from coast to coast: *"We have met the enemy, and he is us."* @ @

Shortly after after Rod's accident, some seven hundred Vietnam veterans tossed their war medals on the West Steps of the Capitol building; the day after that, a half-million Americans marched in Washington D.C., the largest demonstration against the War since the '69 Vietnam Moratorium. Following these events on television filled me with deep sympathy and accord, along with another emotion that was certainly inappropriate and unjust, but I couldn't shake it from my mind nonetheless: I kept thinking that with our cropped hair and wall-mounted homilies, Stanford Track & Field was a gentler version of one of the nameless platoons in the jungles of South Vietnam, taking bullets (and discuses) for clueless Generals in Saigon, while doing everything we could to keep ourselves together and alive. @ @ @

"THE BIG MEET," 1971

The week of The Big Meet that year, a terrorist bomb ripped through the office of Stanford President Richard "Dick" Lyman. The grim, Groucho-worthy quip of Chuck Francis about this was: "Fortunately no one was hurt, unlike at track practice." We Breezy Injun Spikers were of no mind to be beaten down by circumstances. We tuned out the negative and accentuated the positive, packed up our troubles in our old kit bags and recalibrated our sights. The cultural Cold War on our team faded like a bad dream. We metaphysically fragged Coach Jordan with Get-Lost Bombs! We even showed Coach Clark a back seat for a while. Our Side of the Bay put everything aside, which is frankly what athletes have done to coaches good and bad since time immemorial, and determined to do what Men of Stanford have strived to do since the late nineteenth century: shave Golden Bears! We would meet the Enemy, and they were Them! This was the Big Meet! This was Stanford v. Cal!

Cal Berkeley was the prohibitive favorite that afternoon, having won the N.C.A.A. Team Championship the year before, only to have it taken away from them because one of their star sprinters, future Cincinnati Bengals Wide Receiver Isaac Curtis, hadn't properly taken his SATs. (The crown was divided between B.Y.U., Kansas and Oregon, on the heels of Pre's bloody Three-Mile win.) Trying times had not tampered with an event widely-anticipated among Bay Area Track mavens, as Big Meets had historically produced inspired competitions, with athletes from both schools running, throwing, leaping and jumping faster, higher and farther than they ever had before. If we could Beat Cal in our season finale, wouldn't that be sweet? @ @

The competitions that day were fierce, each team battling toe-to-toe in event after event. The Half-Mile saw Stanford's Tom Jordan – future author of the definitive Steve Prefontaine biography and director of the finest of all non-Olympic-related American Track & Field meets, the Prefontaine Classic in Eugene – take out the first lap in a suicidal 53 seconds to burn down Cal's future N.C.A.A. runner-up Rick Brown, successfully handing the victory to our Pete Fairchild. The Quarter-Mile Relay was the race of the day, featuring last year's N.C.A.A. champion Cal quartet anchored by Eddie Hart, last year's national 100-yard-dash champion (9.4) and the future Olympic Gold Medal Relay anchorman in the Munich Games. But Hart was hurt that day, and so was Curtis, his N.C.A.A. runner-up (also in 9.4), who would run anyway, with his thigh heavily-bandaged. Kenny Curl had a great first leg and made a perfect pass to our 25-foot Long Jumper Tom Anderson, who delivered the baton seamlessly to Chuck Francis, who ran a killer third carry to hand the stick to our anchorman, hurdler Rick Tipton with a ten-foot lead. Curtis went after him like a rocket, limping heavily on his bad leg. The two men were shoulder-to-shoulder at the tape, where Tipton just managed to nip Curtis with a world-class lean. Incredible! – although our jubilation was tempered by the knowledge of how lucky we had been, because for all our talent, our sprint quartet was only the sixth-fastest in conference, and even that day ran nowhere near a qualifying time for the national championship.

A major upset was in the works, but to pull it off some of our distance runners would need to double – come back in a second race. I would run only the Mile, joining Duncan and Don against Cal's Cliff West, who was still trying to become the first Black American Miler under Four Minutes. The rivalry that had been prophesied for Cliff and I freshman year had so far failed to materialize, and wouldn't that day, either: earlier in the year Cliff had run a Mile/Two-Mile double against S.C. in 4:06.9 and 9:01.4, well beyond what I was capable of that day. Cal also had John Drew, the pony-tailed Texan who had won the 4-A Regional Mile Championship our senior year in high school, who had already clocked a swift 4:03.7 that spring, and hadn't lost a Mile all year.

Duncan, Don and I met ten yards behind the starting line just before the race and grabbed hands.

"Don't look back," I said. What prompted me to quote Bob Dylan at that moment, I had no idea. But these two future Olympians bought it. We double-slapped palms, turned, and trotted to the line. @ @

What a thrill it was, to be poised at last on the Stanford Stadium track, moments away from racing alongside our two great distance stars and two studs from Cal! We were about to become participants in the most exciting individual event in Track & Field, in the estimation of more people than just me: an event in which speed and strength count in equal measure. I wasn't thinking of the great Milers who had preceded us as we stood on the line, but all of us had heard the pistol's report that set us loose on what the former world-record-holder and second sub-four Miler John Landy once called "a drama in four acts."

Act One – Lap One – sent us around the first curve and on to the backstretch, where we established our characters: leader of follower, and if the latter, where. There was no way I would be racing from the front that day, so I tucked in behind my four competitors, cruising with all the economy and relaxation I could summon – keeping my gaze diffuse and steps as close to the rail as possible, so as to cover the least amount of distance, hopefully less than my opponents. My plan was short and sweet: hang with the pack for as long as possible.

"*Sixty-one*," Coach Clark shouted as we hurtled by in a pack, cheered by our teammates and the several thousand spectators in attendance.

Act Two – Lap Two – I focused on maintaining my pace and relaxation. I felt I was pressing but still together, still in the mix – still close to the leaders – my mind still, my thoughts muted, focused –

"Two-oh-three" Coach Clark called out as we passed through the starting point a second time. Our second lap had taken sixty-two seconds: 2:03 at the half… This was all happening so fast that I failed to register the order of the runners ahead of me, or much of anything, for that matter. I had no worries about anything except sticking with the pack…

Act Three – Lap Three – is key to most Mile races. Everyone is suffering if the pace is decent, but no one could afford to slacken off, even though we knew the final rush to the finish line was less than a minute away. I needed to keep as controlled and relaxed as I could manage, even though I was hurting –

"Three-oh-five, three-oh-SIX, three-oh-seven…"

The bell clanged for Act Four with me a second and a half behind the leaders now, but in a three-quarter mile split of 3:06.0: my fastest ever en route to a four-lapper. I could only watch as Kardong, Macdonald, West and Drew pulled steadily away. Then I noticed Drew fading as he entered the backstretch, so I dug down and passed him without facing any resistance on his part. (I would be disappointed to learn that he had been fighting a nasty stomach flu that week and wasn't at full strength. Drew would return at the end of the year as an N.C.A.A. finalist, finishing 7th in the Half-Mile in 1:50.3.)

As I rounded the final curve I caught a glimpse of Herbie the Hat, Kauf's father, filming us with his eight-millimeter movie camera. (I wouldn't see that footage until a year later.) Kardong passes through the frame first, then Macdonald, then West (who unbeknownst to me was getting married in another two weeks), and finally me, looking strong. Even though I am in next to last place I am holding my form and working my arms, knowing I had a shot at a PR.

Don won in 4:03.5, besting his PR 4:03.8 from mid-March; Duncan was second and Cliff West third, the final scorer in the Cal-Stanford Mile. My fourth-place finish didn't score any points, but I had run a perfect race under ideal conditions. Whatever my time was, I didn't think I could have run any faster that day. I doubted I could have run another ten yards at that pace. Knowing that I had done the very best I could was a very rare and very special feeling indeed. Coach Clark found me on the infield a minute later, stopwatch in hand. "4:07.6, Robert." After nine weeks of training, I had PR'ed in the Mile. Not quite an All-Time Top Ten performance at Stanford, but close. A moment later I realized I had also qualified for the Conference Championship.

My junior Track season wasn't over after all. @ @

And The Big Meet wasn't over, either. The score remained close, with PRs by athletes on both sides, as always in these Bay Area confrontations. (Decades later when the college dual meet system was all but extinct, the Stanford-Cal "Big Meet" would continue to thrive on fierce competitions and many PRs for years into the future.)

I felt an almost feverish excitement. All I could think of was how I might contribute more to the team. The research I had done at UGLY about Mono never crossed my mind. The fact that I was still recovering from Mono never crossed my mind, either. Ten minutes after the Mile, I approached Coach Clark with a plan.

"Coach, listen! Cal doesn't have anybody who can beat me in the Two. Don and Arv will go 1-2, but maybe I can score a point today! I feel great! Honest! Put me in, Coach! I'm ready to go!"

Coach Clark studied my face, assessing how quickly I had recovered from my earlier race. He wasn't thinking of my Mono, either.

"Give it a try if you want," he said, accompanied by a half-smile that I couldn't interpret. I was about to ask him what that smile meant, but somebody came over and dragged him away.

I walked away from people and lay down on the Stadium infield grass to breathe, gaze up at that bluest sky, and wonder what the next race would mean, and how I might do.

After a brief warm-up I made my way to the starting line of the Two

Mile to find Kretz and Kardong, the latter with "Indian" war paint slathered on his face. He must have been feeling cocky after logging 100-mile training weeks consistently for months "to impress the girls," as he joked to a local running newsletter. (Some years later he would observe that while a lot of people thought of 100-Mile weeks as a benchmark and a good target to go for, "88" was "a rounder number.") Earlier that season Don had lowered the school Two-Mile mark to a quick 8:37.8, and he had just PR'ed in the Mile; no one was beating him that day, and I knew better than to try. But after only one lap I knew I had made a mistake. One dirt-slow 69-second tour of the oval took it out of me. I ran the whole distance, but as I reached the top of the last curve on the final lap I looked far down the track and saw Don and Arvid crossing the finish together and leaping into the arms of Captain Al Meredith. With their one-two finish Stanford had sewed up a Big Meet win, Jordan's eighth in his fifteen years on The Farm.

I wasn't competitive, and I didn't score that point I was running for: third place went to Cal's Vic Cary with a PR 9:04.0. No one greeted me at the finish line, because I didn't deserve a greeting. My time didn't interest me at all, and I never asked for it.

The Big Meet ended as Track meets always do, with the Mile Relay, and I probably paid attention to it at the time, although I don't remember a thing about it. What was I thinking when I showed up for that Two-Mile, when I had the biggest race of my life two weeks away? I was thinking I could score a point for my school, despite its possible effect on my performance at the Conference Mile. What inspired my decision was a pathetic lack of self-control, even common sense. But I pushed these thoughts aside, as there were too many good things going on – my Mile PR and a team victory – to worry about the past.

Afterwards Coach Jordan was everywhere, patting butts, squeezing arms and shoulders, beaming with paternal pride, congratulating one and all. He even found a moment to squeeze my arm and whisper in my ear, "You're going to the Pac-8s, Bobby!"

For seniors like Don, Duncan, Kauf and Chuck Francis, the '71 Big

Meet 89-74 win was their Rose Bowl victory, a Last Hurrah overshadowing an otherwise long and discouraging season. The Big Meet cumulative record on that day stood at 40-32-2, Stanford. With the continuing decline of Track & Field on The Farm, Stanford would not win another Big Meet for another twenty-six years. @ @

Creedence Clearwater Revival's new song "Proud Mary" floated through open dorm windows as I loafed on the big lawn behind Wilbur Hall. Frisbees curled above the grass, pursued by barking dogs; people sat around or lay around, reading books, drinking coffee or beer, smoking joints, talking and soaking up the ambient sunlight. I let disjointed thoughts play through my mind, day-dreaming about my fourth-place PR go-around in The Big Meet Mile. Man o man what a *faaan*-tastic day! To miss six weeks with a bum knee; get better; get Mononucleosis and then German Measles; get better, but not really; blow a Devil-Take-the-Hindmost Mile at the Cow Palace; quit the team; train for nine weeks on your own and then drop *a 4:07 mile?* Get outta town! *Proud Mary keep on churning...* I just PR'ed in the Big Meet Mile! *Rolling...* Top Ten Stanford all time! *Rolling...* Well not quite... *Rolling on the rivvv-er...* We were battered and bruised, but this moment was all we had and what this thing was all about. This was why we put in the work. This was why we did all those intervals and miles. Or at least that was what we told ourselves at moments like this, although of course a great deal more was involved: an abstract yet practical culture of inspiration and aspiration, a "service" that we did for one another; each of us contributing to a culture that becomes the foundation for other people's aspirations as well as your own: *"Left a good job in the city... Working for the Man every night and day... But I never saw the good side of a city... Till I hitched a ride on a River Boat Queen..."* @ @

The sun lowered, the sky darkened, and I wandered over to Jordan House for dinner. Afterwards I hooked up with Decker, who had watched the Big Meet from the stands, and headed over to a dorm party in Wilbur, where we hovered over a designated punch bowl.

"Should we?" "I dunno." "Let's ask around..."

After careful inquiries as to the proper dosage – everybody at the party was throwing themselves around to vinyl records and having a high old time – we drank just enough of the mescaline-laced punch to know we would get a buzz. Then we strolled over to Toyon, graduate student housing behind Branner, to "come on," as the saying went, over a game of Ping-Pong. Ping-Pong had been in the news three weeks ago, when the U.S. National team visited Nagoya, Japan for the 31st World Table Tennis Championship and received a formal invitation to visit Mainland China as the first official guests of that closed society in decades. Decker and I were tripping so nicely by the time we headed over to his on-campus mobile home, 14Z in the trailer park named Escondido Village. A party was going on there, lights sparking on faces, including that of a very nice, unassuming sophomore tennis player and Physics major who in a few years would read an ad in the *Daily* about how NASA was looking for female astronauts for the space program. Years later Decker would swear I did not meet his friend-through-tennis Sally Ride, who would go on to become the first American woman in deep space in 1983. (Who do you choose to believe? If you say Decker, I won't mind.) I clearly remember sitting with my legs resting on Decker's ottoman, listening to the new cast album of *Jesus Christ Superstar* and feeling everything flowing together in the alluring, uncontrived way Life can for a five-foot, nine-inch, 151-pound 4:07 Stanford Miler tripping on mescaline in May of 1971. At one in the morning I said goodnight and walked back to my room in College Terrace with the phantasmagorical cosmos swirling over my head, feeling warmed, comforted, and very much at home.

For the longest time writing this book, I found it difficult to admit to myself, that I tripped on the night of my junior year Big Meet Mile. I considered not mentioning it at all, because I knew that for some readers it would be one of those "Gotcha!" moments, which they think proves that I wasn't serious enough to realize the promise still held out for me; that I was just another promising Jock lost to the darker undercurrents of the counterculture. (That's what The Hulk would pretend to think, when I told him about it.) Whatever the case, I did what I did and slept in the next morning, and when I woke up I did what distance runners all over the world were doing that Sunday morning: I went for a Long Run – a thirteen-mile jaunt through Woodside, running alone for ninety minutes, aware of passing cars on the roadside and shady trees and buildings with barrel-tile roofs, moving in and out of sunlight and shadow as I meditated on the road that lay ahead of me. I was surprised by how good I felt just one day after my Big Meet efforts – fresh enough to push a little over the last three miles. It felt like a thirteen-mile recovery run after my ill-advised Big Meet double, and certainly a good start in my preparation for the biggest race of my Track career: the Pac-8 Mile. @ @

Those two weeks after The Big Meet and before the Conference Championship felt weird. I didn't have a better word for it. Maybe "not right." Hard interval workouts knocked the slats, stuffing, and goo out of me. Coach Jordan put me through one of his specially-designed workout himself, one of the only occasions in which I ran under Jordan's stopwatch. Also on this interval session was the school's best Half-Miler, Pete Fairchild, Duncan's peer and a former Cal State High School runner-up from Sacramento. His Mile Relay teammate Kauf had nicknamed him "Smooth Strider," because that was how he ran. In the summer of '68 Pete had written Brook Thomas about how anxious he was to return to "the old feelings of competition, the anxiety and fear of now knowing how you'll do, the struggle of man against society, the doing of your thing," and Brook had published these remarks in our team newsletter. Pete was on our side of the culture gulch, although Half-Milers from the "speed" side of his event almost never trained hard enough to satisfy me.

That day in the stadium Jordan took us through a 56-second quarter, then a quick-jog lap in ninety seconds, then a 62-second quarter, quick-jog another lap, then another 56-second quarter, quick-jog a lap, and so on – a shoulder-to-shoulder pattern we continued for four miles. Decades later, a former rival would dub this workout "Prefontaine-ish," which would make me wonder if I was remembering it correctly. (He also said Fairchild would never have finished that.) It was definitely one of the better "quality" workouts I had ever done – "quality" being what Jordan was into, even if it meant running people "into the ground," as I had noted in a freshman letter home.

Watching Pete and me cruise around the track, Jordan exuded a paternal enthusiasm that anyone would think was genuine:

"Way to go, Pete, way to go! Looking sharp! Way to go, Bobby!"

At that moment I was everything Coach Jordan ever wanted in a runner – everything, that is, except obedient, durable, and cautious.

I had promised I would never again be seduced by Payt's admiration, but that day on the track I succumbed a little, the two of us embracing the illusion that nothing untoward had ever passed between us, because he was the Great Coach and I was his Golden Boy. I think I was probably not as evolved as I had thought. @ @

On the bright, sunny afternoon of the Pac-8 Conference Track & Field Championship, on the same Seattle track where we run had our dual meet against Washington three weeks earlier, a slight wind fluttered colorful flags and pennants, but not enough to have an impact on field events or races. The infield was packed with a hundred athletes in bright school colors, while several thousand spectators scattered across the stands wearing sunglasses against the glare. When the stadium public address announcer summoned Milers to the starting line, I felt I had a chance to do okay. But I also knew that running is 90% preparation and that I didn't have the background to be competitive. Maybe I could run faster than in The Big Meet. I had no idea.

The field was large – over twenty-five runners – but I broke well at the gun, found a rail in the middle of the front-running pack, and felt okay through one lap. As we crossed the starting line for the first time, Duncan took the lead, as he often did: he liked to push the pace to negate his opponents' superior kicks. Without giving it a second thought I went with him, sweeping around three or four runners to tuck in behind Dunc 500 yards into the race. I heard the announcer in Husky Stadium with crystal clarity. "That's Macdonald of Stanford in the lead, followed by teammate..." – pausing, presumably to consult his program – "Robert Coe..."

My Fitzgeraldian moment and the summit of my Track & Field career to date: holding down second place for 140 yards in the Pac-8 Conference Mile!

Midway around the second curve of Lap Two, Duncan began putting distance between us. I pushed to close the gap, but made up no ground. Just before the straightaway an Oregon runner shot by me on my outside shoulder – I knew he was from Oregon because of the bright green shorts and yellow singlet, which I saw from the corner of my eye. When I lifted my head I saw it was Pre, sweeping by and pulling away... Another runner went by mid-straightway... Then another... I was falling back precipitously. I had nothing to do about it. No response. No gas in the tank. Out of fuel. I could have dropped out during that disgraceful Act Three and no one would have faulted me, or cared much, either, to speak the truth. But I had never quit a race in my life, unless I was incapacitated or dragged off the track, and I wasn't going to start now. After about a 2:20 second half-mile (I never asked) I almost trotted across the finish line in 4:26.0, slower than my high-school best. Pre had won in 4:01.5, with Oregon's Rich Ritchie and Archie Kvalheim (actually Arne, a Norwegian) in second and third: three Ducks in a row. Duncan finished fifth in 4:05.1; Cliff West, just behind him in 4:06.0. I can't recall if I came in last or not, but I very well might have. Decades later, when I got my hands on the 1971 conference meet press release, I wouldn't even see my name mentioned in the category "Also Ran."

My problem was not that I dropped mescaline the night after my PR Mile. My problem wasn't a self-fulfilling prophesy that had turned me into a heap of organic rubble, and I hadn't "choked," either. My problem was that I had run a hard 1320 and two hard Miles over three consecutive weekends leading up to this meet, while recovering from Mono. And that hard interval workout that Coach Jordan gave me probably hadn't helped, either, although I didn't question it at the time because it was so much fun. But the truly stupid thing I had done I could have avoided: I ran the Big Meet Two-Mile. I didn't have the background to double that day. I should have exercised some restraint and thought ahead to Seattle. But instead I had convinced my coach to let me try to score a single point – one lousy point – for our team.

None of the Coaches ever spoke to me about my Conference meltdown. Jordan had never said a word to me about my Mononucleosis, either, even though he had been Jim Ryun's nominal baby sitter in Mexico City. @ @

I skulked around Husky Stadium afterwards, too bummed to watch the Three-Mile; I had to hear about it later. Kardong went through two miles in 8:57, then claimed the lead from Pre and held it for a lap before Pre took it back. Don passed Pre again, but then Pre grabbed the lead for good, scorching the final quarter in 60-flat. Afterwards he told my teammate that if he had gone hard for a couple of laps, he would have had him. He told the press much the same thing, but in the form of a put-down: "If [Kardong] would have played it smart, he could have won it with three laps to go. If he would have put in a hard lap, I would have let him go [because] I was dead and my feet felt like a furnace underneath me." Don finished two seconds behind in a Stanford school record 13:19.8; Arvid was fourth in 13:45.7. Don would graduate in less than a month with the school record over Six Miles, too, a nationally swift 28:00.6. Pre would shortly dip under 13 minutes for Three Miles – 12:58.0 – and in June set his first non-junior national record: 13:30.5 for the Olympic distance, 5,000 meters.

"Cal meet was last Saturday, and Stanford won," I wrote my grandparents on May 12th, entirely eliding the conference meet, where Jordan's best-ever dual meet team finished sixth with 36 points, ahead of Oregon State and Washington State – an improvement over last year's last-place showing. "I ran 4:07.6 for the mile, which is my best ever… I'm not running hard but doing OK. I think this will be my last year. Next year I only need 39 units total [to graduate] so I think I'll get into some plays and some other things… I'm really fed up with school – all these books, books, and more books…" That was my disappointment talking. Or maybe I was trying to express my disappointment with Track in a way that would make them feel better. But I really did have little fire in my gut just then. I did not want my junior year to be my last, but given my health and injury issues, I didn't think twice about shutting myself down for the year. @ @

On a hot afternoon not long after school let out, I ran Arastradero for maybe the two hundredth time and afterwards trotted shirtless in my running shorts to one of the eating clubs behind Branner, where I knew I could find a TV set that wasn't being used. I flicked on ABC Sports smack dab in the middle of one of the Half-Mile Heats at the N.C.A.A. Track & Field Championship, again in Seattle, and there was Pete Fairchild, finishing well behind the leaders and not advancing, but in a time of 1:49.6 – breaking 1:50 in his final college race and for the first time since his sophomore year. Sail on, Smooth Strider! Stanford sent five athletes to Nationals that year, but none came close to becoming All-American, including the future Stanford Hall-of-Famers Don Kardong and Duncan Macdonald in their last college track meet. I stuck around long enough to watch Villanova senior Marty Liquori win his third straight N.C.A.A. Mile title in a meet record 3:57.6, and wonder if I could be in this race a year from now. It was time I began planning my one last assault on the slippery slope of that Big Rock Candy Mountain, senior year. 1972 would be an Olympic year, so events would be contested at international distances. Next year's 1,500-Meter Final would be a heavy lift for me, but not impossible.

But after the vaudeville of calamity that was my junior year, begun in glory in Sacramento before spiraling down to a series of traumatic disappointments and ending with a two-second improvement in my best Mile time and a total wash-out at the Conference Championship, I also needed to re-ignite the passion that could make running make sense and re-establish my reasons for running at all. And those reasons had better be good, because my experiences of the past year had affected me in ways that could prove difficult to control. My life as a college athlete felt like it was opening up and closing down at the same time. I wasn't exhausted, just very tired. *"For Stanford I Will"* – nothing would ever change that. But the idea I had taken to heart at the end of my freshman year – that all I had to do was put in the work and everything else would take care of itself – had been blasted away forever by the spring of my junior year. Going forward I would forever have to train under a coach who chose to exacerbate his conflicts with athletes by refusing to look at us for how we played the game; going forward I would forever be under a constant threat of injury – under the perpetual chance that some cruel fate was lying in wait for me just around the corner, ready to freeze my knees, invade my blood, and thwart me again entirely. I still believed that how I handled setbacks would eventually correlate with my success or failure, but I also knew that I needed months if not years of training in order to become the distance-running champion I had envisioned myself becoming. I needed more time than I had. It wasn't that I didn't think I could do it; it was that I had also lost a measure of innocence in Europe, and another big chunk of it during my snake-bit junior year.

But I made my calculation all the same. I set my anti-goal and a goal: I wasn't going to run cross-country for Stanford in the fall of my senior year. I was going to train, but with sights on a sub-four minute Mile in the spring, along with a path to the starting line of the N.C.A.A. 1,500-Meter Championship Final in June, 1972. @ @

Everything was continuing – football, swimming, middle- and long-distance running, all of it – but nothing would ever feel the same, to me and many other people. The Revolution was not being televised, even if the N.C.A.A. Track & Field Championship was. Like the world at large, college athletics were reorganizing, kaleidoscopic, volatile, electric, with old signposts and benchmarks vanishing around us, leaving us little to cling to except one another, our visions of greatness and how to get there. As I sat in front of that eating club TV over my bowl of soggy Cheerios, I thought about all of the hard roads I had traveled and battery endured over the course of my junior season and before, both as a Jock and as a hippie, and found it incredible to realize that I was barely twenty-one years old, but now had only one year left to make my collegiate running dreams a reality. @ @ @

THE LAST "WILD INDIANS" OF CALIFORNIA

Summers are an important season for college distance runners. Summers are when we re-assemble ourselves after our grueling spring campaigns, putting in serious miles on road & trail as a base for our upcoming cross country season and dreams for the future. Summers had always been restorative for me, but also the season when I did some of my most consistent training. Every summer since leaving home I had trained hard in the hottest months, and my intention was to do so again, preparing for my last go-round senior year. The only question I had was where to do it. I had out-grown my grandparents' beach house in San Clemente and my parents in the Netherlands weren't welcoming me with open arms. I hadn't seen my Mom or my brothers since the summer of '69, or my Dad since the Pac-8 meet in November of '69. So without any better idea of where to go I boarded the "California Zephyr" in Oakland and returned to the Sierra Nevadas for another eight-week tour of duty – my first in two years – as a camp counselor at Walton's Grizzly Lodge, elevation: 5,500 feet.

I found gorgeous new mountain trails through second-growth forests that year, which meant I didn't always have to kick it with the truckers on the highway on my morning ten-mile run. But managing a cabin full of rambunctious eight-year-olds in a noisy bunkhouse felt different this time around. I was a different person than I had been at age nineteen, and even then getting up at 6:30 for a single daily training run on less than optimum sleep had been far from ideal. My life had broadened, maybe even atomized. Long hours in a mid-altitude training camp had been a bad idea from the get-go, so after five weeks I asked to be released from the last three weeks of my contract and left Grizzly Lodge, drove to Palo Alto, re-packed my station wagon, then headed over the coastal range and down U.S. 1 to Carmel Highlands, just north of Big Sur, where my freshman dorm mate and fellow Beta bro Mark Shelley was living with a bunch of marine biology students, all of them studying the sewage outfall in Monterrey Bay on a grant from the National Science Foundation. I wasn't there to scuba dive, although I did once anyway, in Jade Cove, a nature preserve located below Kim Novak's house in Big Sur, while tripping on mescaline, which was maybe not the safest way to dive for the first time, but that's what I did, and it was unforgettable. Natural wonders aside, the main reason I went to Carmel Highlands was to hang out with the former World-Record Butterflyer, two-time Olympic Medalist and Wannabe Writer John Ferris, who had been hanging out like I would be, reading novels and generally decompressing from his senior year on The Farm. @ @

The divers would rise before dawn, throw their gear into the back of Mark's battered Chevy pick-up, and split for the chilly ocean, leaving John Ferris and me to rouse ourselves at eleven or thereabouts (I was sleeping on the sofa), make a pot of strong coffee and spend the rest of the afternoon either reading, writing, or talking about books and fictions. Both of us were immersing ourselves in canonical novels that summer, devouring D.H. Lawrence's "Bright Book of Life" like so many buckets of squids from Cannery Row. We worked our way through all of Lawrence Durrell's letters to and from his fellow bohemian Henry Miller, a former Big Sur resident down the coast, whose great essay "Big Sur and the Oranges of Hieronymus Bosch" (one of Ferris' favorites) was written not far from where we were lodged. Both of us were reading Durrell's *Alexandria Quartet* – "

– which I think of as a 'Book of the Dead,'" I pronounced one fogged-in morning, "because all four parts climax in death, as you mentioned a few days ago. I think of the *Quartet* as the ultimate exposé of romantic illusion –"

" – death being where all illusions end up one day –" John said, making a vague sign of the cross above his head somewhere.

"– and meanwhile all the characters are bound in these elaborate webs of political and sexual intrigue, with each novel revealing a different aspect of 'the truth.' This is the kind of relativism the novel is all about," I said as I poured each of us another cup of coffee.

"But if all we have are aspects of 'the truth,'" John making those little "quote marks" in the air, "then what's to stop us from living in any illusion we please? What's to stop us from doing that, if all we have are these mutable versions of 'the truth?' Durrell seems to think that truth and illusion are practically interchangeable. And maybe he's right, Bob! Maybe there are no 'truths' at all, only these brief moments of clarity that fiction can provide, which pass for truth and give us a little deceptive comfort until a better story comes along..." The wannabe writers moved on to another one of Durrell's über-bohemian notions: that "any effort of the will displaces life."

"– although I'm not sure if that's 'true,' either," I said. "What effort of our wills has surpassed what you've done in the pool and what I've done as a runner? Our educations, absolutely. But nothing else springs to mind. And now we're supposed to believe this wasn't 'life?'"

John and I could spend hours in these undergraduate book-chats. We were thoughtful young readers who hoped to become writers one day, and couldn't think of a better way to prepare than to feel our way along with each other and with friends, then sit down and write about it, which both of us did every day, too. Death & Illusion & Truth were matters of great importance at that moment in our country's history and our individual lives. My grandparents were none too thrilled about me daydreaming away the last half of my final undergraduate summer in an adobe house in Carmel Highlands, instead of earning money for school. I defended my un-American activities to the provisioners of my education by explaining how I had stumbled on a way of life that felt important right now: "I feel like I'm completing something in myself that began before I went to Europe and has been working inside me by fits and starts ever since... I think this was what Henry Miller meant when he asked, 'How can we find ourselves if we don't lose ourselves first?'" Quoting a reprobate like Henry Miller to convince a retired California Probate Judge of the wisdom of a course of action might not have been the soundest approach, but I honestly believed I needed to unpack for a while, cool out, not test myself, and simply live. My countercultural life took another turn: I grew my beard out and lived in flannel shirts, worn-out jeans and hiking boots when I wasn't in Onitsuka Tigers. Think about it: from Preppie freshman to early sophomore Austin Powers, than later sophomore High Hippie (tie-dyed pants, see-through Indian shirts) to Junior Salvation Army cast-offs. And now my latest anti-style: Hippie Mountain Man. @ @

So Ferris and I did what we did until nightfall, when the scuba team returned from the freezing waters of Monterrey Bay, famished for hot food. Lengthy meal preparations became preludes to orgiastic feasts, with friends dropping in from the neighborhood and the road to share fresh squid from Cannery Row, buckets of fresh mussels, giant artichokes from the Salinas Valley (along with our own home-made mayonnaise), and mouth-watering summer corn on the cob. After a late supper guitars came out, followed by hours of singing and talking and toking up in front of a roaring fireplace, not to mention listening on a great sound system to the music of "Blue" (Joni Mitchell), "Tea for the Tillerman" (Cat Stevens), and Rod Stewart's "Maggie May," all of which echoed around our adobe architectural showplace.

"Wake up Maggie I think I got something to say to you/ It's late September and I really should be back at school..."

Losing myself in Carmel Highlands was easy. Getting back in shape for long distance racing, not so much. The roads leading from our house were too steep to initiate long runs comfortably, so when I wanted to train I had to drive to Point Lobos, where I ran along cliff side trails past windswept cypresses, above waves crashing on the rocks below.

Point Lobos is one of the most dramatic meetings of land and water in the world, according to many people, but its trails were narrow, treacherous and rocky, and having to drive to get to them was another nuisance that kept my mileage low. I would wrack my brain years later to remember why I didn't train harder that summer, until I remembered: my last two cross country seasons had ended in burn-out and injury, and I did not want that to happen again. I wanted a college track season, and I knew that if I returned to campus in shape I would be tempted to run cross, and I did not want to do that; I wanted one last go-around in Track, come hell or high water. Successful distance runners all have a highly-developed work ethic, but a lot of us also have a gnawing guilt that works in tandem with it, so of course I worked out. Just not a lot: maybe 45 to 50 miles a week, with the idea that once I got back to school I would put myself into heavy training again.

I did hitchhike down U.S. 1 in mid-August to train for a few days with two former teammates registered now on the U.C. Santa Barbara campus: Greg Brock, in a master's program in Exercise Physiology; and Brook Thomas, a Ph.D. candidate in English. One of the least remarked-upon aspects of participating in college sports is the loss of upperclassmen – your friends – to graduation. It was almost like old times, running with Brock and Brook along looping trails and dirt roads, through panoramic farms and fields, into Mozartian sunsets. On one long solo run with Greg described his recent stab at the ten-year-old American record in the One Hour Run. The distance he had covered only weeks ago on July 24th – twelve miles, 197 yards, an average of 4:57 per mile for sixty minutes – made him National A.A.U. Champ and earned him U.S.A. sweats and a uniform to compete in the Marathon San Blas in Coamo, Puerto Rico come February.

"A very hot day to miss the American record by 35 yards," he told me as we tooled along through an enormous potato field at dusk.

"But not too shabby, Greg!"

"It's a pretty mediocre record I didn't break," Brock replied with his usual understatement. "I went out my first three miles in 4:50, 4:46 and

4:48, so I definitely did not negative split… Still, not bad for a strictly solo run…" I later learned it was second all-time on the American list.

Back from our run, Greg ran an idea by me. "When you graduate next year, why don't you move down to Santa Barbara? We could train together. Brook won't push past a 75% effort on our long runs, because he doesn't like to leave his comfort zone. Don't answer me right now, but give it some thought." Brock knew I had barely begun to approach what I was capable of in our sport, so he assumed I planned to keep running after graduation. Long-distance running enclaves were cropping up coast-to-coast in those days. Living at altitude would probably be better, if I could find a way to afford it, but otherwise Santa Barbara was ideal for distance training, because of the consistently-mild weather and many dirt trails. Gerry Lindgren had lived in Santa Barbara for a while not long ago, and Jim Ryun had moved to town permanently. (He would stay for nine years before returning to Kansas to win election to the House and become the single most conservative member of Congress, according to the non-partisan *National Journal.*) Finally I decided I would apply for graduate school in English at U.C.S.B, as Brook had done. Applying to law school seemed remote, but I had not dismissed the idea outright. I had no doubt that my best running years were ahead of me, if I could only recover the momentum I had before. @ @

Back in Carmel Highlands I discussed this all at length with Ferris.

"I'm not training much this summer, at least by my previous standards, but I don't think it's a mistake, John! I also don't think it's unreasonable for me to think about going sub-four in the Mile next June. The Coaches projected a 3:57 for me over a year ago, and my best time last year was only eight seconds away, and I did it on nine weeks of training. Once school starts I'll have ten months to step it up. This is it, John! Senior year! Last Shot! Last time around! Tell me what you think?"

Not until our weeks together in the Highlands had I realized that ever since the Olympic Games three long years ago, John had been more-

or-less finished in the water. "I've hated swimming for years," he told me that summer. "Hours under water, no sound, no socializing, no redeeming influences – nothing but beating yourself up. What's to like about it?" Taking stock of the training he had endured at Arden Hills, logging fifty-to-eighty mile weeks in two- and even three-a-day summer sessions – Michael Phelps and Ryan Lochte swim not much more than half that distance today – John fully realized what he had been put through at a time when many people were thinking about what it meant to be a human being, not a guinea pig or machine. After his N.C.A.A. title at 200-Yards, John had taken the summer off for the first time in a decade. He felt he had no more hills left to climb. I had never realized that he had attended less than half the team workouts as a junior and senior, swimming 12,000 to 15,000 yards a day only three times a week, but still sweeping the 100- and 200-yard Fly at the Pac-8s for three straight years and making a U.S. Team at the 1970 World University Games in Turin, Italy, where he won three Golds – all with the same half-assed attitude. The only reason John hadn't quit swimming outright was because of his half-scholarship and his respect for his coach, Marshall Clark's good friend Jim Gaughran. Steve Prefontaine reportedly said, "To give anything less than your best, is to sacrifice the gift." Ferris's nonchalant attitude about his gift had made him *persona non grata* in the swimming world. One rumor was making the rounds that he had become a heroin addict. Mark Spitz, meanwhile, was winning four national titles and setting two world records at the national championship in Houston the same month we were futzing around Carmel Highlands. Spitz's new WR in the 200-Meter Fly was over two seconds faster than John's best. The prick would go on to be named World Swimmer of the Year, as well as winner of the Sullivan Award, presented to America's top amateur athlete in any sport.

I listened closely and understood what motivated John – quitting the pool was a hugely-positive step for him – but I also privately thought he was a bit crazy for not sucking it up for another twelve months in order to challenge Spitz's stated goal of winning a record seven Gold Medals in Munich. I think this was a similar moment to when I didn't get *The Loneliness of the Long Distance Runner:* quitting for John was the greatest existential victory of his life. Most Fly guys probably would have said Ferris couldn't take down Spitz, who was a year younger and coming on, while John would have to come back. But all of Ferris' Stanford friends thought he could do it, if he only put his mind to it. In the 200-Butterfly, John was as strong as anyone in the world, and a solid bet to medal at his second consecutive Games. But Ferris wasn't training, nor would he be in the pool that fall – and at some point in the early winter he would separate his shoulder skiing at Sugar Bowl in the Sierra Nevadas, giving himself a solid excuse for not swimming a stroke. Don't imagine this wasn't a big deal to John: swimming was a cornerstone of his identity. He had set his first world age-group record at the age of eight. But something else had captured his imagination, as it had mine: the Modern Continental Novelists – James Joyce, Vladimir Nabokov, Joseph Conrad, E.M. Forster and Virginia Woolf – fueled John's fierce loathing of the watery hand that fate had dealt him.

"Go get that Four-Minute Mile," John told me. "What's to stop you?"

"What's to stop me?" I laughed. "How about not training?"

With school three weeks away, I loaded up my wagon and headed back over the mountains to Palo Alto, where I could put in serious miles on happier terrain, and also earn some money for school. @ @

Decker Underwood hooked me up with a construction job on a 42-inch-wide, three-hundred-foot-long sewage tunnel construction project under a crossroads that he and I had run countless times on our way to Alpine or Woodside. Two Stanford undergrads took turns lying belly-down on a flatbed rail car and scooting 150 yards down a narrow tunnel strung with electric lights to the end of the tunnel, where we wielded a heavy jackhammer, shoveled the loosened rubble on our wheeled flatbed, then push-crawled it back to daylight. When we struck something too large to remove, we would jack-hammer holes for dynamite, which Decker's friend and foreman kept stored (illegally) in a chest under his bed at the Delt House where he and Decker lived – enough dynamite to reduce the former home of Jim Plunkett and the

Thunder Chickens to a smoking pile of rubble. The hardest physical labor I had ever done made training difficult, but it paid a king's ransom: ten dollars an hour in cash, under the table, after our contractor bribed a corrupt union official. But I quit after two weeks, because it was impossible to do this job and properly train. Early that summer I had made up excuses for not training, but not anymore.

Freed from the cave of Hephaestus and with school around the corner, I pushed my mileage up to 70 a week, almost all of it on the roads, and almost all of it fast.

"I am in fair shape," I wrote my grandparents two days before school was to start. "I hope I can resist Coach and peer pressure and not run cross country... I'm reading more Virginia Woolf, *Mysticism: The Sacred and the Profane*, and a biography of Ishi, the last 'wild Indian' in North America. I feel about ready to run down game..."

But not ready to run cross country. I paid a courtesy call on Coach Clark in his office to tell him what I wasn't doing that fall. I probably should have prepared him for this little bombshell, but I had felt too conflicted to make a firm decision until I absolutely had to, and that moment was now.

"I'm training hard, Coach, but my goal is to be ready for track. So I'm skipping cross country, just like Duncan did in '69, before he went sub-four. Making it to the end of a long season is tough enough, and I haven't managed to do it since my junior year in high school. This will be my last go-around, Coach! I want to make it count!"

How could Coach Clark not be disappointed, losing one of his top runners out of the blue? But he didn't try to talk me out of it, and I respected him for, although a part of me wanted to hear him try.

"Stay in touch," he said as I left.

Quitting meant I missed the annual team run on San Gregorio Beach and our other traditional fall workout in Foothill Park the weekend after. The defending Champion of the Sacramento State Invitational would not be on the starting line that year. Cal State Fullerton, led by

Mark Covert, would destroy us, as would San Diego State. I knew our team needed me. Kardong, third in the nation at last year's N.C.A.A Cross-Country Championship, had been lost to graduation., but Duncan was back as a fifth-year senior, along with Kretz, Mittelstaedt and Lahde, all rumored to be stronger than they had ever been before.

I didn't know what I found scarier: the team without me, or me without a team that I felt so much part of, but needed to stay away from for a while. @ @

All sorts of new feelings attended the fall of my senior year. Being enrolled on campus and not competing in an intercollegiate sport was something new. So was a life off campus: Ferris and I wanted to keep living together (he had some incompletes to finish and the Draft to deal with), so I signed a lease on a three-bedroom on a South Palo Alto *cul de sac* called Wintergreen, where we had two other housemates: Katie Soleau, a modern dancer and the girlfriend of Kauf and Ferris's good friend Jim Squeri, and Kitty Allport, an Anthropology and Religious Studies major and Mark Shelley's girlfriend. The women each had their own room; John and I shared the master. Out of the blue my '62 Impala gave up the ghost, so Kauf's parents leased me one of their vintage cars, an incredibly-cool five-on-the-floor Rover that I drove to campus and the trailheads of Arastradero and Woodside for my afternoon runs. Surrounded by asphalt in South Palo Alto, I couldn't just step out the door to train, which meant fewer morning runs than in previous years, but if the trade-off was to live with these people, I was okay with that. I also had a Stanford "girlfriend" that quarter – my first, for reasons that would stand up to a half-dozen theories. I'll call her "Evelyn," not because our relationship ended badly, but just because.

Evelyn was the daughter of a conservative arts-loving Oregon lumberman, a French major and equestrienne, and she stayed with us on Wintergreen often that quarter. But the lion's share of my attention went to one of my housemates. Kitty and I had met the previous spring in the living room of the Beta House, when she was living with Mark in the cottage behind the volleyball court. Our first conversation had been about her honors thesis – "The 'I-Thou' Relationship in Martin Buber" – and before long we had formed an "I-Thou" relationship of our own. This was problematic, because Mark was practically living with us, too, abandoning his cabin in the redwoods of La Honda for Kitty's waterbed nearly every night.

"The Loneliness of the Long Distance Runner," I had come to believe, arises from a desire to possess one's own soul. But eventually every soul must reach out to others – a team, a beloved, a "Thou," a something. Running eighty-mile training weeks was helping me to reclaim something of my old self again. My spirit and pride as an athlete was returning, but there were still mornings that fall when I would skip my first workout of the day to hang around the house and have breakfast with Kitty. I knew that I was only 90% focused on my goals, and that this wouldn't cut it if I meant to reach them. I would need hard intervals in the near future, hopefully with teammates, if I was serious about going sub-four and qualifying for the N.C.A.A. Mile championship in the spring. But the remove I felt from training at that time of year, together with the closeness I felt with Kitty (and Evelyn, too), were good for me, I thought. Being in love can change an athlete faster than anything except bad training, not training, injury, illness, and burn-out. But Love – Love is worth it anyway. @ @

The landscape of former Jocks had a special topography in the countercultural heyday of 1971. There were plenty of ex-athletes around in boats like mine: burned down, alienated, reborn; some with eligibility remaining, like I had; others opting to abandon their sport rather than compromise their individuality or bow to stone-age coaching; still more turned off by the depths of commitment required; others simply discouraged, distracted, or despairing about star-crossed careers, ordeals of fumbled glory, de-mystifying athletics. The former All-Conference Offensive Left Tackle and Protector of Jim Plunkett's Blind Side, Steve Jubb, had become lead guitarist for the best rock band on campus, a Grateful Dead-like ensemble that jammed at dorm parties into the wee hours. Defensive Tackle Pierre Perrault didn't play much that fall, as I remember it, although the following season he would be an Honorable Mention All-Conference and a low-round draft choice of the Montreal Alouettes, a Canadian pro football outfit that undoubtedly liked his name. In the spring of '72 Pierre and I would go camping for a night above Lake Tahoe in Desolation Valley, and in the morning drop mescaline and hike down to our car, swimming in ice-cold ponds along the way. Pierre wasn't sure he would bother suiting up next season – he no longer liked the violence of the gridiron – but he also didn't have a clue about what to do with himself once college was over. One afternoon I was thumbing through the *Last Whole Earth Catalogue*, the new Bible for the Back-to-the-Land phenomenon sweeping the Bay Area (with Bill Anders' photo of an "earth rise" on the cover) and came across an ad that made me think of Pierre.

"Pierre!" I told him. "There's this really cool blacksmith school in Oregon…" His face lit up.

"Wow! Thanks, Robert! I'm gonna check that out!" With his brawn and his love of animals, horses in particular, an old-fashioned blacksmithing gig was a natural fit for him. That he would be a Stanford Graduate pounding out horseshoes under a spreading chestnut tree didn't matter to him, or to me, either, at least not at that moment in our lives. *The Stanford Daily* was full of ads for full-time employment at places like I.B.M. and Hughes Aircraft, with starting salaries of twenty-five grand a year for kids just out of school. But nobody I knew was going straight into business, or if they were, they weren't talking about it with me. Graduate schools were the destinations of most of my classmates, and probably mine as well. I was thinking about paying the rent with a Graduate Assistantship or a dead-end job in Santa Barbara. Law School was out of the picture for the moment. A lot of seniors besides Pierre and me were abandoning conventional aspirations, or else not thinking any more about the future than we absolutely had to, which was also how I trained. @ @

Mountain Man showed up for Stanford's team time trial on October 2nd after Coach Clark agreed to let me run alongside the Stanford team and the two-year-old West Valley Track Club. Duncan competed for the Indians; Don, the fifth American in the A.A.U. Championship Six-Mile on the track only months before, was running for West Valley now; and I was running unattached, wearing a circular black target in the middle my dull red jersey. I took the pace out hard and had a three-second lead after one mile, but in the end Dunc, Don and I tied for first over our 4.2 mile course. Our time was 25 seconds slower than the course record and nothing to get too excited about, but it was my course PR and it didn't feel that hard. As always, Stanford was short of personnel; Decker raced that day, but finished ninety seconds behind us, not ready to go. So I was not altogether surprised when Coach Clark called me at Wintergreen two weeks later and asked if I wouldn't mind dropping by the office the next morning. Of course I knew what this was about, but I still showed up with my long curls and bushy beard. I was grateful that Jordan was not around. Pressure I might have resisted, but in all our years of working together my Coach had never asked me for anything except the best I had to offer plus a haircut.

"We have a tough three-way meet with U.C.L.A. and S.C. on the Westwood campus this Saturday. I'd like to ask if you would consider re-joining the team."

It was almost as if I had been waiting for him to ask me.

"Sure, Coach. Let's go beat the Trojans and Bruins!"

I had said I didn't want to run cross-country that fall, but in the blink of an eye I had changed my mind. I decided on the spot that having a few fall races under my belt would be a good thing,

I didn't have to be told what else I needed to do: I went home to Wintergreen and shaved and trimmed my hair over the sink, leaving only modest muttonchops and a moustache, which I was sure I could get away with, because Coach Jordan never seemed to be around. @ @

On October 15th, 1971, Coach, Duncan, Arvid, Bernie, Dave Whiteing. three newcomers to our team, and I flew to L.A. for what would be my first team race senior year: six miles, 410 yards, starting in the vast soccer field close by the U.C.L.A. track in Westwood. We had raced there the year before, but were back this year (instead of alternating venues) to give the Bruins a chance to test their course newly-lengthened for the Conference Championship in November. I cannot recall if my grandparents were in San Clemente for the weekend or if I didn't tell them I was coming, but quite honestly I suspect the latter.

The first mile and the first climb up Sunset felt quick, which wasn't surprising, given that none of my training runs had been anywhere near race pace and I hadn't done quality intervals in months. I was strong, but I badly needed the "quality work" that Coach Clark had warned me not to neglect in his first letter in the summer of '68. I hung with the leaders until the top of the second climb up Sunset Boulevard, roughly Mile Four, which was where Duncan, Bernie Lahde and S.C.'s Tom Lipski pulled away, just as Don and Arvid had done the year before. In trying to go with them I left all of the Bruins behind; Arvid and Freddie Ritcherson, too. I ran the rest of the way alone and hurting, again like the year before. Duncan shattered the course mark by 70 seconds, with S.C.'s Lipski twenty-one seconds behind him; Bernie was third, five seconds ahead of me in fourth. I was ten seconds ahead of Arvid in seventh. The first eight finishers, including me, all broke the old record over the newish course – the second time I had surpassed a U.C.L.A. cross-country course record. The Trojans and the Bruins were weaker than Coach had anticipated: Stanford 27, U.C.L.A. 40, U.S.C. 56. Do the math: evidently we would have won without me. Of course now I wished I had trained hard over the summer, because one last time, say it loud, say it proud: *For Stanford I Will.* @ @

For my Sunday workout I hooked up with Duncan and Don at the house they shared in Menlo Park. We took an easy noon run through Woodside's flickering light and dappled shade, along a curving, two-lane road under towering Eucalypti, talking as we went.

The sun was hot for that time of year and the tempo quicker than I expected. I had done very few road runs with Duncan over the years, and we stayed together the whole way – an excellent workout, with just the right balance of relaxation and pushing. (From Don's training log:

"Noon: Woodside from home with Bob and Dunc and horsepuns. Legs tired at first, which was the mane problem I was saddled with, and there was a colt breeze to stirrup the dust a bit. 11 Miles...") Afterwards I hung out with them in their Menlo Park driveway, enjoying the shade and working out with Duncan's home-made weights: poured concrete in two coffee cans, strung them between a metal rod. After his routine of lunges, curls and presses, Duncan taught me how to "shoot" a beer: poke a hole in the bottom of the can, put the hole to your lips, pull the pop-top, and open your throat to a rush of suds. I never got as good at it as he was. Dunc would bring his Mile down to 3:58.4 that spring and be the fastest qualifier in the 1,500-Meter U.S. Olympic trial heats, leading the field through the half in 2:05.4 – a slower pace than our Big Meet Mile – before being blown off the track by Jim Ryun, Dave Wottle and three others, but ahead of Cal graduate Cliff West in tenth. Duncan would end the year ranked as the seventh-best 1,500-Meter/Miler in America by *Track & Field News*.

Don had a little savings in the bank that fall and winter and would do nothing except read books and work out. "Tough moderation" was giving way to the "heavy training" the Seventies would be famous for: a 132-mile training week in early February would end with Don's world-class 8:34.6 Two-Mile at the Athens Indoor Meet in Oakland. The very next day he would run an excellent 2:18:06 in his first marathon, a few minutes ahead of Duncan and Brook Thomas, all of them under the U.S. Olympic Trials qualifying time. Six days later, Don would beat Frank Shorter and Gerry Lindgren in an indoor Two Mile. Don's heavy mileage created a monster, but Mono would knock him out for most of the outdoor season. He would recover enough to finish sixth in the Olympic Trial 10K and sixth in the Marathon trial in Eugene three weeks later, his 2:22:42 was twelve seconds behind Brock, who finished fifth: the first two runners to cross a finish line in a pair of Nike running shoes. Mark Covert has often been credited with being first, but he came in seventh that day, behind two ex-Stanford guys who were my training partners that day on the Woodside run.

The sun was going down by the time I drove home alone in the Rover after our Woodside session, thinking about the Mile Reps I would run on the golf course with the team the following afternoon. The Big Cross Country Meet was on Saturday in Berkeley. I was thinking about maybe doing some racing indoors that winter. Knowing how important keeping an even keel was in any consistent preparation, I curbed my enthusiasm in anticipation of a ten-hour sleep and a morning run, maybe on the old campus trail this time, since I had found a very convenient place to park the Rover. @ @

When I swung my legs out of bed that morning I felt a sharp pain in my left knee. I tried to stand, but had to sit back down again. It felt exactly like what had knocked me before the Pac-8 cross country race in Pullman, except in the other knee this time.

I woke up my roommate. "I can't believe it, John. I'm screwed again."

The pain and bewilderment I experienced over the next several days were more than I could handle. After managing barely three months of serious training in the past twelve, I was already far behind, and now this new injury would blow another six-week hole in my preparations for the last year of "there's always next year." If I had been attending school on an athletic scholarship – in effect paid to run for my education – I would have begun rehab immediately in the pool and training room so I could return as soon as possible. But faced with the prospect of still more lost time, combined with the disturbing circumstances of my injury, which came like a kick in the groin after I had responded to Coach Clark's call to help the team, on top of all the other matters absorbing my energy and attention just then, not least being my senior honor's thesis and Kitty – I said *no mas*. This Indian made the decision to head off to his Happy Hunting Ground.

I would not spend the next six weeks in Dave's Animal Kingdom, as I had my junior year. I would not go sub-four as a collegian. There would be no N.C.A.A. Championship Mile for me, just as there had been no State Track Meet for me as a high school senior. I had put my body "upon the gears and upon the wheels, upon the levers, upon all the apparatus," as Berkeley's Mario Savio had asked, and my body had broken. My wax wings had melted, and I was tumbling into the sea. I wasn't gonna work on Payton's Farm no more. The Big Rock Candy Mountain was vanishing in the mist, exactly as the legend had it.

As flies to wanton boys, are we to the Gods. @ @

Duncan would continue to light up the West Coast cross-country circuit, setting course records in every meet (including a school record on our old 4.2-mile course) until an illness caught him just before the conference meet at U.C.L.A., which Pre won by over 45 seconds, shattering Dunc's course mark by over a minute, while the Cougars upset the Ducks for the team title. Bernie was Stanford's top man in 15th; Kurt Schoenrock, an earnest young steeplechaser, nudged out Duncan for our second spot, in 30th. Arvid finished back in 48th place, for reasons unknown to me. A team we had thrashed earlier in the season, U.C.L.A. finished third on their home course, while Stanford finished next to last. Two weeks later, at the University of Tennessee in Knoxville, Pre would suffer an attack of sciatica and have to make up a hundred yards on Western Kentucky's English distance star Nick Rose, but managed to win his second individual title, leading Oregon to the first of three straight N.C.A.A. championships. Only Duncan ran for us, coming in an out-of-the-picture 55th. After our third-place finishes at Conference in '69 and '70, no Stanford cross country team would finish higher than fourth until 1985, and the Athletic Department would not send a full team to Nationals until 1994. Decades later, Coach Clark would tell me that the '71 conference meet was "the end of an era" in distance running on The Farm. It would still irk him that we didn't race in the N.C.A.A. meets of '69 and '70, "when we were at least a top five team," although he was forgetting that in 1970, with my knee trashed in Pullman, we wouldn't have been competitive.

Jim Morrison had died on July 3rd; Jimi Hendryx on September 18th; Janis Joplin on October 4th. All of the worlds I ran through were fragmenting. All the cultures I lived in were countercultures.

Our Wintergreen contingent made plans to go to Death Valley together over Thanksgiving, but at the last moment everyone pulled out except

Kitty and me. Death had become a leitmotif that fall: her teenage sister had been struck and killed by a hit-and run-driver in Boulder, Colorado, and Kitty had left Wintergreen for a time to be with her family Back East. In Death Valley we slept outdoors on sand dunes under a full moon, dropped mescaline, wandered narrow canyons, read water-scarred rocks, talked and empathized for hours about Life & Death & Grief & Time. In the barren gullies of Zabriskie Point we shot a Super-8 parody of Michelangelo Antonioni's eponymous apocalyptic countercultural film fantasy, which I had seen in London in 1970; our version segued into Kubrick's discovery-of-tools scene from *2001,* another film epic from my high hippie days. Kitty filmed me running naked down these dry arroyos and across these empty dunes; my knee had healed without treatment in six weeks, the same time it had taken the year before, when I had spent hours in the pool and soaking in a hot tub. All of my relatives, including my parents, had met their future life partners at Stanford, and I imagined I had, too. But I still was with Evelyn, and Kitty was with Mark – two problems that ably distracted me for a time from the loss of my running career. @ @

Anybody who cared to pay attention had a preoccupation that fall: the 1971 Stanford football team opened its season with a 19-0 trouncing of a middling Missouri team that didn't manage a First Down until its eighth possession. Jim Plunkett had gone to the New England Patriots as the first pick in last year's N.F.L. Draft, and his two best receivers and five other starters had graduated, too, but the Rock was now in the capable hands of Plunkett's former backup, fifth-year redshirt senior Don Bunce, second in the nation in total offense that year (229 yards per game), whose long blonde hair flowed out of the back of his helmet. But this would be a rare Indian team led by its defense: the Thunder Chickens had lost only one starter – Dave Tipton, a Fourth Round Pick of the New York Giants – and were better this year than they were the year before, allowing just 12 points a game during the regular season. The team's sole loss in conference was to lowly Washington State at home. Like the team the year before, this was a team that needed to be inspired to play its best, and it did so when it pounded undefeated U.S.C. in the Coliseum, 33-18 – our first road victory over the Trojans since 1957 and one that opened a direct path to a second-straight Rose Bowl appearance. Eighty-six thousand people crammed Stanford Stadium for the '71 Big Game, the second largest crowd in history, tying the attendance at the S.C. bomb-scare battle the year before. Avenging last year's upset loss, we crushed an ordinary Golden Bear team, 14-0, holding Cal to just 38 yards rushing. Our three losses against 15-18-1 teams didn't matter: Stanford was going back to the Rose Bowl – our first back-to-back New Year's Day appearance since the Thirties – to renew a rivalry with the University of Michigan that had begun with the first Rose Bowl game in 1902. @ @

The '72 Rose Bowl team was if anything more "countercultural" than the year before. I ran into D in White Plaza one afternoon that fall. His knee had kept him out of last year's bowl game, but surgery had allowed him to play extremely well in this, his senior campaign, alongside Pimo and Middle Linebacker Jeff Siemon, a future 10th overall pick in the N.F.L. draft and college Hall of Famer. "Hey Robert!" D said. "Good t' see ya, man! I gotta tell ya – I'm into something amazing!" He gazed searchingly into my eyes, a feat I had never seen him manage before his knee repair. "*Stretching!* Stretching is the *best,* man! I got Hollywood into it, too! I'm telling ya, it changes the way you think about things!" An Outside Linebacker had invented Yoga – a good thing he did, because he and his teammates would need every jolt of Kundalini energy they could summon against a third-ranked 11-0 Michigan team seeking to complete its first undefeated season since 1948. Future Midwest football mavens would later call this the best team third-year Wolverine Head Coach Bo Schembechler would ever field in his twenty-one seasons in Ann Arbor, after breezing through a tough non-conference schedule, thumping all of their Big Ten opponents by wide margins, then defeating another great Ohio State team, 10-7, after handing their arch-rival their only regular season loss the season before. Schembechler was on record railing against "those goddamn hippies," and would set up another Big Ten-style monastic training camp in the graveyard known as Bakersfield. Two-thirds of his players signed an anti-war petition anyway.

I avoided the Indians' training camp this year, needless to say, but which the grapevine described as a much more relaxed place than the season before. Jim Murray, the decidedly un-hip Pulitzer-Prize-winning *L.A. Times* sports columnist, filed this report: "This is not a team, it's a Capra comedy. You all know what a football team looks like, right? I mean, those crew cuts, uptight, nights in a monastery. These kooks all got their hair sticking out in back of their helmets. They wear – so help me! – yellow shoes. Also red ones and white ones. You would think they picked up this cast of characters at the Passion Play – or a rock festival. You felt like asking them what they did with the guitars."

After two days of partying in Pasadena (I would share the details, but I don't remember them), I filed into the Rose Bowl along with 103,154 other spectators and took my seat low on the 20-yard line, prepared to watch friends do what few people thought they could do: snatch another Rose Bowl victory from a Midwestern Goliath – although first we were privileged to experience the single most surreal pre-game show I have ever witnessed, starring our Incomparable Band – the Campus Id – spelling out "SMUT" on the field and playing The Grass Roots' "Midnight Confessions" while Rose Parade Grand Marshall Lawrence Welk of TV's "Champagne Music Makers" rode into the stadium in a 19th-century horse-drawn carriage and four U.S. Air Force jets shrieked overhead to honor America's 1,600 M.I.A. and P.O.W.'s in Southeast Asia, including five Michigan and four Stanford grads. Not on the sidelines that afternoon was my classmate and friend, Fullback Hillary Shockley, arguably Stanford's best ball carrier, an Honorable Mention All-Coast player his junior year and future Second Team Stanford "All-70s" player (*thebootleg.com*.) "Shocker" had scored seven TDs and rushed for 622 yards in his junior season and had never been stopped for a loss in his college career, despite playing through many painful injuries, including a serious bone chip in his ankle. I was unaware of these conflicts at the time – specific complaints about Ralston tended to get folded into the team's grumbling generally – but Hillary was not the only Black player who felt that "Indian" Coaches treated them like machines, expecting them to return from injuries more quickly than white players did. So two days before Bowl Day, Shockley quit the team, despite a personal appeal from Ralston – Shocker reportedly telling his Head Coach, in a word-play on Dave the Trainer, "You can't hit the field until you're healed." I had run hurt in a cross country meet in Pullman because I chose to; Shocker wasn't playing in Pasadena because he was fed up with feeling used. Hillary Shockley, a philosophy major from L.A. and a walk-on like I was, was headed to a Harvard M.B.A. program in the fall. Stanford's featured Rose Bowl back would be the former freshman sprinter Jackie Brown, soon to be drafted by the outlaw Oakland Raiders, but who would choose to go to Stanford Law School instead. *The times they are a' changin'…* @ @

Stanford brought three primary tools to the 58th Rose Bowl Game: Brains, Brawn, and Trickery. *Brains:* on Michigan's first offensive play from scrimmage on a soggy field, Schembechler sent All-American senior Halfback Billy Taylor straight at Stanford's undersized outside linebacker Pat Moore, behind the blocking of Michigan's Goliath: six-foot-six, 250-pound All-American Tight End Paul Seymour. Pat weighed 190 soaking wet, but he knew from film study that the massive Wolverine would try to block him outside. So my dog Pimo head-faked Seymour and cut inside for a clean drop of Michigan's career rushing leader. (Moore had been one of the leading tacklers on the team all season, but PR flack Murph had declined to nominate him for a Pac-8 Honor, Pat thought, because he had his ear pierced in Istanbul while attending Stanford-in-England.) Michigan continued to run the same offensive plays that had made them nearly invincible all year, so our defense knew what to expect all day, and the supposedly-great Bo Schembechler couldn't or simply wouldn't adjust. A game that was supposed to be a blow-out turned into a nail-biter: 3-0 Wolverines at the Half – at which point the Incomparable Stanford Band took the field (including women for the first time) to play Santana's "Evil Ways" while standing in a formation that shaped and spelled out the word "RAY-GUN," sending a message to a certain Governor of California who was not a big favorite on Stanford campus that year.

344

Michigan took the Second Half kick-off the length of the field, only to be stopped at the goal line on Fourth and inches in the missile-like forms of future New Orleans Saints Linebacker Jim Merlo and future eleven-year Dallas Cowboy Defensive Back Benny Barnes. Our defense had serious *Brawn:* at six-foot-six-inches and 250 pounds, Greg Sampson, my freshman dorm mate, was fast enough to catch the All-American Running Back Taylor from behind by the neck hole (still legal in those days) and toss him to the ground like a used Kleenex – a move that would help him become the sixth overall pick in the N.F.L. draft, despite having made only 35 tackles his senior year. Late in the Third period, our five-foot-nine-inch, 165-pound Chilean-born placekicker Rod Garcia put Stanford on the board with a 42-yard field goal, kicking soccer-style when not many people did. But then Michigan Fullback Fritz Seyferth capped a seventy-one-yard drive with a one-yard TD plunge, leaving Ann Arbor up 10-3 early in the Fourth.

This was when Ralston resorted to *Trickery:* faced with a seemingly-insurmountable Fourth and Ten from his own 33, Ralston called a play that would probably settle the game one way or the other: the ball was snapped not to the punter but to Fullback Jim Kehl, who handed the Rock *between his legs* to Jackie Brown, who scampered up the left sideline for 33 yards, and followed it with 24-yard bolt that tied the game. Then the gods willed disaster: Stanford defensive back Jim Ferguson fielded Michigan's failed field-goal attempt at the Six-Yard-Line and was met by defenders who pushed him back to the Three, then threw him into the end zone for what officials inexplicably ruled a Safety. Ralston's appeal cited forward progress, but failed, leaving the score 12-10 Michigan with only 3:18 left. Was a blown call going to decide a Rose Bowl Game? But Stanford's defense held on Michigan's next possession, forcing the Wolverines to punt with 1:48 left. This left the outcome of the game in the hands of Stanford's two-minute drill, utilizing five wide receivers. The team had this package in its playbook, of course, but hadn't practiced it since pre-season, and had yet to use it in a game, because we hadn't been in a close one all season.

"All I said [in the huddle] was 'Reba,'" Don Bunce later recalled. "We had a two-minute offense named after our training table cook... It was like a movie and there was a part of me that felt like I was acting out a role..." Several electrifying Bunce scrambles and five consecutive pass completions later, Stanford was within field goal range. Two more plays, three yards gained and two timeouts taken left the clock at 14 seconds. The Rose Bowl game would come down to a 31-yard field goal attempt by junior placekicker Rod Garcia, who had already missed two long first-quarter attempts that day, after Ralston let him try from 52 and 55 yards, although he had made that 42-yarder, too. Six weeks earlier Rod had missed *five* field goal attempts and an extra point in a game that Stanford lost to San Jose State, 13-12. Ralston called it "the darkest day in Stanford football history," a gross exaggeration that fell entirely the shoulders of our All-Conference kicker. In the minutes before the kick, a delegation of players went up to Ralston and said, "Don't talk to him." To Ralston's credit, he listened and left Rod alone. A wise coach sometimes lets his team manage him... As both teams' kicking units rumbled on to the field, every Stanford fan crossed every finger, toe and limb we had. Mine were crossed especially hard, since the last time I had seen Rod on campus he had been dead drunk and passed out in the backseat of a car, his boot heels on the sidewalk of Mayfield Avenue in front of Story House. A year away from setting an N.C.A.A. record of 42 career three-pointers during his senior season, Rod would have a brief stint with the Oakland Raiders that ended when owner Al Davis told him to cut his hair, and Rod said no.

Almost before anyone realized the lines were set, the ball was snapped, Rod's twilight kick went up – and for a second straight year, Stanford's crew of motley stoners, psychedelic party animals and Mystic Others had *almost* beaten another unbeaten Midwestern giant for a Rose Bowl title. Michigan got the ball back with seconds left, but their offense sputtered and their shot at perfection went up in smoke as Stanford fans stormed down from the stands to flood the field with hosannas. Michigan's vaunted offense had not been stopped inside the Ten-once all season; the Thunder Chickens stopped them there five times that New Year's Day. *The New York Times* would call this "a Rose Bowl game they'll be talking about for another 70 years." @ @

The upset of the Michigan Wolverines would become a benchmark in the lives of all our players on the field, just as the game had been for the team that defeated the Buckeyes the year before. It was also the last football game Stanford ever played as "Indians," as well as the final appearance of Prince Lightfoot, who hadn't missed a home or away game since 1951. The last time Stanford played in a Rose Bowl, young Lightfoot had gone toe-to-toe with Chief Illiniwek of the Illinois Fighting Illini, an Indian "mascot" who would survive until 2007 before going the way of most team "redskins." The Indians would become "the Cardinal" in the fall – the color, not the bird. (Other names suggested: Sequoias, Trees, Railroaders, Spikes, Huns, and my personal favorite, "the Robber Barons," but the uniform would have been tricky.) Five days after his Rose Bowl win Ralston resigned, claiming he had accomplished everything he had set out to do on The Farm. Decades later he would be voted Stanford's "Coach of the Century" over Glenn "Pop" Warner, who coached the 1926 national championship team. My sense was that many players on Ralston's rosters would come to appreciate the man more in hindsight than they did at the time, as is frequently the case when an overbearing Head Coach manages to produce more than one legendary victory.

The Admissions Office, meanwhile, surveying the damage left in the wake of the Cambodia/Kent & Jackson State riots of May 1970, had already given up on accepting the more unusual individuals they had admitted in the late Sixties and returned to the Future Leaders of the American Power Elite types that had traditionally comprised the Stanford student body. I cannot prove that any change in admission standards had anything to do with the mediocre teams (and, as always, occasional stars) that Stanford fielded over the next two decades. But it should not be forgotten that dozens of countercultural types played a major role in a Mini-Golden Age of Stanford sports, highlighted by those two astonishing Rose Bowl victories. Farm football would not make it back to that particular field of dreams for another 28 years. @ @ @

ALL-AMERICAN (ALMOST)

Quitting running in my senior year was different than when I quit after the Devil-Take-The-Hindmost Mile. This time I had quit for good. I knew I wouldn't go back, because there was no way I could perform anywhere near the level I had imagined for myself as a senior, and the results so paltry compared to what I had hoped for and dreamed of that it would have been too painful even to try. And so I drove the Kauffman Family Rover to and from campus, read books, wrote, and studied at the library, Wintergreen and the Beta House. I hung out with my housemates, all while pretending that the derailment of my college running career – my highest dream, my deepest aspiration, whatever term you cared to apply – was no big deal; just bad luck; a rotten shame, to tell truth. It was easier to pretend that it didn't really matter in the larger scheme of things, the Big Picture I had in mind. My Humanities Special Program Honors Essay, "'Netting the Fin:' Vision and Image in the Novels of Virginia Woolf," presented a microcosm of my situation: in it I argued that each of Woolf's nine novels was designed around a single image or metaphor: the sight of a shark's fin across a flat sea, a blossoming flower, a pebble tossed in a lake. My professor liked it but only gave me an A-minus because he felt I hadn't done enough to place Woolf in the context of her community and her times. The fact was, I wasn't finding much context in mine, although I still believed that only the strictest Puritanical conscience would attribute my derailment to my engagements with the counterculture. I didn't even feel defensive about it. My two knee injuries were surely related to the spinal fusion I had when I was fourteen. I wasn't like Decker, who had trashed his knee in a motorcycle accident, or Kauf, who hurt his in a rugby game he wasn't supposed to be playing, who also had his shoulder trashed by O.J. Simpson, which not only kept him out of the draft; it kept him out of the Decathlon. There were people everywhere telling us that we needed to change the world, but all too often it was the world that was changing us.

I decided that my L-5 Vertebrae was my Tragic Flaw.

I wasn't an intercollegiate distance runner anymore. So what was I? And what athletic story did I have left to share? Then one day it occurred to me that my college running may be over, but that didn't mean I had to stop running entirely. Post-collegiate runners ran after college by definition, and I would be post-collegiate soon enough in any case. I brooded over this possibility; told myself that getting up off the floor was easy, since we all do it every day when we get out of bed. But I wasn't sure if I wanted to go back into serious training if the result would likely be more of the same. I went through this internal debate at the end of my junior year: the threat of being felled by injury or illness made the investment of time and emotion in hard training feel risky. This line of thinking immediately churned up a host of impressive clichés, including these: success needs no explanation, failure can never be explained; winners never quit and quitters never win ("nobody likes a quitter"); adversity doesn't build character, it reveals it; you only fail when you stop trying; etc. etc. etc.

"I'm running a bit, too, for old time's sake," I wrote my grandparents in mid-February, "and not enjoying it much but who knows? – maybe I'll hit the comeback trail one of these days? I can hardly believe it myself..." I don't remember when I started thinking of "running a bit" as "training," but I remember how inevitable it felt once I did. Training on my own would mean I likely wouldn't run as hard or as far as I once had, at least not right away' it would not entirely eliminate the chances of getting hurt again. But if I only competed when I felt ready I could listen more closely to my body, which would help prevent the breakdowns that had done me in before. So within two weeks I was back to eating like a horse, sleeping like a dog, and getting up like a fisherman – running again, hitting the books, running again, hitting the mattress, getting up and running some more, as I had done more-or-less steadily, when I wasn't sick or injured, since my freshman year. Training once again returned me to my second nature, like breathing out and breathing in. Running felt like one of the few unequivocal things I had left, just as it had when I returned from Europe in the late summer of 1970. But at the same time I had never been obsessed with running to the point of excluding other things. (As I had written Decker from Cliveden House: "Running isn't everything.") I had many other interests, including schoolwork. Even running only forty or fifty miles a week, I immediately felt some of my old strength return, but was never tempted to rejoin a team soon to be lost in its usual spring doldrums; no desire to be out there taking my licks from better-trained runners I used to beat with regularity. Ever since freshman year I had wanted to be more than a decent runner; I had wanted to *blaze*. And although this wasn't going to happen, I still needed to feel my way back into who I used to be. Carl Jung would have called this a classic "regressive restoration of the persona," in which a protagonist "laboriously tries to patch up his social reputation within the confines of a much more limited personality... pretending that he is as he was *before* the crucial experience." The idea was to see if I could run for myself, not my coach, my teammates and my school this time. @ @

Wintergreen unraveled winter quarter. Kitty had plans to move to Aspen to ski, which never happened; Mark was about to graduate and begin work as a marine biologist and soon afterwards, a documentary filmmaker; John and our other housemate Katie weren't sure what they were going to do; and I was still in school. Tensions in the household, stemming from my all-too-obvious feelings for Kitty, escalated until one Friday evening I ignited a weekend-long psychodrama that dragged in the entire household, including my soon-to-be ex Evelyn (who a few years later would marry one of my cross-country teammates.) Bitter volleys were exchanged, although most retained their sanity, most admirably Mark, whose girlfriend I was putting the moves on, after all. But by Sunday evening it was clear that the result I had fantasized – Kitty and me together – wasn't going to happen. So I moved out, and Big Brother Willy, who had been crashing on our living room sofa for a few months, took over my spot in the master bedroom. Two unhappy months passed before I returned for a visit and happily found that our friendships could resume, most of them stronger than before.

Meanwhile I had found an amazing new place to live: my mother's old sorority house at 620 Mayfield Avenue had been re-invented as Stanford's first on-campus co-operative, or "Intentional Community," fully funded and run by the people who lived there. (A "non-violence" house named Columbae was about to open, in a related instance of a "trend," as the *Daily* would note, "towards transforming dying fraternities into co-ed houses.") I had taken many dinners as a guest at Jordan – named not after a certain track Coach but the school's first President, who was still around in my grandfather's era – enjoying the cordial atmosphere and home-cooked meals prepared by residents. But actually moving in, sleeping and studying at Jordan House gave me first full taste of the unexpurgated up-side of the countercultural revolution: Jordan was all about fun, adventure, sharing, intellectual stimulation, gourmet food, first-class home-brewed beer, sex of many varieties, exercise (in-house meditation and yoga classes), dance parties and lots of music, not to mention the first co-ed bathrooms in official on-campus student housing anywhere in the nation. (You should have heard the plotting that went on when Marsha Hallet took a shower.) Some people at Jordan actually "jogged!" And some of these "joggers" were women! Jordan was a breeding nest for genius physicists and computer nerds; future award-winning architects and Deans of Architecture and Medicine; future lawyers, nurses, and doctors; the future founder and CEO of iVillage; the daughter of Warren Buffett's chief business partner; a future Rhodes Scholar and Harvard Med School Professor; and many others who would graduate to more modest but equally helpful professions. Jordanites was Eco-Friendly, too: Tree Huggers, every one of them! My roommate at Jordan had been allowed to skip classes his freshman year in order to write a book about our freshman experience, for credit; David Osborne was the future author of *Re-inventing Government*, a book that would launch a hundred think tanks and win the favor of a sitting American Vice President and future Democratic Presidential candidate, Harvard's own Al Gore. Think about it: my senior roommates were a former world-record swimmer and two-time Olympic medalist, and a future U.S. Vice Presidential Advisor. And my roommate junior year had been an All-American Football Center. Such was life at Stanford U.

Jordan House helped me free myself from the wreckage of my running career and the sadness that engulfed me after the collapse of Wintergreen. I had never felt fully part of my Cliveden group, but at Jordan I felt like I belonged. My mother and father began their first date there, but that wasn't why I thrived. Jordan made me realize that being a Jock had meant I missed some important colors of my college years – like the way teamwork and cooperation didn't have to be based on competition, to give only one example. At Jordan we composted table scraps for our own organic backyard vegetable garden, ordered our own groceries, made our own world-class granola, and washed our own dishes on a semi-voluntary sign-up basis. There were co-ed volleyball games on the front lawn and Deadhead guitar jams in the living room at all hours day and night. We took responsibility for our lives and had fun doing it – an aspect of the Bay Area countercultural revolution that I had barely touched before, largely because of my athletic commitments. But now that I was no longer running seriously – now that I was no longer a Stanford Jock – I discovered that I had been missing some important songs and colors all along. @ @

With my honors thesis finished and all requirements fulfilled – those 17 units of science I had thought I would need had been dropped from the curriculum years ago – I already had enough units to graduate after winter quarter. But I was in no hurry to leave Jordan or a campus that had quieted down considerably since the Computer Center Occupation the year before. Without any serious training to worry about, I did more things I had never had time to do before. For starters, I accessorized and bought a dog – what's a hippie without one? I made friends with people who weren't Jocks. I learned to drive a motorcycle for a short film directed by a classmate who a few years later assisted Roman Polanski on *Chinatown*. I took a small role in a student production of *Richard III* at Branner Hall. I enrolled in a photography class, where I learned to make my own prints, and I took "Introduction to Architecture" pass-fail, befriending my Israeli-born T.A., who took me sailing in San Francisco Bay and later drove "Bowzer" and me to the vet after somebody kicked him in the ribs and he needed an abscess drained. To qualify for a scuba class I had to swim 400 yards in the pool for time, and Ferris came to watch; his compliment on my stroke made my week. I also took a modern dance class taught by a follower of the late Meher Baba, who used to cable his American followers from Europe, "Don't worry, be happy." Dancing made me happy, and I was good at it, too. I found time to apply to Stanford Law, per my grandparents' request, although half-heartedly was not the best way to get in that door. I wouldn't learn until years later how disappointed they were when I was rejected, but Law School was not my dream.

My greatest incitement that spring came from a class taught by Professor Albert Guerard, a famous writing teacher and a wonderful gentleman whose former students included John Updike, as I liked to remind myself. Personally never been much of a Jock himself, Albert followed Stanford sports religiously, and once spoke to me about his admiration for Don Kardong's prose style, after teaching him at Stanford-in-England. Albert's writing seminar stressed the importance of discovering your own voice, and the notion that if you could feel your story, you could find words to get it down. Albert called one of my short stories publishable – "I've been teaching for thirty years," he told me, "and I know a talented writer when I see one." I decided then and there that I would not fail to become a writer for lack of trying. By the end of the quarter Albert would also tell me, "You started out with such promise!" Shades of my running career! "It's too early to say if he will become a professional writer," he later wrote in an otherwise glowing recommendation for English grad schools. Looking back I think my stories for Albert would give juvenilia a bad name.

And through all this I ran, maybe forty or fifty miles a week, no more. It felt good. Sometimes I challenged myself and pushed a little. Maybe this break from competition was what I needed to make running a part of a more balanced "lifestyle." I was trying to think "holistically" in those days, whether running was a part of it or not. @ @

I trained enough to think I could hook up occasionally with former teammates for long runs. One afternoon I met Brian Mittelstaedt at the locker room to run Arastradero. Brian had seemed unsure of himself when he first arrived on The Farm, as if he didn't quite know what he was doing among all these smart and talented people. Slow to come into his own, he had looked good winning the Mile in our dual meet against U.C.L.A., the future National Champions. (I was on the track that day taking photographs.) He was also on his way to a third-place finish in the conference Mile, running 4:05.3 behind Oregon State Ethiopian Hailu Ebba and Cal senior Cliff West, and also ahead of my old high school teammate, Oregon's Mike McClendon., who had run a 4:00.7 Mile as a teenage sophomore. Otherwise Mike's career had been even more injury-plagued than mine – mostly, it was said, because he kept trying to go with Pre. That day on Arastradero Brian and I were humming along at what I thought was a fairly healthy clip when Brian decided to turn it up a notch. I did my best to stay with him, but after a half-mile he disappeared down the road ahead. This was a little unkind, given my fitness level, but I didn't feel any resentment at all – maybe some chagrin. But you can't expect a serious runner to hold back on a serious workout, just because you're not as strong as he is.

I shared this story later with Coach Clark, mostly to give Brian a pat on the back. Coach smiled back at me crookedly: "Payback time for all those years before he lost the weight." Brian would clock a 4:00.1 his senior year – a near-miss at the four-minute barrier and the second-fastest time in school history. He would also qualify for the N.C.A.A. Final, as I had once hoped to do. On that day on the road with Mittelstaedt, Arastradero was my Boulevard of Broken Dreams. @ @

With former Also-Rans spanking me on long runs, I had no legitimate reason to be cocky, but I ended my Stanford enrollment with one last stunt anyway, and got Decker involved in it. His various stabs at rejoining the team had led to multiple ankle sprains, but I knew he was in decent shape, so I phoned his on-campus office job and in the voice of a Southern California Surf Nazi we sometimes played around with, I said, "Dude! I'm choosin' you off!"

"I'm game, 'Bert! What's the plan?

We arrived at the Stadium in the middle of practice wearing our street clothes, shaggy locks and bushy beards, looking like a couple of Mountain Men... *Former stars, lost on the long climb to the Stanford Hall of Fame... Ghost members of Stanford's track fraternity, like The Hulk had been for years... Runners re-surfacing from a past that would have been receding even if our careers had been as glorious as the ones once predicted for us...* Underwood, Ferris, Kauffman – all of my rebel friends could have done more during their years as Stanford Jocks, but the same could be said for practically everybody. Around this time I tried to look up my old freshman pal Jack Lawson, but he appeared to have vanished from campus. I learned later that Jack's friends had called Coach Clark when Jack wouldn't leave his dorm room. Coach had to call Jack's family to come from Modesto to bring him home. Years later I would be glad to learn that he did graduate with our class and a degree in History. Remembering how carefully he kept his running logs, I thought a history major suited him well. I would also learn that his father had won Midwestern college conference championships in Cross Country and Track. Jack had never mentioned this to me. Not even once.

"Hey, Coach!" I blurted that day in the Stadium, hoping to air our intentions before he could say anything to stop us. "We were wondering if we could run a little race-slash-time-trial 660 today!

Would you mind if we stepped in for a few minutes?" When he didn't seem averse or unwelcoming – Coach Jordan was nowhere to be seen, although this was an official late season practice – we asked if he would time us, too. I promptly discovered that in my haste to get to the Stadium on time I had forgotten to bring my running shorts, and had nothing to wear except a jock and an extra-long white sweatshirt that looked like a form-fitting mini-dress. Decker and I had shown up nude for a cross country practice at San Gregorio Beach, and I had attended soccer field workouts in water polo outfit. And now, if I wanted to be really flamboyant about it, I could claim that I cross-dressed for my final practice with Stanford Track & Field.

With old friends on the infield urging us on – don't think Decker and I weren't taking this seriously – we burst from the starting line and streamed through a lap in under fifty-five seconds. At the lap and a half mark I managed to nip Decker by a foot in 1:23.8, with the bottom of my butt-cheeks flapping in the breeze. Our times were roughly equivalent to 1:58 Half-Miles, which was more or less what we had run in high school. All the same, they were PRs in the 660 for us both. Coach Clark told us our times, but otherwise made no comment about our appearance or the minor thing we had just done. I sensed that he would have liked to have a conversation, but a team practice was neither the time nor the place. So he simply acknowledged our feat with a nod of his head, perhaps surprised that we were in any kind of shape at all, and returned to the business of working out the team.

"Bye guys, have fun running those intervals," I called out as Decker and I jogged away to finish our day with an easy five miles. I was only pretending to feel lucky to be off the hook. I had been lying to myself for months. The truth was I missed being part of the team – even after it got hammered in The Big Meet that year, 92-53, marking the first of twenty-six consecutive Cal victories.

The Pac-8 Conference Championship was held at Stanford Stadium that May, but I don't remember it, and I'm quite sure I did not attend. I did not see Stanford take another step back after its sixth-place showing the year before, coming in next to last in my senior year, ahead of only Washington State. Coach Jordan did not send a single athlete to the N.C.A.A. championships in 1972 for the first time in his sixteen years on The Farm. Casey Carrigan and Don Kardong's fourth-place finishes in the Pole Vault and Three-Mile, respectively, were the only All-American Track & Field performances during my four years on The Farm, when over two thousand such honors were given out, indoors and out. I would watch the N.C.A.A. Championships at Hayward Field in Eugene on a neighbor's black & white TV in College Terrace, as Bowling Green State's Dave Wottle, four months younger than I was, triumph in a meet record 3:39.7 in the 1,500-Meters, only months before his incredible sprint from last place on the backstretch to first in the 800-Meters at the Munich Olympic Games.

No knock on cross-dressing, but that Metric Mile that Wottle won was where I had hoped to complete my college running career.

My last class at Stanford was a graduate-student-level seminar on James Joyce's *Finnegans Wake*, a book some critics considered the last work in the Western literary tradition. As I left the professor's home that afternoon and stepped into bright sunlight, I breathed a lungful of an immeasurable wind of freedom. I had never felt so disburdened in all my life.

That's the way it goes in college athletics, and academics, too: the Admissions Office Giveth, and the Diploma Taketh Away. @ @

Stanford's Eightieth Commencement Exercises convened on June 10th, 1972 under a cool, slightly-overcast sky, with temperatures in the mid-sixties. I had invited my parents, who were back from Amsterdam, to attend the close of my required education and the best years of my youth, but they had declined to come without explanation. Travel would have been expensive, for one thing. Or maybe my Dad didn't want to come because as a former J.F.K. liberal on his way to becoming (briefly) a Reagan Democrat, he disapproved of my hippie ways. I thought he also might have felt guilty about not contributing financially to my education, and in that sense not measuring up in the eyes of his former in-laws, who would attend of course. My parents had no choice but to show up for my sister's graduation, since she was getting married in MemChu a day or two later. But if my father didn't feel comfortable attending my graduation ceremony, I had no problem with it, or at least allowed myself to feel no disappointment at all. My grandparents attended, of course, beginning with my installation into Stanford's Phi Beta Kappa chapter: I had been tagged as the top student in the Humanities Special Program, graduating with Honors, Distinction and a GPA of 3.65, despite my delinquent quarters at Cliveden House. I boast about my grades mostly to fill out an anecdote about how thoroughly competition and numbers imbued my Stanford years: an acquaintance from my Cliveden group was in my major with a 3.97 GPA, but his only two B's in were in the program, where I had only that one B, in my "Introduction to the Novel" class junior year. This meant I was the Special Program's only Phi Beta Kappa graduate, and why my friendly acquaintance never spoke to me again.

My grandfather's films of my actual graduation day include images of an anti-war protest outside MemChu, where dozens of students staged a "Die-In," lying on the asphalt and gravel while a long-haired student spoke through a megaphone about the calamity in Southeast Asia. (A process Nixon called "Vietnamization," begun in 1969, had gradually drawn down the number of American troops on the ground, but this past April the President had authorized the bombing of North Vietnam south of the 18th Parallel for the first time – yet another action that wouldn't win a war we would in fact lose. Also at the ceremony that day, I could only presume, were two classmates I had never met: Claude Terry, a future six-year N.B.A. veteran and the second-leading hoops scorer in Pac-8 history, behind U.C.L.A.'s Lew Alcindor. (The latter had converted to Islam a year ago and was known now as Kareem-Abdul Jabbar. Also in my class was Bob Kammeyer, who later pitched in eight games for the New York Yankees. I had been a fan of baseball and basketball for as long as I could remember, but never attended a single game in either sport in all my years on The Farm.

By an accident of the draw I was in the front row of our huge procession winding into Frost Amphitheater. (Still leading the pack!) I will never forget the moment I entered Frost and heard my grandfather's resonant baritone bellowing: *"Wait! Wait!"* His cameras weren't ready. *"Wait,"* as Brook Thomas had told me in the U.S.C.-Stanford Two-Mile my freshman year... *People were always telling me to wait...* The commencement speaker that afternoon was James "Scotty" Reston of the *New York Times,* who talked to us about the importance of remaining compassionate and open to new ideas, urging us to take heart in knowing that "staying the course" is often success enough. Eight years later, freelancing at Reston's newspaper, I would be unable to remember a word he said. @ @

After the convocation my grandparents and I strolled across campus all the way to Jordan House, my mother's World War Two-era Tri-Delt sorority, where my father allegedly picked up my mother for their first date, saw her walking down the spiral staircase and fell in love at first sight. Thirty years later the front door of the old Tri-Delt House had the huge lips and gaping tongue of the Rolling Stones "Sticky Fingers" album cover mounted in the middle of it. Where my grandparents' daughter had worn cashmere and pearls, empty beer kegs and papers cups littered the living room floor, along with some badly-broken furniture and the feces of several illegal house dogs, including my Bowzer, who would shortly run away for less troubling pastures. After taking a few photos of my grandmother and I gamely sitting on a tilting, three-legged sofa, my grandfather led us out to Jordan's front steps for my official graduation portrait. Thick curly locks cover my ears. I sport a beard worthy of ZZ-Top and a Vietnamese National Liberation Front armband on the sleeve of my academic gown. *(Go, Go, Viet Cong! U.S. out of Vietnam!)* I remember not feeling perfectly comfortable wearing the armband of a combat group killing American soldiers, but given how wrong our involvement was, I wore it anyway.

I agreed to accompany my grandparents to the reception at President Lyman's house on top of a nearby hill under one condition: that I not have to stand in a receiving line for a half-hour to shake hands with Richard Lyman, who I considered little better than a war criminal. My grandparents did not insist that I behave, although I suspected at the time that they thought I didn't have the common sense god gave a sparrow. I did not mention that I knew about my grandfather's graduation in 1919, when he had dressed as a "Mad Poet" and raced up and down the aisles of matriculating students with hair streaming and eyes wild, making a thorough spectacle of himself. He and I had never talked much about his Stanford experiences, but I knew he had marched as an R.O.T.C. candidate on fields I ran on, hoping that the War to End All Wars would end before he had to go over to the slaughter in France. I had read about this in the book of his life, which I was free to look at, so perhaps it was in the back of his mind.

From the perspective of years, I don't think I was entirely misguided in my condemnation of Stanford's active involvement in the War, even though I also know that President Lyman had personally written President Nixon in April, urging him to end the war now and warning that massive bombing from the air "only reinforces the will to win of the enemy against whom it is practiced." All the same, this newly-minted third-generation graduate of The Farm believed he had every right to be angry with the Promised Land of his youth, which in his view was being run by war criminals, as our nation was, too. And yet I continued to love my alma mater with a mystical tie that would never be broken. I did not need to embrace its current leadership in order to love Stanford with all my heart and soul. Please just soften your complicity in war and truly let the Winds of Freedom Blow! @ @

I took no special notice of the definitive end of my college running days, other than sensing a vague emptiness inside me. I had become good at pushing away thoughts I didn't care to entertain. I did want to say a goodbye to Coach Clark before too much time passed, so shortly after my grandparents returned to L.A. I phoned him with a plan.

"Hey Coach!" I didn't have to say who was calling, because of course he knew. "Since school let out I've been training more and I've had some fairly decent workouts lately. I've never been timed over Three Miles, and I'm curious to see what I can do. Would you mind timing me down at the stadium, any time that's convenient for you?"

"Are you free tomorrow morning at eleven?" It was as if he had been waiting for me to call so he could do something for me. Maybe he wanted to assuage the guilt about throwing me into the cross country meet in L.A. and me coming up injured, essentially ending my college career. I had not a drop of bitterness about how that unfolded; I had made the decision myself. But guilt wasn't why he volunteered. I think he wanted to end our four-year involvement on a positive note.

An azure sky hung over the track that day, as on my first day on campus: another perfect early summer morning for running in the mid-peninsula. Coach Clark and I were the only people in that 85,000-seat bowl. When I came through my first lap a few seconds faster than we had discussed, Coach said *"Sixty-six! Take it easy..."* I settled down, hit my marks, and closed with a modestly-fast 64-second last lap. When I was done I decelerated on the infield grass, propped my arms on my knees, and caught my breath for twenty seconds or so. Then I straightened up and jogged over to Coach by the finish line, more or less recovered. He gave me my time with a mild "what-might-have-been" smile on his face. My 13:54.0 was fifty-six seconds slower than Pre's best, so at least he wouldn't have lapped me.

Less than ten years ago, Stanford's Harry McCalla had won a Conference championship with a 14:13.3. Freshman Dave Deubner set a school record 13:57.0 that year, and afterwards Coach Jordan told him, "You're going to be quite an addition, Dave, as soon as I break your spirit." (Deubner's close friend Kenny Moore would report this story in his 2006 Bowerman biography. Deubner thought Jordan was joking, but Jordan wasn't. Deubner ran a 4:03.6 Mile his senior year, but never turned a faster Three Mile on The Farm.) Indulge my inner nerd for another moment: Duncan Macdonald, the future American record-holder at the metric equivalent, never ran faster than 13:56.0 in college; Bernie Lahde's PR was 13:56.4; Chuck Menz's, 14:05.4; Brook Thomas's, 14:15.6. My time was faster than Arvid and Freddie Ritcherson's at the Pac-8 Championship two weeks earlier, where steeplechase champion Bill Koss took sixth in 13:50.0, scoring a point for Washington in a race that Pre won in a run-to-win 13:32.2 and becoming an All-Conference Three-Miler. I had just solo'ed in a time only four seconds slower than Koss'. Had I made a mistake not re-joining the team and becoming All-Conference myself? I didn't know if I made a mistake or not, but I was fine with it. I was now (unofficially) the fourth-fastest Three-Miler in school history, running the equivalent of a 4:10 Mile and an 8:53 Two-Mile, according to International Tables. And I had done it without competition, with minimal training, on a sunny morning in June 1972. As Brock had told me the previous summer, "Not bad for a strictly solo run." (Years later I asked myself from "the loneliness of the long distance runner" if this was an existential victory or a Pyrrhic one. My answer: a little of both.)

"I don't think Kardong or Brock could have run that fast by themselves at this time of year," Coach told me. It made me proud to hear myself compared to runners like Don and Greg, who were the real deals. I started babbling: "Competition would have been worth at least a second a lap, don't you think? I'm probably in 13:40 shape right now, don't you think? And I did this off fifty-mile weeks, Coach! I haven't been doing any two-a-days at all…" I carried on like this for another half-minute before I noticed Coach only half listening, which was when I realized this talk was cheap, so I stopped. @ @

We jogged back to the locker room together, where he disappeared into the equipment closet for a minute or two, giving me time to realize I shouldn't make more of this performance than was actually there. My 13:54 would have won the Southeast Conference title that year, although the heat and humidity at race time in the South were surely more gruesome than Palo Alto's. My time was faster than the American Junior College Record, if that meant anything. I was also faster than "The Flying Finn," Paavo Nurmi, the greatest distance runner of the Twenties, which meant even less. Brock ran 13:37.2 as a sophomore. Kardong's 13:48.8 eighth-place finish in his last college race – the 1971 N.C.A.A. championship in Seattle – left him ready to quit the sport, until Coach Clark caught him on the track just after the race and told him not to give up, because he could have a future in this sport if he wanted one. My 13:54 would have left me in the dust at the N.C.A.A.'s that year – college distance running was exploding under the impact of Pre, the arrival of African runners, all-weather tracks and better shoes. And yet for the entirety of the Sixties my time would have placed me no worse than fifth at every Division I national championship. So this was "almost" an All-American-caliber performance in a year when Stanford had no All-Americans at all.

When Coach emerged from the equipment room he had a new nylon Stanford racing singlet, which he gave me to keep. (Maybe he had been looking for the one with "COE" on the back, only to find that it had already been thrown out.) Then he told me he was going to letter me for my senior year in cross country, even though I had only run the one meet against U.S.C. and U.C.L.A., which ended my college career. This made me a three-year cross country letterman, entitled to a jacket, a blanket and a ring; I gave the latter to my father, who would hold on to it for a decade before returning it to me, when I was better able to reflect on what I had and had not achieved.

The career highlights of the freshman walk-on "everybody connected with Stanford track" had been excited about, who the Buck Club Bulletin picked to be "one of the greatest distance runners ever to attend the Farm?" A freshman school Mile record that stood for nine years; top man for most of the '69 cross-country season and an "Athlete of the Week" that fall; and a first place at the Sacramento State Invitational during junior cross. For a Walk-On I had done pretty well. But the career Varsity Track & Field scoring for "the most talented distance runner" in Payton Jordan's fifteen years at Stanford? Second place in a dual meet at the University of Washington. My best time? That 4:07.6 Mile as a non-scorer in the Big Meet of '71. The Baby-Faced Assassin, the Golden Boy, the Chosen One had some great stories to share about his four years in Palo Alto, but he never won a single Varsity letter in Track. In the grand scheme of things, I was just another washout of the Payton Jordan era. @ @

I was accepted into U.C. Santa Barbara's doctoral program in English, but decided to become a supermarket check-out clerk instead. It was the same job I had the summer before starting college, only now I worked at the nation's first organic supermarket, New Age Natural Foods on California Avenue, a few blocks south of campus. Frank Shorter's Olympic Marathon Victory in Munich inspired my first 100-mile training week that fall: 101 miles in seven days. I showed up for the Pacific A.A.U. 10,000-Meter Cross Country Championship in San Francisco's rolling, muddy Golden Gate Park – the transition from yards to meters was underway in the American running scene, although this course was ¾ of a mile short for some reason. Running for the West Valley Track Club, I was fifty yards ahead of everybody at the mile mark. I clearly didn't know what I was doing anymore. I ended up fourth, soundly beaten by the winner, Nevada's Peter Duffy (fifth in the 10K at the N.C.A.A, Championships that spring), the soon-to-be four-time Columbian Olympian Domingo Tibaduiza, and in third, the Oregon Track Club's Jon Anderson, a 1972 American Olympian in the 10K who would win next year's Boston Marathon. (In a few years he would serve as one of Pre's pall bearers.) I gave my medal to my girlfriend Lorrie – the first girlfriend who ever saw me race. Lorrie worked the next cash register over at "New Age Natural," whose owner Fred Rohé – my new girlfriend's ex – had recently authored a self-published pamphlet, "The Zen of Running," in which he extolled the virtues of a joyful, gentle, "centered" approach to the sport.

"We're all entitled to our opinions, Fred, and I think distance running should be *tough*. I *like* that running long distances makes me suffer. I *like* feeling pride in what I do! You get to know yourself when you become a warrior – a Spartan! And a suffering Athenian, too, if you wanna be... We're all aspirants, Fred! We're all temple runners! Running in a 'gentle' way isn't the only way to be 'spiritual' and high-minded... Running long distances can cut through that part of your Ego that thinks you're special. To run really hard over long distances you need to get out there and *just do it*. You work hard to be the best runner you can be, and when you do that, running will cut through your Ego like a swift, clean blade! Running – at least the way we did it at Stanford – running exacts a *price*. It's not some joyous nature romp – at least not until you got into really fierce shape and then it sometimes does have an element of effortlessness – the 'Zone' people talk about. But serious distance runners – we're *wolves*, Fred. So let's just say that I think about the 'Zen' of long-distance running a whole lot different than you do…" Fred listened, nodding his head and stroking his long beard from time to time. He still preferred running ten-minute miles for hours, like the "Marathon Monks" Decker had told me about who ran around Mount Hiei. More power to Fred. But that wasn't me. @ @

I flew to Chicago in mid-November to compete over six miles at the 1972 A.A.U. national Cross-Country Championship, under the auspices of the West Valley Track Club. The night before the race I snuck into a Cheech & Chong concert on the Loop by climbing up a fire escape, then slept in the basement of a local church on a lumpy sofa under a thin blanket, freezing my ass off. The pace in Washington Park the next morning felt ridiculously fast, probably because I had done almost no interval training and not much more preparation than a lot of hard ten-milers through Los Altos Hills. I hung on behind the future Olympian Dick Buerkle (recognizable because he's completely hairless), getting splattered by his mud and ice and hurting like hell before being waxed over the last mile and finishing 31st, a full minute behind Olympic Marathon champ Frank Shorter, that year's Sullivan Award winner. (I did beat Greg Brock, but not Brook Thomas.)

Back in Palo Alto I had to admit to myself that my first experience of a national championship had not rocked my world. Our West Valley team had finished fourth in the country, but I only met my teammates at the starting line. I decided that the reason it didn't mean much to me was because I hadn't felt part of anything except the discipline of my sport. Coach Jordan often expressed a Reagan-esque belief in the primacy of the individual: "I didn't expect [the boys] to run for me or for the school," he told a journalist. "I wanted them to run for themselves. That's what athletics is about; it's an expression of yourself." (On another occasion he remarked, "If you work only for

yourself, sometimes your performance is not quite so high in standard"
– a foolish consistency being the hobgoblin of little minds) But for me,
the freedom to express myself was only part of what running was. At a
depth I wouldn't comprehend for years, I had run for myself, but also
for my teammates, my Coach, and the greater glory of Stanford
University. The ironies were rich: the "weenie" in the water polo outfit
had come across as such a rebel and maverick, but in fact he was Joe
College, running for his school – his *family's* school, mind you, whether
his family cared about his running or not. As Joe College I had doubled
and tripled for the Indians; I had given up my shot at a freshman
school record for the sake of my teammates' cause; I had raced in six-
mile competitions week in and week out in the toughest long-distance
running conference in the nation. Maybe putting up with Bob Murphy
and Dave Blanchard and Payton Jordan had been part of my service,
too, as Kenny Moore had told me running could be. As Gerry
Lindgren would write forty years later: "The best way to enjoy running
is to freely dedicate yourself to others." And now that my participation
in intercollegiate athletics had gone the way of the "Redskin," the joys
and camaraderie and challenges I had found as a Stanford distance
runner were not being replaced by other things. I hadn't lost interest in
running or in competition, but without the incentive of my school and
my team, I had lost my deepest reason for doing it at all. @ @

On December 7th, 1972, Apollo 17, the eleventh and final manned
American mission to the Moon, launched at 9:33 a.m. PST. The three-
member crew included our family friend Ron Evans, who lived with his
wife and two kids in the cul-de-sac more-or-less cattycorner across the
street from our house. When "Mr. Evans," as the Coe boys always
called him, first set foot on the lunar surface, his first words were "Hot
diggity dog!" Apollo 17 splashed down in the Atlantic ten days later,
having established records for the longest manned lunar landing flight,
the longest lunar surface extravehicular activity, the largest lunar sample
return, and the longest time in lunar orbit. No one from our planet has
set foot on an extraterrestrial body since. Five or six weeks later, I
don't remember the exact date and have no record of it, I stepped on

to the rock-hard semi-asphalt track perched on the side of a mountain halfway up the peninsula at the College of San Mateo, and raced a Mile in a Saturday all-comers meet, breaking the tape in pelting rain and gusty winds as the announcer declared: "That was a 4:13 Mile by former Stanford runner Robert Coe. It looks like he's going to have a big year this year!" I had never been called a "former Stanford runner" before, and I found it jarring. My time didn't impress me at all, despite the horrible conditions and lack of competition and the fact that I hadn't done any speed work in months. For someone four months shy of twenty-three, a 4:13 Mile was "no great shakes," as my father would have said, although it was the fourth-fastest four-lapper of my short, soon-to-be aborted career.

It was the last serious race I would ever run. A month later I left Palo Alto to become a Track & Field Coach for the Peace Corps in Ghana, West Africa. (Arvid Kretz had gone to African on a Mission while still in school.) I won a regional 5K championship, racing against barefoot men in slacks. For weeks afterwards strangers approached me on the streets in the capital city of Accra, calling "Hey! Mister Five Thousand!" But I was never especially fit over there, and when I returned to the Bay Area three months later – the "Sports College" where I was supposed to join the faculty didn't exist – I never got in racing shape again. I will say from the perspective of years that the distractions of the counterculture may have made it more difficult for me to sustain the long view to train much beyond college. I actually stopped running entirely for years, except for a few mildly-psychotic episodes, like after watching Don and Duncan make the '76 Olympic team. Otherwise I was unaware of any regrets. The four-time Olympic champion Al Oerter once asked, "Have you ever seen a longer face than on an athlete who has quit in his prime?" But I wasn't wearing a long face at all. As Oscar Wilde wrote, "Youth has a kingdom waiting for it." I was studying dance by then, so I packed up memories of my running career, my achievements and disappointments, and without a bang, a whimper, a fanfare, or a *hasta luego*, quietly moved on. @ @ @

POST-SCRIPT: WE WERE BORN TO RUN

I was a Stanford runner once, and in my dreams I remained one. All through the coming decades, the Cosmic Marathon that I entered on my first day on campus was without beginning or end, just as I had imagined. On countless nights, fast asleep under my covers, I ran. Almost never in any discomfort or distress, I ran. *Why?* James Thurber: "All men should strive to learn before they die what they are running from, and to, and why." What did my years as a runner mean to me? What was I to make of my long trip across The Farm? Who (to me now) was this person who had lived through these adventures and misadventures and survived them? Or had I survived? Did the "great potential" that Payton Jordan and my grandfather see in me land in other life endeavors? Anthropologists sweetened the pot by claiming that homo sapiens' ability to run long distances in acts of "persistence hunting" is a quality that distinguishes us from all other mammals, and goes to the core of our humanity. These would be a number of reasons why I began to think about writing this book about my college running days, almost thirty years after they were well behind me.

Before this idea took hold, I did not pay much attention to running during my daylight and evening hours. I followed the Olympics closely, and in 1978, the year I wrote my qualified denunciation of the jogging boom in the *Village Voice,* I also reported for the *Voice* on the eighth annual New York City Marathon, which gave me an opportunity to catch up with an old teammate, an elementary school teacher from Spokane, Washington. Don Kardong had missed a Bronze Medal in the Montreal Olympic Marathon by a scant three seconds. After finishing eighth through the five boroughs that day, Don asked, "Why did you quit running, Robert? You had so much talent!" Another former teammate had also qualified for Montreal, where a case of food poisoning kept him from advancing out of his heat. But nine days after the Olympic flame was extinguished, Duncan Macdonald had stunned the world of Track & Field by becoming the first American to run 5,000 meters in under thirteen minutes and twenty seconds. Duncan's time – 13:19.7 – broke the late Steve Prefontaine's American record and was only seven seconds shy of the world mark. Kenny Moore in *Sports Illustrated* called Dunc "the most promising runner in the world." Not long afterwards I caught up with Duncan at a party at his home on the mid-peninsula. Among other things I told him about my new life in the New York dance world. "I'm glad you found something you love," he told me. Then he went out to his garage and came back with a new pair of Size Nine Nike training flats that had never fit him right. "I thought you might like to have these," he said, "in case you ever change your mind." Gonzo journalist Hunter S. Thompson, covering the Honolulu Marathon a few years later, would marvel at how "Duncan MacDonald, a local boy and previous two time winner, had taken command of the race somewhere around the 15 mile-mark and was so far ahead that the only way he could lose this race would be by falling down – which was not likely, despite his maverick reputation and good-natured disdain for traditional training habits. Even drunk [sic], he was a world-class racer, and a hard man for anybody to catch once he got in front... moving like Secretariat in the stretch at Churchill Downs, he looked about 10 feet tall... It was like watching Magic Johnson run the fast break or Walter Payton turning the corner..." At least two of my teammates reached the pinnacle. @ @

While Ronald Reagan triumphed in the political realm, Payton Jordan became the greatest master sprinter of all time, shattering age-group world records from the 55 to 80, when "the Silver Streak," as he was known in some quarters – Coach always did love nicknames – threw down a 14.35 100-Meters, likely faster than I could have run that day. The university program he coached did not fare as well: by the time Jordan retired in 1979 – "As far as coaching goes, I feel I've done everything any man could ask for" – Stanford Track & Field had devolved into a cast of walk-ons finishing last in the Pac-10 Conference season after season. There were occasional stars, as always on The Farm, but with only nine scholarships – three for men, six for women – and a department budget of $78,000, the program couldn't even afford to maintain a dedicated office, much less an elite Track & Field program. The inside lane of the Stadium track was allowed to wear down to a path of rubble. This decline continued under Jordan's successor. Then Vin Lananna arrived from Dartmouth in 1992 and after only a few years of savvy recruitment and investment produced one of the most respected long-distance college programs in the nation: "The Machine," winner of four N.C.A.A. cross country titles between 1996 and 2003, in that final year placing six runners in the top thirteen for the second-greatest team performance in the history of the meet.

The Internet was around by then, and I was following Cardinal sports religiously. I firmly believed that the things that challenge us the most are the things that most define us, and running was that for me, as Stanford was, too. I also know that nothing haunts us like promise unfulfilled. But early on I decided not to write a book about my disappointments, but rather a book that would include my successes and my failures, because in the end these things cannot be extricated. I did what I did, there can be no denying that. I won some and I lost some, and all of it came from the deepest parts of who I was. @ @

The changes that overtook Stanford Track & Field and Cross Country over the past two decades are mind-blowing to an old alumnus like me. The modernization and down-sizing of the Stadium in 2007 included the removal of the track, despite the crocodile tears of some of us old-timers, but the loss was insignificant to the program, since Stanford Track & Field teams had been training and racing for more than a decade in a state-of-the-art facility at fully revamped Angell Field, the north entrance of which was re-named Payton Jordan Plaza in a 1999 ceremony that Jordan and his wife (and college sweetheart) Marge attended. Today's runners have trails to train in Huddart and Wunderlich Parks, a Canada Road horse trail and a wood chip loop on campus; all of which mean nothing to me. Cross Country has its own designated physical therapist and masseur (not just Scottie and Dave with his fire hose); a camp at Mammoth Lakes in the Sierra Nevada for altitude training at 7,880 feet for five weeks before fall quarter (no more camp counseling in the mountains or running on nude beaches, unless you wanted to); an on-campus high school training camp offering summer employment (no more cleaning the cages of cancer-ridden mice at the Medical Center, or being a tunnel rat yourself), and a share in the university's multi-million dollar shoe deal with Nike, meaning that you are not limited to a single pair of flats a year.

These young men and women have earned it: the undergraduate men's program produces times surpassing world records in my day, not to mention fourteen sub-four-minute Milers. Each spring more than two hundred college kids nationwide run faster Miles than my PR 4:07, while Stanford swimmer Elaine Breeden came within inches (in 2009) of taking down John Ferris' old American men's record in the 200-yard Fly. Stanford women's Cross Country teams – that Title IX innovation – won N.C.A.A. titles in 2005 and 2006 and were invited to the White House, where three of the last five sitting Presidents – George W. Bush, Bill Clinton and Jimmy Carter – have been committed runners-in-office. Distance running has come a long way since people made fun of it at a Buck Club Breakfast. Most impressively (to me), Coach Lanana led a Stanford team to an N.C.A.A. Track & Field Title in 2000, the school's first since 1934, on the heels of a superb crop of middle- and long-distance runners and a future Olympic Silver Medalist in the Pole Vault. Lanana told Kardong, a visiting journalism from *Runners World*, "we just followed what you guys did." I suspected Lananna was flattering a fourth-place Olympic marathoner and influential Stanford alumnus, but all the same, when I read those words

I felt a warm glow inside. So Don, Duncan, Greg, Arvid, Brian, Chuck, Bernie, Large, Brook, me and all the rest – Decker and Jack, too – were the founders of a legacy! Today's runners are much better informed and better trained than we were, but I am sure they still speak and dream of the things we spoke and dreamt about in our day. It all happens over and over, time and time again, and therein lies part of the greatness of our sport: long-distance running endures. @ @

I had my own on-campus meeting with Coach Lananna, a few years before he left Stanford to take the head job at the University of Oregon and turn Bill Bowerman's old team into a Track & Field powerhouse again. During a brief meeting in his trailer office by the Stadium track (I remember a day bed that looked slept in), I could sense Lananna's distraction at having to be polite to an alumnus who hadn't come in the door with an open checkbook and a pen. But soon enough I was having many more private meetings with Lanana, only in my dreams. In more than one of these dreams I pleaded my case: "Vin, Coach, look, I may be an old guy, but I still have my stuff! I know I can still *perform*, I can still *do it!* Just give me a chance! I'm not saying I'll be your top guy. But I could be your fifth man! One of your top seven, easy!" You think I'm making this up, but I swear I'm not. Coach Lananna never believed me – not even in my dreams. More than once I showed up in a dream for a Stanford cross-country team time trial on the golf course and set out to compete against the current crop of runners, determined to prove myself against long odds. And in other dreams I search for, but cannot find, the starting line at all.

The impetus behind this book was these dreams I have had for years. I thought I should run down these "royal roads to the unconscious," as Freud called them – to see if I could discover what unfinished business these dreams expressed. I thought that my daytime research and recollection might reduce the frequency of these nighttime runs, or even alter them, but I soon found myself contemplating not just the rise of Stanford Track & Field, but Farm Athletics generally. Driven by the growth of "Silicon Valley" (a term coined my senior year), tens of millions of dollars have poured into the Athletic Department, not just for scholarships and endowed professorships but to replace deteriorating facilities and enhance existing ones. Thirty-six Cardinal teams and 900 undergraduate students now compete intercollegiately (16 for men, 20 for women), and our football program has been consistently one of the finest in the country. Stanford has basically retired the Directors' Cup, presented annually to the deepest and best athletic university in the country, winning every year for the past twenty. The Farm has become "Disneyland for Athletes," as one Coach told a young recruit. Stanford has become so thoroughly suffused with athletic excellence that it became another reason for me to go back and conjure why it mattered so much to me when it was only a shadow of what it is today. @ @

I sat down with my notes, but all that poured out of me at first were Facts. Stats. Races. Places. Names. Faces. Workouts. Times. Splits. Reps. Distances. Images. Numbers. Matters of Public Record. The challenge became recovering the excitement, the fireworks, and the magic that have faded into the mists of time for the Frank Shorters, Duncan Macdonalds and Don Kardongs of the world, and most definitely for me. My time as Stanford runner was a Biblical Forty Years ago and counting. My #1 Cross-Country Jersey from 1969 acquired some holes, morphed into a dishcloth, and disappeared years ago; my letterman's jacket, which I had almost outgrown (I had put on a little weight), was stolen from my closet by a conniving sub-letter; the nylon racing jersey Coach Clark gave me that last day in the locker room, vanished; my Buck Club necktie barely made it out of the Hyatt. My freshman school Mile record lasted until 1978, and I can't say I was heartbroken to see it go. Honestly: it felt good not to hold on to something that had given me so much pride, and not let somebody else have the fun of owning it for a while. Fun is important. As I began to rediscover the feelings of our running world, I also had to admit the real reason I was going to so much trouble: not for some high-minded self-discovery, but for the sheer pleasure I found. Any gregarious sort who has ever played competitive sports knows what a trip it can be to remember that last-second Hail Mary pass, that walk-off home run in the bottom of the ninth, that impossible comeback with no time left on the clock. Sharing these old tales – singing these old songs – is as much a cliché as any sports story ever told – old Jocks sitting around in a sharing mood, spare us or pass me the remote! But every one of us has done something memorable in our physical lives. Why should we deprive ourselves of the pleasure of that PR in the J.V. Half-Mile against Dickinson, or that winning TD catch in Middle School in front of your Dad and Sally Parker, or that unexpected victory in a cross-country meet in Sacramento, or being called "Mister Five Thousand" on the sidewalks of Africa? In moments like these we mere mortals enter a God Realm where private experience blurs with mythic events, and we taste the best kind of immortality: the human kind. @ @

Cinematic immortality is okay, too, yet no more than a half-dozen souls sat with me in a darkened Beverly Center shopping-mall cinema at 11:30 in the morning for the first public screening in L.A. of the Steve Prefontaine bio-pic *Without Limits* (1998). Bill Bowerman (played by Donald Sutherland) tells the cocky freshman (Billy Crudup, who trained down to a 4:24 Mile for the role), "Grant me those Stanford Three-Milers are no slouches, especially that fellow Kardong." Pre's reply: "Don Kardong? He's not bad..." Bowerman (an Oregon Beta, by the way) instructs his prodigy to run 70-second laps against us, which would have resulted in a nothing-special 14:00 Three-Mile. Pre disobeys and un-corks a snake-quick 13:12.8, the fastest Three-Mile in the world so far that year, crushing Don and Arvid (actors played them) in a scene that conflated three historical races. I briefly considered standing on my seat and shouting at the screen, "Kardong only beat me once that year," but of course I did no such thing. *Without Limits* provoked all sorts of memories half-forgotten or too impacted to recall. Building on the structure of facts I had already built – the next of meets and workouts – I began to remember how amazing our running years had been, and all the great things we accomplished in the war-torn, wanton, dazzling, depressing late Sixties and early Seventies. I ran through an era when many of our dreams went south, but what remains most alive to me now is the spirit of liberation we felt and the joy of the discoveries and adventures and challenges we shared as we pursued our dreams. Those tumultuous, harrowing years did not steal my chance for glory; the late Sixties and early Seventies fanned, flavored and inflamed my aspirations. I was not a victim of the time any more than anyone else who was swept up in the momentum and fervor of college years. If I was a victim of anything, it was my physical durability. But I didn't want to spend more than a moment lamenting or condemning my wasted talent. Good god no! I was immensely fortunate to have been where I was and doing what I did in a career almost perfectly framed by the Apollo Missions to the Moon.

My portrait hung in the Stanford locker room for nine years! I raced against Frank Shorter, Gerry Lindgren, Martin Liquori and Steve Prefontaine, and in meets with Bob Seagren, O.J. Simpson, Lee Evans, and John Carlos! I led Pre for 800 yards in the 1971 Pac-8 Conference Mile! Before the first race Jim Ryun contested as a Born-Again Christian, I was dragged off the track in the Devil-Take-the-Hindmost Mile! I could run a 50-second Quarter and also out-run long-distance All-Americans and Olympians, past, present and future! I logged thousands of miles with truly great runners and aspired with them to national championships! I competed for the London Track Club at the Crystal Palace, and at the Oakland Coliseum and San Francisco's Cow Palace for Stanford! I trained on trails in the Sierra Nevadas and on the track at Berlin's Olympiastadion! I coursed through the cypresses of Point Lobos and risked my life running along the Rhine! I was a forest creature in Munich, a Yank between the hedgerows of the English countryside and on the cobblestones around Buckingham Palace, and a naked hippie on the Costa Blanca! When the great Australian Ron Clarke set his last world record, he flung his arms around my neck and said, "Thanks, mate!" I was present at the births of West Coast cross country and the West Coast Offense! I rolled joints for the Thunder Chickens and brought measles into their Rose Bowl Camp! I may or may not have met Sally Ride on the night of my PR Mile! I had been there, and done that. But I also decided early on that my book would no more grovel over long-sought victories than it would trade in long-vanished defeats. What I wanted to do was to open a window on an era, and confirm that I felt like the Stanford All-American basketball star Nneka Ogwumike when she addressed a crowd at Maples at the end of her final college season in 2012: "I wouldn't have traded these four years for any other place with any other community, any other team, any other coach." With tears in my eyes all these decades later, I can say the words spoken in TV ads during Cardinal football broadcasts and on gostanford.com: *"I am Stanford."*

There was what I desired to do as a runner, and what I actually achieved. But why should I regret any of it, or anything at all? @ @

So I ran with the "facts." I fleshed out my "Tales of Brave Ulysses" (Cream.) I painted my "Portrait of the Runner as a Young Man" (Joyce). I launched my own Race to the Moon up that old oak tree we used to climb. I Googled. I You-Tubed. I went the Extra Mile. I dredged up letters, phoning and emailing former teammates, digging out my old Blue Adidas spikes to heirloom like a pair of baby shoes. I framed my Apollo 8 moon patch and telegram from Bill Anders, in which he hoped he would do as well on his lunar injection as I did in my cross-country race in Sacramento, and hung it over my desk. I thought to look up John Ferris, who made leaving the pool sound so brutally simple, by searching online and discovering he was living in Europe and had written and self-published a novel about swimming and swimmers, *Olimpix,* which is best book I have ever read about the nature and nurture of athletic aspiration. I opened up a long-closed filing cabinet and pulled out my bulging running scrapbook, a water-warped tome stuffed with track memorabilia, training logs and race results from high school to the end of college and beyond. And on the page near the *San Francisco Examiner* clipping that read, "Bill Moultrie, Head Coach Payton Jordan and everybody else connected with Stanford track are excited by Freshman Bill [sic] Coe," I recognized The Hulk's ungainly scrawl, a penciled message: *"Coe, you egotistical cocksucker."* Yes, my Ego is in play, no doubt about that, and thanks for reminding me, Hulk. I had lost touch with the Team Trickster after graduation, but had heard that he blossomed into a fairly decent road runner, winning some big local races; other rumors had him going off to sea as a smuggler of illegal contraband and making a lot of money, which he used to purchase a sailing vessel that he soloed to Hawaii. In our last contact in the mid-Seventies he mailed me a postcard from Honolulu, informing me that "Chinese women have big nipples." The message was obnoxious (no doubt intentionally), but I was glad to hear from him anyway. It was good just knowing The Hulk was alive.

One of the best rewards this book gave me was getting back in touch with Marshall Clark. When Jordan retired in 1979, his assistant was passed over for the top job, so "Coach" (I could never call him "Marshall") left for the head job at the University of Montana, and two years later moved to San Jose State, first to coach men's cross country and assist with the men's Track & Field, then as the Head Coach of both storied programs in 1984. Four years later, when the university dropped them both and turned the "Speed City" track into an asphalt parking lot, Coach Clark denounced the move to local media and eventually returned to high school ranks. In 2005, San Jose State would honor its former students Smith and Carlos with a 22-foot high statue of their medal stand protest that remains a vivid image of a civil rights movement that has continued to reshape American society.

Decker and I visited Coach in at his home in San Jose in the late Eighties. He talked a little about his time in the Coast Guard, which he spent freezing in boats off the coast of South Korea, and wondered why we never learned anything about Southeast Asia from the French. I mentioned in passing that I had met one of his runners in a hotel elevator in Reno. "He was wearing San Jose State team sweats," I said. "I don't remember his name, but he was kind of a good-looking kid –"

Coach's dead-pan reply: "Then he couldn't have been one of ours..."

Marshall Clark was our leader, our witness and our rock during a time that was tough on authority and tough on us all. The late Sixties and early Seventies were difficult years for him: after fathering twin girls he went through a painful divorce. Were we a factor in his marriage collapsing, or were we his escape from it? I would never ask Coach a question like that in a million years, but I didn't miss the opportunity to tell him via email: "You had the respect and attention of every person on those teams." That he never responded to this compliment was typical of the man. He had never tried to talk me into sticking with our sport, as he had Kardong; perhaps he saw something in me, and Don was more accomplished than I was anyway. And he had asked me to run against U.S.C. and U.C.L.A., and I had turned up injured afterwards. He had made a few mistakes with me, I can admit now, like letting me double and triple at meets just because I wanted to. But during the brief time we corresponded he did email me: "I would like to have seen what you could have done." He sounded very content in his second marriage. He remembered as much about the old days as I did, along with a few things I had quite forgotten. I wanted to, but I never found a way to tell him I was writing a book. @ @

On September 30, 2002, Decker phoned from his law office in San Jose with shocking news: Coach Clark had dropped dead on the side of a road, jogging with his girls' high school cross country team. He was only 69. A thousand people would attend his memorial service at Saratoga High School, including some old-timers: Decker, a lawyer with a Bay Area practice in worker's compensation; Arvid Kretz, Director of Retail Inventory Management for Williams-Sonoma; Chuck Menz, who had left electrical engineering and become a gastroenterologist in Ventura County; and Greg Brock, President of the Santa Cruz Track Club and the Track and Cross-Country Coach at Santa Cruz High School. Payton Jordan flew in from his retirement in Santa Barbara, took one look at Brook Thomas – the Captain of our national runner-up cross country team, who had traveled north from his job as Chairman of the English Department at the University of California at Irvine – and burst into tears, which was almost enough for me to forgive the man for all the havoc he wreaked during my years on The Farm. Most of his former Indians had buried the hatchet with Jordan years ago. Brock, Kardong, and Macdonald (an anesthesiologist in Honolulu who also coaches runners at Punahou School, where his daughters ran and Obama played hoops), and even Chuck Francis (before his death in 2010) had been on decent terms with our former Head Coach for a while. "One of the sunshine boys," as a journalist wrote during my years on The Farm, Jordan remained the recipient of great good will and veneration in his sunset years. Stanford's Payton Jordan Invitational has become the marquee distance running carnival in the nation, famous for fast times. A few days before he knew he would to die at the age of ninety-one, he would write this in a letter: "Listen to your heart and express your love. Share life fully with those you hold close to your heart. Be content with what God has in store."

I very much wanted to attend Coach Clark's memorial, but work and a new family made it unreasonable to leave the West Village in New York City. None of Coach's three Olympians were able to attend – a group that included Tony Sandoval, who enrolled at Stanford the fall I left and went on to set a U.S. Olympic Trial Marathon record that would stand for over thirty years. In 1980 Frank Shorter called Tony "the fastest runner in the world." As a running eminence and author – "the only spiritual descendent of Mark Twain ever to bring his unsparing eye and antic voice to running," according to *Sports Illustrated,* as well as the founder of the Lilac Bloomsday Run in Spokane, where he has a footbridge named after him – Don Kardong forwarded words that were read aloud. In them he noted that Coach Clark "was equally happy coaching runners who no one has ever heard of, runners who simply wanted to be better." Marshall's respect for people – something he infallibly showed towards me – was much commented on that day.

But my favorite story came from a former high school runner who some years earlier had emptied the contents of his stomach after his first race and figured he would go to Coach Clark, who had a reputation for being such a nice guy, to beg off his leg on the Mile Relay. "Coach, I feel really sick. Do you think you could get someone else to run my relay leg?"

Coach Clark looked at him and without expression said, "You have a race to run in fifteen minutes." In other words: tough beans. @ @

I have now spent three times more years writing this book – fifteen –

than I did running it. The era's remoteness in time – those Biblical four decades and more – is part of why this story has a dreamlike quality for me now. My grandfather, who died eighteen months after I graduated and never saw what became of me, was an avid Shakespearean who particularly loved a line from *Midsummer Night's Dream:* "And it shall be called Bottom's Dream, which hath no bottom." These words – spoken by the leader of the "Rude Mechanicals," Nick Bottom, a role I played in high school, much to the disapproval of my track coach, who would rather have me running the cindered oval than trodding the histrionic boards – resonate with me now in ways it never did when I was younger. Was I ever really a cross country champion and a 4:07 Miler at a great western university? Did I really lead twenty runners down the wrong path at the 1969 Sac State Invitational? Did I truly turn down a motorcycle ride to Altamont so I could go out and run thirteen miles hard?

Or is it all Bottom's Dream, which hath no bottom?

The visual evidence is scant – only two dozen photographs and two silent films, one shot by Jim Kauffman's late father; the other, of the Stanford-U.C.L.A. cross country meet in Westwood, the other shot by my Grandfather in the days before the Camcorder and presently preserved in a climate-controlled vault at the American Academy of Motion Picture Arts & Sciences and copied to DVDs. I recently showed a photograph of the finish of the Stanford-S.C.-San Jose State cross-country meet in 1970 to a young friend, who studied the picture, then me, then the picture. Then she asked, "Is that really you?"

"Yes," I laughed, "that's really me." I may no longer closely resemble the boy in the photographs – when I see someone in a pair of 30 x 32 trousers, I can hardly believe I ever fit in them – but I am that boy's Shadow, as he is mine. ("I let my shadow write it," Gerry Lindgren wrote in the preface to a memoir that took him twenty-five years to complete. "My shadow was there through every step, knows my deepest thoughts and the agony kept hidden deep inside my heart.") I recently emailed Kardong the line from Herman Hesse's I had mailed my grandparents in December '69 – "The hardest road to travel is the road into yourself" – and Don emailed back: "The road into myself is also the road less traveled. I don't like the scenery." Don was kidding, sort of – the late Jim Fixx, author of the 1977 best-selling *The Complete Book of Running*, called him "the funniest guy in running" – but Don was on to something all the same. A great distance runner, which Don was, needs to walk a steady path and live a stable life, remain humble (apologies, Pre, wherever you are) but also feisty and competitive. And he has to put in the miles. But I also know that a serious runner can dream rhododendron forests, too, as long as he (or she) maintains a grounded, working-class existence, which at one time I did embody. As Coach Clark wrote in one of his last emails to me: *"You were there."*

And in my dreams, I still am. I have not stopped running in my sleep. And I am certain that no matter how old I get, or how far the counterculture recedes in history and memory, I will always be a Stanford Jock. @ @

It's my daughter who gets it now – or some of it, from a child's perspective, of course. We used to run on a synthetic grass pier on the nearby Hudson River Park, which we called "The Running Park." Sometimes we did 25-yard intervals on the Astroturf, which had these little black grains of soft rubberized sand that showed up in our clothes and shoes and hair – what's left of mine – when we got home. My goal some seasons back was to still be beating her over twenty-five-yards until she turned eight. After that, we were on our own.

"I promise you'll be the only eight-year-old I'll ever race!" Watching her prepare, I regret nothing and see only the future, which is where I am headed anyway. "Ready... Set... *Go!*" And off we do go.

"I won! I won!" she tells me at the finish line. She has her mother's coloring and manual skills, and my features, my (former) flowing curls and my tireless metabolism. In her spontaneous energy, she's a *doppelganger* of sorts. Whether or not she has the eye of the tiger is for her to discover, although I will assist her in finding her way in anything, as long as it's honorable. But watching her run, for me, is like meeting life all over again. As the Youngbloods sang, in a tune every garage band and dormitory pick-up group played back in my day:

"We are but a moment's sunlight
Fading in the grass..."

I'm still out there sometimes, plodding a mile and a half down to Chambers Street and back. Running may not be the biggest spectator sport, but over forty million Americans practice it now, making it the most popular participatory sport in America and a multi-billion dollar industry with a financial demographic similar to golf. Stanford websites provide maps for over 180 running trails around the mid-peninsula, while the New York City Marathon attracts more than forty thousand participants each year, with an economic impact on the city in the hundreds of millions of dollars. It also has a TV ad: "If you're losing faith in human nature, go out and watch a Marathon." I was never one of those people who ran twenty-six-plus miles – never happened and never will, since asphalt has never been my friend. I am at best a jogger, in the sense that I "jog/walk" occasionally, and that's about it.

But you might still see me sometimes, an older man, white-haired where there's any left, heading south down the path along the Hudson, spying someone twenty-five yards ahead – and twenty-five years younger, most likely – and with all the pride and dare-I-say gusto of the old college Jock I am, deciding that I'm going after him (or her).

Catch up by Canal Street? Optimistic. How about just before the Traveler's Building? Better. So I set out to do what I have challenged myself to do, and go for the burn, hoping my knees can handle it.

Being a runner is primal. I only run for buses and trains when it's a sure thing these days, but we're not just cardiovascular systems with legs. Running is the purest form of human endeavor. All of us are wired that way. Caught in the human race. @ @ @ @

ABOUT THE AUTHOR

Robert Coe is a writer living in New Jersey. His journalism has appeared in *The New York Times Sunday Magazine* and *Arts and Leisure* section, *Rolling Stone, Vanity Fair, Esquire, New York, The Village Voice, American Theatre Magazine*, and *Tricycle: The Buddhist Review*. *War Babies* – his first play, and the first world premiere produced by the Tony award-winning La Jolla Playhouse – received four nominations from the San Diego Theater Critics Circle, including Best New Play, and a *Drama-Logue* Award for Best Play. Coe's original book for *The Photographer* (music by Philip Glass) opened the first NEXT WAVE Festival at the Brooklyn Academy of Music (BAM.) The production subsequently toured the eastern United States. Coe also served as the dramaturge and occasional co-writer for Laurie Anderson's *UNITED STATES: PARTS I-IV*, a two-evening-long work that premiered at BAM and went on to introduce performance art into the international arts mainstream. In the commercial theater he wrote a new book for the national tour of the Tim Rice/ABBA musical *Chess,* directed by three-time Tony winner Des McAnuff, who was also Coe's co-writer on *PERFECT LIGHT*, a screenplay for Touchstone Pictures and The Walt Disney Company. Coe has also performed as a dancer with Bill T. Jones/Arnie Zane and Jane Comfort, and later wrote the official companion book to PBS's long-running television series, *Dance in America* (E.P. Dutton, 1985.) The author of catalogues for the First NEXT WAVE at BAM and for the first New York International Festival of the Arts, the largest performing arts festival of the twentieth century, Coe is currently working on two new books: *NOTHING LIKE I THOUGHT IT WOULD BE: An Autobiography of Downtown New York, 1974-1989*, and a novel, *The Princess of the Leafy Suburbs*.

Made in the USA
San Bernardino, CA
12 February 2016